AIRCRAFT MECHANIC'S
Shop Manual

AIRCRAFT MECHANIC'S Shop Manual

Compiled and Edited by
Larry Reithmaier

Second Printing 1981
Third Printing 1983
5th Printing 1989

Palomar Books

P.O. Box 915
Marquette, MI 49855

Library of Congress Cataloging in Publication Data

Reithmaier, Larry W.
    Aircraft mechanic's shop manual.
    1. Airplanes—Maintenance and repair. I. Title.
TL671.9.R37   629.134'6   78-25800

ISBN 0-932882-00-5

Table of Contents

Acknowledgements

Grateful acknowledgement is extended to the manufacturers of aircraft and aircraft components for their cooperation in making material available for inclusion in this manual.

Photographs, illustrations, data and catalogs were provided by:
Cessna Aircraft Co.
Beech Aircraft Corp.
Piper Aircraft Corp.
U.S. Industrial Tool & Supply Co.
Cherry Fasteners (Townsend Textron)
Snap-on Tools Corp.
The L.S. Starrett Co.
DeVilbis
Dzus Fastener Co., Inc.
Hi-shear Corp.
Aeroquip Corp.
Sterling Laquer Mfg. Co.
Reynolds Metals
Aluminum Co. of America
Chicago Pneumatic
Bild Industries, Inc.
John Hassell, Inc.
SPS Aerospace Products Div.
AAA Aircraft Supply Co.
ESNA Division, Amerace Corp.
United Supply Co.
Tiernary Metals
Superior Pneumatic, Inc.
Binks Mfg. Co.
U.S. Paint, Laquer & Chemical Co.
Randolph Products Co.
E.I. Du Pont De Nemours & CO., Inc.
Magnaflux Corp.
AIMSCO
Standard Pressed Steel Co.
Lawrence Engineering & Supply Co.
Aero Engineering & Mfg. Co.
Gates Learjet Corp.
Magnaflux Corp.

Chapter Heading Illustrations by Gretchen Egge

Preface

This manual was compiled using selected material from various Federal Aviation Administration (FAA) and military publications as well as photographs, illustrations and data supplied by aircraft manufacturers and parts supply companies.

Aircraft Mechanic's Shop Manual provides the mechanic or student mechanic with the techniques and procedures involved in basic shop practices such as inspection, repair of sheet metal structures, welding, riveting, use of standard hardware, installation of plumbing and electrical wiring and painting and finishing. Aircraft systems and their maintenance will be presented in a future manual.

This manual was compiled to aid the practicing mechanic as well as the student mechanic studying for his Airframe and Powerplant (A&P) mechanics certificate. It is designed for use in a formal course of instruction or by an individual studying on his own.

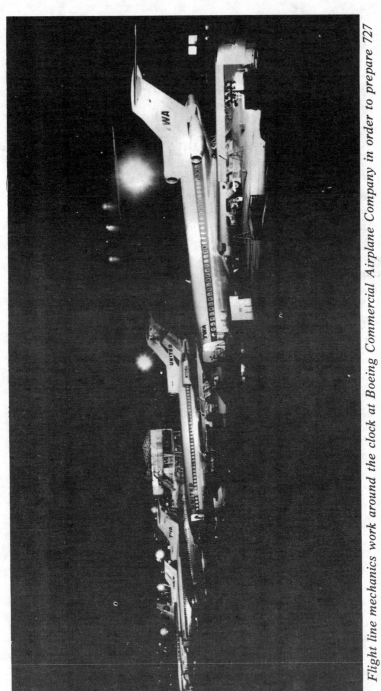

Flight line mechanics work around the clock at Boeing Commercial Airplane Company in order to prepare 727 jetliners for delivery to airline customers.

Chapter 1

Introduction

AIRCRAFT MAINTENANCE

Maintenance means the inspection, overhaul, and repair of aircraft, including the replacement of parts. A PROPERLY MAINTAINED AIRCRAFT IS A SAFE AIRCRAFT.

The purpose of maintenance is to ensure that the aircraft meets acceptable standards of airworthiness throughout its operational life.

Although maintenance requirements will vary for different types of aircraft, experience shows that most aircraft will need some type of preventive maintenance every 25 hours of flying time or less, and minor maintenance at least every 100 hours. This is influenced by the kind of operation, climatic conditions, storage facilities, age, and construction of the aircraft. Most manufacturers supply service information which should be used in maintaining an aircraft.

Inspections

FAR Part 91 places primary responsibility on the owner or operator for maintaining an aircraft in an airworthy condition. Certain inspections must be performed on an aircraft, and the airworthiness of the aircraft must be maintained between required inspections by having any defects corrected.

Federal Aviation Regulations require the inspection of all civil aircraft at specific intervals to determine the overall condition. The interval depends generally upon the type of operations engaged in. Some aircraft need to be inspected at least once each 12 calendar months, while inspection is required for others after each 100 hours of operation. In other instances, an aircraft may be inspected in accordance with an inspection system set up to provide for total inspection of the aircraft on the basis of calendar time, time in service, number of system operations, or any combination of these.

To determine the specific inspection requirements and rules for the performance of inspections, refer to the Federal Aviation Regulations which prescribe the requirements for various types of operations. (See Appendix II).

Annual Inspection. Any reciprocating-powered light aircraft, 12,500 pounds and under, flown for pleasure is required to be inspected at least annually by a certificated airframe and powerplant mechanic holding an inspection authorization, or a certificated repair station that is appropriately rated, or the manufacturer of the aircraft. The aircraft may not be operated unless the annual inspection has been performed within the preceding 12 calendar months. A period of 12 calendar months extends from any day of any month to the last day of the same month the following year. However, an aircraft with the annual inspection overdue may be operated under a special flight permit for the purpose of flying the aircraft to a location where the annual inspection can be performed.

100-Hour Inspection. Any reciprocating-powered light aircraft, 12,500 pounds and under, used to carry passengers or for flight instruction for hire must be inspected within each 100 hours of time in service by a certificated airframe and powerplant mechanic, a certificated repair station that is appropriately rated, or the aircraft manufacturer. An annual inspection is acceptable as a 100-hour inspection, but the reverse is not true.

Other Inspection Programs. The annual and 100-hour inspection requirements do not apply to large airplanes, turbojet, or turbo-propeller-powered multiengine airplanes, or to airplanes for which the owner or operator complies with the progressive inspection requirements. Details of these requirements may be determined by reference to Parts 43 and 91 of the Federal Aviation Regulations and by inquiry at a local FAA General Aviation or Flight Standards District Office.

Preflight Inspection. Although not required by Federal Aviation Regulations, a careful pilot will always conduct a thorough preflight inspection before every flight to satisfy himself that the aircraft is safe for flight.

Preventive Maintenance

Simple or minor preservation operations and the replacement of small standard parts, not involving complex assembly operations, are considered preventive maintenance. Certificated pilots may perform preventive maintenance on any aircraft owned or operated by them that are not used in air carrier service. Preventive maintenance operations are found in FAR Part 43, Maintenance, Preventive Maintenance, Rebuilding, and Alteration. Part 43 also contains other rules to be followed in the maintenance of aircraft.

Repairs and Alterations

Except as noted under the previous paragraph, Preventive Maintenance, all repairs and alterations are classed as either major or minor. Major repairs or alterations must be approved for return to service by an appropriately rated certificated repair station, an airframe and powerplant mechanic holding an inspection authorization, or a representative of the FAA. Minor repairs and alterations may be returned to service by a certificated airframe and powerplant mechanic or an appropriately certificated repair station.

USE OF MANUFACTURER'S MAINTENANCE MANUALS

The majority of aircraft built today are more complex than those built in the past. New materials and fabrication methods are used and sophisticated equipment is being installed, all of which require maintenance instructions and techniques which are not common knowledge or used on older aircraft. This complexity makes it more and more important that the owner and operator consider the manufacturer's information and recommendations concerning servicing, repairing, and maintaining aircraft, engines, and propellers. Owners and operators should find the information contained in manufacturer's maintenance manuals an invaluable source of data to meet the maintenance requirements discussed in the previous paragraphs.

Maintenance Manual Contents

Maintenance manuals which are issued under the FARs Part 23, Section 23.1529 and Part 25, Section 25.1529, and some earlier manuals, contain information the manufacturer considers essential for proper maintenance of the aircraft, engines, and propellers. Some manuals may contain a complete recommended detailed continuous maintenance program that the owner/operator may choose to adopt. In general, the manuals are likely to be structured as follows:

A step-by-step recipe format that should provide for continuity of recommended work schedules.

Information logically sequenced to make it easy to find and use.

Easy to follow expanded view drawings, charts or photographs supported by text.

Subject matter likely to be displayed in the manner of 1, 2, and 3 above are:
- Description of systems such as electrical, hydraulic, fuel controls, etc.
- Lubrication instructions setting forth the manufacturer's recommended frequency and the lubricants and fluids which are to be used in the various systems.
- Pressures and electrical loads applicable to the various systems.
- Tolerances and adjustments the manufacturer considers necessary

for proper functioning of the aircraft.
- Methods of leveling, raising, and towing.
- Methods of balancing control surfaces.
- Identification of primary and secondary structures.
- Frequency and extent of inspections the manufacturer considers necessary for proper maintenance of the aircraft.
- Special repair methods applicable to the aircraft.
- Special inspection techniques such as X-ray, ultrasonic, magnetic particle inspection, etc.
- List of special tools.

Manual Changes

Maintenance practices and requirements are not static and may change as information is developed during the service life of an aircraft. Manufacturers may provide a systematic manual revision system to implement changes to their maintenance instructions.

AIRCRAFT PARTS CATALOG

A companion to the manufacturer's Maintenance/Service manuals is the aircraft illustrated Parts Catalog issued for each aircraft model.

The illustrated parts catalogs is an amazingly detailed publication containing exploded views of every component of the aircraft showing every detail part and its part number.

AIRCRAFT MANUFACTURER'S TRAINING PROGRAMS

The major aircraft manufacturers provide training courses for maintenance personnel to familiarize them with the systems of their various aircraft. These courses include component nomenclature, location, operation, inspection, servicing and maintenance. When applicable, troubleshooting, test procedures, and adjustments are demonstrated on the actual aircraft, aircraft components, or mockups.

These courses are normally provided to dealer personnel without charge. They are also available to non-dealer personnel at a nominal charge for tuition.

Gates Learjet

Chapter 2
Basic Tools
and
Shop Equipment

By the time a mechanic studies for his A & P certificate, he already has a basic knowledge of tools and their use. However, a summary of the basic tools with emphasis on aircraft practices, is in order. Also, tools and equipment peculiar to the aircraft industry, are discussed.

This information, however, cannot replace sound judgment on the part of the individual. There are many times when ingenuity and resourcefulness can supplement the basic rules. A sound knowledge is required of these basic rules and of the situations in which they apply. The use of tools may vary, but good practices for safety, care, and storage of tools remain the same.

GENERAL-PURPOSE TOOLS

Hammers and Mallets

Figure 2-1 shows some of the hammers that the aviation mechanic may be required to use. Metal-head hammers are usually sized according to the weight of the head without the handle.

Occasionally it is necessary to use a soft-faced hammer, which has a striking surface made of wood, brass, lead, rawhide, hard rubber, or plastic. These hammers are intended for use in forming soft metals and striking surfaces that are easily damaged. Soft-faced hammers should not be used for rough work. Striking punch heads, bolts, or nails will quickly ruin this type hammer.

A mallet is a hammerlike tool with a head made of hickory, raw-hide, or rubber. It is handy for shaping thin metal parts without denting them. Always use a wooden mallet when pounding a wood chisel or gouge.

When using a hammer or mallet, choose the one best suited for the job. Ensure that the handle is tight. When striking a blow with the hammer, use the forearm as an extension of the handle. Swing the hammer by bending the elbow, not the wrist. Always strike the work squarely with the full face of the hammer.

Always keep the faces of hammers and mallets smooth and free from dents to prevent marring the work.

BALL PEEN   STRAIGHT PEEN   CROSS PEEN   TINNERS MALLET   RIVETING HAMMER

Figure 2-1. Various types of hammers.

Screwdrivers

Figure 2-2 shows several different types of screwdrivers. Always select the largest screwdriver whose blade will make a good fit in the screw which is to be turned.

A common screwdriver must fill at least 75 percent of the screw slot. If the screwdriver is the wrong size, it cuts and burrs the screw slot, making it worthless. A screwdriver with the wrong size blade may slip and damage adjacent parts of the structures. The common screwdriver is used only where slotted head screws or fasteners are found on aircraft.

The two types of recessed head screws in common use are the Phillips and the Reed and Prince. As shown in figure 2-2, the Reed and Prince recessed head forms a perfect cross. The screwdriver used with this screw is pointed on the end. Since the Phillips screw has a slightly larger center in the cross, the Phillips screwdriver is blunt on the end. The Phillips screwdriver is not interchangeable with the Reed and Prince. The use of the wrong type screwdriver results in mutilation of the screwdriver and the screwhead.

A screwdriver should not be used for chiseling or prying.

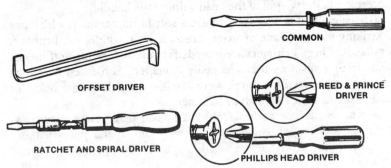

COMMON

OFFSET DRIVER

REED & PRINCE DRIVER

RATCHET AND SPIRAL DRIVER

PHILLIPS HEAD DRIVER

Figure 2-2. Typical screwdrivers.

Pliers and Plier Type Cutting Tools

There are several types of pliers, but those used most frequently in aircraft repair work are the diagonal, adjustable combination, needlenose, and duckbill. The size of pliers indicates their overall length, usually ranging from 5 to 12 inches. Figure 2-3 shows several types of pliers.

INTERLOCKING PLIERS

SLIP-JOINT PLIERS

NEEDLE NOSE PLIERS

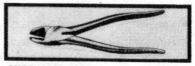

CUTTING PLIERS

Figure 2-3. Several types of pliers.

The 6-inch slip-joint plier, is the preferred size for use in repair work.

Flatnose pliers are very satisfactory for making flanges.

Roundnose pliers are used to crimp metal. They are not made for heavy work however.

Needlenose pliers have half-round jaws of varying lengths. They are used to hold objects and make adjustments in tight places.

Duckbill pliers resemble a "duck's bill" in that the jaws are thin, flat, and shaped like a duck's bill. They are used exclusively for twisting safety wire.

Water pump (channel locks) pliers are slip-joint pliers with the jaws set at an angle to the handles. The most popular type has the slip-joint channeled, hence the name channel locks. These are used to grasp packing nuts, pipe, and odd shaped parts.

Diagonal pliers are usually referred to as diagonals or "dikes." The diagonal is a short-jawed cutter with a blade set at a slight angle on each jaw. This tool can be used to cut wire, rivets, small screws, and cotter pins, besides being practically indispensible in removing or installing safety wire. The duckbill pliers and the diagonal cutting pliers are used extensively in aviation for the job of safety wiring.

An important rule for using pliers is:

Do not use pliers to turn nuts. In just a few seconds, a pair of pliers can damage a nut more than years of service.

Punches

Punches are used to start holes for drilling, to punch holes in sheet metal, to remove damaged rivets, pins or bolts and for aligning two or more parts for bolting together. Figure 2-4 shows the most common punches used in aircraft repair work.

7

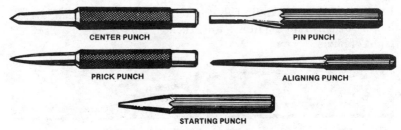

Figure 2-4. Typical punches.

Wrenches

The wrenches most often used in aircraft maintenance are classified as open-end, box-end, socket, adjustable, and special wrenches. The allen wrench, although seldom used, is required on one special type of recessed screw. One of the most widely used metals for making wrenches is chromevanadium steel. Wrenches made of this metal are almost unbreakable.

Box-end wrenches are ideal to break loose tight nuts or pull nuts tighter. However, after a nut is broken loose, it can be completely backed off or unscrewed more quickly with an open-end than with a box-end wrench. Figure 2-5 shows several typical wrenches.

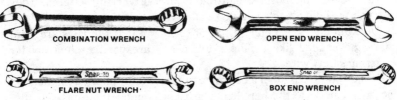

Figure 2-5. Box end and open end wrenches.

A socket wrench is made of two parts: (1) The socket, which is placed over the top of a nut or bolthead, and (2) a handle, which is attached to the socket. Figure 2-6 shows a typical socket wrench set.

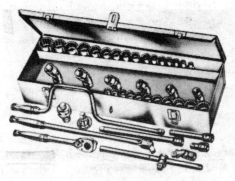

Figure 2-6. Typical socket wrench set.

8

The adjustable wrench is a handy utility tool which has smooth jaws and is designed as an open-end wrench. One jaw is fixed, but the other may be moved by a thumbscrew or spiral screwworm adjustment in the handle. The width of the jaws may be varied from 0 to ½ inch or more. One adjustable wrench does the work of several open-end wrenches. Although versatile, they are not intended to replace the standard open-end, box-end, or socket wrenches. When using any adjustable wrench, always exert the pull on the side of the handle attached to the fixed jaw of the wrench.

Special Wrenches

The category of special wrenches includes the spanner, torque, and allen wrenches. The hook spanner is for a round nut with a series of notches cut in the outer edge. This wrench has a curved arm with a hook on the end which fits into one of the notches on the nut.

There are times when definite pressure must be applied to a nut or bolt. In such cases a torque wrench must be used. The torque wrench is a precision tool consisting of a torque-indicating handle and appropriate adapter or attachments. It measures the amount of turning or twisting force applied to a nut, bolt, or screw.

The three most commonly used torque wrenches are the deflecting beam, dial-indicating, and micrometer-setting types. When using the deflecting beam and the dial-indicating torque wrenches, the torque is read visually on a dial or scale mounted on the handle of the wrench. The micrometer-setting torque wrench is preset to the desired torque. When this torque is reached, a sharp impulse or breakaway is noticed by the operator. Figure 2-7 shows a dial-indicating torque wrench.

Figure 2-7. Dial indicating torque wrench.

Before each use, the torque wrench should be visually inspected for damage. If a bent pointer, cracked or broken glass (dial type), or signs of rough handling are found, the wrench must be tested. Torque wrenches must be tested at periodic intervals to ensure accuracy.

Most headless setscrews are the allen type and must be installed and removed with an allen wrench. Allen wrenches are six-sided bars in the shape of an L. They range in size from 3/64 to ½ inch and fit into a hexagonal recess in the setscrew.

METAL CUTTING TOOLS

Hand Snips

There are several kinds of hand snips, each of which serves a different purpose. Straight, curved, hawksbill, and aviation snips are in common use (figure 2-8). Straight snips are used for cutting straight lines when the distance is not great enough to use a squaring shear and for cutting the outside of a curve. The other types are used for cutting the inside of curves or radii. Snips should never be used to cut heavy sheet metal.

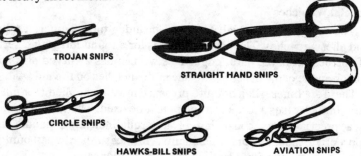

Figure 2-8. Various types of snips.

Aviation snips are designed especially for cutting heat-treated aluminum alloy and stainless steel. They are also adaptable for enlarging small holes. The blades have small teeth on the cutting edges and are shaped for cutting very small circles and irregular outlines. The handles are the compound leverage type, making it possible to cut material as thick as 0.051 inch. Aviation snips are available in two types, those which cut from right to left and those which cut from left to right.

Unlike the hacksaw, snips do not remove any material when the cut is made, but minute fractures often occur along the cut. Therefore, cuts should be made about one-thirty-second inch from the layout line and finished by hand-filing down to the line.

Hacksaws

The common hacksaw has a blade, a frame, and a handle. The handle can be obtained in two styles, pistol grip and straight (figure 2-9).

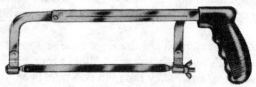

Figure 2-9. Pistol grip hacksaw.

When installing a blade in a hacksaw frame, mount the blade with the teeth pointing forward, away from the handle.

Blades are made of high-grade tool steel or tungsten steel and are available in sizes from 6 to 16 inches in length. The 10-inch blade is most commonly used. There are two types, the all-hard blade and the flexible blade. In flexible blades, only the teeth are hardened. Selection of the best blade for the job involves finding the right type and pitch. An all-hard blade is best for sawing brass, tool steel, cast iron, and heavy cross-section materials. A flexible blade is usually best for sawing hollow shapes and metals having a thin cross section.

The pitch of a blade indicates the number of teeth per inch. Pitches of 14, 18, 24, and 32 teeth per inch are available. A blade with 14 teeth per inch is preferred when cutting machine steel, cold-rolled steel, or structural steel. A blade with 18 teeth per inch is preferred for solid stock aluminum, bearing metal, tool steel, and cast iron. Use a blade with 24 teeth per inch when cutting thick-walled tubing, pipe, brass, copper, channel, and angle iron. Use a 32-teeth-per-inch blade for cutting thin-walled tubing and sheet metal.

When using the hacksaw, make each stroke as long as the hacksaw frame will allow. This will prevent the blade from overheating. Apply just enough pressure on the foreward stroke to cause each tooth to remove a small amount of metal. The strokes should be long and steady with a speed of not more than 50 or 60 strokes per minute.

Chisels

A chisel is a hard steel cutting tool which can be used for cutting and chipping any metal softer than the chisel itself. It can be used in restricted areas and for such work as shearing rivets, or splitting seized or damaged nuts from bolts (figure 2-10).

Figure 2-10. Chisels.

The size of a flat cold chisel is determined by the width of the cutting edge. Lengths will vary, but chisels are seldom under 5 inches or over 8 inches long.

Chisels are usually made of eight-sided tool steel bar stock, carefully hardened and tempered. Since the cutting edge is slightly

11

convex, the center portion receives the greatest shock when cutting, and the weaker corners are protected. The cutting angle should be 60 degrees to 70 degrees for general use, such as for cutting wire, strap iron, or small bars and rods.

When using a chisel, hold it firmly in one hand. With the other hand, strike the chisel head squarely with a ball-peen hammer.

When cutting square corners or slots, a special cold chisel called a cape chisel should be used. It is like a flat chisel except the cutting edge is very narrow. It has the same cutting angle and is held and used in the same manner as any other chisel.

Rounded or semicircular grooves and corners which have fillets should be cut with a roundnose chisel. This chisel is also used to recenter a drill which has moved away from its intended center.

The diamond point chisel is tapered square at the cutting end, then ground at an angle to provide the sharp diamond point. It is used for cutting B-grooves and inside sharp angles.

Files

Files are used to square ends, file rounded corners, remove burrs and slivers from metal, straighten uneven edges, file holes and slots, and smooth rough edges.

Files are usually made in two types of cuts, single-cut and double-cut. The single-cut file has a single row of teeth extending across the face at an angle of 65 degrees to 85 degrees with the length of the file. The size of the cuts depends on the coarseness of the file. The double-cut file has two rows of teeth which cross each other. For general work, the angle of the first row is 40 degrees to 45 degrees. The first row is generally referred to as "overcut," and the second row as "upcut"; the upcut is somewhat finer and not so deep as the overcut.

Files—Care and Use

Files and rasps are cataloged in three ways:

Length. Measuring from the tip to the heel of the file. The tang is never included in the length.

Shape. Refers to the physical configuration of the file (circular, rectangular, or triangular or a variation thereof).

Cut. Refers to both the character of the teeth or the coarseness; rough, coarse and bastard for use on heavier classes of work and second cut, smooth and dead smooth for finishing work.

Most Commonly Used Files (see figure 2-11)

Hand files. These are parallel in width and tapered in thickness. They have one safe edge (smooth edge) which permits filing in corners, and on other work where a safe edge is required. Hand files are double-cut and used principally for finishing flat surfaces and similar work.

Flat files. These files are slightly tapered toward the point in both width and thickness. They cut on both edges as well as on the sides. They are the most common files in use. Flat files are double-cut on both sides and single-cut on both edges.

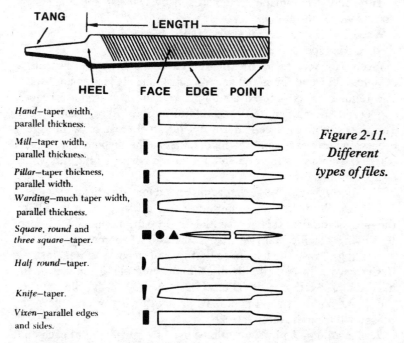

Figure 2-11. Different types of files.

Mill files. These are usually tapered slightly in thickness and in width for about one-third of their length. The teeth are ordinarily single-cut. These files are used for drawfiling and to some extent for filing soft metals.

Square files. These files may be tapered or blunt and are double-cut. They are used principally for filing slots and key seats, and for surface filing.

Round or rattail files. These are circular in cross section and may be either tapered or blunt and single- or double-cut. They are used principally for filing circular openings or concave surfaces.

Triangular and Three-square files. These files are triangular in cross section. Triangular files are single-cut and are used for filing the gullet between saw teeth. Three-square files, which are double-cut, may be used for filing internal angles, clearing out corners, and filing taps and cutters.

Half-round files. These files cut on both the flat and round sides.

13

They may be single- or double-cut. Their shape permits them to be used where other files would be unsatisfactory.

Lead float files. These are especially designed for use on soft metals. They are single-cut and are made in various lengths.

Warding file. Rectangular in section and tapers to narrow point as to width. Used for narrow space filing where other files cannot be used.

Knife file. Knife-blade section. Used by tool and die makers on work having acute angles.

Wood file. Same section as flat and half round files. Has coarser teeth and is especially adaptable for use on wood.

Vixen (Curved tooth files). Curved tooth files are especially designed for rapid filing and smooth finish on soft metals and wood. The regular cut is adapted for tough work on cast iron, soft steel, copper, brass, aluminum, wood, slate, marble, fibre, rubber, etc. The fine cut gives excellent results on steel, cast iron, phosphor bronze, white brass, and all hard metals. The smooth cut is used where the amount of material to be removed is very slight, but where a superior finish is desired.

The following methods are recommended for using files:

1. **Crossfiling.** Before attempting to use a file, place a handle on the tang of the file. This is essential for proper guiding and safe use. In moving the file endwise across the work (commonly known as crossfiling), grasp the handle so that its end fits into and against the fleshy part of the palm with the thumb lying along the top of the handle in a lengthwise direction. Grasp the end of the file between the thumb and first two fingers. To prevent undue wear, relieve the pressure during the return stroke.

2. **Drawfiling.** A file is sometimes used by grasping it at each end, crosswise to the work, then moving it lengthwise with the work. When done properly, work may be finished somewhat finer than when crossfiling with the same file. In drawfiling, the teeth of the file produce a shearing effect. To accomplish this shearing effect, the angle at which the file is held with respect to its line of movement varies with different files, depending on the angle at which the teeth are cut. Pressure should be relieved during the backstroke.

3. **Rounding Corners.** The method used in filing a rounded surface depends upon its width and the radius of the rounded surface. If the surface is narrow or only a portion of a surface is to be rounded, start the forward stroke of the file with the point of the file inclinded downward at approximately a 45 degree angle. Using a rocking chair motion, finish the stroke with the heel of the file near the curved surface. This method allows use of the full length of the file.

4. **Removing Burred or Slivered Edges.** Practically every cutting operation on sheet metal produces burrs or slivers. These must be

removed to avoid personal injury and to prevent scratching and marring of parts to be assembled. Burrs and slivers will prevent parts from fitting properly and should always be removed from the work as a matter of habit.

Lathe filing requires that the file be held against the work revolving in the lathe. The file should not be held rigid or stationary but should be stroked constantly with a slight gliding or lateral motion along the work. A standard mill file may be used for this operation, but the long angle lathe file provides a much cleaner shearing and self-clearing action. Use a file with "safe" edges to protect work with shoulders from being marred.

Particles of metal collect between the teeth of a file and may make deep scratches in the material being filed. When these particles of metal are lodged too firmly between the teeth and cannot be removed by tapping the edge of the file, remove them with a file card or wire brush (figure 2-12). Draw the brush across the file so that the bristles pass down the gullet between the teeth.

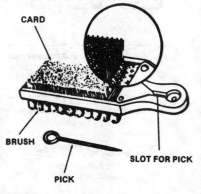

Figure 2-12. File card used for cleaning files.

Drills

Holes ¼ inch in diameter and under can be drilled using a hand drill however, power drills are almost universally used. Electric and pneumatic power drills are available in various shapes and sizes. Pneumatic drills are preferred for use around flammable materials, since sparks from an electric drill are a fire or explosive hazard.

Twist Drills

Twist drills are made of carbon steel or high-speed alloy steel. Carbon steel twist drills are satisfactory for the general run of work and are relatively inexpensive. The more expensive high-speed twist drills are used for the tough materials such as stainless steels. See figure 2-13 and 2-14.

Straight shank twist drills (figure 2-14), are generally used in hand and portable electric drills. Tapered shanks generally are used in

15

machine shop drill presses.

The diameter of a twist drill may be given in one or three ways: (1) By fractions, (2) letters, or (3) numbers. Fractionally, they are classified by sixteenths of an inch (from 1/16 to 3½ in.), by thirty-seconds (from 1/32 to 2½ in.), or by sixty-fourths (from 1/64 to 1¼ in.). For a more exact measurement a letter system is used with decimal equivalents: **A** (0.234 in.) to **Z** (0.413 in.). The number system of classification is most accurate: No. 80 (0.0314 in.) to No. 1 (0.228 in.). Drill sizes to ½ inch are shown in figure 2-15. Figure 2-16 shows a drill gage.

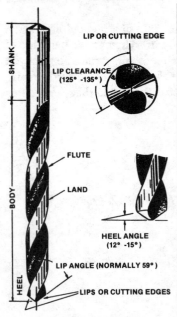

Figure 2-13. Twist drill details.

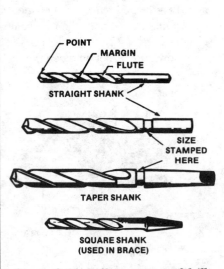

Figure 2-14. Different types of drills.

The twist drill should be sharpened at the first sign of dullness. For most drilling, a twist drill with a cutting angle of 118 degrees (59 degrees on either side of center) will be sufficient; however, when drilling soft metals, a cutting angle of 90 degrees may be more efficient.

Drill speeds are generally a function of the material being drilled. Soft materials such as aluminum should be drilled at high speeds whereas hard materials such as stainless steels require low drill speeds. Cutting speed tables are available, however, most shop equipment has no speed indications, therefore experience is the best factor in determining drill speeds.

Extensive drilling, normally not encountered in aircraft repair work may require use of a coolant.

Drill No.	Frac.	Deci.	Drill No.	Frac.	Deci.	Drill No.	Frac.	Deci.	Drill No.	Frac.	Deci.
80	—	.0135	42	—	.0935	7	—	.201	X	—	.397
79	—	.0145	—	3/32	.0938	—	13/64	.203	Y	—	.404
—	1/64	.0156	41	—	.0960	6	—	.204	—	13/32	.406
78	—	.0160	40	—	.0980	5	—	.206	Z	—	.413
77	—	.0180	39	—	.0995	4	—	.209	—	27/64	.422
76	—	.0200	38	—	.1015	3	—	.213	—	7/16	.438
75	—	.0210	37	—	.1040	—	7/32	.219	—	29/64	.453
74	—	.0225	36	—	.1065	2	—	.221	—	15/32	.469
73	—	.0240	—	7/64	.1094	1	—	.228	—	31/64	.484
72	—	.0250	35	—	.1100	A	—	.234	—	1/2	.500
71	—	.0260	34	—	.1110	—	15/64	.234	—	33/64	.516
70	—	.0280	33	—	.1130	B	—	.238	—	17/32	.531
69	—	.0292	32	—	.116	C	—	.242	—	35/64	.547
68	—	.0310	31	—	.120	D	—	.246	—	9/16	.562
—	1/32	.0313	—	1/8	.125	—	1/4	.250	—	37/64	.578
67	—	.0320	30	—	.129	E	—	.250	—	19/32	.594
66	—	.0330	29	—	.136	F	—	.257	—	39/64	.609
65	—	.0350	28	—	.141	G	—	.261	—	5/8	.625
64	—	.0360	27	—	.144	—	17/64	.266	—	41/64	.641
63	—	.0370	26	—	.147	H	—	.266	—	21/32	.656
62	—	.0380	25	—	.150	I	—	.272	—	43/64	.672
61	—	.0390	24	—	.152	J	—	.277	—	11/16	.688
60	—	.0400	23	—	.154	—	9/32	.281	—	45/64	.703
59	—	.0410	—	5/32	.156	K	—	.281	—	23/32	.719
58	—	.0420	22	—	.157	L	—	.290	—	47/64	.734
57	—	.0430	21	—	.159	M	—	.295	—	3/4	.750
56	—	.0465	20	—	.161	—	19/64	.297	—	49/64	.766
—	3/64	.0469	19	—	.166	N	—	.302	—	25/32	.781
55	—	.0520	18	—	.170	—	5/16	.313	—	51/64	.797
54	—	.0550	—	11/64	.172	O	—	.316	—	13/16	.813
53	—	.0595	17	—	.173	P	—	.323	—	53/64	.828
—	1/16	.0625	16	—	.177	—	21/64	.328	—	27/32	.844
52	—	.0635	15	—	.180	Q	—	.332	—	55/64	.859
51	—	.0670	14	—	.182	R	—	.339	—	7/8	.875
50	—	.0700	13	—	.185	—	11/32	.344	—	57/64	.891
49	—	.0730	—	3/16	.188	S	—	.348	—	29/32	.906
48	—	.0760	12	—	.189	T	—	.358	—	59/64	.922
—	5/64	.0781	11	—	.191	—	23/64	.359	—	15/16	.938
47	—	.0785	10	—	.194	U	—	.368	—	61/64	.953
46	—	.0810	9	—	.196	—	3/8	.375	—	31/32	.969
45	—	.0820	8	—	.199	V	—	.377	—	63/64	.984
44	—	.0860				W	—	.386	—	1	1.000
43	—	.0890				—	25/64	.391			

Figure 2-15. Sizes and designations of fraction, number and letter drills.

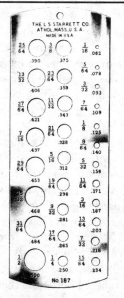

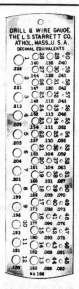

Figure 2-16. Drill gages; fraction on the left and number on the right.

Decimal equivalents are also given.

17

Reamers

Reamers are used to smooth and enlarge holes to exact size. Hand reamers have square end shanks so that they can be turned with a tap wrench or similar handle. The various types of reamers are illustrated in figure 2-17.

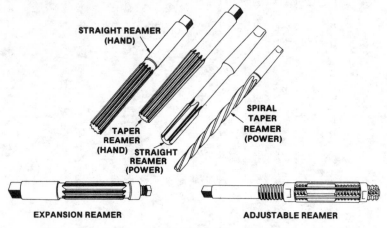

Figure 2-17. Typical reamers.

A hole that is to be reamed to exact size must be drilled about 0.003- to 0.007-inch undersize. A cut that removes more than 0.007 inch places too much load on the reamer and should not be attempted.

Reamers are made of either carbon tool steel or high-speed steel. The cutting blades of a high-speed steel reamer lose their original keenness sooner than those of a carbon steel reamer; however, after the first super-keeness is gone, they are still serviceable. The high-speed reamer usually lasts much longer than the carbon steel type.

Reamer blades are hardened to the point of being brittle and must be handled carefully to avoid chipping them. When reaming a hole, rotate the reamer in the cutting direction only. Turn the reamer steadily and evenly to prevent chattering, or marking and scoring of the hole walls.

Reamers are available in any standard size. The straight-fluted reamer is less expensive than the spiral-fluted reamer, but the spiral type has less tendency to chatter. Both types are tapered for a short distance back of the end to aid in starting. Bottoming reamers have no taper and are used to complete the reaming of blind holes.

For general use, an expansion reamer is the most practical. This type is furnished in standard sizes from ¼ inch to 1 inch, increasing in diameter by 1/32-inch increments.

Taper reamers, both hand- and machine-operated, are used to smooth and true tapered holes and recesses.

Countersink

A countersink is a tool which cuts a cone-shaped depression around the hole to allow a rivet or screw to set flush with the surface of the material. Countersinks are made with various angles to correspond to the various angles of the countersunk rivet and screwheads. The angle of the standard countersink shown in figure 2-18 is 100 degrees.

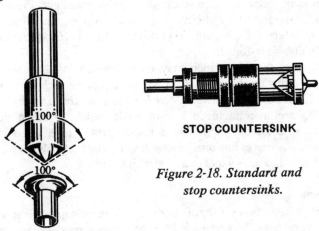

STOP COUNTERSINK

Figure 2-18. Standard and stop countersinks.

STANDARD COUNTERSINK

Special stop countersinks are available. Stop countersinks (figure 2-18) are adjustable to any desired depth, and the cutters are interchangeable so that holes of various countersunk angles may be made. Some stop countersinks have a micrometer set arrangement (in increments of 0.001 inch) for adjusting the cutting depths.

When using a countersink, care must be taken not to remove an excessive amount of material since this reduces the strength of flush joints.

LAYOUT AND MEASURING TOOLS

Layout and measuring devices are precision tools. They are carefully machined, accurately marked and, in many cases, are made up of very delicate parts. When using these tools, be careful not to drop, bend, or scratch them. The finished product will be no more accurate than the measurements or the layout; therefore, it is very important to understand how to read, use, and care for these tools.

Rules

Rules are made of steel and are either rigid or flexible. The flexible steel rule will bend, but it should not be bent intentionally as it may be broken rather easily. See figure 2-19.

Figure 2-19. Steel rules are available in various lengths.

In aircraft work the unit of measure most commonly used is the inch. The inch may be divided into smaller parts by means of either common or decimal fraction divisions. The fractional divisions for an inch are found by dividing the inch into equal parts—halves (½), quarters (¼), eighths (⅛), sixteenths, (1/16), thirty-seconds (1/32), and sixty-fourths (1/64).

The fractions of an inch may be expressed in decimals, called decimal equivalents of an inch; for example, ⅛ inch is expressed as 0.0125 (one hundred twenty-five ten-thousandths of an inch).

Rules are manufactured in two basic styles, those divided or marked in common fractions and those divided or marked in decimals or divisions of one one-hundredth of an inch. A rule may be used either as a measuring tool or as a straightedge.

Combination Sets

The combination set (figure 2-20), as its name implies, is a tool that has several uses. It can be used for the same purposes as an ordinary tri-square, but it differs from the tri-square in that the head slides along the blade and can be clamped at any desired place. Combined with the square or stock head are a level and scriber. The head slides in a central groove on the blade or scale, which can be used separately as a rule.

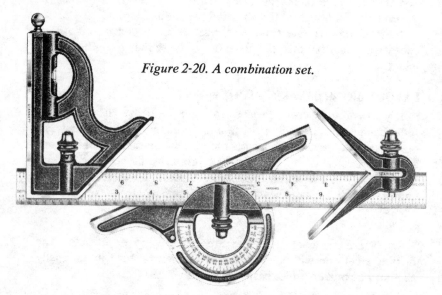

Figure 2-20. A combination set.

The spirit level in the stock head makes it convenient to square a piece of material with a surface and at the same time tell whether one or the other is plumb or level. The head can be used alone as a simple level.

The combination of square head and blade can also be used as a marking gage to scribe lines at a 45 degree angle, as a depth gage, or as a height gage.

Scriber

In general, the scriber (figure 2-21) is used to scribe or mark lines on metal surfaces.

Figure 2-21. A scriber.

Dividers and Calipers

Dividers have two legs tapered to a needle point and joined at the top by a pivot. They are used to scribe circles and for transferring measurements from the rule to the work.

Calipers are used for measuring diameters and distances or for comparing distances and sizes. The most common types of calipers are the inside and the outside calipers. (see figure 2-22).

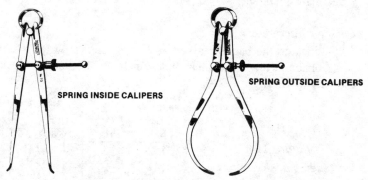

SPRING INSIDE CALIPERS

SPRING OUTSIDE CALIPERS

Figure 2-22. Typical inside and outside calipers.

Micrometer Calipers

There are four types of micrometer calipers, each designed for a specific use. The four types are commonly called outside micrometer, figure 2-23, inside micrometer, depth micrometer, and thread micrometer. Micrometers are available in a variety of sizes, either 0 to ½ inch, 0 to 1 inch, 1 to 2 inch, 2 to 3 inch, 3 to 4 inch, 4 to 5 inch, or 5 to 6 inch sizes. Even larger sizes are available.

The 0 to 1 inch outside micrometer (figure 2-23) is used by the mechanic more often than any other type. It may be used to measure the outside dimensions of shafts, thickness of sheet metal stock, diameter of drills, and for many other applications.

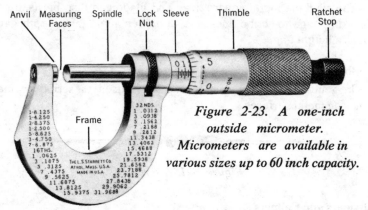

Figure 2-23. A one-inch outside micrometer. Micrometers are available in various sizes up to 60 inch capacity.

The smallest measurement which can be made with the use of the steel rule is one sixty-fourth of an inch in common fractions, and one one-hundredth of an inch in decimal fractions. To measure more closely than this (in thousandths and ten-thousandths of an inch), a micrometer is used. If a dimension given in a common fraction is to be measured with the micrometer, the fraction must be converted to its decimal equivalent.

Reading a Micrometer

The lines on the barrel marked 1, 2, 3, 4, etc., indicate measurements of tenths, or 0.100 inch, 0.200 inch, 0.300 inch, 0.400 inch, respectively (see figure 2-24).

Figure 2-24. Reading a micrometer.

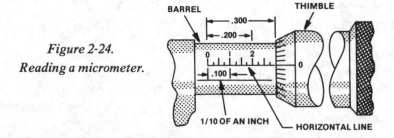

Each of the sections between the tenths divisions (between 1, 2, 3, 4, etc.) is divided into four parts of 0.025 inch each. One complete revolution of the thimble (from zero on the thimble around to the same zero) moves it one of these divisions (0.025 inch) along the barrel.

The bevel edge of the thimble is divided into 25 equal parts. Each of these parts represents one twenty-fifth of the distance the thimble travels along the barrel in moving from one of the 0.025-inch divisions to another. Thus, each division on the thimble represents one one-thousandth (0.001) of an inch. These divisions are marked for convenience at every five spaces by 0, 5, 10, 15, and 20. When 25 of these graduations have passed the horizontal line on the barrel, the spindle (having made one revolution) has moved 0.025 inch.

The micrometer is read by first noting the last visible figure on the horizontal line of the barrel representing tenths of an inch. Add to this the length of barrel between the thimble and the previously noted number. (This is found by multiplying the number of graduations by 0.025 inch.) Add to this the number of divisions on the bevel edge of the thimble that coincides with the line of the graduation. The total of the three figures equals the measurement.

Using a Micrometer

The micrometer must be handled carefully. If it is dropped, its accuracy may be permanently affected. Continually sliding work between the anvil and spindle may wear the surfaces. If the spindle is tightened too much, the frame may be sprung permanently and inaccurate readings will result.

To measure a piece of work with the micrometer, hold the frame of the micrometer in the palm of the hand with the little finger or third finger, whichever is more convenient. This allows the thumb and forefinger to be free to revolve the thimble for adjustment.

TAPS AND DIES

A tap is used to cut threads on the inside of a hole, while a die is for cutting external threads on round stock. They are made of hard-tempered steel and ground to an exact size. There are four types of threads that can be cut with standard taps and dies. They are: National Coarse, National Fine, National Extra Fine, and National Pipe.

Hand taps are usually provided in sets of three taps for each diameter and thread series. Each set contains a taper tap, a plug tap, and a bottoming tap. The taps in a set are identical in diameter and cross section; the only difference is the amount of taper (see figure 2-25).

The taper tap is used to begin the tapping process, because it is tapered back for 6 to 7 threads. This tap cuts a complete thread when it is needed when tapping holes that extend through thin sections. The plug tap supplements the taper tap for tapping holes in thick stock.

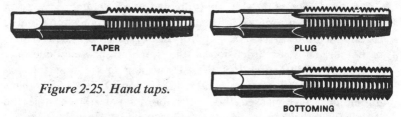

TAPER

PLUG

Figure 2-25. Hand taps.

BOTTOMING

The bottoming tap is not tapered. It is used to cut full threads to the bottom of a blind hole.

Dies may be classified as adjustable round split die, and plain round split die (see figure 2-26). The adjustable-split die has an adjusting screw that can be tightened so that the die is spread slightly. By adjusting the die, the diameter and fit of the thread can be controlled.

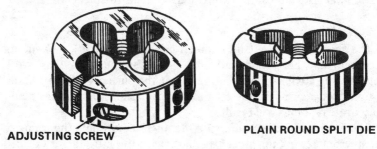

ADJUSTING SCREW

PLAIN ROUND SPLIT DIE

ADJUSTABLE ROUND SPLIT DIE

Figure 2-26. Types of dies.

Solid dies are not adjustable; therefore, a variety of thread fits cannot be obtained with this type.

There are many types of wrenches for turning taps, as well as turning dies. The T-handle, the adjustable tap wrench, and the diestock for round split dies down in figure 2-27 are a few of the more common types.

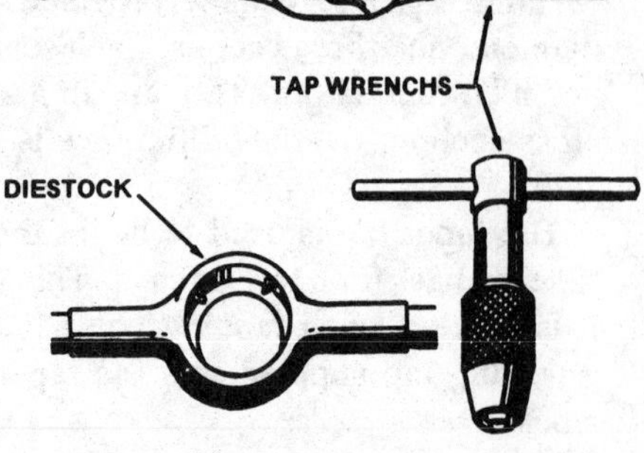

Figure 2-27.
Diestock and tap wrenches.

TAP WRENCHS

DIESTOCK

Information on thread sizes, fits, types, etc., is shown in figure 2-28.

NATIONAL COARSE THREAD SERIES MEDIUM FIT. CLASS 3 (NC)					NATIONAL FINE THREAD SERIES MEDIUM FIT. CLASS 3 (NF)				
Size and Threads	Dia. of body for thread	Body Drill	Tap Drill		Size and threads	Dia. of body for thread	Body Drill	Tap Drill	
			Pref'd dia. of hole	Nearest stand'd Drill Size				Pref'd dia. of hole	Nearest stand'd Drill Size
					0-80	.060	52	.0472	3/64
1-64	.073	47	.0575	#53	1-72	.073	47	.0591	#53
2-56	.086	42	.0682	#51	2-64	.086	42	.0700	#50
3-48	.099	37	.078	5/64	3-56	.099	37	.0810	#46
4-40	.112	31	.0866	#44	4-48	.112	31	.0911	#42
5-40	.125	29	.0995	#39	5-44	.125	25	.1024	#38
6-32	.138	27	.1063	#36	6-40	.138	27	.113	#33
8-32	.164	18	.1324	#29	8-36	.164	18	.136	#29
10-24	.190	10	.1472	#26	10-32	.190	10	.159	#21
12-24	.216	2	.1732	#17	12-28	.216	2	.180	#15
1/4-20	.250	1/4	.1990	#8	1/4-28	.250	F	.213	#3
5/16-18	.3125	5/16	.2559	#F	5/16-24	.3125	5/16	.2703	I
3/8-16	.375	3/8	.3110	5/16"	3/8-24	.375	3/8	.332	Q
7/16-14	.4375	7/16	.3642	U	7/16-20	.4375	7/16	.386	W
1/2-13	.500	1/2	.4219	27/64"	1/2-20	.500	1/2	.449	7/16"
9/16-12	.5625	9/16	.4776	31/64"	9/16-18	.5625	9/16	.506	1/2"
5/8-11	.625	5/8	.5315	17/32"	5/8-18	.625	5/8	.568	9/16"
3/4-10	.750	3/4	.6480	41/64"	3/4-16	.750	3/4	.6688	11/16"
7/8-9	.875	7/8	.7307	49/64"	7/8-14	.875	7/8	.7822	51/64"
1-8	1.000	1.0	.8376	7/8"	1-14	1.000	1.0	.9072	49/64"

Figure 2-28. American (National) screw threads. Standard AN aircraft bolts are threaded in National Fine, class 3 (NF) thread series.

Final assembly line for Cessna 152. (Cessna Aircraft Co. photo.)

Chapter 3
Materials and Processes

STRUCTURAL METALS

Knowledge and understanding of the uses, strengths, limitations, and other characteristics of structural metals is vital to properly construct and maintain any equipment, especially airframes. In aircraft maintenance and repair, even a slight deviation from design specification, or the substitution of inferior materials, may result in the loss of both lives and equipment. The selection of the correct material for a specific repair job demands familiarity with the most common physical properties of various metals.

Properties of Metals

Of primary concern in aircraft maintenance are such general properties of metal and their alloys as hardness malleability, ductility, elasticity, toughness, density, brittleness, fusibility, conductivity contraction and expansion, and so forth.

The tensile strength of a material is its resistance to a force which tends to pull it apart. Tensile strength is measured in p.s.i. (pounds per square inch) and is calculated by dividing the load, in pounds, required to pull the material apart by its cross-sectional area, in square inches.

The compression strength of a material is its resistance to a crushing force which is the opposite of tensile strength. Compression strength is also measured in p.s.i.

Shear is the tendency on the part of parallel members to slide in opposite directions. It is like placing a cord or thread between the blades of a pair of scissors. The shear strength is the shear force in p.s.i. at which a material fails. It is the load divided by the shear area.

Bending can be described as the deflection or curving of a member due to forces acting upon it. The bending strength of material is the resistance it offers to deflecting forces.

Torsion is a twisting force. Such action would occur in a member fixed at one end and twisted at the other. The torsional strength of material is its resistance to twisting.

Corrosion is the eating away or pitting of the surface or the internal structure of metals. Because of the thin sections and the safety factors used in aircraft design and construction, it would be dangerous to select a material possessing poor corrosion-resistant characteristics.

Another significant factor to consider in maintenance and repair is the ability of a material to be formed, bent, or machined to required shapes. The hardening of metals by cold-working or forming is termed work-hardening. If a piece of metal is formed (shaped or bent) while cold, it is said to be cold-worked.

Any process which involves controlled heating and cooling of metals to develop certain desirable characteristics (such as hardness, softness, ductility, tensile strength, or refined grain structure) is called heat treatment or heat treating. With steels the term "heat treating" has a broad meaning and includes such processes as annealing, normalizing, hardening, and tempering.

In the heat treatment of aluminum alloys, only two processes are included: (1) The hardening and toughening process, and (2) the softening process. The hardening and toughening process is called heat treating, and the softening process is called annealing.

Metalworking Processes

There are three methods of metalworking: (1) Hot-working, (2) cold-working, and (3) extruding. The method used will depend on the metal involved and the part required, although in some instances both hot- and cold-working methods may be used to make a single part.

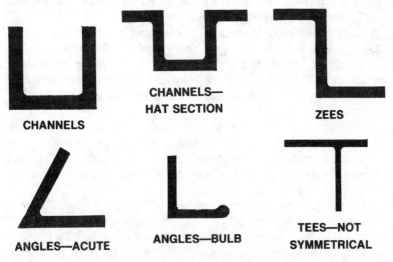

CHANNELS

CHANNELS—
HAT SECTION

ZEES

ANGLES—ACUTE

ANGLES—BULB

TEES—NOT
SYMMETRICAL

Figure 3-1. Typical aluminum alloy extrusions.

27

Practically all the work an aviation mechanic does on metal is cold-work. While this is convenient, it causes the metal to become harder and more brittle.

Many structural parts, such as channels, angles, T-sections, and Z-sections are formed by the extrusion process. (See figure 3-1).

NONFERROUS AIRCRAFT METALS

The term "nonferrous" refers to all metals which have elements other than iron as their base or principal constituent. This group includes such metals as aluminum, titanium, copper, and magnesium, as well as such alloyed metals as Monel and babbit.

ALUMINUM AND ALUMINUM ALLOYS

Aluminum is one of the most widely used metals in modern aircraft construction. It is vital to the aviation industry because of its high strength-to-weight ratio and its comparative ease of fabrication. The outstanding characteristic of aluminum is its light weight. Aluminum melts at the comparatively low temperature of 1,250° F. It is non-magnetic and is an excellent conductor.

Commercially pure aluminum is a white lustrous metal. Aluminum combined with various percentages of other metals forms alloys which are used in aircraft construction.

Aluminum alloys in which the principal alloying ingredients are either manganese, chromium, or magnesium and silicon show little attack in corrosive environments. Alloys in which substantial percentages of copper are used are more susceptible to corrosive action. The total percentage of alloying elements is seldom more than 6 or 7 percent in the wrought alloys.

Commercially pure aluminum has a tensile strength of about 13,000 p.s.i., but by rolling or other cold-working processes its strength may be approximately doubled. By alloying with other metals, or by using heat-treating processes, the tensile strength may be raised to as high as 65,000 p.s.i. or to within the strength range of structural steel.

Aluminum alloys, although strong, are easily worked because they are malleable and ductile. Most aluminum alloy sheet stock used in aircraft construction ranges from .016 to .096 inch in thickness; however, some of the larger aircraft use sheet stock which may be as thick as .356 inch.

The various types of aluminum may be divided into two general classes: (1) The casting alloys (those suitable for casting in sand, permanent mold, die castings), and (2) the wrought alloys (those which may be shaped by rolling, drawing, or forging). Of these two, the wrought alloys are the most widely used in aircraft construction, being used for stringers, bulkheads, skin, rivets, and extruded sections.

Aluminum Casting Alloys

Aluminum casting alloys are divided into two basic groups. In one, the physical properties of the alloys are determined by the alloying elements and cannot be changed after the metal is cast. In the other, the alloying elements make it possible to heat treat the casting to produce the desired physical properties.

The casting alloys are identified by a letter preceding the alloy number. When a letter precedes a number, it indicates a slight variation in the composition of the original alloy. This variation in composition is simply to impart some desirable quality. In casting alloy 214, for example, the addition of zinc to improve its pouring qualities is indicated by the letter A in front of the number, thus creating the designation A214.

When castings have been heat treated, the heat treatment and the composition of the casting is indicated by the letter T, followed by an alloying number. An example of this is the sand casting alloy 355, which has several different compositions and tempers and is designated by 355-T6, 355-T51, or C355-T51.

Aluminum alloy castings are produced by one of three basic methods: (1) Sand mold, (2) permanent mold, or (3) die cast. In casting aluminum, different types of alloys are used for different types of castings. Sand castings and die castings require different types of alloys than those used in permanent molds.

Wrought Aluminum and Alloys

Wrought aluminum and wrought aluminum alloys are divided into two general classes, nonheat-treatable alloys and heat-treatable alloys.

Nonheat-treatable alloys are those in which the mechanical properties are determined by the amount of cold-work introduced after the final annealing operation. The mechanical properties obtained by cold working are destroyed by any subsequent heating and cannot be restored except by additional cold working, which is not always possible. The "full hard" temper is produced by the maximum amount of cold-work that is commercially practicable. Metal in the "as fabricated" condition is produced from the ingot without any subsequent controlled amount of cold working or thermal treatment. There is, consequently, a variable amount of strain hardening, depending upon the thickness of the section.

For heat-treatable aluminum alloys the mechanical properties are obtained by heat treating to a suitable temperature, holding at that temperature long enough to allow the alloying constituent to enter into solid solution, and then quenching to hold the constituent in solution. The metal is left in a supersaturated, unstable state and is then age hardened either by natural aging at room temperature or by artificial aging at some elevated temperature.

Aluminum Designations

Wrought aluminum and wrought aluminum alloys are designated by a four-digit index system. The system is broken into three distinct groups: 1xxx group, 2xxx through 8xxx group, and 9xxx group (which is at present unused).

The first digit of a designation identifies the alloy type. The second digit indicates specific alloy modifications. Should the second number be zero, it would indicate no special control over individual impurities. Digit 1 through 9, however, when assigned consecutively as needed for the second number in this group, indicate the number of controls over individual impurities in the metal.

The last two digits of the 1xxx group are used to indicate the hundredths of 1 percent above the original 99 percent designated by the first digit. Thus, if the last two digits were 30, the alloy would contain 99 percent plus 0.30 percent of pure aluminum, or a total of 99.30 percent pure aluminum. Examples of alloys in this group are:

1100—99.00 percent pure aluminum with one control over individual impurities.

1130—99.30 percent pure aluminum with one control over individual impurities.

1275—99.75 percent pure aluminum with two controls over individual impurities.

In the 2xxx through 8xxx groups, the first digit indicates the major alloying element used in the formation of the alloy as follows:

2xxx—copper.

3xxx—manganese.

4xxx—silicon.

5xxx—magnesium.

6xxx—magnesium and silicon.

7xxx—zinc.

8xxx—other elements.

In the 2xxx through 8xxx alloy groups, the second digit in the alloy designation indicates alloy modifications. If the second digit is zero, it indicates the original alloy, while digits 1 through 9 indicate alloy modifications.

The last two of the four digits in the designation identify the different alloys in the group.

Where used, the temper designation follows the alloy designation and is separated from it by a dash; i.e., 7075-T6, 2024-T4, etc. The temper designation consists of a letter indicating the basic temper which may be more specifically defined by the addition of one or more digits. These designations are as follows:

—F As fabricated.

—O Annealed, recrystallized (wrought products only).

—H Strain hardened.

    —H1 (plus one or more digits) strain hardened only.

    —H2 (plus one or more digits) strain hardened and partially annealed.

    —H3 (plus one or more digits) strain hardened and stabilized.

—W Solution heat treated, unstable temper.

—T Treated to produce stable tempers other than —F, —O, or —H.

    —T2 Annealed (cast products only).

    —T3 Solution heat treated and then cold worked.

    —T4 Solution heat treated.

    —T5 Artificially aged only.

    —T6 Solution heat treated and then artificially aged.

    —T7 Solution heat treated and then stabilized.

    —T8 Solution heat treated, cold worked, and then artificially aged.

    —T9 Solution heat treated, artificially aged, and then cold worked.

    —T10 Artificially aged and then cold worked.

In the wrought form, commercially pure aluminum is known as 1100. It has a high degree of resistance to corrosion and is easily formed into intricate shapes. It is relatively low in strength, however, and does not have the strength required for structural aircraft parts. Higher strengths are generally obtained by the process of alloying. The resulting alloys are less easily formed and, with some exceptions, have lower resistance to corrosion than 1100 aluminum.

Alloying is not the only method of increasing the strength of aluminum. Like other materials, aluminum becomes stronger and harder as it is rolled, formed, or otherwise cold-worked. Since the hardness depends on the amount of cold working done, 1100 and some wrought aluminum alloys are available in several strain-hardened tempers. The soft or annealed condition is designated O. If the material is strain hardened, it is said to be in the H condition.

The most widely used alloys in aircraft construction are hardened by heat treatment rather than by cold-work. These alloys are designated by a somewhat different set of symbols: —T4 and W indicate solution heat treated and quenched but not aged, and T6 indicates an alloy in the heat treated hardened condition.

Aluminum alloy sheets are marked with the specification number on approximately every square foot of material. If for any reason this identification is not on the material, it is possible to separate the heat-treatable alloys from the nonheat-treatable alloys by immersing a sample of the material in a 10-percent solution of caustic soda (sodium hydroxide). The heat-treatable alloys will turn black due to the copper content, whereas the others will remain bright. In the case of clad material, the surface will remain bright, but there will be a dark area in the middle when viewed from the edge.

CLAD ALUMINUM

The terms "Alclad and Pureclad" (tradenames) are used to designate sheets that consist of an aluminum alloy core coated with a layer of pure aluminum to a depth of approximately 5½ percent on each side. The pure aluminum coating affords a dual protection for the core, preventing contact with any corrosive agents, and protecting the core electrolytically by preventing any attack caused by scratching or from other abrasions.

HEAT TREATMENT OF ALUMINUM ALLOYS

Heat treatment is a series of operations involving the heating and cooling of metals in the solid state. Its purpose is to change a mechanical property or combination of mechanical properties so that the metal will be more useful, serviceable, and safe for a definite purpose. By heat treating, a metal can be made harder, stronger, and more resistant to impact. Heat treating can also make a metal softer and more ductile. No one heat-treating operation can produce all of these characteristics. In fact, some properties are often improved at the expense of others. In being hardened, for example, a metal may become brittle.

The various heat-treating processes are similar in that they all involve the heating and cooling of metals. They differ, however, in the temperatures to which the metal is heated, the rate at which it is cooled, and, of course, in the final result.

Successful heat treating requires close control over all factors affecting the heating and cooling of metals. Such control is possible only when the proper equipment is available and the equipment is selected to fit the particular job. Thus, the furnace must be of the proper size and type and must be so controlled that temperatures are kept within the limits prescribed for each operation. Even the atmosphere within the furnace affects the condition of the part being heat treated. Further, the quenching equipment and the quenching medium must be selected to fit the metal and the heat-treating operation. Finally, there must be equipment for handling parts and materials, for cleaning metals, and for straightening parts.

Heat treating requires special techniques and equipment which are usually associated with manufacturers or large repair stations. Since these processes are usually beyond the scope of the field mechanic, the heat treatment of aluminum alloys will only be discussed briefly.

There are two types of heat treatments applicable to aluminum alloys. One is called solution heat treatment, and the other is known as precipitation heat treatment. Some alloys, such as 2017 and 2024, develop their full properties as a result of solution heat treatment followed by about 4 days of aging at room temperature. Other alloys, such as 2014 and 7075, require both heat treatments.

The alloys that require precipitation heat treatment (artificial aging) to develop their full strength also age to a limited extent at room temperature; the rate and amount of strengthening depends upon the alloy. Some reach their maximum natural or room-temperature aging strength in a few days, and are designated as —T4 or —T3 temper. Others continue to age appreciably over a long period of time. Because of this natural aging, the —W designation is specified only when the period of aging is indicated, for example, 7075-W (½ hour). Thus, there is considerable difference in the mechanical and physical properties of freshly quenched (—W) material and material that is in the —T3 or —T4 temper.

The hardening of an aluminum alloy by heat treatment consists of four distinct steps:

1. Heating to a predetermined temperature.
2. Soaking at temperature for a specified length of time.
3. Rapidly quenching to a relatively low temperature.
4. Aging or precipitation hardening either spontaneously at room temperature, or as a result of a low-temperature thermal treatment.

The first three steps above are known as solution heat treatment, although it has become common practice to use the shorter term, "heat treatment". Room-temperature hardening is known as natural aging, while hardening done at moderate temperatures is called artificial aging, or precipitation heat treatment.

SOLUTION HEAT TREATMENT

Temperature

The temperatures used for solution heat treating vary with different alloys and range from 825 degrees F. to 980 degrees F. As a rule, they must be controlled within a very narrow range (plus or minus 10 degrees) to obtain specified properties. Heating is accomplished in either a fused salt bath or an air furnace. The soaking time varies, depending upon the alloy and thickness from 10 minutes for thin sheets to approximately 12 hours for heavy forgings. For the heavy sections, the nominal soaking time is approximately 1 hour for each inch of cross-sectional thickness. The soaking time is chosen so that it will be the minimum necessary to develop the required physical properties.

Quenching

After the soluble constituents are in solid solution, the material is quenched to prevent or retard immediate re-precipitation. Three distinct quenching methods are employed. The one to be used in any particular instance depends upon the part, the alloy, and the properties desired.

Cold Water Quenching

Parts produced from sheet, extrusions, tubing, small forgings, and similar type material are generally quenched in a cold water bath. The temperature of the water before quenching should not exceed 85 degrees F. Such a drastic quench ensures maximum resistance to corrosion. This is particularly important when working with such alloys as 2017, 2024, and 7075. This is the reason a drastic quench is preferred, even though a slower quench may produce the required mechanical properties.

Hot Water Quenching

Large forgings and heavy sections can be quenched in hot or boiling water. This type of quench minimizes distortion and alleviates cracking which may be produced by the unequal temperatures obtained during the quench. The use of a hot water quench is permitted with these parts because the temperature of the quench water does not critically affect the resistance to corrosion of the forging alloys. In addition, the resistance to corrosion of heavy sections is not as critical a factor as for thin sections.

Spray Quenching

High-velocity water sprays are useful for parts formed from clad sheet and for large sections of almost all alloys. This type of quench also minimizes distortion and alleviates quench cracking. However, many specifications forbid the use of spray quenching for bare 2017 and 2024 sheet materials because of the effect on their resistance to corrosion.

Lag Between Soaking and Quenching

The time interval between the removal of the material from the furnace and quenching is critical for some alloys and should be held to a minimum.

Re-heat Treatment

The treatment of material which has been previously heat treated is considered a re-heat treatment. The unclad heat-treatable alloys can be solution heat treated repeatedly without harmful effects.

The number of solution heat treatments allowed for clad sheet is limited due to increased diffusion of core and cladding with each re-heating. Existing specifications allow one to three re-heat treatments of clad sheet depending upon cladding thickness.

Straightening After Solution Heat Treatment

Some warping occurs during solution heat treatment, producing kinks, buckles, waves, and twists. These imperfections are generally removed by straightening and flattening operations.

Where the straightening operations produce an appreciable increase in the tensile and yield strengths and a slight decrease in the percent of elongation, the material is designated —T3 temper. When the above values are not materially affected, the material is designated —T4 temper.

PRECIPITATION HEAT HEATING

As previously stated, the aluminum alloys are in a comparatively soft state immediately after quenching from a solution heat-treating temperature. To obtain their maximum strengths, they must be either naturally aged or precipitation hardened.

Precipitation hardening produces a great increase in the strength and hardness of the material with corresponding decreases in the ductile properties. The process used to obtain the desired increase in strength is therefore known as aging, or precipitation hardening.

The aging practices used depend upon many properties other than strength. As a rule, the artificially aged alloys are slightly overaged to increase their resistance to corrosion. This is especially true with the artificially aged high-copper-content alloys that are susceptible to intergranular corrosion when inadequately aged.

The heat-treatable aluminum alloys are subdivided into two classes, those that obtain their full strength at room temperature and those that require artificial aging.

The alloys that obtain their full strength after 4 or 5 days at room temperature are known as natural aging alloys. Precipitation from the supersaturated solid solution starts soon after quenching, with 90 percent of the maximum strength generally being obtained in 24 hours. Alloys 2017 and 2024 are natural aging alloys.

The alloys that require precipitation thermal treatment to develop their full strength are artificially aged alloys. However, these alloys also age a limited amount at room temperature, the rate and extent of the strengthening depending upon the alloys.

Many of the artificially aged alloys reach their maximum natural or room temperature aging strengths after a few days. These can be stocked for fabrication in the —T4 or —T3 temper. High-zinc-content alloys such as 7075 continue to age appreciably over a long period of time, their mechanical property changes being sufficient to reduce their formability.

The advantage of —W temper formability can be utilized, however, in the same manner as with natural aging alloys; that is, by fabricating shortly after solution heat treatment, or retaining formability by the use of refrigeration.

Refrigeration retards the rate of natural aging. At 32 degrees F., the beginning of the aging process is delayed for several hours, while dry ice (—50 degrees F. to —100 degrees F.) retards aging for an extended period of time.

Precipitation Practices

The temperatures used for precipitation hardening depend upon the alloy and the properties desired, ranging from 250 degrees F. to 375 degrees F. They should be controlled within a very narrow range (plus or minus 5 degrees) to obtain best results. (See figure 3-2.)

Alloy	Aging temperature (°F.)	Aging-time (hours)	Temper designation
2014	315–325	10	—T6
2017	Room temperature	96	—T4
2024	Room temperature	96	—T4
6061	315–325	18	—T6
6061	345–355	8	—T6
6161	335–345	10	—T6
7075	245–255	24	—T6

Figure 3-2. Typical precipitation (aging) cycles for wrought aluminum alloys.

The time at temperature is dependent upon the temperature used, the properties desired, and the alloy. It ranges from 8 to 96 hours. Increasing the aging temperature decreases the soaking period necessary for proper aging. However, a closer control of both time and temperature is necessary when using the higher temperatures.

After receiving the thermal precipitation treatment, the material should be air cooled to room temperature. Water quenching, while not necessary, produces no ill effects. Furnace cooling has a tendency to produce overaging.

ANNEALING OF ALUMINUM ALLOYS

The annealing procedure for aluminum alloys consists of heating the alloys to an elevated temperature, holding or soaking them at this temperature for a length of time depending upon the mass of the metal, and then cooling in still air. Annealing leaves the metal in the best condition for cold-working. However, when prolonged forming operations are involved, the metal will take on a condition known as "mechanical hardness" and will resist further working. It may be necessary to anneal a part several times during the forming process to avoid cracking. Aluminum alloys should not be used in the annealed state for parts or fittings.

Clad parts should be heated as quickly and carefully as possible, since long exposure to heat tends to cause some of the constituents of the core to diffuse into the cladding. This reduces the corrosion resistance of the cladding.

HEAT TREATMENT OF ALUMINUM ALLOY RIVETS

Heat treatment of aluminum alloy rivets is discussed in Chapter 4 "Fasteners and Hardware and their Installation".

TITANIUM AND TITANIUM ALLOYS

The use of titanium is widespread. It is used in many commercial enterprises and is in constant demand for such items as pumps, screens, and other tools and fixtures where corrosion attack is prevalent. In aircraft construction and repair, titanium is used for fuselage skins, engine shrouds, firewalls, longerons, frames, fittings, air ducts, and fasteners.

Titanium is used for making compressor disks, spacer rings, compressor blades and vanes, through bolts, turbine housings and liners, and miscellaneous hardware for turbine engines.

Titanium falls between aluminum and stainless steel in terms of elasticity, density, and elevated temperature strength. It has a melting point of from 2,730 degrees F. to 3,155 degrees., low thermal conductivity, and a low coefficient of expansion. It is light, strong, and resistant to stress-corrosion cracking. Titanium is approximately 60 percent heavier than aluminum and about 50 percent lighter than stainless steel.

Because of the high melting point of titanium, high-temperature properties are disappointing. The ultimate yield strength of titanium drops rapidly above 800 degrees F. The absorption of oxygen and nitrogen from the air at temperatures above 1,000 degrees F. makes the metal so brittle on long exposure that it soon becomes worthless. However, titanium does have some merit for short-time exposure up to 3,000 degrees F. where strength is not important. Aircraft firewalls demand this requirement.

Titanium is nonmagnetic and has an electrical resistance comparable to that of stainless steel. Some the base alloys of titanium are quite hard. Heat treating and alloying do not develop the hardness of titanium to the high levels of some of the heat-treated alloys of steel. It was only recently that a heat-treatable titanium alloy was developed. Prior to the development of this alloy, heating and rolling was the only method of forming that could be accomplished. However, it is possible to form the new alloy in the soft condition and heat treat it for hardness.

Iron, molybdenum, and chromium are used to stabilize titanium and produce alloys that will quench harden and age harden. The addition of these metals also adds ductility. The fatigue resistance of titanium is greater than that of aluminum or steel.

Titanium Designations

The A-B-C classification of titanium alloys was established to provide a convenient and simple means of describing all titanium alloys. Titanium and titanium alloys possess three basic types of crystals: A (alpha), B (beta), and C (combined alpha and beta). Their characteristics are:

A (alpha)—All-around performance; good weldability; tough and strong both cold and hot, and resistant to oxidation.

B (beta)—Bendability; excellent bend ductility; strong both cold and hot, but vulnerable to contamination.

C (combined alpha and beta for compromise performances)—Strong when cold and warm, but weak when hot; good bendability; moderate contamination resistance; excellent forgeability.

Titanium is manufactured for commercial use in two basic compositions; commercially pure titanium and alloyed titanium. A-55 is an example of a commercially pure titanium. It has a yield strength of 55,000 to 80,000 p.s.i. and is a general-purpose grade for moderate to severe forming. It is sometimes used for nonstructural aircraft parts and for all types of corrosion-resistant applications, such as tubing.

Type A-70 titanium is closely related to type A-55 but has a yield strength of 70,000 to 95,000 p.s.i. It is used where higher strength is required, and it is specified for many moderately stressed aircraft parts. For many corrosion applications, it is used interchangeably with type A-55. Both type A-55 and type A-70 are weldable.

One of the widely used titanium-base alloys is designated as C-110M. It is used for primary structural members and aircraft skin, has 110,000 p.s.i. minimum yield strength, and contains 8 percent manganese.

Type A-110AT is a titanium alloy which contains 5 percent aluminum and 2.5 percent tin. It also has a high minimum yield strength at elevated temperatures with the excellent welding characteristics inherent in alpha-type titanium alloys.

Corrosion Characteristics

The corrosion resistance of titanium deserves special mention. The resistance of the metal to corrosion is caused by the formation of a protective surface film of stable oxide or chemi-absorbed oxygen. Film is often produced by the presence of oxygen and oxidizing agents.

Corrosion of titanium is uniform. There is little evidence of pitting or other serious forms of localized attack. Normally, it is not subject to stress corrosion, corrosion fatigue, intergranular corrosion, or galvanic corrosion. Its corrosion resistance is equal or superior to 18-8 stainless steel.

HEAT TREATMENT OF TITANIUM

Titanium is heat treated for the following purposes:
1. Relief of stresses set up during cold forming or machining.
2. Annealing after hot working or cold working, or to provide maximum ductility for subsequent cold working.
3. Thermal hardening to improve strength.

Stress Relieving

Stress relieving is generally used to remove stress concentrations resulting from forming of titanium sheet. It is performed at temperatures ranging from 650 degrees F. to 1,000 degrees F. The time at temperature varies from a few minutes for a very thin sheet to an hour or more for heavier sections. A typical stress-relieving treatment is 900 degree F. for 30 minutes, followed by an air cool.

The discoloration or scale which forms on the surface of the metal during stress relieving is easily removed by pickling in acid solutions. The recommended solution contains 10 to 20 percent nitric acid and 1 to 3 percent hydrofluoric acid. The solution should be at room temperature or slightly above.

Full Annealing

The annealing of titanium and titanium alloys provides toughness, ductility at room temperature, dimensional and structural stability at elevated temperatures, and improved machinability.

The full anneal is usually called for as preparation for further working. It is performed at 1,200 degrees F. to 1,650 degrees F. The time at temperature varies from 16 minutes to several hours, depending on the thickness of the material and the amount of cold work to be performed. The usual treatment for the commonly used alloys is 1,300 degrees F. for 1 hour, followed by an air cool. A full anneal generally results in sufficient scale formation to require the use of caustic descaling, such as sodium hydride salt bath.

Thermal Hardening

Unalloyed titanium cannot be heat treated, but the alloys commonly used in aircraft construction can be strengthened by thermal treatment, usually at some sacrifice in ductility. For best results, a water quench from 1,450 degree F., followed by re-heating to 900 degrees F. for 8 hours is recommended.

Casehardening

The chemical activity of titanium and its rapid absorption of oxygen, nitrogen, and carbon at relatively low temperatures make casehardening advantageous for special applications. Nitriding, carburizing, or carbonitriding can be used to produce a water-resistant case of 0.0001 to 0.0002 inch in depth.

MAGNESIUM AND MAGNESIUM ALLOYS

Magnesium, the world's lightest structural metal, is a silvery-white material weighing only two-thirds as much as aluminum. Magnesium does not possess sufficient strength in its pure state for structural uses, but when alloyed with zinc, aluminum, and manganese it produces an alloy having the highest strength-to-weight ratio of any of the commonly used metals.

Some of today's aircraft require in excess of one-half ton of this metal for use in hundreds of vital spots. Some wing panels are fabricated entirely from magnesium alloys, weigh 18 percent less than standard aluminum panels, and have flown hundreds of satisfactory hours. Among the aircraft parts that have been made from magnesium with a substantial savings in weight are nosewheel, doors, flap cover skin, aileron cover skin, oil tanks, floorings, fuselage parts, wingtips, engine nacelles, instrument panels, radio masts, hydraulic fluid tanks, oxygen bottle cases, ducts, and seats.

Magnesium alloys possess good casting characteristics. Their properties compare favorably with those of cast aluminum. In forging, hydraulic presses are ordinarily used, although, under certain conditions, forging can be accomplished in mechanical presses or with drop hammers.

Magnesium alloys are subject to such treatments as annealing, quenching, solution heat treatment, aging, and stabilizing. Sheet and plate magnesium are annealed at the rolling mill. The solution heat treatment is used to put as much of the alloying ingredients as possible into solid solution, which results in high tensile strength and maximum ductility. Aging is applied to castings following heat treatment where maximum hardness and yield strength are desired.

Magnesium embodies fire hazards of an unpredictable nature. When in large sections, its high thermal conductivity makes it difficult to ignite and prevents it from burning. It will not burn until the melting point is reached, which is 1,204 degrees F. However, magnesium dust and fine chips are ignited easily. Precautions must be taken to avoid this if possible. Should a fire occur, it can be extinguished with an extinguishing powder, such as powdered soapstone, or graphite powder. Water or any standard liquid or foam fire extinguishers cause magnesium to burn more rapidly and can cause explosions.

Magnesium alloys produced in the United States consist of magnesium alloyed with varying proportions of aluminum, manganese, and zinc. These alloys are designated by a letter of the alphabet, with the number 1 indicating high purity and maximum corrosion resistance.

HEAT TREATMENT OF MAGNESIUM ALLOYS

Magnesium alloy castings respond readily to heat treatment, and about 95 percent of the magnesium used in aircraft construction is in the cast form.

The heat treatment of magnesium alloy castings is similar to the heat treatment of aluminum alloys in that there are two types of heat treatment: (1) Solution heat treatment and (2) precipitation (aging) heat treatment. Magnesium, however, develops a neglibible change in its properties when allowed to age naturally at room temperatures.

Solution Heat Treatment

Magnesium alloy castings are solution heat treated to improve tensile strength, ductility, and shock resistance. This heat-treatment condition is indicated by using the symbol —T4 following the alloy designation. Solution heat treatment plus artificial aging is designated —T6. Artificial aging is necessary to develop the full properties of the metal.

Solution heat-treatment temperatures for magnesium alloy castings range from 730 degrees F. to 780 degrees F., the exact range depending upon the type of alloy. The temperature range for each type of alloy is listed in Specification MIL-H-6857. The upper limit of each range listed in the specification is the maximum temperature to which the alloy may be heated without danger of melting the metal.

The soaking time ranges from 10 to 18 hours, the exact time depending upon the type of alloy as well as the thickness of the part. Soaking periods longer than 18 hours may be necessary for castings over 2 inches in thickness. Magnesium alloys must **never** be heated in a salt bath as this may result in an explosion.

A serious potential fire hazard exists in the heat treatment of magnesium alloys. If through oversight or malfunctioning of equipment, the maximum temperatures are exceeded, the casting may ignite and burn freely. For this reason, the furnace used should be equipped with a safety cutoff that will turn off the power to the heating elements and blowers if the regular control equipment malfunctions or fails.

Some magnesium alloys require a protective atmosphere of sulfur dioxide gas during solution heat treatment. This aids in preventing the start of a fire even if the temperature limits are slightly exceeded.

Air-quenching is used after solution heat treatment of magnesium alloys since there appears to be no advantage in liquid cooling.

Precipitation Heat Treatment

After solution treatment, magnesium alloys may be given an aging treatment to increase hardness and yield strength. Generally, the aging treatments are used merely to relieve stress and stabilize the alloys in order to prevent dimensional changes later, especially during or after machining. Both yield strength and hardness are improved somewhat by this treatment at the expense of a slight amount of ductility. The corrosion resistance is also improved, making it closer to the "as cast" alloy.

Precipitation heat-treatment temperatures are considerably lower than solution heat-treatment temperatures and range from 325 degrees F. to 500 degrees F. Soaking time ranges from 4 to 18 hours.

OTHER NONFERROUS AIRCRAFT METALS

Copper and its alloys (brass, muntz metal, beryllium copper and bronze are used in limited quantities in aircraft construction, mostly for non-structural and/or electrical components.

Monel is a leading high-nickel alloy, combining the properties of high strength and excellent corrosion resistance. Monel has been successfully used for gears and chains to operate retractable landing gears, and for structural parts subject to corrosion. In aircraft, Monel is used for parts demanding both strength and high resistance to corrosion (such as exhaust manifolds and carburetor needle valves and sleeves).

FERROUS AIRCRAFT METALS

The term "ferrous" applies to the group of metals having iron as their principal constituent.

Identification

If carbon is added to iron, in percentages ranging up to approximately 1 percent, the product is vastly superior to iron alone and is classified as carbon steel. Carbon steel forms the base of those alloy steels produced by combining carbon steel with other elements known to improve the properties of steel. A base metal (such as iron) to which small quantities of other metals have been added is called an alloy. The addition of other metals changes or improves the chemical or physical properties of the base metal for a particular use.

The steel classification of the SAE (Society of Automotive Engineers) is used in specifications for all high-grade steels used in automotive and aircraft construction. A numerical index system identifies the composition of SAE steels.

Each SAE number consists of a group of digits, the first of which represents the type of steel; the second, the percentage of the principal alloying element; and, usually, the last two or three digits, the percentage, in hundredths of 1 percent, of carbon in the alloy. For example, the SAE number 4130 indicates a molybdenum steel containing 1 percent molybdenum and 0.30 percent carbon. Refer to the SAE numerical index table in figure 3-3.

Type of Steel	Classification
Carbon	1xxx
Nickel	2xxx
Nickel-chromium	3xxx
Molybdenum	4xxx
Chromium	5xxx
Chromiun-vanadium	6xxx
Tungsten	7xxx
Silicon-manganese	9xxx

Figure 3-3. SAE numerical index.

Metal stock is manufactured in several forms and shapes, including sheets, bars, rods, tubings, extrusions, forgings, and castings. Sheet metal is made in a number of sizes and thicknesses. Specifications designate thicknesses in thousandths of an inch. Bars and rods are supplied in a variety of shapes, such as round, square, rectangular, hexagonal, and octagonal. Tubing can be obtained in round, oval, rectangular, or streamlined shapes. The size of tubing is generally specified by outside diameter and wall thickness.

The sheet metal is usually formed cold in such machines as presses, bending brakes, drawbenches, or rolls. Forgings are shaped or formed by pressing or hammering heated metal in dies. Castings are produced by pouring molten metal into molds. The casting is finished by machining.

Types, Characteristics, and Uses of Alloyed Steels

Steel containing carbon in percentages ranging from 0.10 to 0.30 percent is classed as low-carbon steel. The equivalent SAE numbers range from 1010 to 1030. Steels of this grade are used for making such items as safety wire, certain nuts, cable bushings, or threaded rod ends. This steel in sheet form is used for secondary structural parts and clamps, and in tubular form for moderately stressed structural parts.

Steel containing carbon in percentages ranging from 0.30 to 0.50 percent is classed as medium-carbon steel. This steel is especially adaptable for machining or forging, and where surface hardness is desirable. Certain rod ends and light forgings are made from SAE 1035 steel.

Steel containing carbon in percentages ranging from 0.50 to 1.05 percent is classed as high-carbon steel. The addition of other elements in varying quantities add to the hardness of this steel. In the fully heat-treated condition it is very hard, will withstand high shear and wear, and will have little deformation. It has limited use in aircraft. SAE 1095 in sheet form is used for making flat springs and in wire form for making coil springs.

The various nickel steels are produced by combining nickel with carbon steel. Steels containing from 3 to 3.75 percent nickel are commonly used. Nickel increases the hardness, tensile strength, and elastic limit of steel without appreciably decreasing the ductility. It also intensifies the hardening effect of heat treatment. SAE 2330 steel is used extensively for aircraft parts, such as bolts, terminals, keys, clevises, and pins.

Chromium steel is high in hardness, strength, and corrosion-resistant properties, and is particularly adaptable for heat-treated forgings which require greater toughness and strength than may be obtained in plain carbon steel. It can be used for such articles as the balls and rollers of anti-friction bearings.

Chrome-nickel or stainless steels are the corrosion-resistant metals. The anticorrosive degree of this steel is determined by the surface condition of the metal as well as by the composition, temperature, and concentration of the corrosive agent.

The principal alloy of stainless steel is chromium. The corrosion-resistant steel most often used in aircraft construction is known as 18-8 steel because of its content of 18 percent chromium and 8 percent nickel. One of the distinctive features of 18-8 steel is that its strength may be increased by coldworking.

Stainless steel may be rolled, drawn, bent, or formed to any shape. Because these steels expand about 50 percent more than mild steel and conduct heat only about 40 percent as rapidly, they are more difficult to weld. Stainless steel can be used for almost any part of an aircraft. Some of its common applications are in the fabrication of exhaust collectors, stacks and manifolds, structural and machined parts, springs, castings, tie rods, and control cables.

The chrome-vanadium steels are made of approximately 18 percent vanadium and about 1 percent chromium. When heat treated, they have strength, toughness, and resistance to wear and fatigue. A special grade of this steel in sheet form can be cold-formed into intricate shapes. It can be folded and flattened without signs of breaking or failure. SAE 6150 is used for making springs; and chrome-vanadium with high-carbon content, SAE 6195, is used for ball and roller bearings.

Molybdenum in small percentages is used in combination with chromium to form chrome-molybdenum steel, which has various uses in aircraft. Molybdenum is a strong alloying element. It raises the ultimate strength of steel without affecting ductility or workability. Molybdenum steels are tough and wear resistant, and they harden throughout when heat treated. They are especially adaptable for welding and, for this reason, are used principally for welded structural parts and assemblies. This type steel has practically replaced carbon steel in the fabrication of fuselage tubing, engine mounts, landing gears, and other structural parts. For example, a heat-treated SAE X4130 tube is approximately four times as strong as an SAE 1025 tube of the same weight and size.

A series of chrome-molybdenum steel most used in aircraft construction is that series containing 0.25 to 0.55 percent carbon, 0.15 to 0.25 percent molybdenum, and 0.50 to 1.10 percent chromium. These steels, when suitably heat treated, are deep hardening, easily machined, readily welded by either gas or electric methods, and are especially adapted to high-temperature service.

Inconel is a nickel-chromium-iron alloy closely resembling stainless steel in appearance. Because these two metals look very much alike, a distinguishing test is often necessary. One method of identification is to use a solution of 10 grams of cupric chloride in 100 cubic centimeters of hydrochloric acid. With a medicine dropper, place 1 drop of the solution on a sample of each metal to be tested and allow it to remain for 2 minutes. At the end of this period, slowly add 3 or 4 drops of water to the solution on the metal samples, 1 drop at a time; then wash the samples in clear water and dry them. If the metal is stainless steel, the copper in the cupric chloride solution will be deposited on the metal leaving a copper-colored spot. If the sample is inconel, a new-looking spot will be present.

The tensile strength of inconel is 100,000 p.s.i. annealed, and 125,000 p.s.i., when hard rolled. It is highly resistant to salt water and is able to withstand temperatures as high as 1,600 degrees F.

Inconel welds readily and has working qualities quite similar to those of corrosion-resistant steels.

HEAT TREATMENT OF FERROUS METALS

The first important consideration in the heat treatment of a steel part is to know its chemical composition. This, in turn, determines its upper critical point. When the upper critical point is known, the next consideration is the rate of heating and cooling to be used. Carrying out these operations involves the use of uniform heating furnaces, proper temperature controls, and suitable quenching mediums.

Heat treating requires special techniques and equipment which are usually associated with manufacturers or large repair stations. Since these processes are normally beyond the scope of the field mechanic, the heat treatment of steel alloys will only be discussed briefly.

Behavior of Steel During Heating and Cooling.

Changing the internal structure of a ferrous metal is accomplished by heating to a temperature above its upper critical point, holding it at that temperature for a time sufficient to permit certain internal changes to occur, and then cooling to atmospheric temperature under predetermined, controlled conditions.

At ordinary temperatures, the carbon in steel exists in the form of particles of iron carbide scattered throughout an iron matrix known as "ferrite." The number, size, and distribution of these particles determine the hardness of the steel. At elevated temperatures, the carbon is dissolved in the iron matrix in the form of a solid solution called "austenite," and the carbide particles appear only after the steel has been cooled. If the cooling is slow, the carbide particles are relatively coarse and few. In this condition, the steel is soft. If the cooling is rapid, as by quenching in oil or water, the carbon precipitates as a cloud of very fine carbide particles, and the steel is hard. The fact that the carbide particles can be dissolved in austenite is the basis of the heat treatment of steel. The temperatures at which this transformation takes place are called the critical points and vary with the composition of the steel. The element normally having the greatest influence is carbon.

Hardening

For most steels, the hardening treatment consists of heating the steel to a temperature just above the upper critical point, soaking or holding for the required length of time, and then cooling it rapidly by plunging the hot steel into oil, water, or brine. Although most steels must be cooled rapidly for hardening, a few may be cooled in still air. Hardening increases the hardness and strength of the steel but makes it less ductile.

46

When hardening carbon steel, it must be cooled to below 1,000 degrees F. in less than 1 second. Should the time required for the temperature to drop to 1,000 degrees F. exceed 1 second, the austenite begins to transform into fine pearlite. This pearlite varies in hardness, but is much harder than the pearlite formed by annealing and much softer than the martensite desired. After the 1,000 degree F. temperature is reached, the rapid cooling must continue if the final structure is to be all martensite.

When alloys are added to steel, the time limit for the temperature drop to 1,000 degrees F. increases above the 1-second limit for carbon steels. Therefore, a slower quenching medium will produce hardness in alloy steels.

Because of the high internal stresses in the "as quenched" condition, steel must be tempered just before it becomes cold. The part should be removed from the quenching bath at a temperature of approximately 200 degrees F., since the temperature range from 200 degrees F. down to room temperature is the cracking range.

Tempering

Tempering reduces the brittleness imparted by hardening and produces definite physical properties within the steel. Tempering always follows, never precedes, the hardening operation. In addition to reducing brittleness, tempering softens the steel.

Tempering is always conducted at temperatures below the low critical point of the steel. In this respect, tempering differs from annealing, normalizing, or hardening, all of which require temperatures above the upper critical point. When hardened steel is reheated, tempering begins at 212 degrees F. and continues as the temperature increases toward the low critical point. By selecting a definite tempering temperature, the resulting hardness and strength can be predetermined. Tempered steels used in aircraft work have from 125,000 to 200,000 p.s.i. ultimate tensile strength.

Generally, the rate of cooling from the tempering temperature has no effect on the resulting structure; therefore, the steel is usually cooled in still air after being removed from the furnace.

Annealing

Annealing of steel produces a fine-grained, soft, ductile metal without internal stresses or strains. In the annealed state, steel has its lowest strength. In general, annealing is the opposite of hardening.

Annealing of steel is accomplished by heating the metal to just above the upper critical point, soaking at that temperature, and cooling very slowly in the furnace. To produce maximum softness in steel, the metal must be cooled very slowly. Slow cooling is obtained by shutting off the heat and allowing the furnace and metal to cool together to 900 degrees F. or lower, then removing the metal from the furnace and cooling in still air. Another method is to bury the heated steel in ashes, sand, or other substance that does not conduct heat readily.

Normalizing

Normalizing of steel removes the internal stresses set up by heat treating, welding, casting, forming, or machining. Stress, if not controlled, will lead to failure. Because of the better physical properties, aircraft steels are often used in the normalized state, but seldom, if ever, in the annealed state.

One of the most important uses of normalizing in aircraft work is in welded parts. Welding causes strains to be set up in the adjacent material. In addition, the weld itself is a cast structure as opposed to the wrought structure of the rest of the material. These two types of structures have different grain sizes, and to refine the grain as well as to relieve the internal stresses, all welded parts should be normalized after fabrication.

Normalizing is accomplished by heating the steel above the upper critical point and cooling in still air. The more rapid quenching obtained by air cooling, as compared to furnace cooling, results in a harder and stronger material than that obtained by annealing.

CASEHARDENING

Casehardening produces a hard wear-resistant surface or case over a strong, tough core. Casehardening is ideal for parts which require a wear-resistant surface and, at the same time, must be tough enough internally to withstand the applied loads. The steels best suited to casehardening are the low-carbon and low-alloy steels. If high-carbon steel is casehardened, the hardness penetrates the core and causes brittleness.

In casehardening, the surface of the metal is changed chemically by introducing a high carbide or nitride content. The core is unaffected chemically. When heat treated, the surface responds to hardening while the core toughens. The common forms of casehardening are carburizing, cyaniding, and nitriding. Since cyaniding is not used in aircraft work, only carburizing and nitriding are discussed in this section.

Carburizing

Carburizing is a casehardening process in which carbon is added to the surface of low-carbon steel. Thus, a carburized steel has a high-carbon surface and a low-carbon interior. When the carburized steel is heat treated, the case is hardened while the core remains soft and tough.

A common method of carburizing is called "pack carburizing." When carburizing is to be done by this method, the steel parts are packed in a container with charcoal or some other material rich in carbon. The container is then sealed with fire clay, placed in a furnace, heated to approximately 1,700 degrees F., and soaked at that temperature for several hours. As the temperature increases, carbon monoxide gas forms inside the container and, being unable to escape, combines with the gamma iron in the surface of the steel. The depth to which the carbon penetrates depends on the length of the soaking period. For example, when carbon steel is soaked for 8 hours, the carbon penetrates to a depth of about 0.062 inch.

In another method of carburizing, called "gas carburizing," a material rich in carbon is introduced into the furnace atmosphere. The carburizing atmosphere is produced by the use of various gases or by the burning of oil, wood, or other materials. When the steel parts are heated in this atmosphere, carbon monoxide combines with the gamma iron to produce practically the same results as those described under the pack carburizing process.

A third method of carburizing is that of "liquid carburizing." In this method the steel is placed in a molten salt bath that contains the chemicals required to produce a case comparable with one resulting from pack or gas carburizing.

Alloy steels with low-carbon content as well as low-carbon steels may be carburized by either of the three processes. However, some alloys, such as nickel, tend to retard the absorption of carbon. As a result, the time required to produce a given thickness of case varies with the composition of the metal.

Nitriding

Nitriding is unlike other casehardening processes in that, before nitriding, the part is heat treated to produce definite physical properties. Thus, parts are hardened and tempered before being nitrided. Most steels can be nitrided, but special alloys are required for best results. These special alloys contain aluminum as one of the alloying elements and are called "nitralloys."

In nitriding, the part is placed in a special nitriding furnace and heated to a temperature of approximately 1,000 degrees F. With the part at this temperature, ammonia gas is circulated within the specially constructed furnace chamber. The high temperature cracks the ammonia gas into nitrogen and hydrogen. The ammonia which does not break down is caught in a water trap below the regions of the other two gases. The nitrogen reacts with the iron to form nitride. The iron nitride is dispersed in minute particles at the surface and works inward. The depth of penetration depends on the length of the treatment. In nitriding, soaking periods as long as 72 hours are frequently required to produce the desired thickness of case.

Nitriding can be accomplished with a minimum of distortion, because of the low temperature at which parts are casehardened and because no quenching is required after exposure to the ammonia gas.

HARDNESS TESTING

Hardness testing is a method of determining the results of heat treatment as well as the state of a metal prior to heat treatment. Since hardness values can be tied in with tensile strength values and, in part, with wear resistance, hardness tests are a valuable check of heat-treat control and of material properties.

Practically all hardness-testing equipment now uses the resistance to penetration as a measure of hardness. Included among the better known hardness testers are the Brinell and Rockwell.

Details of hardness testing requires equipment normally not available to the field mechanic and will not be discussed in detail.

Factory mechanics applying fuselage skin to a Learjet. (Gates Learjet Corp. photo.)

Chapter 4
Fasteners and Hardware and their Installation

Most aircraft consist of subassemblies such as fuselages, wings etc., which are riveted aluminum alloy units. These separate units are then normally bolted together using steel bolts to complete the aircraft structure. Some highly stressed parts such as engine mounts and landing gears are normally made of welded steel. Steel (and aluminum alloy) forgings are also incorporated in the structure.

Bonded honeycomb (sandwich construction) and wood also find limited use in aircraft structures. However, the specialized fabrication processes using these materials will not be discussed in this handbook.

STANDARD FASTENERS

Only the most commonly used standard fasteners are described in detail in this section. Refer to Appendix 1 for illustrations of the many "standard" fasteners as well as other miscellaneous small items, referred to as "hardware", used in the manufacture and repair of aircraft.

IDENTIFICATION

Most items of aircraft hardware are identified by their specification number or trade name. Threaded fasteners and rivets are usually identified by AN (Air Force-Navy), NAS (National Aircraft Standard), or MS (Military Standard) numbers. Quick-release fasteners are usually identifed by factory trade names and size designations.

RIVETS

To make a good union and a strong joint, aluminum parts can be welded, bolted, or riveted together. Riveting is satisfactory from the standpoint of strength and neatness, and is much easier to do than welding. It is the most common method used to fasten or join aluminum alloys in aircraft construction and repair.

A rivet is a metal pin used to hold two or more metal sheets, plates, or pieces of material together. A head is formed on one end when the rivet is manufactured. The shank of the rivet is placed through matched holes in two pieces of material, and the tip is then upset to form a second head to clamp the two pieces securely together. The second head, formed either by hand or by pneumatic equipment, is called a "shop head." The shop head functions in the same manner as a nut on a bolt. In addition to their use for joining aircraft skin sections, rivets are also used for joining spar sections, for holding rib sections in place, for securing fittings to various parts of the aircraft, and for fastening innumerable bracing members and other parts together.

Two of the major types of rivets used in the aircraft are the common solid-shank type, which must be driven using a bucking bar, and the special (blind) rivets, which may be installed where it is impossible to use a bucking bar.

Solid-Shank Rivets

Solid-shank rivets are generally used in repair work. They are identified by the kind of material of which they are made, their head type, size of shank, and their temper condition. The designation of the solid-shank rivet head type, such as universal head, round-head, flathead, countersunk head, and brazier head, depends on the cross sectional shape of the head (see figure 4-1). The temper designation and strength are indicated by special markings on the head of the rivet (see figure 4-5).

MS20470	MS20435	AN455	MS20426 (100°)	AN441
AN470	AN430	AN456	AN426 (100°)	AN442
UNIVERSAL	AN435	BRAZIER	COUNTERSUNK	FLAT
HEAD	ROUND	HEAD	HEAD	HEAD
	HEAD			

Figure 4-1. Rivet head shapes and code numbers.

The material used for the majority of aircraft solid-shank rivets is aluminum alloy. The strength and temper conditions of aluminum alloy rivets are identified by digits and letters similar to those adopted for the identification of strength and temper conditions of aluminum and aluminum alloy sheet stock. The 1100, 2017-T, 2024-T, 2117-T, and 5056 rivets are the five grades usually available.

The 1100 rivet, which is composed of 99.45 percent pure aluminum, is very soft. It is for riveting the softer aluminum alloys, such as 1100, 3003, and 5052, which are used for nonstructural parts (all parts where strength is not a factor). The riveting of map cases is a good example of where a rivet of 1100 aluminum alloy may be used.

The 2117-T rivet, known as the field rivet, is used more than any other for riveting aluminum alloy structures. The field rivet is in wide demand because it is ready for use as received and needs no further heat-treating or annealing. It also has a high resistance to corrosion.

The 2017-T and 2024-T rivets are used in aluminum alloy structures where more strength is needed than is obtainable with the same size 2217-T rivet. These rivets are annealed and must be kept refrigerated until they are to be driven. The 2017-T rivet should be driven within approximately 1 hour and the 2024-T rivet within 10 to 20 minutes after removal from refrigeration.

The 5056 rivet is used for riveting magnesium alloy structures because of its corrosion-resistant qualities in combinations with magnesium.

Mild steel rivets are used for riveting steel parts. The corrosion-resistant steel rivets are for riveting corrosion-resistant steels in firewalls, exhaust stack brackets, and similar structures.

Monel rivets are used for riveting nickel-steel alloys. They can be substituted for those made of corrosion-resistant steel in some cases.

Metal temper is an important factor in the riveting process, especially with aluminum alloy rivets. Aluminum alloy rivets have the same heat-treating characteristics as aluminum alloy sheet stock. They can be hardened and annealed in the same manner as sheet aluminum. The rivet must be soft, or comparatively soft, before a good head can be formed. The 2017-T and 2024-T rivets are annealed before being driven. They harden with age.

The process of heat treating (annealing) rivets is much the same as that for sheet stock. Either an electric air furnace, a salt bath, or a hot oil bath is needed. The heat treating range, depending on the alloy, is 625 degrees F. to 950 degrees F. For convenient handling, rivets are heated in a tray or a wire basket. They are quenched in cold water (70 degrees F.) immediately after heat treating.

The 2017-T and 2024-T rivets, which are heat-treatable rivets, begin to age-harden within a few minutes after being exposed to room temperature. Therefore, they must be used immediately after quenching or else be placed in cold storage. The most commonly used means for holding heattreatable rivets at low temperature (below 32 degrees F.) is to keep them in an electric refrigerator. They are referred to as "icebox" rivets. Under this storage condition, they will remain soft enough for driving for periods up to 2 weeks. Any rivets not used within that time should be removed for re-heat treating.

Icebox rivets attain about one-half their maximum strength in approximately 1 hour after driving and full strength in about 4 days. When 2017-T rivets are exposed to room temperature for 1 hour or longer, they must be subject to re-heat treatment. This also applies to 2024-T rivets exposed to room temperature for a period exceeding 10 minutes.

Once an icebox rivet has been taken from the refrigerator, it should not be mixed with the rivets still in cold storage. If more rivets are removed from the icebox than can be used in 15 minutes, they should be placed in a separate container and stored for re-heat treatment. Heat treatment of rivets may be repeated a number of times if done properly. Proper heating times and temperatures are shown in figure 4-2.

Heating time—air furnace

Rivet alloy	Time at temperature	Heat treating temperature
2024	1 hour	910° F.—930° F.
2017	1 hour	925° F.—950° F.

Heating time—salt bath

2024	30 minutes	910° F.—930° F.
2017	30 minutes	925° F.—950° F.

Figure 4-2. Air furnace heating time for rivets.

Most metals, and therefore aircraft rivet stock, are subject to corrosion. Corrosion may be the result of local climatic conditions or the fabrication process used. It is reduced to a minimum by using metals which are highly resistant to corrosion and possess the correct strength-to-weight ratio.

Ferrous metals placed in contact with moist salt air will rust if not properly protected. Nonferrous metals, those without an iron base, do not rust, but a similar process known as corrosion takes place. The salt in moist air (found in the coastal areas) attacks the aluminum alloys. It is a common experience to inspect the rivets of an aircraft which has been operated near salt water and find them badly corroded.

If a copper rivet is inserted into an aluminum alloy structure, two dissimilar metals are brought in contact with each other. Remember, all metals possess a small electrical potential. Dissimilar metals in contact with each other in the presence of moisture cause an electrical current to flow between them and chemical-by-products to be formed. Principally, this results in the deterioration of one of the metals.

Certain aluminum alloys react to each other and, therefore, must be thought of as dissimilar metals. The commonly used aluminum alloys may be divided into the two groups shown in figure 4-3.

Group A	Group B
1100	2117
3003	2017
5052	2124
6053	7075

Figure 4-3. Group A aluminum alloys may react with those of group B.

Members within either group A or group B can be considered as similar to each other and will not react to others within the same group. A corroding action will take place, however, if any metal of group A comes in contact with a metal in group B in the presence of moisture.

Avoid the use of dissimilar metals whenever possible. Their incompatibility is a factor which was considered when the AN Standards were adopted. To comply with AN Standards, the manufacturers must put a protective surface coating on the rivets. This may be zinc chromate, metal spray, or an anodized finish.

The protective coating on a rivet is identified by its color. A rivet coated with zinc chromate is yellow, an anodized surface is pearl gray, and the metal-sprayed rivet is identified by a silvery-gray color. If a situation arises in which a protective coating must be applied on the job, paint the rivet with zinc chromate before it is used and again after it is driven.

Identification

Markings on the heads of rivets are used to classify their characteristics. These markings may be either a raised teat, two raised teats, a dimple, a pair of raised dashes, a raised cross, a single triangle, or a raised dash; some other heads have no markings. The different markings indicate the composition of the rivet stock. As explained previously, the rivets have different colors to identify the protective surface coating used by the manufacturers.

Roundhead rivets are used in the interior of the aircraft, except where clearance is required for adjacent members. The roundhead rivet has a deep, rounded top surface. The head is large enough to strengthen the sheet around the hole and, at the same time, offer resistance to tension.

The flathead rivet, like the roundhead rivet, is used on interior structures. It is used where maximum strength is needed and where there isn't sufficient clearance to use a roundhead rivet. It is seldom, if ever, used on external surfaces.

The brazier head rivet has a head of large diameter, which makes it particularly adaptable for riveting thin sheet stock (skin). The brazier head rivet offers only slight resistance to the airflow, and because of this factor, it is frequently used for riveting skin on exterior surfaces, especially on aft sections of the fuselage and empennage. It is used for riveting thin sheets exposed to the slipstream. A modified brazier head rivet is also manufactured; it is simply a brazier head of reduced diameter.

The universal head rivet is a combination of the roundhead, flathead, and brazier head. It is used in aircraft construction and repair in both interior and exterior locations. **When replacement is necessary for protruding heads rivets—roundhead, flathead, or brazier head—they can be replaced by universal head rivets.**

The countersunk head rivet is flat topped and beveled toward the shank so that it fits into a countersunk or dimpled hole and is flush with the material's surface. The angle at which the head slopes may vary from 78 degrees to 120 degrees. The 100 degrees rivet is the most commonly used type. These rivets are used to fasten sheets over which other sheets must fit. They are also used on exterior surfaces of the aircraft because they offer only slight resistance to the slipstream and help to minimize turbulent airflow.

The markings on the heads of rivets, indicate the material of which they are made and, therefore, their strength. Figures 4-4 and 4-5 identify the rivet head markings and the materials indicated by them. Although there are three materials indicated by a plain head, it is possible to distinguish their difference by color. The 1100 is aluminum color; the mild steel is a typical steel color; and the copper rivet is a copper color. Any head marking can appear on any head style of the same material.

Head Markings	Material
Plain head_____	Pure aluminum, 1100; mild steel; or copper.
Dimpled head_____	2117-T aluminum alloy.
Raised teat_____	2017-T aluminum alloy.
Raised double dash_____	2024-T aluminum alloy.
Raised cross_____	5056 aluminum alloy.
Raised triangle_____	Mild steel, countersunk head.
Raised dash_____	Corrision-resistant steel.
Two raised teats___	Monel.

Figure 4-4. Head markings and rivet composition.

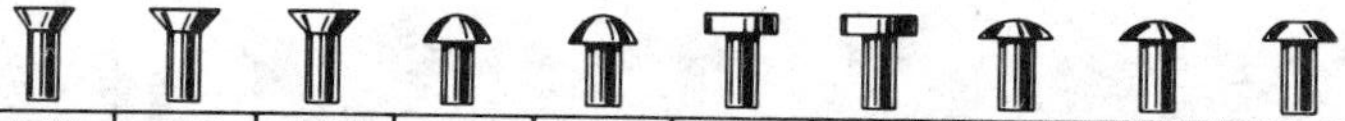

	Material	Head Marking	AN Material Code	AN425 78° Counter-Sunk Head	AN426 100° Counter-Sunk Head MS20426*	AN427 100° Counter-Sunk Head MS20427*	AN430 Round Head MS20430 **	AN435 Round Head MS20613* MS20615*	AN441 Flat Head	AN442 Flat Head **	AN455 Brazier Head **	AN456 Brazier Head **	AN470 Universal Head MS20470*	Heat Treat Before Using	Shear Strength P.S.I.	Bearing Strength P.S.I.
Aluminum & Alum. Alloy	1100	Plain	A	■	■		■			■	■	■	■	No	10000	25000
Aluminum & Alum. Alloy	2117T	Recessed Dot	AD	■	■		■			■	■	■	■	No	30000	100000
Aluminum & Alum. Alloy	2017T	Raised Dot	D	■	■		■			■	■	■	■	Yes	34000	113000
Aluminum & Alum. Alloy	2017T-HD	Raised Dot	D	■	■		■			■	■	■	■	No	38000	126000
Aluminum & Alum. Alloy	2024T	Raised Double Dash	DD	■	■		■			■	■	■	■	Yes	41000	136000
Aluminum & Alum. Alloy	5056T	Raised Cross	B		■		■			■	■	■	■	No	27000	90000
Aluminum & Alum. Alloy	7075-T73	Three Raised Dashes		■	■		■			■	■	■	■	No		
	Carbon Steel	Recessed Triangle				■		■ MS20613*	■					No	35000	90000
	Corrosion Resistant Steel	Recessed Dash	F			■		■ MS20613*						No	65000	90000
	Copper	Plain	C			■		■	■					No	23000	
	Monel	Plain	M			■			■					No	49000	
	Monel (Nickel-Copper Alloy)	Recessed Double Dots	C					■ MS20615*						No	49000	
	Brass	Plain						■ MS20615*						No		
	Titanium	Recessed Large and Small Dot			■ MS 20426				■					No	95000	

* New specifications are for Design purposes

** These rivets have been superceded by AN470 Universal head for most applications

Figure 4-5. Rivet identification chart. Shading indicates head shapes and materials available. See Appendix I for more data.

Each type of rivet is identified by a part number so that the user can select the correct rivet for the job. The type of rivet head is identified by AN or MS standard numbers. The numbers selected are in series and each series represents a particular type of head. (See figure 4-5). The most common numbers and the types of heads they represent are:

AN426 or MS20426—countersunk head rivets (100 degrees).

AN430 or MS20430—roundhead rivets.

AN441—flathead rivets.

AN456—brazier head rivets.

AN470 or MS20470—universal head rivets.

There are also letters and numbers added to a part number. The letters designate alloy content; the numbers, rivet diameter and length. The letters in common use for alloy designation are:

A—Aluminum alloy, 1100 or 3003 composition.

AD—Aluminum alloy, 2117-T composition.

D—Aluminum alloy, 2017-T composition.

DD—Aluminum alloy, 2024-T composition.

B—Aluminum alloy, 5056 composition.

C—Copper.

M—Monel.

The absence of a letter following the AN standard number indicates a rivet manufactured from mild steel.

The first number following the material composition letters expresses the diameter of the rivet shank in 32nds of an inch. Examples: 3, 3/32nds; 5, 5/32nds; etc. (See figure 4-6.)

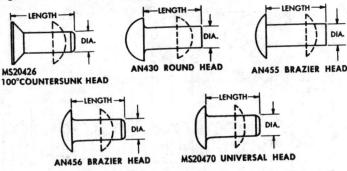

Figure 4-6. Methods of measuring rivet diameter and length.

The last number(s), separated by a dash from the preceding number, expresses the length of the rivet shank in 16ths of an inch. Examples: 3, 3/16ths; 7, 7/16ths; 11, 11/16ths; etc. (See figure 4-6).

An example of identification marking of a rivet is:

AN470AD3-5—complete part number.

AN—Air Force-Navy standard number.
470—universal head rivet.
AD—2117-T aluminum alloy.
3—3/32nds in diameter.
5—5/16ths in length.

A countersunk rivet (AN426), ⅛ inch diameter and ¾ inch long, made of 1100 aluminum, using the MS designation, would be: MS20426A4-12.

Special (Blind) Rivets

There are many places on an aircraft where access to both sides of a riveted structure or structural part is impossible, or where limited space will not permit the use of a bucking bar.

Also, in the attachment of many nonstructural parts such as aircraft interior furnishings, flooring, deicing boots, and the like, the full strength of solid shank rivets is not necessary.

For use in such places, special rivets have been designed which can be bucked from the front. They are sometimes lighter than solid-shank rivets, yet amply strong for their intended use. These rivets are produced by several manufacturers and have unique characteristics that require special installation tools, special installation procedures, and special removal procedures. Because these rivets are often inserted in locations where one head (usually the shop head) cannot be seen, they are called blind rivets.

Mechanically Expanded Rivets

Two classes of mechanically expanded rivets will be discussed here:
(1) Non-structural, figure 4-7.
  (a) Self-plugging (friction lock) rivets
  (b) Pull-thru rivets (hollow)
(2) Mechanical lock, flush fracturing, self-plugging rivets, figure 4-8.

Self-Plugging

The self-plugging (friction lock) blind rivets are manufactured by several companies: the same general basic information about their fabrication, composition, uses, selection, installation, inspection, and removal procedures apply to all of them.

Self-plugging (friction lock) rivets are fabricated in two parts: A rivet head with a hollow shank or sleeve, and a stem that extends through the hollow shank.

Several events, in their proper sequence, occur when a pulling force is applied to the stem of the rivet: (1) The stem is pulled into the rivet shank; (2) the mandrel portion of the stem forces the rivet

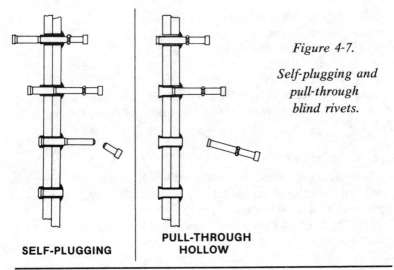

Figure 4-7.

Self-plugging and pull-through blind rivets.

SELF-PLUGGING | **PULL-THROUGH HOLLOW**

Figure 4-8.

A mechanical lock self-plugging blind rivet.

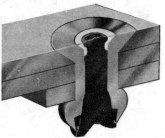

shank to expand; and (3) when friction (or pulling action pressure) becomes great enough it will cause the stem to snap at a breakoff groove on the stem. The plug portion (bottom end of the stem) is retained in the shank of the rivet giving the rivet much greater shear strength than could be obtained from a hollow rivet.

Self-plugging (friction lock) rivets are fabricated in two common head styles: (1) A protruding head similar to the MS20470 or universal head, and (2) a 100 degree countersunk head. See figure 4-9. Other head styles are available from some manufacturers.

The stem of the self-plugging (friction lock) rivet may have a knot or knob on the upper portion, or it may have a serrated portion as shown in figure 4-9.

Self-plugging (friction lock) rivets are fabricated from several materials. Rivets are available in the following material combinations: stem 2017 aluminum alloy and sleeve 2117 aluminum alloy; stem 2017 aluminum alloy and sleeve 5056 aluminum alloy; and stem steel and sleeve steel.

The stem of the self-plugging (friction lock) rivet may have a knot or knob on the upper portion, or it may have a serrated

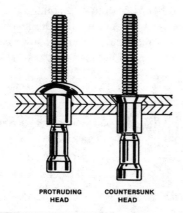

Figure 4-9.

Self-plugging
(friction lock) rivets.

PROTRUDING HEAD   COUNTERSUNK HEAD

Figure 4-10.

Two different types of pulling heads
are available for friction lock rivets.

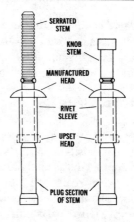

SERRATED STEM
KNOB STEM
MANUFACTURED HEAD
RIVET SLEEVE
UPSET HEAD
PLUG SECTION OF STEM

portion as shown in figure 4-10 depending on the type of pulling tool available.

Self-plugging (friction lock) rivets are designed so that installation requires only one person; it is not necessary to have the work accessible from both sides. The pulling strength of the rivet stem is such that a uniform job can always be assured. Because it is not necessary to have access to the opposite side of the work, self-plugging (friction lock) rivets can be used to attach assemblies to hollow tubes, corrugated sheet, hollow boxes, etc. Because a hammering force is not necessary to install the rivet, it can be used to attach assemblies to plywood or plastics.

Material composition of the rivet shank will depend upon the type of material being riveted. Aluminum alloy 2117 shank rivets can be used on most aluminum alloys. Aluminum alloy 5056 shank rivets should be used when the material being riveted is magnesium. Steel rivets should always be selected for riveting assemblies fabricated from steel.

The thickness of the material being riveted determines the overall length of the shank of the rivet. As a general rule, the shank of the rivet should extend beyond the material thickness approximately 3/64 inch to ⅛ inch before the stem is pulled (see figure 4-11).

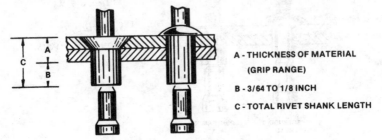

A - THICKNESS OF MATERIAL
(GRIP RANGE)

B - 3/64 TO 1/8 INCH

C - TOTAL RIVET SHANK LENGTH

Figure 4-11. Determining rivet length.

Each company that manufacturers self-plugging (friction lock) rivets has a code number to help users obtain the correct rivet for the grip range or material thickness of a particular installation. In addition, MS numbers are used for identification purposes.

Pull-Thru Rivets

The pull-thru blind rivets are manufactured by several companies; the same general basic information about their fabrication, composition, uses, selection, installation, inspection, and removal procedures apply to all of them.

Pull-thru rivets are fabricated in two parts: A rivet head with a hollow shank or sleeve and a stem that extends through the hollow shank. Figure 4-12 illustrates a protruding head pull-thru rivet.

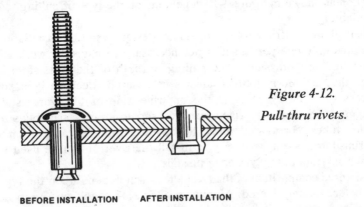

Figure 4-12.
Pull-thru rivets.

BEFORE INSTALLATION   AFTER INSTALLATION

Several events, in their proper sequence, occur when a pulling force is applied to the stem of the rivet: (1) The stem is pulled thru the rivet shank; (2) the mandrel portion of the stem forces the shank

62

to expand forming the blind head.

Pull-thru rivets are fabricated in two common head styles: (1) Protruding head similar to the MS20470 or universal head, and (2) a 100 degrees countersunk head. Other head styles are available from some manufacturers.

Pull-thru rivets are fabricated from several materials. The most commonly used are: 2117-T4 aluminum alloy, 5056 aluminum alloy, and monel.

Pull-thru rivets are designed so that installation requires only one person; it is not necessary to have the work accessible from both sides.

Since they are structurally weak, pull-thru rivets are used to a limited extent in the airframe field.

Self-Plugging Rivets (mechanical lock)

Self-plugging (mechanical lock) rivets are similar to self-plugging (friction lock) rivets, except for the manner in which the stem is retained in the rivet sleeve. This type of rivet has a positive mechanical locking collar to resist vibrations that cause the friction lock rivets to loosen and possibly fall out. (See figure 4-13.) Also, the mechanical locking type rivet stem breaks off flush with the head and usually does not require further stem trimming when properly installed. Self-plugging (mechanical lock) rivets display all the strength characteristics of solid shank rivets and in most cases can be substituted rivet for rivet.

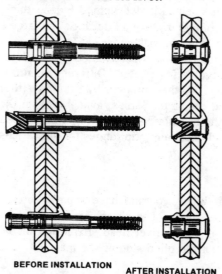

Figure 4-13.

Self-plugging (mechanical lock) rivets. Also see figure 4-8.

BEFORE INSTALLATION   AFTER INSTALLATION

Self-plugging (mechanical lock) rivets are fabricated in two sections—a head and shank (including a conical recess and locking collar in the head), and a serrated stem that extends through the shank. Unlike the friction lock rivet, the mechanical lock rivet has a locking collar that forms a positive lock for retention of the stem in the shank of the rivet. This collar is seated in position during the installation of the rivet.

Three operations are performed in the installation of the mechanical lock rivet. When a pulling force is exerted on the stem, it is pulled into position and tightens the rivet heads (manufactured and shop heads) against the material. At a predetermined point, an inner anvil incorporated in the driving assembly forces the locking collar into position in the manufactured head, and the rivet stem snaps off approximately even with the head of the rivet. (Figure 4-13 illustrates the final position of the locking collar in the rivet head.)

Self-plugging (mechanical lock) rivets are available from at least two manufacturers. They are fabricated with sleeves (rivet shanks) of 2017 and 5056 aluminum alloys, Monel, or stainless steel.

The mechanical lock type of self-plugging rivet can be used in the same applications as the friction lock type of rivet. In addition, because of its greater stem retention characteristic, installation in areas subject to considerable vibration is recommended.

The same general requirements must be met in the selection of the mechanical lock rivet as for the friction lock rivet. Composition of the material being joined together determines the composition of the rivet sleeve, for example, 2017 aluminum alloy rivets for most aluminum alloys and 5056 aluminum rivets for magnesium.

Shank diameter of the rivet selected is determined by the thickness of the material and the strength of the joint desired. Too large a diameter should not be used in thin material.

The length of the selected rivet shank is determined by the thickness of the material (grip range) being riveted. Different manufacturers designate the grip range for their product by symbols either on the head of the rivet or on the stem. Tables, available from the manufacturers, will provide the numbering or lettering system used by each, and the minimum and maximum grip ranges for the various diameters available.

Explosive Rivets

Explosive rivets are of the blind type and have a partly hollow shank filled with an explosive charge. The charge is detonated by applying a heated electric iron to the rivet head. Explosion of the charge forms a bulged head on the blind side of the material. It is used for nonstructural repair.

The outward appearance of the explosive rivet is the same as the solid-shank aluminum alloy rivet. Two types of explosive rivets are manufactured. The newer type has a cavity drilled the length of the shank and will expand to fill a drilled hole. Only the blind end of the old type explosive rivet expands. Both types are made of 2017-T aluminum alloy. These rivets are available with either brazier or countersunk heads and in three shank diameters, 1/8, 5/32, and 3/16 inch.

Brazier head explosive rivets have a grip length range from .025 inch to .244 inch in steps of .020 inch. The countersunk (78 degrees or 100 degrees) explosive rivet has a grip length range from .045 inch to .224 inch in steps of .020 inch.

The part number of explosive rivets designates the shank diameter, type of head, and grip length.

Other Blind Rivets

Other blind rivets known by their trade names are used in fabricating aircraft components such as Rivnuts, Dill Lok-Skrus, Dill Lok-Rivets and Deutsch Rivets.

Pin Rivets (Hi-Shear)

Pin (Hi-shear) rivets are classified as special rivets but are not of the blind type. Access to both sides of the material is required to install this type of rivet. Pin rivets have the same shear strength as bolts of equal diameters, are about 40 percent of the weight of a bolt, and require only about one-fifth as much time for installation as a bolt, nut, and washer combination. They are approximately three times as strong as solid-shank rivets.

Pin rivets are essentially threadless bolts. The pin is headed at one end and is grooved about the circumference at the other. A metal collar is swaged onto the grooved end effecting a firm, tight fit (see figure 4-14.)

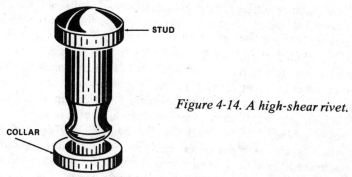

Figure 4-14. A high-shear rivet.

Pin rivets are fabricated in a variety of materials (usually steel) but should be used only in shear applications. They should never be used where the grip length is less than the shank diameter.

Part numbers for pin rivets can be interpreted to give the diameter and grip length of the individual rivets. A typical part number break-down would be:

$$NAS \quad 177 - 14 - 17$$

└─ Maximum grip length in 16ths of an inch.

└─ Nominal diameter in 32nds of an inch.

177 = 100° countersunk head rivet.

178 = flathead rivet.

└─ National Aircraft Standard.

THREADED FASTENERS

Various types of fastening devices allow quick dismantling or re-placement of aircraft parts that must be taken apart and put back together at frequent intervals. Riveting or welding these parts each time they are serviced would soon weaken or ruin the joint. Further-more some joints require greater tensile strength and stiffness than rivets can provide. Bolts and screws are two types of fastening devices which give the required security of attachment and rigidity. Generally, bolts are used where great strength is required, and screws are used where strength is not the deciding factor.

Bolts and screws are similar in many ways. They are both used for fastening or holding, and each has a head on one end and screw threads on the other. Regardless of these similarities, there are several distinct differences between the two types of fasteners. The threaded end of a bolt is always blunt while that of a screw may be either blunt or pointed.

The threaded end of a bolt usually has a nut screwed onto it to complete the assembly. The threaded end of a screw may fit into a female receptacle, or it may fit directly into the material being secured. A bolt has a fairly short threaded section and a compara-tively long grip length or unthreaded portion, whereas a screw has a longer threaded section and may have no clearly defined grip length. A bolt assembly is generally tightened by turning the nut on the bolt; the head of the bolt may or may not be designed for turning. A screw is always tightened by turning its head.

When it becomes necessary to replace aircraft fasteners, a dupli-cate of the original fastener should be used if at all possible. If duplicate fasteners are not available, extreme care and caution must be used in selecting substitutes.

Classification of Threads

Aircraft bolts, screws, and nuts are threaded in either the NC (American National Coarse) thread series, the NF (American National Fine) thread series, the UNC (American Standard Unified Coarse) thread series, or the UNF (American Standard Unified Fine) thread series. There is one difference between the American National series and the American Standard Unified series that should be pointed out. In the 1-inch-diameter size, the NF thread specified 14 threads per inch (1-14NF), while the UNF thread specifies 12 threads per inch (1-12UNF). Both type threads are designated by the number of times the incline (threads) rotates around a 1-inch length of a given diameter bolt or screw. For example, a 4-28 thread indicates that a ¼-inch-diameter bolt has 28 threads in 1 inch of its threaded length.

Threads are also designated by Class of fit. The Class of a thread indicates the tolerance allowed in manufacturing. Class 1 is a loose fit, Class 2 is a free fit, Class 3 is a medium fit, and Class 4 is a close fit. **Aircraft bolts are almost always manufactured in the Class 3, medium fit.** A Class 4 fit requires a wrench to turn the nut onto a bolt, whereas a Class 1 fit can easily be turned with the fingers. Generally, aircraft screws are manufactured with a Class 2 thread fit for ease of assembly. The general purpose aircraft bolt, AN3 thru AN20 has UNF-3 threads (American Standard Unified Fine, Class 3, medium fit).

Bolts and nuts are also produced with right-hand and left-hand threads. A right-hand thread tightens when turned clockwise; a left-hand thread tightens when turned counterclockwise. Except in special cases, all aircraft bolts and nuts have right hand threads.

AIRCRAFT BOLTS

Aircraft bolts are fabricated from cadmium- or zinc-plated steel, (usually nickel steel SAE2330), unplated corrosion-resistant steel, and anodized aluminum alloys. By far the most common is the cadmium plated steel bolt. Most bolts used in aircraft structures are either general-purpose, AN bolts, or NAS internal-wrenching or close-tolerance bolts, or MS bolts. In certain cases, aircraft manufacturers make bolts of different dimensions or greater strength than the standard types. Such bolts are made for a particular application, and it is of extreme importance to use like bolts in replacement. Special bolts are usually identified by the letter "S" or "spec" stamped on the head.

AN bolts come in three head styles—hex-head, clevis, and eyebolt (see figure 4-15). NAS bolts are available in hex-head, internal-wrenching, and countersunk head styles. MS bolts come in hex-head and internal-wrenching styles.

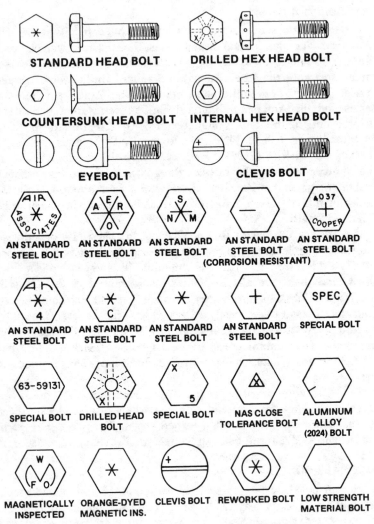

Figure 4-15. Aircraft bolt identification.

General-Purpose Bolts

The hex-head aircraft bolt (AN-3 through AN-20) is an all-purpose structural bolt used for general applications involving tension or shear loads where a light-drive fit is permissible. (.006-inch clearance for a ⅝-inch hole, and other sizes in proportion). See figure 4-16.

Alloy steel bolts smaller than No. 10-32 (3/16-inch diameter, AN3-) and aluminum alloy bolts smaller than ¼-inch diameter are not used in primary structures. Aluminum alloy bolts and nuts are not used where they will be repeatedly removed for purposes of maintenance and inspection. Aluminum alloy nuts may be used with cadmium-plated steel bolts loaded in shear on land airplanes, but are not used on seaplanes due to the increased possibility of dissimilar-metal corrosion.

The AN73-AN81 (MS20073-MS20074) drilled-head bolt is similar to the standard hex-bolt, but has a deeper head which is drilled to receive wire for safetying. The AN-3, AN-20 and the AN-73, AN-81 series bolts are interchangeable, for all practical purposes, from the standpoint of tension and shear strengths.

Close-Tolerance Bolts

This type of bolt is machined more accurately than the general-purpose bolt. Close-tolerance bolts may be hex-headed (AN-173 through AN-186) or have a 100 degrees countersunk head (NAS-80 through NAS-86). They are used in applications where a tight-drive fit is required (the bolt will move into position only when struck with a 12- to 14-ounce hammer).

Internal-Wrenching Bolts

These bolts, (MS-20004 through MS-20024 or NAS-495) are fabricated from high-strength steel and are suitable for use in both tension and shear applications. When they are used in steel parts, the bolthole must be slightly countersunk to seat the large corner radius of the shank at the head. In aluminum alloy material, a special heat-treated washer must be used to provide an adequate bearing surface for the head. The head of the internal-wrenching bolt is recessed to allow the insertion of an internal wrench when installing or removing the bolt. Special high-strength nuts are used on these bolts. Replace an internal-wrenching bolt with another internal-wrenching bolt. Standard AN hex-head bolts and washers cannot be substituted for them as they do not have the required strength.

Identification and Coding

Bolts are manufactured in many shapes and varieties. A clear-cut method of classification is difficult. Bolts can be identified by the shape of the head, method of securing, material used in fabrication, or the expected usage.

AN-type aircraft bolts can be identified by the code markings on the boltheads. The markings generally denote the bolt manufacturer, the material of which the bolt is made, and whether the bolt is a standard AN-type or a special-purpose bolt. **AN standard steel bolts are marked with either a raised dash or asterisk;** corrosion-resistant steel is indicated by a single raised dash; and AN aluminum alloy bolts are marked with two raised dashes. Additional information, such as bolt diameter, bolt length, and grip length may be obtained from the bolt part number. AN standard steel bolts are shown in figure 4-16. Figure 4-17 shows the identification of many other bolts.

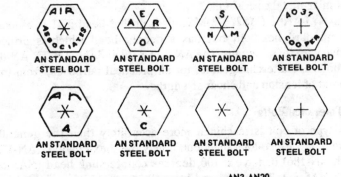

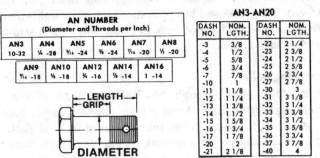

Figure 4-16. The general purpose structural bolt (AN3 through AN20) cadmimum-plated high strength steel alloy is identified by a cross or asterisk. The manufacturer's name may also be included as shown in these examples.

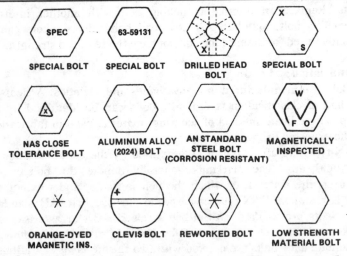

Figure 4-17. Bolt identification for bolts other than the general purpose steel bolt.

70

For example, in the bolt part number AN3DD5A, the "AN" designates that it is an Air-Navy Standard bolt, the "3" indicates the diamter in sixteenths of an inch (3/16), the "DD" indicates the material is 2024 aluminum alloy. The letter "C" in place of the "DD" would indicate corrosion-resistant steel, and the absence of the letters would indicate cadmium-plated steel (the most (common). The "5" indicates the length in eighths of an inch (⅝), and the "A" indicates that the shank is undrilled. If the letter "H" preceded the "5" in addition to the "A" following it, the head would be drilled for safetying.

Close-tolerance NAS bolts are marked with either a raised or recessed triangle. The material markings for NAS bolts are the same as for AN bolts, except that they may be either raised or recessed. Bolts inspected magnetically (Magna-flux) or by fluorescent means (Zyglo) are identified by means of colored lacquer, or a head marking of a distinctive type.

SPECIAL-PURPOSE BOLTS

Bolts designed for a particular application or use are classified as special-purpose bolts. Clevis bolts, eyebolts, and lock bolts are special-purpose bolts. See figure 4-15.

Clevis Bolts

The head of a clevis bolt is round and is either slotted to receive a common screwdriver or recessed to receive a crosspoint screwdriver. This type of bolt is used only where shear loads occur and never in tension. It is often inserted as a mechanical pin in a control system.

Eyebolt

This type of special-purpose bolt is used where external tension loads are to be applied. The eye is designed for the attachment of such devices as the fork of a turnbuckle, a clevis, or a cable shackle. The threaded end may or may not be drilled for safetying.

AIRCRAFT NUTS

Aircraft nuts are made in a variety of shapes and sizes. They are made of cadmium-plated carbon steel, stainless steel, or anodized 2024T aluminum alloy, and may be obtained with either right- or left-hand threads. No identifying marking or lettering appears on nuts. They can be identified only by the characteristic metallic luster or color of the aluminum, brass, or the insert when the nut is of the self-locking type. They can be further identified by their construction.

Aircraft nuts can be divided into two general groups: Non-self-locking and self-locking nuts. Non-self locking nuts are those that must be safetied by external locking devices, such as cotter pins, safety wire, or locknuts. Self-locking nuts contain the locking feature as an integral part.

Non-self-locking Nuts

Most of the familiar types of nuts, including the plain nut, the castle nut, the castellated shear nut, the plain hex nut, the light hex nut, and the plain check nut are the non-self-locking type. (See figure 4-18.)

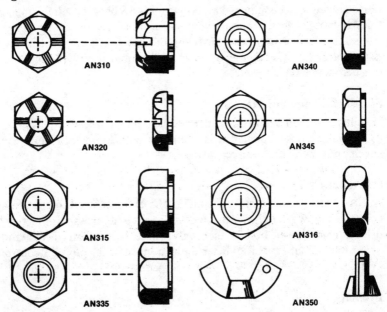

Figure 4-18. Non-self-locking nuts. The AN310 castellated steel nut is the most common and is used with the general purpose steel bolt (AN3 through AN20.)

The castle nut, AN310, is used with drilled-shank AN hex head bolts, clevis bolts, eyebolts, drilled head bolts, or studs. It is fairly rugged and can withstand large tension loads. Slots (called castellations) in the nut are designed to accommodate a cotter pin or lock wire for safety. The AN310 castellated, cadmium plated steel nut as shown in figure 4-18 is by far the most commonly used airframe nut.

The castellated shear nut, AN320, is designed for use with devices (such as drilled clevis bolts and threaded taper pins) which are normally subjected to shearing stress only. Like the castle nut, it is castellated for safetying. Note, however, that the nut is not as deep or as strong as the castle nut; also that the castellations are not as deep as those in the castle nut.

The plain hex nut, AN315 and AN335 (fine and coarse thread), is of rugged construction. This makes it suitable for carrying large tensional loads. However, since it requires an auxiliary locking device such as a check nut or lockwasher, its use on aircraft structures is somewhat limited.

The light hex nut, AN340 and AN345 (fine and coarse thread), is a much lighter nut than the plain hex nut and must be locked by an auxiliary device. It is used for miscellaneous light-tension requirements.

The plain check nut, AN316, is employed as a locking device for plain nuts, set screws, threaded rod ends, and other devices.

The wing nut, AN350, is intended for use where the desired tightness can be obtained with the fingers and where the assembly is frequently removed.

Self-locking Nuts

As their name implies, self-locking nuts need no auxiliary means of safetying but have a safetying feature included as an integral part of their construction. Many types of self-locking nuts have been designed and their use has become quite widespread. Common applications are: (1) Attachment of antifriction bearings and control pulleys; (2) attachment of accessories, anchor nuts around inspection holes and small tank installation openings; and (3) attachment of rocker box covers and exhaust stacks. Self-locking nuts are acceptable for use on certificated aircraft subject to the restrictions of the manufacturer.

Self-locking nuts are used on aircraft to provide tight connections which will not shake loose under severe vibration. **Do not use self-locking nuts at joints which subject either the nut or bolt to rotation.** They may be used with antifriction bearings and control pulleys, provided the inner race of the bearing is clamped to the supporting structure by the nut and bolt. Plates nuts must be attached to the structure in a positive manner to eliminate rotation or misalignment when tightening the bolts or screws.

The two general types of self-locking nuts currently in use are the all-metal type and the fiber-lock type. For the sake of simplicity, only two typical kinds of self-locking nuts are considered in this handbook: The Boots self-locking nut, representing the all-metal type; and the elastic stop nut, representing the fiber-insert type.

The Boots self-locking nut is of one-piece, all-metal construction, designed to hold tight in spite of severe vibration. Note in figure 4-19 that it has two sections and is essentially two nuts in one, a locking

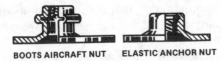

BOOTS AIRCRAFT NUT

ELASTIC ANCHOR NUT

Figure 4-19.

Self-locking nuts.

FLEXLOC NUT   FIBER LOCKNUT   ELASTIC STOP NUT

nut and a load-carrying nut. The two sections are connected with a spring which is an integral part of the nut. The spring keeps the locking and load-carrying sections such a distance apart that the two sets of threads are out-of-phase; that is, so spaced that a bolt which has been screwed through the load-carrying section must push the locking section outward against the force of the spring to engage the threads of the locking section properly.

Thus, the spring, through the medium of the locking section, exerts a constant locking force on the bolt in the same direction as a force that would tighten the nut. In this nut, the load-carrying section has the thread strength of a standard nut of comparable size, while the locking section presses against the threads of the bolt and locks the nut firmly in position. Only a wrench applied to the nut will loosen it. The nut can be removed and reused without impairing its efficiency.

Boots self-locking nuts are made with three different spring styles and in various shapes and sizes. The wing type, ranges in size from No. 6 up to ¼ inch, the Rol-top ranges from ¼ inch to 9/16 inch, and the bellows type ranges in size from No. 8 up to ⅜ inch. Wing-type nuts are made of anodized aluminum alloy, cadmium-plated carbon steel, or stainless steel. The Rol-top nut is cadmium-plated steel, and the bellows type is made of aluminum alloy only.

Elastic Stop Nut

The elastic stop nut, AN365 (MS20365) the most commonly used self-locking nut, is a standard nut with the height increased to accommodate a fiber-locking collar. This fiber collar is very tough and durable and is unaffected by immersion in hot or cold water or ordinary solvents such as ether, carbon tetrachloride, oils and gasoline. It will not damage bolt threads or plating.

As shown in figure 4-20, the fiber-locking collar is not threaded and its inside diameter is smaller than the largest diameter of the threaded portion or the outside diameter of a corresponding bolt. When the nut is screwed onto a bolt, it acts as an ordinary nut until the bolt reaches the fiber collar. When the bolt is screwed into the

74

fiber collar, however, friction (or drag) causes the fiber to be pushed upward. This creates a heavy downward pressure on the load-carrying part and automatically throws the load-carrying sides of the nut and bolt threads into positive contact. After the bolt has been forced all the way through the fiber collar, the downward pressure remains constant. This pressure locks and holds the nut securely in place even under severe vibration.

Figure 4-20. Elastic stop nut, AN365 (MS20365).

Nearly all elastic stop nuts are steel or aluminum alloy. However, such nuts are available in practically any kind of metal. Aluminum alloy elastic stop nuts are supplied with an anodized finish. Steel nuts are cadmium plated.

Normally, elastic stop nuts can be used many times with complete safety and without detriment to their locking efficiency. When re-using elastic stop nuts, be sure the fiber has not lost its locking friction or become brittle.**If a nut can be turned with the fingers, replace it.**

After the nut has been tightened, make sure the rounded or chamfered end of the bolts, studs, or screws extends at least the full round or chamfer through the nut. Flat end bolts, studs, or screws should extend least 1/32 inch through the nut. Bolts of 5/16-inch diameter and over with cotter pin holes may be used with self-locking nuts, but only if free from burrs around the holes. Bolts with damaged threads and rough ends are not acceptable. Do not tap the fiber-locking insert. The self-locking action of the elastic stop nut is the result of having the bolt threads impress themselves into the un-tapped fiber.

Do not install elastic stop nuts in places where the temperature is higher than 250 degrees F., because the effectiveness of the self-locking action is reduced beyond this point. Self-locking nuts may be used on aircraft engines and accessories when their use is speci-fied by the engine manufacturer.

Self-locking nut bases are made in a number of forms and materials for riveting and welding to aircraft structure or parts. (See figure 4-21.) Certain applications require the installation of self-locking nuts in channels, an arrangement which permits the attachment of many nuts with only a few rivets. These channels are track-like bases with regularly spaced nuts which are either removable or nonremovable. The removable type carries a floating nut, which can be snapped in or out of the channel, thus making possible the easy removal of damaged nuts. Nuts such as the clinch-type and spline-type which depend on friction for their anchorage are not acceptable for use in aircraft structures.

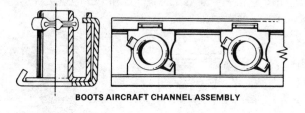

BOOTS AIRCRAFT CHANNEL ASSEMBLY

ELASTIC STOP NUT CHANNEL ASSEMBLY

Figure 4-21.

Self-locking nut bases.

Sheet Spring Nuts

Sheet spring nuts, sometimes called speed nuts, are used with standard and sheet-metal self-tapping screws in **nonstructural locations** . They find various uses in supporting line clamps, conduit clamps, electrical equipment, access doors, and the like, and are available in several types. Speed nuts, are made from spring steel and are arched prior to tightening. This arched spring lock prevents the screw from working loose. These nuts should be used only where originally used in fabrication of the aircraft. See figure 4-22.

Figure 4-22. Sheet spring nuts are used with self-tapping screws in non-structural locations.

Identification and Coding

Part numbers designate the type of nut. The common types and their respective part numbers are: Plain, AN315 and AN335; castle AN310; plain check, AN316; light hex, AN340 and AN345; and castellated shear, AN320. The patented self-locking types are assigned part numbers ranging from MS20363 through MS20367. The Boots, the Flexloc, the fiber locknut, the elastic stop nut, and the self-locking nut belong to this group. Part number AN350 is assigned to the wing nut.

Letters and digits following the part number indicate such items as material, size, threads per inch, and whether the thread is right or left hand. The letter "B" following the part number indicates the nut material to be brass; a "D" indicates 2017-T aluminum alloy; a "DD" indicates 2024-T aluminum alloy; a "C" indicates stainless steel; and a dash in place of a letter indicates cadmium-plated carbon steel.

The digit (or two digits) following the dash or the material code letter is the dash number of the nut, and it indicates the size of the shank and threads per inch of the bolt on which the nut will fit. The dash number corresponds to the first figure appearing in the part number coding of general-purpose bolts. A dash and the number 3, for example, indicates that the nut will fit an AN3 bolt (10-32); a dash and the number 4 means it will fit an AN4 bolt (¼-28); a dash and the number 5, an AN5 bolt (5/16-24); and so on.

The code numbers for self-locking nuts end in three- or four-digit numbers. The last two digits refer to threads per inch, and the one or two preceding digits stand for the nut size in 16ths of an inch.

Some other common nuts and their code numbers are:

Code Number AN310D5R:

    AN310 = aircraft castle nut.

    D = 2024-T aluminum alloy.

    5 = 5/16-inch diameter.

    R = right-hand thread (usually 24 threads per inch).

Code Number AN320-10:

    AN320 = aircraft castellated shear nut, cadmium-plated carbon steel.

    10 = ⅝-inch diameter, 18 threads per inch (this nut is usually right-hand thread).

Code Number AN350B1032.

    AN350 = aircraft wingnut.

    B = brass.

    10 = number 10 bolt.

    32 = threads per inch.

AIRCRAFT WASHERS

Aircraft washers used in airframe repair are either plain, lock, or special type washers.

Plain Washers

The plain washer (figure 4-23), the AN960 is used under hex nuts. It provides a smooth bearing surface and acts as a shim in obtaining correct grip length for a bolt and nut assembly. It is used to adjust the position of castellated nuts in respect to drilled cotter pin holes in bolts. Plain washers should be used under lockwashers to prevent damage to the surface material.

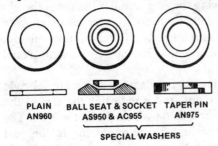

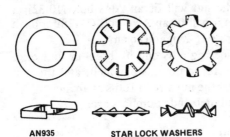

Figure 4-23.

Various types of washers. The AN960 plain washer is the most common and is used with AN3 thru AN20 bolts and AN310 nuts.

Aluminum and aluminum alloy washers may be used under bolt heads or nuts on aluminum alloy or magnesium structures where corrosion caused by dissimilar metals is a factor. When used in this manner, any electric current flow will be between the washer and the steel bolt. **However, it is common practice to use a cadmium-plated steel washer under a nut bearing directly against a structure** as this washer will resist the cutting action of a nut better than an aluminum alloy washer.

The AN970 steel washer provides a greater bearing area than the AN960 washer and is used on wooden structures under both the head and the nut of a bolt to prevent crushing the surface.

Lockwashers

Lockwashers, both the AN935 and AN936, are used with machine screws or bolts where the selflocking or castellated type nut is not appropriate. The spring action of the washer (AN935) provides enough friction to prevent loosening of the nut from vibration. (These washers are shown in figure 4-23).

Lockwashers should never be used under the following conditions:
1. With fasteners to primary or secondary structures.
2. With fasteners on any part of the aircraft where failure might result in damage or danger to the aircraft or personnel.
3. Where failure would permit the opening of a joint to the airflow.

4. Where the screw is subject to frequent removal.
5. Where the washers are exposed to the airflow.
6. Where the washers are subject to corrosive conditions.
7. Where the washer is against soft material without a plain washer underneath to prevent gouging the surface.

Shakeproof Lockwashers

Shakeproof lockwashers are round washers designed with tabs or lips that are bent upward across the sides of a hex nut or bolt to lock the nut in place. There are various methods of securing the lockwasher to prevent it from turning, such as an external tab bent downward 90 degrees into a small hole in the face of the unit, or an internal tab which fits a keyed bolt.

Shakeproof lockwashers can withstand higher heat than other methods of safetying and can be used under high-vibration conditions safely. They should be used only once because the tabs tend to break when bent a second time.

Special Washers

The ball-socket and seat washers, AC950 and AC955, are special washers used where a bolt is installed at an angle to a surface, or where perfect alignment with a surface is required. These washers are used together. They are shown in figure 4-23.

The NAS143 and MS20002 washers are used for internal wrenching bolts of the NAS144 through NAS158 series. This washer is either plain or countersunk. The countersunk washer (designated as NAS143C and MS20002C) is used to seat the bolt head shank radius, and the plain washer is used under the nut.

AIRCRAFT SCREWS

Screws differ from bolts inasmuch as they are generally made of lower strength materials. They can be installed with a loose-fitting thread, and the head shapes are made to engage a screwdriver or wrench. Some screws have a clearly defined grip or unthreaded portion while others are threaded along their entire length. See figure 4-24.

Several types of structural screws differ from the standard structural bolts only in head style. The material in them is the same, and a definite grip length is provided. The AN525 washer-head screw and the NAS220 through NAS227 series are such screws.

Commonly used screws are classified in three groups: (1) Structural screws which have the same strength as equal size bolts; (2) machine screws, which include the majority of types used for general repair; and (3) self-tapping screws, which are used for attaching lighter parts.

Figure 4-24. Several types of aircraft screws. (Also see Appendix I.)

Structural Screws

Structural screws are made of alloy steel, are properly heat treated, and can be used as structural bolts. These screws are found in the NAS204 through NAS235 and AN509 and AN525 series. They have a definite grip and the same shear strength as a bolt of the same size. Shank tolerances are similar to AN hex-head bolts, and the threads are National Fine. Structural screws are available with round, brazier, or countersunk heads. The recessed head screws are driven by either a Phillips or a Reed and Prince screwdriver.

The AN509 (100 degree) flathead screw is used in countersunk holes where a flush surface is necessary.

The AN525 washer-head structural screw is used where raised heads are not objectionable. The washer-head screw provides a large contact area.

Machine Screws

Machine screws are usually of the flathead (countersunk), round-head, or washer-head types. These screws are general-purpose screws and are available in low-carbon steel, brass, corrosion-resistant steel, and aluminum alloy.

Roundhead screws, AN515 and AN520, have either slotted or recessed heads. The AN515 screw has coarse threads and the AN520 has fine threads.

Countersunk machine screws are listed as AN505 and AN510 for 82 degrees, and AN507 for 100 degrees. The AN505 and AN510 correspond to the AN515 and AN520 roundhead in material and usage.

The fillister-head screw, AN500 through AN503, is a general-purpose screw and is used as a capscrew in light mechanisms. This could include attachments of cast aluminum parts such as gearbox cover plates.

The AN500 and AN501 screws are available in low-carbon steel, corrosion-resistant steel, and brass. The AN500 has coarse threads while the AN501 has fine threads. They have no clearly defined grip length. Screws larger than No. 6 have a hole drilled through the head for safetying purposes.

The AN502 and AN503 fillister-head screws are made of heat-treated alloy steel, have a small grip, and are available in fine and coarse threads. These screws are used as capscrews where great strength is required. The coarse-threaded screws are commonly used as capscrews in tapped aluminum alloy and magnesium castings because of the softness of the metal.

Self-tapping Screws

Machine self-tapping screws are listed as AN504 and AN506. The AN504 screw has a roundhead, and the AN506 is 82 degrees countersunk. These screws are used for attaching removable parts, such as nameplates, to castings and parts in which the screw cuts its own threads.

AN530 and AN531 self-tapping sheet-metal screws, such as the Parker-Kalon Z-type sheetmetal screw, are blunt on the end. They are used in the temporary attachment of sheet metal for riveting, and in the permanent assembly of nonstructural assemblies. Self-tapping screws should not be used to replace standard screws, nuts, bolts, or rivets.

Drive Screws

Drive screws, AN535, correspond to the Parker-Kalon U-type. They are plain-head self-tapping screws used as capscrews for attaching nameplates in castings and for sealing drain holes in corrosion proofing tubular structures. They are not intended to be removed after installation.

Identification and Coding

The coding system used to identify screws is similar to that used for bolts. There are AN and NAS screws. NAS screws are structural screws. Part numbers 510, 515, 550, and so on, catalog screws into classes such as roundhead, flathead, washerheads, and so forth. Letters and digits indicate their material composition, length, and thickness.

OTHER STANDARD PARTS

Appendix I shows a partial listing of the many standard parts available.

RIVETS AND RIVETING

RIVET LAYOUT

Rivet layout consists of determining (1) the number of rivets required; (2) the size and style of rivet to use; (3) its material, temper condition, and strength; (4) the size of the rivet holes; (5) distance of the rivet holes and rivets from the edges of the patch; and (6) the spacing of the rivets throughout the repair. Since distances are measured in terms of rivet diameters, application of the measurements is simple once the correct rivet diameter is determined.

Singe-row, two-row, and three-row layouts designed for small repair jobs are discussed in this section. More complicated layouts for large repairs, which require the application of rivet formulas, are discussed in chapter 6, Aircraft Structural Repairs.

The type of head, size, and strength required in a rivet are governed by such factors as the kind of forces present at the point riveted, the kind and thickness of the material to be riveted, and location of the riveted part on the aircraft.

The type of head required for a particular job is determined by its installation location. Where a smooth aerodynamic surface is required, countersunk head rivets should be used. Universal head rivets may be used in most other locations. If extra strength is required and clearance permits, roundhead rivets may be used; if the necessary clearance is not available, flathead rivets may be used.

The size (or diameter) of the selected rivet shank should correspond in general to the thickness of the material being riveted. If too large a rivet is used in a thin material, the force necessary to drive the rivet properly will cause an undesirable bulging around the rivet head. On the other hand, if too small a rivet diameter is selected for thick material the shear strength of the rivet will not be great enough to carry the load of the joint. **As a general rule, the rivet diameter should be not less than three times the thickness of the thicker sheet.** Rivets most commonly chosen in the assembly and repair of aircraft range from 3/32-in. to 3/8-in. diameter. Ordinarily, **rivets smaller than 3/32-in. diameter are never used on any structural parts which carry stresses.**

When determining the total length of a rivet for installation, the combined thickness of the materials to be joined must be known. This measurement is known as grip length (B of figure 4-25). The total length of the rivet (A of figure 4-25) should be equal to grip length plus the amount of rivet shank necessary to form a proper shop head.

**The length of rivet required to form a shop head is 1½ times the dia-
meter of the rivet shank** (C of figure 5-36).

A—TOTAL RIVET LENGTH

B—GRIP LENGTH

C—AMOUNT OF RIVET LENGTH NEEDED FOR
    PROPER SHOP HEAD (1½ × RIVET DIA.)

D—INSTALLED RIVETS

Figure 4-25.

*Determining
length of rivet.*

Using figure 4-25 and the above information, the formula
$A = B + C$ was developed. (A, total rivet length; B, grip length;
C, material needed to form a shop head.)

Properly installed rivets are shown in D of figure 4-25. Note carefully the method used to measure total rivet lengths for countersunk
rivets and the other types of heads.

Whenever possible, select rivets of the same alloy number as the
material being riveted. For example, use 1100 and 3003 rivets on
parts fabricated from 1100 and 3003 alloys, and 2117-T and 2017-T
rivets on parts fabricated from 2017 and 2024 alloys.

The 2117-T rivet is usually used for general repair work, since it
requires no heat treatment, is fairly soft and strong, and is highly
corrosion resistant when used with most types of alloys. The 2024-T
rivet is the strongest of the aluminum alloy rivets and is used in
highly stressed parts. However, it must be soft when driven. Never
replace 2024-T rivets with 2117-T rivets.

The type of rivet head to select for a particular repair job can be
determined by referring to the type used within the surrounding area
by the manufacturer. A general rule to follow on a flush-riveted aircraft is to apply flush rivets on the upper surface of the wing and
stabilizers, on the lower leading edge back to the spar, and on the
fuselage back to the high point of the wing. Use universal head rivets
in all other surface areas.

In general, try to make the spacing of the rivets on a repair conform
to that used by the manufacturer in the area surrounding the damage.
Aside from this fundamental rule, there is no specific set of rules
which governs spacing of rivets in all cases. However, there are
certain minimum requirements which must be observed.

The edge distance, or distance from the center of the first rivet
to the edge of the sheet, should be not less than two rivet diameters
nor more than four. The recommended edge distance is about two
and one-half rivet diameters. If rivets are placed too close to the
edge of the sheet, the sheet is likely to crack or pull away from the

rivets; and if they are spaced too far from the edge, the sheet is apt to turn up at the edges.

Rivet pitch is the distance between the centers of adjacent rivets in the same row. The smallest allowable rivet pitch is three rivet diameters. The average rivet pitch usually ranges from six to eight rivet diameters, although rivet pitch may range from four to 10 rivet diameters. Tranverse pitch is the perpendicular distance between rivet rows; it is usually equal to 75% of the rivet pitch. The smallest allowable tranverse pitch is two and one-half rivet diameters.

When splicing a damaged tube and the rivets pass completely through the tube, space the rivets four to seven rivet diameters apart if adjacent rivets are at right angles to each other, and space them five to seven rivet diameters apart if the rivets are in line (parallel to each other). The first rivet on each side of the joint should be not less than two and one-half rivet diameters from the end of the sleeve.

The general rules of rivet spacing, as applied to straight-row layout, are quite simple. In a single-row layout, first determine the edge distance at each end of the row then lay off the rivet pitch (distance between rivets) as shown in figure 4-26. In the two-row layout, lay off the first row as just described, place the second row a distance equal to the transverse pitch from the first row, and then lay off rivet spots in the second row so that they fall midway between those in the first row. In the three-row layout, first lay off the first and third rows, then determine the second row rivet spots by using a straight-edge. (See figure 4-26.)

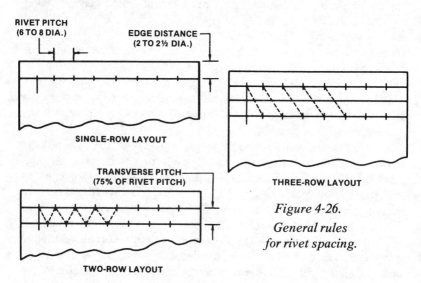

Figure 4-26.
General rules
for rivet spacing.

84

RIVET INSTALLATION

The various tools needed in the normal course of driving and up-setting rivets include drills, reamers, rivet cutters or nippers, bucking bars, riveting hammers, draw sets, dimpling dies or other types of countersinking equipment, rivet guns, and squeeze riveters. Self-tapping screws, C-clamps, and fasteners are riveting accessories commonly used to hold sheets together when riveting. Tools and equipment needed in the installation of rivets are discussed in the following paragraphs.

The shop head of a rivet is normally formed by means of a rivet gun and bucking bar or a squeezer. See figure 4-27.

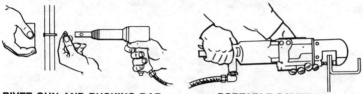

RIVET GUN AND BUCKING BAR   PORTABLE SQUEEZER

Figure 4-27. The shop head of a rivet is normally formed by means of a rivet gun and bucking bar or a portable squeezer.

Hole Duplicators

When sections of skin are replaced with new sections, the holes in the replacement sheet or in the patch must be drilled to match existing holes in the structure. These holes can be located with a hole duplicator. The peg on the bottom leg of the duplicator fits into the existing rivet hole. The hole in the new part is made by drilling through the bushing on the top leg. If the duplicator is properly made, holes drilled in this manner will be in perfect alignment. A separate duplicator must be used for each diameter of rivet.

Rivet Cutters

In cases where rivets of the required length are unavailable, rivet cutters can be used to cut rivets to the desired length. When using the rotary rivet cutter, insert the rivet in the correct hole, place the required number of shims under the rivet head, and squeeze as though it were a pair of pliers. Rotation of the disks will cut the rivet to give the right length, which is determined by the number of shims inserted under the head. When using a large rivet cutter, place it in a vise, insert the rivet in the proper hole, and cut by pulling the handle, thus shearing off the rivet. If regular rivet cutters are not available, diagonal cutting pliers can be used as a substitute cutter.

Bucking Bars

A bucking bar is a tool which is held against the shank end of a rivet while the shop head is being formed. Most bucking bars are made of alloy bar stock, but those made of better grades of steel last longer and require less reconditioning. Bucking bars are made in a number of different shapes and sizes to facilitate rivet bucking in all places where rivets are used. Some of the various bucking bars are shown in figure 4-28.

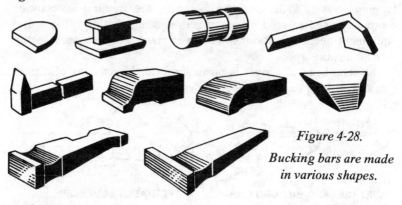

Figure 4-28.

Bucking bars are made in various shapes.

The bars must be kept clean, smooth, and well polished. Their edges should be slightly rounded to prevent marring the material surrounding the riveting operation.

Hand Rivet and Draw Sets

A hand rivet set is a tool equipped with a die for driving a particular type rivet. Rivet sets are available to fit every size and shape of rivet head. The ordinary set is made of ½-in. carbon tool steel about 6 in. long and is knurled to prevent slipping in the hand. Only the face of the set is hardened and polished.

Sets for round and brazier head rivets are recessed (or cupped) to fit the rivet head. In selecting the correct set, be sure that it will provide the proper clearance between the set and the sides of the rivet head and between the surfaces of the metal and the set. Flush or flat sets are used for countersunk and flathead rivets. To seat flush rivets properly, be sure that the flush sets are at least 1 in. in diameter.

Special draw sets are used to "draw up" the sheets to eliminate any opening between them before the rivet is bucked. Each draw set has a hole 1/32 in. larger than the diameter of the rivet shank for which it is made. Occasionally, the draw set and rivet header are incorporated into one tool. The header part consists of a hole sufficiently shallow so that the set will expand the rivet and head it when struck with a hammer.

Countersinks

The countersink is a tool which cuts a coneshaped depression around the rivet hole to allow the rivet to set flush with the surface of the skin. Countersinks are made with various angles to correspond to the various angles of the countersunk rivet heads, however, the 100 degrees angle is the most common.

Special stop countersinks are available. Stop countersinks are adjustable to any desired depth, and the cutters are interchangeable so that holes of various countersunk angles can be made. Some stop countersinks have a micrometer set arrangement, in increments of 0.001 in., for adjusting the cutting depths. See figure 2-18 in Chapter 2.

Dimpling Dies

The process of making an indentation or a dimple around a rivet hole so that the top of the head of a countersunk rivet will be flush with the surface of the metal is called dimpling. Dimpling is done with a male and female die, or forms, often called punch and die set. The male die has a guide the size of the rivet hole and is beveled to correspond to the degree of countersink of the rivet head. The female die has a hole into which the male guide fits, and is beveled to a corresponding degree of countersink.

Pneumatic Rivet Guns

The most common upsetting tool used in airframe repair work is the slow-hitting pneumatic hammer called a rivet gun. Pneumatic guns are available in various sizes and shapes (figure 4-29). The capacity of each gun, as recommended by the manufacturer, is usually stamped on the barrel; pneumatic guns operate on air pressures of from 90 to 100 p.s.i.

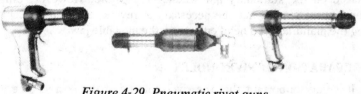

Figure 4-29. Pneumatic rivet guns.

Pneumatic guns are used in conjunction with interchangeable rivet sets. Each set is designed to fit the type of rivet and location of the work. The shank of the set is designed to fit into the rivet gun. Force to buck the rivet is supplied by an air-driven hammer inside the barrel of the gun. The sets are made of high-grade carbon tool steel and are heat treated to give them strength and wear resistance.

Some precautions to be observed when using a rivet gun are:
(1) Never point a rivet gun at anyone at any time. A rivet gun should be used for one purpose only—to drive or install rivets.

(2) Never depress the trigger mechanism unless the set is held tightly against a block of wood or a rivet.

(3) Always disconnect the air hose from the rivet gun when it will not be in use for any appreciable length of time.

Squeeze Riveters

The squeeze method of riveting is limited since it can be used only over the edges of sheets or assemblies where conditions permit, and where the reach of the squeeze riveter is deep enough. There are three types of rivet squeezers—hand, pneumatic, and pneudraulic. See figure 4-27. They are basically alike except that in the hand rivet squeezer, compression is supplied by hand pressure; in the pneumatic rivet squeezer, by air pressure; and in the pneudraulic, by a combination of air and hydraulic pressure. One jaw is stationary and serves as a bucking bar, the other jaw is movable and does the upsetting. Riveting with a squeezer is a quick method and requires only one operator.

Squeeze riveters are usually equipped with either a C-yoke or an alligator yoke. Yokes are available in various sizes to accommodate any size of rivet. The working capacity of a yoke is measured by its gap and its reach. The gap is the distance between the movable jaw and the stationary jaw; the reach is the inside length of the throat measured from the center of the end sets.

End sets for squeeze riveters serve the same purpose as rivet sets for pneumatic rivet guns and are available with the same type heads. They are interchangeable to suit any type of rivet head. One part of each set is inserted in the stationary jaw, while the other part is placed in the movable jaws. The manufactured head end set is placed on the stationary jaw whenever possible. However, during some operations, it may be necessary to reverse the end sets, placing the manufactured head end set on the movable jaw.

PREPARATION OF RIVET HOLES

It is very important that the rivet hole be of the correct size and shape and free from burrs. If the hole is too small, the protective coating will be scratched from the rivet when the rivet is driven through the hole. If the hole is too large, the rivet will not fill the hole completely. When it is bucked, the joint will not develop its full strength, and structural failure may occur at that spot.

If countersinking is required, consider the thickness of the metal and adopt the countersinking method recommended for that thickness. If dimpling is required, keep hammer blows or dimpling pressures to a minimum so that no undue work-hardening occurs in the surrounding area.

Drilling

To make a rivet hole of the correct size, first drill a hole slightly undersize. This is known as predrilling, and the hole is called a pilot hole. Ream the pilot hole with a twist drill of the correct size to get the required dimension. Pilot and reaming drill sizes are shown in figure 4-30. The recommended clearance for rivet holes is from 0.002 to 0.004 in.

Rivet Diameter	Pilot Size	Ream Size
3/32	3/32 (.0937)°	40 (.908)
1/8	1/8 (.125)	30 (.1285)
5/32	5/32 (.1562)	21 (.159)
3/16	3/16 (.1875)	11 (.191)
1/4	1/4 (.250)°	F (.257)
5/16	5/16 (.3125)	O (.316)
3/8	3/8 (.375)	V (.377)

°Note that ream size exceeds the maximum tolerance of .004 inch. This is permissible only if the next larger drill size happens to be so much larger than the tolerance of .004 inch.

Figure 4-30. Pilot and reaming twist drill sizes.

When drilling hard metals the twist drill should have an included angle of 118 degrees and should be operated at low speeds; but for soft metals use a twist drill with an included angle of 90 degrees and it should be operated at higher speeds. Thin sheets of aluminum alloy are drilled with greater accuracy by a drill having an included angle of 118 degrees because the large angle of the drill has less tendency to tear or elongate the hole.

Center punch locations for rivet holes before beginning the actual drilling. The center punch mark acts as a guide and lets the drill grip or bite into the metal with greater ease. Make the center punch mark large enough to prevent the drill from slipping out of position, but punch lightly enough not to dent the surrounding material. Hold a hard, smooth, wooden backing block securely in position behind the hole locations when drilling.

Drilling is usually done with a light power drill. Hold the power drill firmly with both hands. Extend the index and middle fingers of the left hand against the metal to act as a guide in starting a hole, and as a snubber or brake when the drill goes though the material. Before beginning to drill, always test the inserted twist drill for trueness and vibration by running the motor freely and watching the drill end. If the drill wobbles, it may be because of burrs on its shank or because the drill is bent or incorrectly chucked. A drill that wobbles or is slightly bent must not be used because it causes enlarged holes.

Always hold the drill at right angles to the work, regardless of the position of the hole or the curvature of the material. Use an angle drill or drill extensions and adapters when access is difficult with a straight drill. Never tip the drill sideways when drilling or when withdrawing from the material because this causes elongation of the hole.

When holes are drilled through sheet metal, small burrs are formed around the edge of the hole. Remove all burrs with a burr remover before riveting.

Countersinking and Dimpling

An improperly made countersink reduces the strength of a flush-riveted joint and may even cause failure of the sheet or the rivet head. The two methods of countersinking commonly used for flush riveting in aircraft construction and repair are the machine or drill countersinking, and dimpling or press countersinking. The proper method for any particular application depends on the thickness of the parts to be riveted, the height and angle of the countersunk head, the tools available, and accessibility.

As a general rule, use the drill countersink method when the thickness of the material is greater than the thickness of the rivet head, and use the dimpling method on thinner material. Figure 4-31 illustrates general rules for countersinking. Note in figure 4-31A that the material is quite thick and the head of the countersunk rivet extends only about halfway through the upper layer of metal. Countersinking will leave plenty of material for gripping.

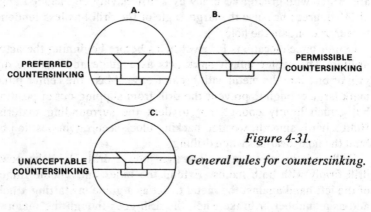

Figure 4-31.

General rules for countersinking.

In figure 4-31B, the countersunk head reaches completely through the upper layer. This condition is permissible but should be avoided.

In figure 4-31C, the head extends well into the second layer of material. This indicates that the material is thin and that most of it would be ground away by drill countersinking; therefore, dimpling is preferred. Dimpling will work best if the material is not over 0.040-in. thick.

Machine or drill countersinking is accomplished by a suitable cutting tool machined to the desired angle. The edge of the hole is cut away so that the countersunk rivet head fits snugly into the recess. The resulting recess is referred to as the "well" or "nest."

During the process of machine countersinking, first drill the original rivet hole to the exact rivet size, as recommended in the table in figure 4-30. The limits within which the head of the rivet may extend either above or below the surface of the metal are close, 0.006 in. in most cases. Therefore, perform the countersinking accurately, using equipment which is capable of producing results within the specified tolerance.

Hold the countersinking tool firmly at right angles to the material. Do not tip it. Tipping elongates the well and prevents the countersunk rivet head from fitting properly. Oversized rivet holes, undersized countersink pilots (in the case of the stop countersink), chattering caused by improper use of the countersink or by a countersink in poor condition, and a countersink not running true in the chuck of the drill are some of the causes of elongated wells.

Press countersinking or dimpling can be accomplished by either of two methods. Male and female die sets can be used, or using the rivet as the male die and the draw die as the female die is acceptable. In either case, the metal immediately surrounding the rivet hole is pressed to the proper shape to fit the rivet head. The depression thus formed, as in machine countersinking, is known as the "well" or "nest."

The rivet must fit the well snugly to obtain maximum strength. The number of sheets which can be dimpled simultaneously is limited by the capacity of the equipment used. The dimpling process may be accomplished by the use of hand tools, by dies placed in a pneumatic squeeze or single shot riveter, or by using a pneumatic riveting hammer.

Dimpling dies are made to correspond to any size and degree of countersunk rivet head available. The dies are usually numbered, and the correct combination of punch and die to use is indicated on charts specified by the manufacturer. Both male and female dies are machined accurately and have highly polished surfaces. The male die or punch is cone shaped to conform to the rivet head and has a small concentric pilot shaft that fits into the rivet hole and female die. The female die has a corresponding degree of countersink into which the male guide fits.

When dimpling a hole, rest the female die on some solid surface, place the material on the female die, insert the male die in the hole to be dimpled, and then hammer the male die. Strike with several solid blows until the dimple is formed.

In some cases, the face of the male die is convex to allow for springback in the metal. Dies of this type are used to advantage when the sheet to be dimpled is curved. Some dies have flat faces and are principally used for flat work. Dimpling dies are usually made so that their included angle is 5 degrees less than that of the rivet. This arrangement allows for springback of the metal.

In die dimpling, the pilot hole of the female die should be smaller than the diameter of the rivet to be used. Therefore, the rivet hole must be reamed to the exact diameter after the dimpling operation has been completed so that the rivet fits snugly.

When using a countersink rivet as the male dimpling die, place the female die in the usual position and back it with a bucking bar. Place the rivet of the required type into the hole and strike the rivet with a pneumatic riveting hammer. This method of countersinking is often called "coin pressing." It should be used only when the regular male die is not available.

Coin pressing has a distinct disadvantage in that the rivet hole must be drilled to correct rivet size before the dimpling operation is accomplished. Since the metal stretches during the dimpling operation, the hole becomes enlarged and the rivet must be swelled slightly before driving to produce a close fit. Because the rivet head will cause slight distortions in the recess, and these are characteristic only to that particular rivet head, it is wise to drive the same rivet that was used as the male die during the dimpling process. Do not substitute another rivet, either of the same size or a size larger.

Thermo-Dimpling

This type of dimpling consists of two processes, radius dimpling and coin dimpling. The major difference between radius and coin dimpling is in the construction of the female die. In radius dimpling, a solid female die is used. Coin dimpling uses a sliding ram female die (figure 4-32) that makes this process superior.

During the coin dimpling process, the metal is coined (made to flow) into the contours of the dies so that the dimple assumes the true shape of the die. The pressure exerted by the coining ram prevents the metal from compressing and thereby assures uniform cross sectional thickness of the sides of the dimple and a true conical shape.

Coin dimpling offers several advantages. It improves the configuration of the dimple, produces a more satisfactory aerodynamic skin surface, eliminates radial and circumferential cracking, ensures a stronger and safer joint, and allows identical dies to be used for both skin and understructure dimpling.

The material being used is a very important factor to consider in any dimpling operation. Materials such as corrosion-resistant steel, magnesium, and titanium each present different dimpling problems.

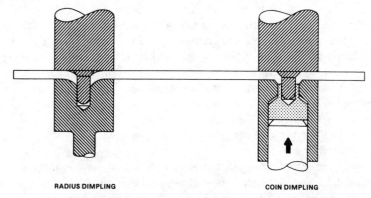

RADIUS DIMPLING   COIN DIMPLING

Figure 4-32. Radius and coin dimpling dies.

The 2024-T aluminum alloy can be satisfactorily coin dimpled either hot or cold. However, cracking in the vicinity of the dimple may result from cold dimpling because of hard spots in the metal. Hot dimpling will prevent such cracking.

The 7075-T6 and 2024-T81 aluminum alloys are always hot dimpled. Magnesium alloys also must be hot dimpled because, like 7075-T6, they have low formability qualities. Titanium is another metal that must be hot dimpled because it is tough and resists forming. The same temperature and dwell time used to hot dimple 7075-T6 is used for titanium.

Corrosion-resistant steel is cold dimpled because the temperature range of the heating unit is not high enough to affect dimpling.

The coin ram dimpling dies are designed with a number of built-in features. The faces of both the male and female dies are dished (the male concave and female convex) at an angle of 2 degrees on the pilot. This facilitates removal of the metal after the dimple has been made.

The female dimpling set has two parts: (1) The body, which is merely a counterpart of the male die; and (2) the coining ram, which extends up through the center of the conical recess of the body. In forming a dimple, the metal is forced down into the female die by the male die. The metal first contacts the coining ram, and this supports the metal as it is forced down into the conical recess. When the two dies close to the point where the forces of both are squeezing the material, the coining ram forces the metal back into the sharp corners of the dies.

When cold dimpling, the dies are used alone. When hot dimpling, a strap or block heater is slipped over either or both dies and connected to an electric current.

The dies should be kept clean at all times and in good working order. It is advisable to clean them regularly with steel wool. Special precautions must be taken when the dies are in the machine. If the machine is operated with the dies in place but without material between them, the male die will enlarge and ruin the coining ram.

When possible, coin dimpling should be performed on stationary equipment and before the assembly of parts. However, many instances arise in which dimpling must be done after parts are assembled to other structures. In such cases, dimpling operations are performed by portable squeeze dimplers. Most squeezers may be used either for cold dimpling or, combined with a junction box, for hot dimpling.

There are dimpling applications in which it is not possible to accommodate any squeezer- or yoke-type equipment. Under these circumstances, it is necessary to use a pneumatic hammer and a bucking bar type of tool to hold the dimpling dies.

DRIVING RIVETS

The methods of driving solid shank rivets can be classified into two types, depending on whether the riveting equipment is portable or stationary. Since stationary riveting equipment is seldom used in airframe repair work, only portable equipment that is used in hand, pneumatic, or squeezer methods is discussed here.

Before driving any rivets, be sure that all holes line up perfectly, all shavings and burrs have been removed, and that the parts to be riveted are securely fastened together.

Two men, a "gunner" and a "bucker," usually work as a team when installing rivets. However, on some jobs the riveter holds a bucking bar with one hand and operates a riveting gun with the other. When team riveting, an efficient signal system can be employed to develop the necessary teamwork. The code usually consists of tapping the bucking bar against the work; one tap may mean "not fully seated, hit it again"; two taps may mean "good rivet"; three taps may mean "bad rivet, remove and drive another" and so on.

Bucking

Selection of the appropriate bucking bar is one of the most important factors in bucking rivets. If the bar does not have the correct shape, it will deform the rivet head; if the bar is too light, it will not give the necessary bucking weight, and the material may become bulged toward the shop head; and, if the bar is too heavy, its weight and the bucking force may cause the material to bulge away from the shop head. Weights of bucking bars range from a few ounces to 8 or 10 lbs., depending upon the nature of the work. Recommended weights of bucking bars to be used with various rivet sizes are given in figure 4-33.

Rivet Diameter (In Inches)	Approx. Weight (In Pounds)
3/32	2 to 3
1/8	3 to 4
5/32	3 to 4½
3/16	4 to 5
1/4	5 to 6½

Figure 4-33. Recommended bucking bar weights.

Always hold the face of the bucking bar at right angles to the rivet shank. Failure to do this will cause the rivet shank to bend with the first blows of the rivet gun, and will cause the material to become marred with the final blows. The bucker must hold the bucking bar in place until the rivet is completely driven. If the bucking bar is removed while the gun is in operation, the rivet set may be driven through the material. Do not bear down too heavily on the shank of the rivet. Allow the weight of the bucking bar to do most of the work. The hands merely guide the bar and supply the necessary tension and rebound action.

Allow the bucking bar to vibrate in unison with the gun set. This process is called coordinated bucking. Coordinated bucking can be developed through pressure and stiffness applied at the wrists; with experience, a high degree of deftness can be obtained.

Lack of proper vibrating action, the use of a bucking bar that is too light or too heavy, and failure to hold the bucking bar at right angles to the rivet can all cause defective rivet heads. A rivet going "clubhead" (malforming) can be corrected by rapidly moving the bucking bar across the rivet head in a direction opposite that of clubhead travel. This corrective action can be accomplished only while the gun is in action and the rivet is partly driven. If a rivet shank bends at the beginning of the bucking operation, place the bar in the corrective position only long enough to straighten the shank.

Hand Driving

Under certain conditions, it may be necessary to rivet by hand driving. Either of two methods can be used depending upon the location and accessibility of the work. In the one method, the manufactured head end of the rivet is driven with a hand set and hammer, the shank end is bucked with a suitable bucking bar. In the other method, the shank end of the rivet is driven with a hand set and a hammer, and the manufactured head is bucked with a hand set held in a vise or a bottle bar (a special bucking bar recessed to hold a rivet set). This method is known as reverse riveting. It is commonly used in hand riveting but is not considered good practice in pneumatic riveting.

When using either of the described methods, keep hammer strokes to a minimum. Too much hammering will change the crystalline structure of the rivet or the material around it, causing the joint to lose some of its strength. Hold the bucking bar and rivet set square with the rivet at all times. Misuse of the rivet set and bucking bar will result in marring or scratching the rivet head or material, and may cause undue corrosion. This, in turn, will weaken the structure of the aircraft.

The diameter of a correctly formed shop head should be one and one-half times the diameter of the rivet shank, and the height should be about one-half the diameter.

Pneumatic Driving

The procedure for pneumatic riveting is practically the same as for hand riveting. Preparation of the sheet, selection of rivets, and drilling of rivet holes are the same. In hand riveting, however, the pressure for bucking the rivet is applied using a hand set and hammer. In pneumatic riveting, the pressure is applied with a set and an air-driven hammer or gun.

To get good riveting results with a pneumatic rivet gun, follow these basic pointers:

(1) Select the right type and size of rivet gun and the correct rivet set for the size of rivet to be driven. Install the rivet set firmly, as shown in figure 4-34.

Figure 4-34. Installing rivet set in rivet gun.

(2) Adjust the speed of the riveting gun (vibrations per minute). Always press set firmly against a block of wood before pressing the trigger. Never operate the gun without resistance against

96

the set because the vibrating action may cause the retaining spring to break, allowing the gun set to fly out of the gun. Also, free vibration may flare or mushroom the gun end of the set, causing it to bind in the barrel of the gun.

(3) Hold the rivet set at right angles to the work to prevent damage to the rivet head or the surrounding material as shown in figure 4-35. Upset the rivet with a medium burst from the rivet gun.

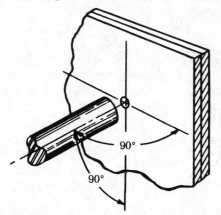

Figure 4-35.

The rivet set must be perpendicular to the surface.

(4) Remove the bucking bar and check the shop head of the rivet. It should be one and one-half times the diameter of the rivet in width and one-half times the rivet diameter in height. If the rivet needs further driving, repeat the necessary procedures to complete the job.

A small piece of adhesive tape applied to the cupped end of the rivet set often corrects an unsatisfactory cupped condition, which occasionally gives trouble in forming uniformly shaped rivet heads.

Squeeze Riveting

The squeeze method of driving a rivet produces the most uniform and balanced type of shop head. Each rivet is upset in a single operation; all rivets are headed over with uniform pressure; all heads are formed alike; and each rivet shank is sufficiently and uniformly expanded to completely fill each rivet hole. Squeeze riveters come equipped with pairs of end sets, each pair being designed for a particular job. Once the correct end set is selected and the squeezer adjusted for a particular application, all the rivets will be driven uniformly, thus providing an efficient method of riveting.

Portable squeezers are particularly suited for riveting large assemblies where the tool must be moved in relation to the work. They are not too heavy and can easily be operated by one person. The preparation of the material for riveting with the squeeze riveter is the same as for hand or pneumatic riveting.

Microshaving

Sometimes it is necessary to use a microshaver when making a repair involving the use of countersunk rivets. If the smoothness of the material (such as skin) requires that all countersunk rivets be driven within a specific tolerance, a microshaver is used. This tool has a cutter, stop, and two legs or stabilizers, as shown in figure 4-36.

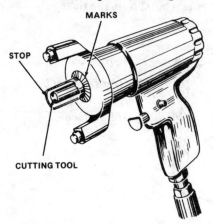

MARKS
STOP
CUTTING TOOL

Figure 4-36.

A microshaver may be necessary to smooth flush rivets with the skin.

The cutting portion of the microshaver is located inside the stop. The depth of cut can be adjusted by pulling outward on the stop and turning it in either direction (clockwise for deeper cuts). The marks on the stop permit adjustments of 0.001 in.

If the microshaver is adjusted and held correctly, it will cut the head of a countersunk rivet to within 0.002 in. without damaging the surrounding material. Adjustments should always be made on scrap material. When correctly adjusted, the shaver will leave a small round dot about the size of a pinhead on the microshaved rivet.

RIVET FAILURES

Generally speaking, the design of riveted joints is based on the theory that the total joint strength is simply the sum of the individual strengths of a whole group of rivets. It is then obvious that, if any one rivet fails, its load must immediately, be carried by others of the group; if they are unable to carry this added load, progressive joint failure then occurs. Stress concentrations will usually cause one rivet to fail first; and careful analysis of such a rivet in a joint will indicate that it has been too highly loaded, with the possibility that neighboring rivets may have partially failed.

Shear Failure

Shear failure is perhaps the most common of rivet failures. It is simply a breakdown of the rivet shank by forces acting along the plane of two adjacent sheets, causing a slipping action which may be severe enough to cut the rivet shank in two. If the shank becomes loaded beyond the yield point of the material and remains overloaded, a permanent shift is established in the sheets and the rivet shank may become joggled.

Bearing Failure

If the rivet is excessively strong in shear, bearing failure occurs in the sheet at the edge of the rivet hole. The application of large rivets in thin sheets brings about such a failure. In that case, the sheet is locally crushed or buckled, and the buckling destroys the rigidity of the joint. Vibrations, set up by engine operation or by air turbulence in flight, may cause the buckled portion to flutter and the material to break off close to the rivet head. If buckling occurs at the end of the sheet, a tear-out may result. In either case, replacement of the sheet is necessary.

Head Failure

Head failure may result from complex loadings occuring at a joint, causing stresses of tension to be applied to the rivet head. The head may fail by shearing through the area corresponding to the rivet shank, or, in thicker sheets, it may fail through a prying action which causes failure of the head itself. Any visible head distortion is cause for replacement. This latter type of head failure is especially common in blind rivets.

Rivet Inspection

To obtain high structural efficiency in the manufacture and repair of aircraft, an inspection must be made of all rivets before the part is put in service. This inspection consists of examining both the shop and manufactured heads and the surrounding skin and structural parts for deformities. A scale or rivet gage can be used to check the condition of the upset rivet head to see that it conforms to the proper requirements. Deformities in the manufactured head can be detected by the trained eye alone. However, on flush rivets, a straightedge can be used as shown in figure 4-37.

Some common causes of unsatisfactory riveting are improper bucking, rivet set slipping off or being held at the wrong angle, and rivet holes or rivets of the wrong size. Additional causes for unsatisfactory riveting are countersunk rivets not flush with the well; work not properly fastened together during riveting; the presence of burrs, rivets too hard, too much or too little driving; and rivets out of line. Figure 4-38 shows some common imperfections.

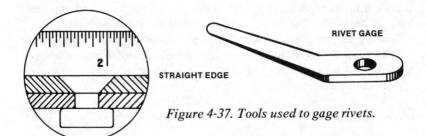

RIVET GAGE
2
STRAIGHT EDGE

Figure 4-37. Tools used to gage rivets.

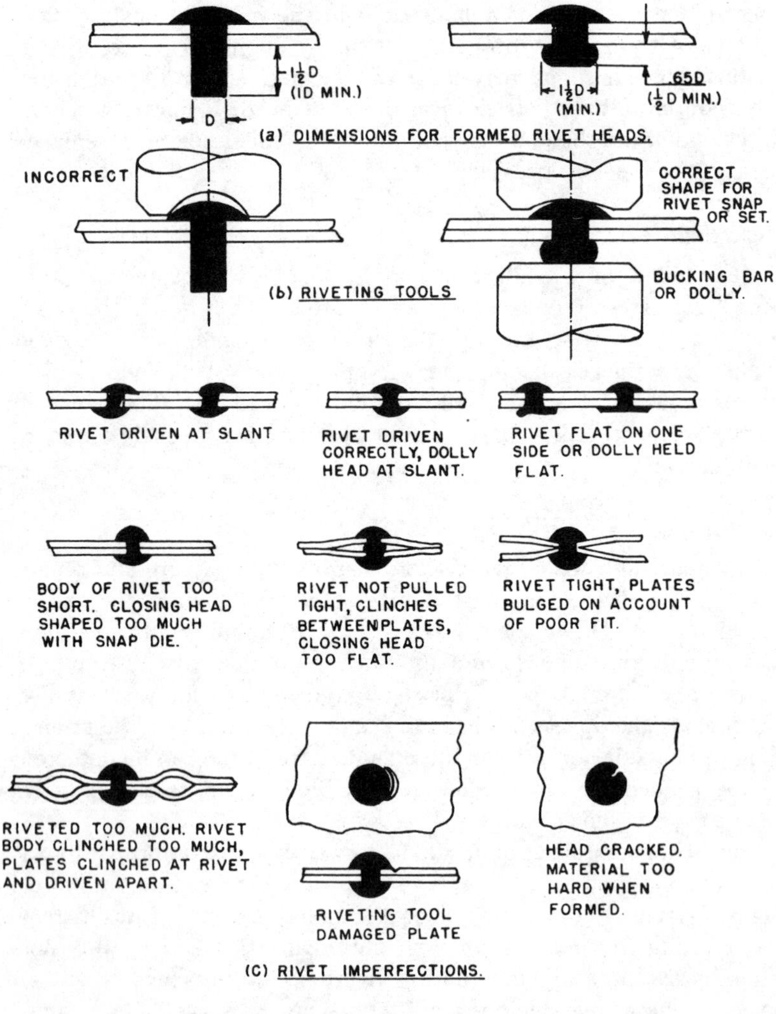

1½D
(1D MIN.)
D
1½D
(MIN.)
.65D
(½D MIN.)
(a) DIMENSIONS FOR FORMED RIVET HEADS.
INCORRECT
CORRECT SHAPE FOR RIVET SNAP OR SET.
BUCKING BAR OR DOLLY.
(b) RIVETING TOOLS
RIVET DRIVEN AT SLANT
RIVET DRIVEN CORRECTLY, DOLLY HEAD AT SLANT.
RIVET FLAT ON ONE SIDE OR DOLLY HELD FLAT.
BODY OF RIVET TOO SHORT. CLOSING HEAD SHAPED TOO MUCH WITH SNAP DIE.
RIVET NOT PULLED TIGHT, CLINCHES BETWEENPLATES, CLOSING HEAD TOO FLAT.
RIVET TIGHT, PLATES BULGED ON ACCOUNT OF POOR FIT.
RIVETED TOO MUCH. RIVET BODY CLINCHED TOO MUCH, PLATES CLINCHED AT RIVET AND DRIVEN APART.
RIVETING TOOL DAMAGED PLATE
HEAD CRACKED. MATERIAL TOO HARD WHEN FORMED.
(C) RIVET IMPERFECTIONS.

Figure 4-38. Riveting practice and rivet imperfections.

Occasionally, during an aircraft structural repair, it is wise to examine adjacent parts to determine the true condition of neighboring rivets. In doing so, it may be necessary to remove the paint. The presence of chipped or cracked paint around the heads may indicate shifted or loose rivets. Look for tipped or loose rivet heads. If the heads are tipped or if rivets are loose, they will show up in groups of several consecutive rivets and will probably be tipped in the same direction. If heads which appear to be tipped are not in groups and are not tipped in the same direction, tipping may have occurred during some previous installation.

Inspect rivets known to have been critically loaded, but which show no visible distortion, by drilling off the head and carefully punching out the shank. If, upon examination, the shank appears joggled and the holes in the sheet misaligned, the rivet has failed in shear. In that case, try to determine what is causing the shearing stress and take the necessary corrective action. Flush rivets that show head slippage within the countersink or dimple, indicating either sheet bearing failure or rivet shear failure, must be removed for inspection and replacement.

Joggles in removed rivet shanks indicate partial shear failure. Replace these rivets with the next larger size. Also, if the rivet holes show elongation, replace the rivets with the next larger size. Sheet failures (such as tear-outs, cracks between rivets, and the like) usually indicate damaged rivets, and the complete repair of the joint may require replacement of the rivets with the next larger size.

The general practice of replacing a rivet with the next larger size (1/32 in. greater diameter) is necessary to obtain the proper joint strength of rivet and sheet when the original rivet hole is enlarged. If the rivet in an elongated hole is replaced by a rivet of the same size, its ability to carry its share of the shear load is impaired and joint weakness results.

REMOVING RIVETS

When removing a rivet for replacement, be very careful so that the rivet hole will retain its original size and shape and replacement with a larger size rivet will not be necessary. If the rivet is not removed properly, the strength of the joint may be weakened and the replacement of rivets made more difficult.

When removing a rivet, work on the manufactured head. It is more symmetrical about the shank than the shop head, and there will be less chance of damaging the rivet hole or the material around it. To remove rivets, use hand tools, a power drill, or a combination of both. The preferred method is to drill through the rivet head and drive out the remainder of the rivet with a drift punch. First, file a flat area on the head of any round or brazier head rivet, and center punch the flat surface for drilling. On thin metal, back up the rivet on the upset head when center punching to avoid depressing the metal. The dimple in 2117-T rivets usually eliminates the necessity of filing and center punching the rivet head.

Select a drill one size smaller than the rivet shank and drill out the rivet head. When using a power drill, set the drill on the rivet and rotate the chuck several revolutions by hand before turning on the power. This procedure helps the drill cut a good starting spot and eliminates the chance of the drill slipping off and tracking across the metal. Drill the rivet to the depth of its head, while holding the drill at a 90 degree angle. Be careful not to drill too deep because the rivet shank will turn with the drill and cause a tear. The rivet head will often break away and climb the drill, which is a good signal to withdraw the drill. If the rivet head does not come loose of its own accord, insert a drift punch into the hole and twist slightly to either side until the head comes off.

Drive out the shank of the rivet with a drift punch slightly smaller than the diameter of the shank. On thin metal or unsupported structures, support the sheet with a bucking bar while driving out the shank. If the shank is exceptionally tight after the rivet head is removed, drill the rivet about two-thirds of the way through the thickness of the material and then drive out the remainder of the rivet with a drift punch.

The procedure for the removal of flush rivets is the same as that just described except that no filing is necessary. Be very careful to avoid elongation of the dimpled or the countersunk holes. The rivet head should be drilled to approximately one-half the thickness of the top sheet.

SPECIAL RIVETS

The various types of mechanically expanded rivets, their fabrication, composition, uses, selection, and identification were discussed previously in this chapter.

INSTALLATION TOOLS

The tools used to install self-plugging (friction lock) rivets depend upon the manufacturer of the rivet being installed. Each company has designed special tools which should always be used to ensure satisfactory results with its product. Hand tools as well as pneumatic tools are available and are discussed later in this chapter.

After selection or determination of the rivet to be used in any installation, the proper size twist drill must be determined. Generally, manufacturers recommend finish drill sizes for common shank diameters as shown in figure 4-39.

Rivet size	Drill size	
4 (1/8 in.)	#30	*Figure 4-39.*
5 (5/32 in.)	#20	*Finish drill sizes for common*
6 (6/32 in.)	#10	*rivet shank diameters.*
8 (1/4 in.)	F	

Be very careful when drilling the material. Hold the drill at right angles to the work at all times to keep from drilling an elongated hole. The self-plugging (friction lock) rivet will not expand as much as a solid shank rivet. If the hole is too large or elongated, the shank will not properly fill the drilled hole. Common hand or pneumatic powered drills can be used to drill the holes. Some manufacturers recommend predrilling the holes; others do not.

Equipment used to pull the stem of the rivet, as previously stated, will depend upon the manufacturer of the rivet. Both manually operated and power-operated guns are manufactured for this purpose. Nomenclature for various tools and assemblies available depends upon the manufacturer. Application and use of the equipment is basically the same. Whether the equipment is called a hand tool, air tool, hand gun, or pneumatic gun (figure 4-40), all of these are used with but one goal, the proper installation of a rivet.

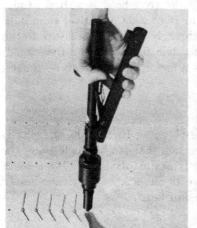 

Figure 4-40. Tools used to install self-plugging (friction lock) rivets.

Pneumatic tools operate on the same air pressure as pneumatic riveting hammers, 90 to 100 p.s.i. Follow the operational procedures and adjustments recommended by the manufacturer.

The choice of installation tools is influenced by several factors: The quality of rivets to be installed, the availability of an air supply, the accessibility of the work, and the size and type of rivet to be installed. In addition to a hand or power riveter, it is necessary to select the correct "pulling head" to complete the installation tool.

Selection of the proper pulling head is of primary importance since it compensates for the variables of head style and diameter. Since your selection will depend on the rivets to be installed, you should consult the applicable manufacturer's literature.

SELF-PLUGGING (FRICTION LOCK) RIVETS

The stem of the self-plugging (friction lock) rivet may have a knot or knob on the upper portion, or it may have a serrated portion as shown in figure 4-10 near the beginning of this chapter.

The sequence of steps to follow in the installation of self-plugging (friction lock) rivets is basically the same as that for solid shank rivets, but the methods and equipment vary. The following steps are typical of any installation:

(1) Select the rivet to be installed—determined by thickness of material to be riveted, strength desired in assembly, and location of installation (protruding or countersunk head).

(2) Drill the hole(s)—determine size of twist drill to be used, do not elongate rivet hole, remove burrs, and use a stop countersink if necessary.

(3) Install the rivet—make certain the rivet head is seated firmly, position the selected tool on the rivet stem, pull rivet stem until the stem snaps, apply approximately 15 lbs. of pressure to the end of the stem, and trim the stem flush with the rivet head. If aerodynamic smoothness is a factor, the stem can be shaved with a rivet shaver.

Inspection

The inspection of installed self-plugging (friction lock) rivets is very limited. Often the only inspection that can be made is on the head of the rivet. It should fit tightly against the metal. The stem of the rivet should be trimmed flush with the head of the rivet whether it is a protruding head or a countersunk head.

Removal Procedures

Self-plugging (friction lock) rivets are removed in the same manner as solid shank rivets except for the preliminary step of driving out the stem. The following steps should be used in their proper sequence:

(1) Punch out the rivet stem with a pin punch.

(2) Drill out the rivet head, using a drill the same size as the rivet shank.

(3) Pry off the weakened rivet head with a pin punch.

(4) Push out the remainder of the rivet shank with a punch. If the shank will not push out, drill the shank, taking care not to enlarge the hole in the material.

SELF-PLUGGING (MECHANICAL LOCK) RIVETS

Self-plugging, mechanical lock rivets are similar to self-plugging, friction lock rivets, except for the manner in which they are retained in the material as discussed previously in this chapter. Self-plugging, mechanical lock rivets display all the strength characteristics of solid shank rivets and in almost all cases can be substituted rivet for rivet.

Self-plugging, mechanical lock rivets require special driving assemblies. It is best to use tools manufactured by the company that produces the rivet.

Installation Procedures

Procedures for installing self-plugging (mechanical lock) rivets are basically the same as those used for installing the friction lock type of rivets. Precautions to be observed are:

(1) Be sure the correct grip range is selected.

(2) Always use the correct nose assembly or pulling tool for the diameter rivet selected.

(3) When inserting the rivet in the tool and the material, hold a slight pressure against the head of the rivet.

(4) Determine that the rivet is completely driven before lifting the tool from the rivet head (The stem should snap.)

(5) Check each rivet after the driving sequence has been completed for proper stem breakage. (The rivet stem should snap off even with the head of the rivet.

Inspection

Visual inspection of the seating of the pin in the manufactured head is the most reliable and simplest means of inspection for mechanical lock rivets. If the proper grip range has been used and the locking collar and broken end of the stem are approximately flush with the manufactured head, the rivet has been properly upset and the lock formed. Insufficient grip length is indicated by the stem breaking below the surface of the manufactured head. Excessive grip length is indicated by the stem breaking off well above the manufactured head. In either case, the locking collar might not be seated properly, thus forming an unsatisfactory lock.

Removal Procedures

The mechanical lock rivet can easily be removed by following the procedures indicated previously for friction lock rivets.

PULL-THRU RIVETS

This type of blind mechanically expanded rivet is used as a tacking rivet to attach assemblies to hollow tubes, and as a grommet. It differs from the two previously discussed rivets in that the stem pulls completely through the sleeve of the rivet during installation. Pull-thru rivets are structurally weak because of the hollow center after installation is completed. Methods and procedures for installation, inspection, and removal are not discussed here because of the limited use for this type rivet in the airframe field. Figure 4-41 illustrates a typical pull-thru rivet before and after installation.

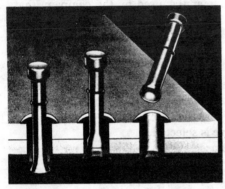

Figure 4-41.

Pull-thru rivet before and after installation.

EXPLOSIVE RIVETS

Explosive rivets are a blind type, having a partly hollow shank filled with an explosive charge that is detonated by applying a heated electric iron to the rivet head. Explosion of the charge forms a bulged head on the blind side of the material. Explosive rivets are used for nonstructural repair. Two types of explosive rivets are manufactured. The shankcharge type has a cavity drilled the length of the shank and will expand to fill a hole, and the blindend type in which only the end expands.

Explosive rivets are driven with a special type of electrically heated iron equipped with a special tip. Heat applied to the head sets off the explosive charge. Most irons have silver tips, of various sizes. An adjustment on the iron controls the temperatures needed.

HI-SHEAR RIVETS

Hi-Shear pin rivets are essentially threadless bolts. The pin is headed at one end and is grooved about the circumference at the other. A metal collar is swaged onto the grooved end, effecting a firm tight fit.

The proper length rivet may be determined by part number or by trial. Part numbers for pin rivets can be interpreted to give the diameter and grip length of the individual rivets. A typical part number and an explanation of the terms have been discussed previously in this chapter.

To determine correct grip length by trial, insert the correct diameter rivet in the hole. The straight portion of the shank should not extend more than 1/16 in. through the material. Place a collar over the grooved end of the rivet. Check the position of the collar.

The collar should be positioned so that the shearing edge of the pin groove is just below the top of the collar. It is permissible to add a 0.032-in. (approximately) steel washer between the collar and the material to bring the collar to the desired location. The washer may be positioned on the rivet head side of the material when using a flathead rivet.

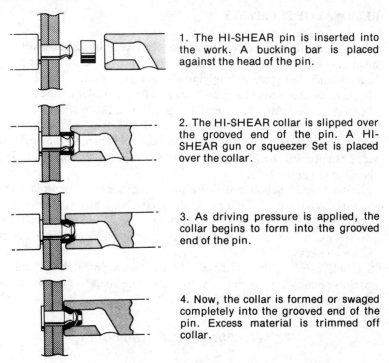

1. The HI-SHEAR pin is inserted into the work. A bucking bar is placed against the head of the pin.

2. The HI-SHEAR collar is slipped over the grooved end of the pin. A HI-SHEAR gun or squeezer Set is placed over the collar.

3. As driving pressure is applied, the collar begins to form into the grooved end of the pin.

4. Now, the collar is formed or swaged completely into the grooved end of the pin. Excess material is trimmed off collar.

Figure 4-42. Steps in the installation of a hi-shear rivet.

Hi-Shear rivets are installed with standard bucking bars and pneumatic riveting hammer. They require the use of a special gun set that incorporates collar swaging and trimming and a discharge port through which excess collar material is discharged. A separate size set is required for each shank diameter.

Prepare holes for pin rivets with the same care as for other close tolerance rivets or bolts. At times, it may be necessary to spot-face the area under the head of the pin so that the head of the rivet can fit tightly against the material. The spot-faced area should be 1/16 in. larger in diameter than the head diameter.

Pin rivets may be driven from either end. Procedures for driving a pin rivet from the collar end are shown in figure 4-42.

INSPECTION

Pin rivets should be inspected on both sides of the material. The head of the rivet should not be marred and should fit tightly against the material.

REMOVAL OF PIN RIVETS

The conventional method of removing rivets by drilling off the head may be utilized on either end of the pin rivet. Center punching is recommended prior to applying drilling pressure. In some cases alternate methods may be more desirable for particular instances.

Grind a chisel edge on a small pin punch to a blade width of ⅛ in. Place this tool at right angles to the collar and drive with a hammer to split the collar down one side. Repeat the operation on the opposite side. Then, with the chisel blade, pry the collar from the rivet. Tap the rivet out of the hole.

Use a special hollow punch having one or more blades placed to split the collar. Pry the collar from the groove and tap out the rivet.

Grind a pair of nippers so that cutting blades will cut the collar in two pieces, or use nippers at right angles to the rivet and cut through the small neck.

A hollow-mill collar cutter can be used in a power hand drill to cut away enough collar material to permit the rivet to be tapped out of the work.

INSTALLATION OF NUTS AND BOLTS

Bolt and Hole Sizes

Slight clearances in boltholes are permissible wherever bolts are used in tension and are not subject to reversal of load. A few of the applications in which clearance of holes may be permitted are in pulley brackets, conduit boxes, lining trim, and miscellaneous supports and brackets.

Boltholes must be normal to the surface involved to provide full bearing surface for the bolthead and nut and must not be oversized or elongated. A bolt in such a hole will carry none of its shear load until parts have yielded or deformed enough to allow the bearing surface of the oversized hole to contact the bolt. In this respect, remember that bolts do not become swaged to fill up the holes as do rivets.

In cases of oversized or elongated holes in critical members, obtain advice from the aircraft or engine manufacturer before drilling or reaming the hole to take the next larger bolt. Usually, such factors as edge distance, clearance, or load factor must be considered. Oversized or elongated holes in noncritical members can usually be drilled or reamed to the next larger size.

Many boltholes, particularly those in primary connecting elements, have close tolerances. Generally, it is permissible to use the first lettered drill size larger than the normal bolt diameter, except where the AN hexagon bolts are used in lightdrive fit (reamed) applications and where NAS close-tolerance bolts or AN clevis bolts are used.

Light-drive fits for bolts (specified on the repair drawings as .0015-inch maximum clearance between bolt and hole) are required in places where bolts are used in repair, or where they are placed in the original structure.

The fit of holes and bolts cannot be defined in terms of shaft and hole diameters; it is defined in terms of the friction between bolt and hole when sliding the bolt into place. A tight-drive fit, for example, is one in which a sharp blow of a 12- or 14-ounce hammer is required to move the bolt. A bolt that requires a hard blow and sounds tight is considered to fit too tightly. A light-drive fit is one in which a bolt will move when a hammer handle is held against its head and pressed by the weight of the body.

Installation Practices

Examine the markings on the bolthead to determine that each bolt is of the correct material. It is of extreme importance to use like bolts in replacement. In every case, refer to the applicable Maintenance Instructions Manual and Illustrated Parts Breakdown.

Be sure that washers are used under both the heads of bolts and nuts unless their omission is specified. A washer guards against mechanical damage to the material being bolted and prevents corrosion of the structural members. An aluminum alloy washer should be used under the head and nut of a steel bolt securing aluminum alloy or magnesium alloy members. Any corrosion that occurs then attacks the washer rather than the members. Steel washers should be used when joining steel members with steel bolts.

Whenever possible, the bolt should be placed with the head on top or in the forward position. This positioning tends to prevent the bolt from slipping out if the nut is accidently lost.

Be certain that the bolt grip length is correct. Grip length is the length of the unthreaded portion of the bolt shank. Generally speaking, the grip length should equal the thickness of the material being bolted together. However, bolts of slightly greater grip length may be used if washers are placed under the nut or the bolthead. In the case of plate nuts, add shims under the plate.

TORQUE AND TORQUE WRENCHES

As the speed of an aircraft increases, each structural member becomes more highly stressed. It is therefore extremely important that each member carry no more and no less than the load for which it was designed. In order to distribute the loads safely throughout a structure, it is necessary that proper torque be applied to all nuts, bolts, studs and screws. Using the proper torque allows the structure to develop its designed strength and greatly reduces the possibility of failure due to fatigue.

Torque Wrenches

The three most commonly used torque wrenches are the flexible beam, rigid frame, and the ratchet types (figure 4-43). When using the flexible beam and the rigid frame torque wrenches, the torque value is read visually on a dial or scale mounted on the handle of the wrench.

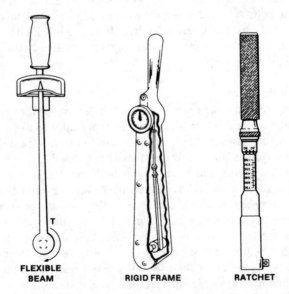

FLEXIBLE BEAM   RIGID FRAME   RATCHET

Figure 4-43. Three common types of torque wrenches.

To use the ratchet type, unlock the grip and adjust the handle to the desired setting on the micrometer type scale, then relock the grip. Install the required socket or adapter to the square drive of the handle. Place the wrench assembly on the nut or bolt and pull in a clockwise direction with a smooth, steady motion. (A fast or jerky motion will result in an improperly torqued unit.) When the applied torque reaches the torque value which indicated on the handle setting, the handle will automatically release or "break" and move freely for a short distance. The release and free travel is easily felt, so there is no doubt about when the torquing process is completed.

To assure getting the correct amount of torque on the fasteners, all torque wrenches must be tested at least once a month or more often if necessary.

NOTE: It is not advisable to use a handle extension on a flexible beam type torque wrench at any time. A handle extension alone has no effect on the reading of the other types. The use of a driveend extension on any type of torque wrench requires the use of a formula supplied by the wrench manufacturer. When applying the formula, force must be applied to the handle of the torque wrench at the point from which the measurements were taken. If this is not done, the torque obtained will be in error.

Torque Tables

The standard torque table should be used as a guide in tightening nuts, studs, bolts, and screws whenever specific torque values are not called out in maintenance procedures. The following rules apply for correct use of the torque table (figure 4-44):

1. To obtain values in foot-pounds, divide inch-pounds by 12.
2. Do not lubricate nuts or bolts except for corrosion-resistant steel parts or where specifically instructed to do so.
3. Always tighten by rotating the nut first if possible. When space considerations make it necessary to tighten by rotating the bolt-head, approach the high side of the indicated torque range. Do not exceed the maximum allowable torque value.
4. Maximum torque ranges should be used only when materials and surfaces being joined are of sufficient thickness, area, and strength to resist breaking, warping, or other damage.
5. For corrosion-resisting steel nuts, use torque values given for shear type nuts.
6. The use of any type of drive-end extension on a torque wrench changes the dial reading required to obtain the actual values indicated in the standard torque range tables. When using a drive-end extension, the torque wrench reading must be computed by use of the proper formula, which is included in the handbook accompanying the torque wrench.

Bolt, Stud or Screw Size		Torque Values in Inch-Pounds for Tightening Nuts			
		On standard bolts, studs, and screws having a tensile strength of 125,000 to 140,000 p.s.i.		On bolts, studs, and screws having a tensile strength of 140,000 to 160,000 p.s.i.	On high-strength bolts, studs, and screws having a tensile strength 160,000 p.s.i. and over
		Shear type nuts (AN320, AN364 or equivalent)	Tension type nuts and threaded machine parts (AN-310,AN365 or equivalent)	Any nut, except, shear type	Any nut, except shear type
8-32	8-36	7-9	12-15	14-17	15-18
10-24	10-32	12-15	20-25	23-30	25-35
1/4-20		25-30	40-50	45-49	50-68
	1/4-28	30-40	50-70	60-80	70-90
5/16-18		48-55	80-90	85-117	90-144
	5/16-24	60-85	100-140	120-172	140-203
3/8-16		95-110	160-185	173-217	185-248
	3/8-24	95-110	160-190	175-271	190-351
7/16-14		140-155	235-255	245-342	255-428
	7/16-20	270-300	450-500	475-628	500-756
1/2-13		240-290	400-480	440-636	480-792
	1/2-20	290-410	480-690	585-840	690-990
9/16-12		300-420	500-700	600-845	700-990
	9/16-18	480-600	800-1,000	900-1,220	1,000-1,440
5/8-11		420-540	700-900	800-1,125	900-1,350
	5/8-18	660-780	1,100-1,300	1,200-1,730	1,300-2,160
3/4-10		700-950	1,150-1,600	1,380-1,925	1,600-2,250
	3/4-16	1,300-1,500	2,300-2,500	2,400-3,500	2,500-4,500
7/8-9		1,300-1,800	2,200-3,000	2,600-3,570	3,000-4,140
	7/8-14	1,500-1,800	2,500-3,000	2,750-4,650	3,000-6,300
1"-8		2,200-3,000	3,700-5,000	4,350-5,920	5,000-6,840
	1"-14	2,200-3,300	3,700-5,500	4,600-7,250	5,500-9,000
1 1/8-8		3,300-4,000	5,500-6,500	6,000-8,650	6,500-10,800
	1 1/8-12	3,000-4,200	5,000-7,000	6,000-10,250	7,000-13,500
1 1/4-8		4,000-5,000	6,500-8,000	7,250-11,000	8,000-14,000
	1 1/4-12	5,400-6,600	9,000-11,000	10,000-16,750	11,000-22,500

Figure 4-44. Torque values in inch-pounds for tightening nuts.

Cotter Pin Hole Line-Up

When tightening castellated nuts on bolts, the cotter pin holes may not line up with the slots in the nuts for the range of recommended values. Except in cases of highly stressed engine parts, the nut may be over tightened to permit lining up the next slot with the cotter pin hole. The torque loads specified may be used for all unlubricated cadmium-plated steel nuts of the fine- or coarse-thread series which have approximately equal number of threads and equal face bearing areas. These values do not apply where special torque requirements are specified in the maintenance manual.

If the head end, rather than the nut, must be turned in the tightening operation, maximum torque values may be increased by an amount equal to shank friction, provided the latter is first measured by a torque wrench.

Safetying of Nuts and Bolts

It is very important that all bolts or nuts, except the self-locking type, be safetied after installation. This prevents them from loosening in flight due to vibration.

Safety Wiring

Safety wiring is the most positive and satisfactory method of safetying capscrews, studs, nuts, boltheads, and turnbuckle barrels which cannot be safetied by any other practical means. It is a method of wiring together two or more units in such a manner that any tendency of one to loosen is counteracted by the tightening of the wire.

Nuts, Bolts, and Screws

Nuts, bolts, and screws are safety wired by the single-wire or double-twist method. The double-twist method is the most common method of safety wiring. The single-wire method may be used on small screws in a closely spaced closed geometrical pattern, on parts in electrical systems, and in places that are extremely difficult to reach.

Figure 4-45 is an illustration of various methods which are commonly used in safety wiring nuts, bolts, and screws. Careful study of Figure 4-45 shows that:

a. Examples 1, 2, and 5 illustrate the proper method of safety wiring bolts, screws, square-head plugs, and similar parts when wired in pairs.

b. Example 3 illustrates several components wired in series.

c. Example 4 illustrates the proper method of wiring castellated nuts and studs. (Note that there is no loop around the nut.)

d. Examples 6 and 7 illustrate a single-threaded component wired to a housing or lug.

e. Example 8 illustrates several components in a closely spaced closed geometrical pattern, using a single-wire method.

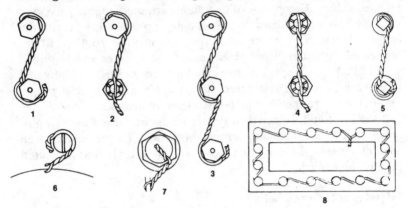

Figure 4-45. Typical safety wiring methods.

When drilled-head bolts, screws, or other parts are grouped together, they are more conveniently safety wired to each other in a series rather than individually. The number of nuts, bolts, or screws that may be safety wired together is dependent on the application. For instance, when safety-wiring widely spaced bolts by the double-twist method, a group of three should be the maximum number in a series.

When safety-wiring closely spaced bolts, the number that can be safety-wired by a 24-inch length of wire is the maximum in a series. **The wire is arranged so that if the bolt or screw begins to loosen, the force applied to the wire is in the tightening direction.**

Parts being safety-wired should be torqued to recommend values and the holes aligned before attempting the safetying operation. Never over torque or loosen a torqued nut to align safety wire holes.

General Safety Wiring Rules

When using the safety wire method of safetying, the following general rules should be followed:

1. A pigtail of ¼ to ½ inch (three to six twists) should be made at the end of the wiring. This pigtail must be bent back or under to prevent it from becoming a snag.
2. The safety wire must be new upon each application.
3. When castellated nuts are to be secured with safety wire, tighten the nut to the low side of the selected torque range, unless otherwise specified, and if necessary, continue tightening until a slot aligns with the hole.
4. All safety wires must be tight after installation, but not under

114

such tension that normal handling or vibration will break the wire.

5. **The wire must be applied so that all pull exerted by the wire tends to tighten the nut.**

6. Twists should be tight and even, and the wire between the nuts as taut as possible without overtwisting.

7. The safety wire should always be installed and twisted so that the loop around the head stays down and does not tend to come up over the bolthead, causing a slack loop.

Cotter Pin Safetying

Cotter pin installation is shown in figure 4-46. Castellated nuts are used with bolts that have been drilled for cotter pins. The cotter pin should fit neatly into the hole, with very little sideplay. The following general rules apply to cotter pin safetying:

1. The prong bent over the bolt end should not extend beyond the bolt diameter. (Cut it off if necessary).

2. The prong bent down should not rest against the surface of the washer. (Again, cut it off if necessary.)

3. If the optional wraparound method is used, the prongs should not extend outward from the sides of the nut.

4. All prongs should be bent over a reasonable radius. Sharp-angled bends invite breakage. Tapping lightly with a mallet is the best method of bending the prongs.

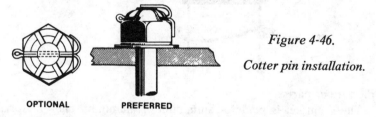

Figure 4-46.

Cotter pin installation.

OPTIONAL   PREFERRED

TURNLOCK FASTENERS

Turnlock fasteners are used to secure inspection plates, doors, and other removable panels on aircraft. Turnlock fasteners are also referred to by such terms as quick-opening, quick-action, and stressed-panel fasteners. The most desirable feature of these fasteners is that they permit quick and easy removal of access panels for inspection and servicing purposes.

Turnlock fasteners are manufactured and supplied by a number of manufacturers under various trade names. Some of the most commonly used are the Dzus, Camloc, and Airloc.

Dzus Fasteners

The Dzus turnlock fastener consists of a stud, grommet, and receptacle. Figure 4-47 illustrates an installed Dzus fastener and

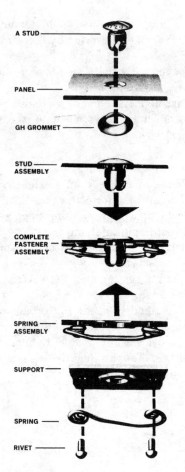

A STUD

PANEL

GH GROMMET

STUD ASSEMBLY

COMPLETE FASTENER ASSEMBLY

SPRING ASSEMBLY

SUPPORT

SPRING

RIVET

Figure 4-47.

The Dzus fastener.

the various parts.

The grommet is made of aluminum or aluminum alloy material. It acts as a holding device for the stud. Grommets can be fabricated from 1100 aluminum tubing, if none are available from normal sources.

The spring is made of steel, cadmium plated to prevent corrosion. The spring supplies the force that locks or secures the stud in place when two assemblies are joined.

The studs are fabricated from steel and are cadmium plated. They are available in three head styles; wing, flush, and oval.

A quarter of a turn of the stud (clockwise) locks the fastener. The fastener may be unlocked only by turning the stud counterclockwise. A Dzus key or a specially ground screwdriver locks or unlocks the fastener.

Special installation tools and instructions are available from the manufacturers.

Chapter 5
Aircraft Welding, Brazing and Soldering

Metals can be joined by mechanical means (bolting or riveting), or by welding, brazing, soldering or adhesive bonding. All of these methods are used in aircraft construction. This chapter will discuss the methods used to join metals by welding, brazing, and soldering.

Welding

Welding is the process of joining metal by fusing the materials while they are in a plastic or molten state. There are three general types of welding: (1) Gas, (2) electric arc, and (3) electric resistance welding. Each of these types of welding has several variations which are used in aircraft construction.

Welding is used extensively in the repair and manufacture of aircraft. Such parts as engine mounts and landing gear are often fabricated in this manner, and many fuselages, control surfaces, fittings, tanks, etc., are also of welded construction. Structures that have been welded in manufacture may generally be repaired economically by using the same welding process. Careful workmanship, both in preparation and actual welding, is of utmost importance.

Welding is one of the most practical of the many metal-joining processes available. The welded joint offers rigidity, simplicity, low weight, and high strength. Consequently, welding has been universally adopted in the manufacture and repair of all types of aircraft. Many structural parts as well as nonstructural parts are joined by some form of welding, and the repair of many of these parts is an indispensable part of aircraft maintenance.

It is equally important to know when not to weld, as it is to know when. Many of the alloy steels or high-carbon steel parts that have been hardened or strengthened by heat treatment cannot be restored to 100% of their former hardness and strength after they have been welded. Aluminum alloys such as 2017, 2024 and 7075, used in fabricating aircraft structural parts, are not weldable. Only nonstructural parts fabricated from aluminum alloys 1100, 3003, 4043 and 5052, are weldable.

Gas Welding

Gas welding is accomplished by heating the ends or edges of metal parts to a molten state with a high-temperature flame. This flame is produced with a torch burning a special gas such as acetylene or hydrogen with pure oxygen. The metals, when in a molten state, flow together to form a union without the application of mechanical pressure or blows.

Aircraft parts fabricated from chrome-molybdenum or mild carbon steel are often gas welded. There are two types of gas welding in common use: (1) Oxyacetylene and (2) oxyhydrogen. Nearly all gas welding in aircraft construction is done with an oxyacetylene flame, although some manufacturers prefer an oxyhydrogen flame for welding aluminum alloys.

Electric Arc Welding

Electric arc welding is used in both the manufacture and repair of aircraft, and can be satisfactorily used in the joining of all weldable metals. The process is based on using the heat generated by an electric arc. Variations of the process are: (1) Metallic arc welding, (2) carbon arc welding, (3) atomic hydrogen welding, (4) inert-gas (helium) welding, and (5) multi-arc welding. Metallic arc and inert-gas welding are the two electric arc welding processes most widely used in aircraft construction.

Electric Resistance Welding

Electric resistance welding is a welding process in which a low-voltage, high-amperage current is applied to the metals to be welded through a heavy, low-resistance copper conductor. The materials to be welded offer a high resistance to the flow of current, and the heat generated by this resistance fuses (welds) the parts together at their point of contact.

Three commonly used types of electric resistance welding are butt, spot, and seam welding. Butt welding is used in aircraft work to weld terminals to control rods. Spot welding is frequently used in airframe construction. It is the only welding method used for joining structural corrosion-resistant steel. Seam welding is similar to spot welding, except that power-driven rollers are used as electrodes. A continuous airtight weld can be obtained using seam welding.

OXYACETYLENE WELDING EQUIPMENT

Oxyacetylene welding equipment may be either stationary or portable. A portable equipment rig consists of the following:
(1) Two cylinders, one containing oxygen and one acetylene.

(2) Acetylene and oxygen pressure regulators, complete with pressure gages and connections.

(3) A welding torch, with a mixing head, extra tips and connections.

(4) Two lengths of colored hose, with adapter connections for the torch and regulators.

(5) A special wrench.

(6) A pair of welding goggles.

(7) A flint lighter.

(8) A fire extinguisher.

Figure 5-1 shows some of the equipment in a typical portable acetylene welding rig.

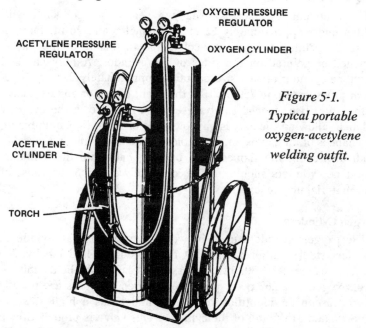

Figure 5-1.
Typical portable
oxygen-acetylene
welding outfit.

Acetylene Gas

Acetylene gas is a flammable, colorless gas which has a distinctive, disagreeable odor, readily detectable even when the gas is heavily diluted with air. Unlike oxygen, acetylene does not exist free in the atmosphere; it must be manufactured. The process is neither difficult nor expensive. Calcium carbide is made to react chemically with water to produce acetylene.

Acetylene is either used directly in a manifold system or stored in cylinders. If ignited, the result is a yellow, smoky flame with a low temperature. When the gas is mixed with oxygen in the proper proportions and ignited, the result is a blue-white flame with temperatures which range from approximately 5,700 degrees to 6,300 degrees F.

Under low pressure at normal temperatures, acetylene is a stable compound. But when compressed in a container to pressures greater than 15 p.s.i., it becomes dangerously unstable. For this reason, manufacturers fill the acetylene storage cylinders with a porous substance (generally a mixture of asbestos and charcoal) and saturate this substance with acetone. Since acetone is capable of absorbing approximately 25 times its own volume of acetylene gas, a cylinder containing the correct amount of acetone can be pressurized to 250 p.s.i.

Acetylene Cylinders

The acetylene cylinder is usually a seamless steel shell with welded ends, approximately 12 in. in diameter and 36 in. long. It is usually painted a distinctive color, and the name of the gas is stenciled or painted on the sides of the cylinder. A fully charged acetylene cylinder of this size contains approximately 225 cu. ft. of gas at pressures up to 250 p.s.i. In the event of fire or any excessive temperature rise, special safety fuse plugs installed in the cylinder will melt, allowing the excess gas to escape or burn, thus minimizing the chances of an explosion. The holes in the safety plugs are made small to prevent the flames from burning back into the cylinder. Acetylene cylinders should not be completely emptied, or a loss of filler material may result.

Oxygen Cylinders

The oxygen cylinders used in welding operations are made of seamless steel of different sizes. A typical small cylinder holds 200 cu. ft. of oxygen at 1,800 p.s.i. pressure. A large size holds 250 cu. ft. of oxygen at 2,265 p.s.i. pressure. Oxygen cylinders are usually painted green for identification. The cylinder has a high-pressure valve located at the top of the cylinder. This valve is protected by a metal safety cap which should always be in place when the cylinder is not in use.

Oxygen should never come in contact with oil or grease. In the presence of pure oxygen, these substances become highly combustible. **Oxygen hose and valve fittings should never be oiled or greased, or handled with oily or greasy hands.** Even grease spots on clothing may flare up or explode if struck by a stream of oxygen. Beeswax is a commonly used lubricant for oxygen equipment and fittings.

Pressure Regulators

Acetylene and oxygen regulators reduce pressures and control the flow of gases from the cylinders to the torch. Acetylene and oxygen regulators are of the same general type, although those designed for acetylene are not made to withstand such high pressures as those designed for use with oxygen. To prevent interchange of oxygen and acetylene hoses, the regulators are built with different threads on the outlet fitting. **The oxygen regulator has a right-hand thread, and the acetylene regulator has a left-hand thread.**

On most portable welding units, each regulator is equipped with two pressure gages, a high-pressure gage which indicates the cylinder pressure and a low-pressure gage which indicates the pressure in the hose leading to the torch (working pressure).

A typical regulator, complete with pressure gages and connections, is shown in figure 5-2. The adjusting screw shown on the front of the regulator is for adjusting the working pressure. When this adjusting screw is turned to the left (counter-clockwise) until it turns easily, the valve mechanism inside the regulator is closed. No gas can then flow to the torch. As the handle is turned to the right (clockwise), the screw presses against the regulating mechanism, the valve opens, and gas passes to the torch at the pressure shown on the working pressure gage. Changes in the working pressure can be made by adjusting the handle until the desired pressure is registered.

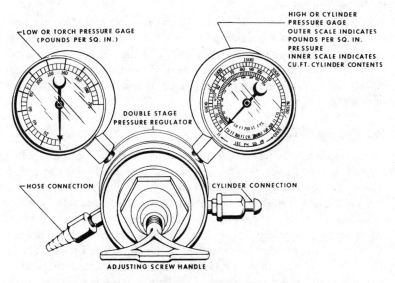

Figure 5-2. Typical oxygen pressure regulator.

Before opening the high-pressure valve on a cylinder, the adjusting screw on the regulator should be fully released by turning it counterclockwise. This closes the valve inside the regulator, protecting the mechanism against possible damage.

Welding Torch

The welding torch is the unit used to mix the oxygen and acetylene together in correct proportions. See figure 5-3. The torch also provides a means of directing and controlling the size and quality of the flame produced. The torches are designed with two needle valves, one for adjusting the flow of acetylene and the other for adjusting the flow of oxygen.

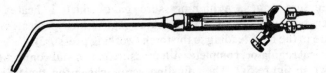

Figure 5-3. A light weight aircraft welding torch.

Welding torches are manufactured in different sizes and styles, thereby providing a suitable type for different applications. They are also available with several different sizes of interchangeable tips in order that a suitable amount of heat can be obtained for welding the various kinds and thicknesses of metals.

Welding torches can be divided into two classes: (1) The injector type and (2) the balanced-pressure type. The injector-type torch is designed to operate with very low acetylene pressure as compared to the oxygen pressure.

In the balanced-pressure torch, the oxygen and acetylene are both fed to the torch at the same pressure. The openings to the mixing chamber for each gas are equal in size, and the delivery of each gas is independently controlled. This type of torch is generally better suited for aircraft welding than the injector type because of the ease of adjustment.

Welding Torch Tips

The torch tip delivers and controls the final flow of gases. It is important that the correct tip be selected and used with the proper gas pressures if a job is to be welded satisfactorily. The nature of the weld, the material, the experience of the welder, and the position in which the weld is to be made, all determine the correct size of the tip opening. The size of tip opening, in turn, determines the amount of heat (not the temperature) applied to the work. If a tip which is too small is used, the heat provided will be insufficient to produce penetration to the proper depth. If the tip is too large, the heat will be too great, and holes will be burned in the metal.

The torch tip sizes are designated by numbers, and each manufacturer has his own arrangement for classifying them. As an example, a number two tip is made with an orifice of approximately 0.040 in. diameter. The diameter of the tip orifice is related to the volume of heat it will deliver.

Torch tips are made of copper or copper alloy and are made so that they seat well when tightened handtight. Torch tips should not be rubbed across fire brick or used as tongs to position work.

With use, the torch tip will become clogged with carbon deposits and, if it is brought in contact with the molten pool, particles of slag may lodge in the opening. A split or distorted flame is an indication of a clogged tip. Tips should be cleaned with the proper size tip cleaners or with a piece of copper or soft brass wire. Fine steel wool may be used to remove oxides from the outside of the tip. These oxides hinder the heat dissipation and cause the tip to overheat.

A flint lighter is provided for igniting the torch. The lighter consists of a file-shaped piece of steel, usually recessed in a cuplike device, and a piece of flint that can be drawn across the steel, producing the sparks required to light the torch. Matches should never be used to ignite a torch since their length requires bringing the hand in close to the tip to ignite the gas. Accumulated gas may envelop the hand and, when ignited, cause a severe burn.

Goggles

Welding goggles, fitted with colored lenses, are worn to protect the eyes from heat, light rays, sparks, and molten metal. A shade or density of color that is best suited for the particular situation should be selected. The darkest shade of lens which will show a clear definition of the work without eyestrain is the most desirable. **Goggles should fit closely around the eyes and should be worn at all times during welding and cutting operations.**

Welding (Filler) Rods

The use of the proper type filler rod is very important in oxyacetylene welding operations. This material not only adds reinforcement to the weld area, but also adds desired properties to the finished weld. By selecting the proper rod, either tensile strength or ductility can be secured in a weld, or both can be secured to a reasonably high degree. Similarly, rods can be selected which will help retain the desired amount of corrosion resistance. In some cases, a suitable rod with a lower melting point will eliminate possible cracks caused by expansion and contraction.

Welding rods may be classified as ferrous or nonferrous. The ferrous rods include carbon and alloy steel rods as well as cast-iron rods. Nonferrous rods include brazing and bronze rods, aluminum and aluminum alloy rods, magnesium and magnesium alloy rods, copper rods, and silver rods.

Welding rods are manufactured in standard 36-in. lengths and in diameters from 1/16 in. to 3/8 in. The diameter of the rod to be used is governed by the thickness of the metals being joined. If the rod is too small, it will not conduct heat away from the puddle rapidly enough, and a burned weld will result. A rod that is too large will chill the puddle. As in selecting the proper size welding torch tip, experience enables the welder to select the proper diameter welding rod.

Setting Up Acetylene Welding Equipment

Setting up acetylene welding equipment and preparing for welding should be done systematically and in a definite order to avoid costly mistakes. The following procedures and instructions are typical of those used to assure safety of equipment and personnel:

(1) Secure the cylinders so they cannot be upset, and remove the protective caps from the cylinders.

(2) Open each cylinder shutoff valve for an instant to blow out any foreign matter that may be lodged in the outlet. Close the valves and wipe off the connections with a clean cloth.

(3) Connect the acetylene pressure regulator to the acetylene cylinder and the oxygen regulator to the oxygen cylinder. Use a regulator wrench and tighten connecting nuts enough to prevent leakage.

(4) Connect the red (or maroon) hose to the acetylene pressure regulator and the green (or black) hose to the oxygen regulator. Tighten the connecting nuts enough to prevent leakage. Do not force these connections, since these threads are made of brass and are easily damaged.

(5) Release both pressure regulator adjusting screws by turning the adjusting screw handle on each regulator counterclockwise until it turns freely. This is to avoid damage to the regulators and pressure gages when the cylinder valves are opened.

(6) Open the cylinder valves slowly and read each of the cylinder pressure gages to check the contents in each cylinder. The oxygen cylinder shutoff valve should be opened fully and the acetylene cylinder shutoff valve is opened approximately one and one-half turns.

(7) Blow out each hose by turning the pressure adjusting screw handle inward (clockwise) and then turning it out again. The acetylene hose should be blown out only in a well-ventilated space which is free from sparks, flame, or other sources of ignition.

(8) Connect both hoses to the torch and check the connections for leaks by turning the pressure regulator screws in, with the torch needle valves closed. When 20 p.s.i. shows on the oxygen

124

working pressure gage and 5 p.s.i. on the acetylene gage, close the valves by turning the pressure regulator screws out. A drop in pressure on the working gage indicates a leak between the regulator and torch tip. A general tightening of all connections should remedy the situation. If it becomes necessary to locate a leak, use the soap suds method. Do this by painting all fittings and connections with a thick solution of the soapy water. **Never hunt for an acetylene leak with a flame,** since a serious explosion can occur in the hose or in the cylinder.

(9) Adjust the working pressure on both the oxygen and acetylene regulators by turning the pressure-adjusting screw on the regulator clockwise until the desired settings are obtained.

Oxyacetylene Flame Adjustment

To light the torch, open the torch acetylene valve a quarter to a half turn. Hold the torch to direct the flame away from the body and ignite the acetylene gas, using the flint lighter. The pure acetylene flame is long and bushy and has a yellowish color. Continue opening the acetylene valve until the flame leaves the tip approximately one-sixteenth of an inch. Open the torch oxygen valve. When the oxygen valve is opened, the acetylene flame is shortened, and the mixed gases burn in contact with the tip face. The flame changes to a bluish-white color and forms a bright inner cone surrounded by an outer flame envelope.

Extinguishing The Torch

The torch can be shutoff simply by closing both needle valves, but it is better practice to turn the acetylene off first and allow the gas remaining in the torch tip to burn out. The oxygen needle valve can then be turned off. If the torch is not to be used again for a long period, the pressure should be turned off at the cylinder. The hose lines should then be relieved of pressure by opening the torch needle valves and the working pressure regulator, one at a time, allowing the gas to escape. Again, it is a good practice to relieve the acetylene pressure and then the oxygen pressure. The hose should then be coiled or hung carefully to prevent damage or kinking.

Oxyacetylene Welding Process

The oxyacetylene process of welding is a method in which acetylene and oxygen gases are used to produce the welding flame. The temperature of this flame is approximately 6,300 degrees F., which is sufficiently high to melt any of the commercial metals to effect a weld. When the oxyacetylene flame is applied to the ends or edges of metal parts, they are quickly raised to a melting state and flow together to form one solid piece when solidified. Usually some additional metal is added to the weld, in the form of a wire or rod, to build up the weld seam to a greater thickness than the base metal.

There are three types of flames commonly used for welding. These are neutral, reducing or carburizing, and oxidizing. The characteristics of the different kinds of flames are shown in figure 5-4.

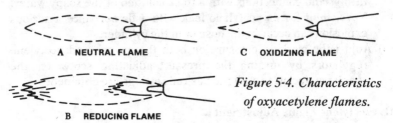

A   NEUTRAL FLAME

C   OXIDIZING FLAME

B   REDUCING FLAME

Figure 5-4. Characteristics of oxyacetylene flames.

The neutral flame (figure 5-4A) is produced by burning acetylene with oxygen in such proportions as to oxidize all particles of carbon and hydrogen in the acetylene. This flame is distinguished by the well-rounded, smooth, clearly defined white central cone at the end of the tip. The envelope or outer flame is blue with a purple tinge at the point and edges. **A neutral flame is generally used for welding and gives a thoroughly fused weld, free from burned metal or hard spots.**

To obtain a neutral flame, gradually open the oxygen valve. This shortens the acetylene flame and causes a "feather" to appear in the flame envelope. Gradually increase the amount of oxygen until the "feather" disappears inside a clearly defined inner luminous cone.

The reducing or carburizing flame is shown in figure 5-4 B. Since the oxygen furnished through the torch is not sufficient to complete the combustion of the acetylene, carbon escapes unburned. This flame can be recognized by the greenish-white brushlike second cone at the tip of the first cone. The outer flame is slightly luminous and has about the same appearance as an acetylene flame burning freely in air alone. This type of flame introduces carbon into the steel.

To obtain a reducing flame, first adjust the flame to neutral; then open the acetylene valve slightly to produce a white streamer or "feather" of acetylene at the end of the inner cone.

An oxidizing flame (figure 5-4C) contains an excess of oxygen, which is the result of too much oxygen passing through the torch. The oxygen not consumed in the flame escapes to combine with the metal. This flame can be recognized by the short, pointed, bluish-white central cone. The envelope or outer flame is also shorter and of a lighter blue color than the neutral flame. It is accompanied by a harsh sound similar to high-pressure air escaping through a small nozzle. This flame oxidizes or burns most metals and results in a porous weld. It is used only when welding brass or bronze.

To obtain the oxidizing flame, first adjust the flame to neutral; then increase the flow of oxygen until the inner cone is shortened by about one-tenth of its length. The oxidizing flame has a pointed inner cone.

With each size of tip, a neutral, oxidizing or carburizing flame can be obtained. It is also possible to obtain a "harsh" or "soft" flame by increasing or decreasing the pressure of both gases.

For most regulator settings the gases are expelled from the torch tip at a relatively high velocity, and the flame is called "harsh". For some work it is desirable to have a "soft" or low-velocity flame without a reduction in thermal output. This may be achieved by using a larger tip and closing the gas needle valves until the neutral flame is quiet and steady. It is especially desirable to use a soft flame when welding aluminum, to avoid blowing holes in the metal when the puddle is formed.

Improper adjustment or handling of the torch may cause the flame to backfire or, in very rare cases, to flashback. A backfire is a momentary backward flow of the gases at the torch tip, which causes the flame to go out. A backfire may be caused by touching the tip against the work, by overheating the tip, by operating the torch at other than recommended pressures, by a loose tip or head, or by dirt or slag in the end of the tip. A backfire is rarely dangerous, but the molten metal may be splattered when the flame pops.

A flashback is the burning of the gases within the torch and is dangerous. It is usually caused by loose connections, improper pressures, or overheating of the torch. A shrill hissing or squealing noise accompanies a flashback; and unless the gases are turned off immediately, the flame may burn back through the hose and regulators and cause great damage. The cause of a flashback should always be determined and the trouble remedied before relighting the torch.

Fundamental Oxyacetylene Welding Techniques

The proper method of holding the acetylene welding torch depends on the thickness of the metal being welded. When welding light-gage metal, the torch is usually held as illustrated in figure 5-5, with the hose draped over the wrist.

Figure 5-6 shows the method of holding the torch during the welding of heavy materials.

The torch should be held so that the tip is in line with the joint to be welded, and inclined between 30 degrees and 60 degrees from the perpendicular. The best angle depends on the type of weld to be made, the amount of preheating necessary, and the thickness and

127

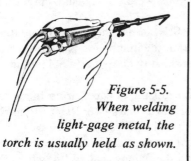

Figure 5-5.
When welding
light-gage metal, the
torch is usually held as shown.

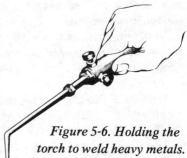

Figure 5-6. Holding the
torch to weld heavy metals.

type of metal. The thicker the metal, the more nearly vertical the torch must be for proper heat penetration. The white cone of the flame should be held about ⅛ in. from the surface of the base metal.

If the torch is held in the correct position, a small puddle of molten metal will form. The puddle should be composed of equal parts of the pieces being welded. After the puddle appears, movement of the tip in a semicircular or circular motion should be started. This movement ensures an even distribution of heat on both pieces of metal. The speed and motion of the torch movement are learned only by practice and experience.

Forehand welding is the technique of pointing the torch flame forward in the direction in which the weld is progressing, as illustrated in figure 5-7. The filler rod is added to the puddle as the edges of the joint melt before the flame. **The forehand method is used in welding most of the lighter tubings and sheet metals.**

Backhand welding is the technique of pointing the torch flame toward the finished weld and moving away in the direction of the unwelded area, melting the edges of the joint as it is moved (figure 5-8). The welding rod is added to the puddle between the flame and the finished weld.

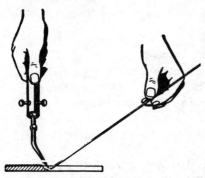

Figure 5-7. The forehand method is used in welding most of the lighter tubings and sheet metals.

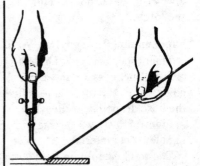

Figure 5-8. Backhand welding is preferred for metals having a thick cross section.

Backhand welding is seldom used on sheet metal because the increased heat generated in this method is likely to cause overheating and burning. It is preferred for metals having a thick cross section. The large puddle of molten metal required for such welds is more easily controlled in backhand welding, and it is possible to examine the progress of the weld and determine if penetration is complete.

WELDING POSITIONS

There are four general positions in which welds are made. These positions are shown in figure 5-9 and are designated as flat, overhead, horizontal, and vertical.

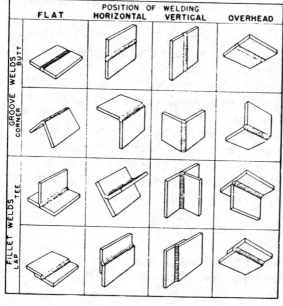

Figure 5-9.

Four basic welding positions.

Welding is done in the flat position whenever possible, since the puddle is much easier to control in this position. Quite often, though, it is necessary to weld in the overhead, vertical, or horizontal position in aircraft repair.

The flat position is used when the material can be laid flat, or inclined at an angle of less than 45 degrees and welded on the topside. The welding torch is pointed downward toward the work. This weld may be made by either the forehand or backhand technique, depending upon the thickness of the metal being welded.

The horizontal position is used when the line of the weld runs horizontally across a piece of work, and the torch is directed at the material in a horizontal or nearly horizontal position. The weld is made from right to left across the plate (for the right-handed welder).

The flame is inclined upward at an angle of from 45 degrees to 60 degrees. The weld can be made using the forehand or backhand technique. Adding the filler rod to the top of the puddle will help prevent the molten metal from sagging to the lower edge of the bead.

The overhead position is used when the material is to be welded on the underside with the seam running horizontally or in a plane that requires the flame to point upward from below the work. In welding overhead, a large pool of molten metal should be avoided, as the metal will drip or run out of the joint. The rod is used to control the size of the molten puddle. The volume of flame used should not exceed that required to obtain good fusion of the base metal with the filler rod. The amount of heat needed to make the weld is best controlled by selecting the right tip size for the thickness of metal to be welded.

When the parts to be joined are inclined at an angle of more than 45 degrees, with the seam running vertically, it is designated as a vertical weld. In a vertical weld, the pressure exerted by the torch flame must be relied upon to a great extent to support the puddle. It is highly important to keep the puddle from becoming too hot, to prevent the hot metal from running out of the puddle onto the finished weld. Vertical welds are begun at the bottom, and the puddle is carried upward using the forehand technique. The tip should be inclined from 45 degrees to 60 degrees, the exact angle depending upon the desired balance between correct penetration and control of the puddle. The rod is added from the top and in front of the flame.

WELDED JOINTS

The five fundamental types of welded joins (figure 5-10) are the butt joint, tee joint, lap joint, corner joint, and edge joint.

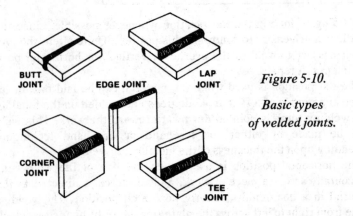

BUTT JOINT

EDGE JOINT

LAP JOINT

CORNER JOINT

TEE JOINT

Figure 5-10.

Basic types of welded joints.

Butt Joints

A butt joint is made by placing two pieces of material edge to edge, so that there is no overlapping, and then welded. Some of the various types of butt joints are shown in figure 5-11. The flanged butt joint can be used in welding thin sheets, 1/16 in. or less. The edges are prepared for welding by turning up a flange equal to the thickness of the metal. This type of joint is usually made without the use of filler rod.

Figure 5-11. Types of welded butt joints.

FLANGED PLAIN

SINGLE BEVEL DOUBLE BEVEL

A plain butt joint is used for metals from 1/16 in. to 1/8 in. in thickness. A filler rod is used when making this joint to obtain a strong weld.

If the metal is thicker than ⅛ in., it is necessary to bevel the edges so that the heat from the torch can penetrate completely through the metal. These bevels may be either single- or double-bevel type or single- or double-V type. A filler rod is used to add strength and reinforcement to the weld.

Cracks

Repair of cracks by welding may be considered just another type of butt joint. A stop drill hole is made at either end of the crack, then the two edges are brought together. The use of filler rod is necessary.

Tee Joints

A tee joint is formed when the edge or end of one piece is welded to the surface of another, as shown in figure 5-12. These joints are quite common in aircraft work, particularly in tubular structures. The plain tee joint is suitable for most aircraft metal thicknesses, but heavier thicknesses require the vertical member to be either single or double beveled to permit the heat to penetrate deeply enough. The dark areas in figure 5-12 show the depth of heat penetration and fusion required.

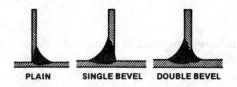

PLAIN SINGLE BEVEL DOUBLE BEVEL

Figure 5-12. Types of welded tee joints.

Edge Joints

An edge joint may be used when two pieces of sheet metal must be fastened together and load stresses are not important. Edge joints are usually made by bending the edges of one or both parts upward, placing the two bent ends parallel to each other or placing one bent end parallel to the upright unbent end, and welding along the outside of the seam formed by the two joined edges. Figure 5-13 shows two types of edge joints. The type shown in figure 5-13A requires no filler rod, since the edges can be melted down to fill the seam. The type shown in figure 5-13B, being thicker material, must be beveled for heat penetration; filler rod is added for reinforcement.

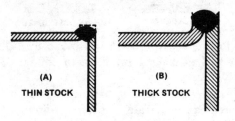

(A) THIN STOCK

(B) THICK STOCK

*Figure 5-13.
Welded edge joints.*

Corner Joints

A corner joint is made when two pieces of metal are brought together so that their edges form a corner of a box or enclosure as shown in figure 5-14. The corner joint shown in figure 5-14A requires little or no filler rod, since the edges fuse to make the weld. It is used where load stress is unimportant. The joint shown in figure 5-14B is used on heavier metals, and filler rod is added for roundness and strength. If much stress is to be placed on the corner, the inside is reinforced as shown in figure 5-14C.

*Figure 5-14.
Welded corner joints.*

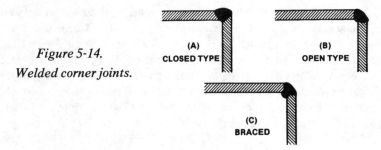

(A) CLOSED TYPE

(B) OPEN TYPE

(C) BRACED

Lap Joints

The lap joint is seldom used in aircraft structures when welding with oxyacetylene, but is commonly used when spot welding. The single lap joint (figure 5-15) has very little resistance to bending. and will not withstand the shearing stress to which the weld may be subjected under tension or compression loads. The double lap joint (figure 5-15) offers more strength, but requires twice the amount of welding required on the simpler, more efficient butt weld.

SINGLE LAP **DOUBLE LAP**

Figure 5-15. Single and double lap welded joints.

EXPANSION AND CONTRACTION OF METALS

Heat causes metals to expand; cooling causes them to contract. Uneven heating, therefore, will cause uneven expansion, or uneven cooling will cause uneven contraction. Under such conditions, stresses are set up within the metal. These forces must be relieved, and unless precautions are taken, warping or buckling of the metal will take place. Likewise, on cooling, if nothing is done to take up the stress set up by the contraction forces, further warping may result; or if the metal is too heavy to permit this change in shape, the stresses remain within the metal itself.

The coefficient of linear expansion of a metal is the amount in inches that a 1 in. piece of metal will expand when its temperature is raised 1 degree F. The amount that a piece of metal will expand when heat is applied is found by multiplying the coefficient of linear expansion by the temperature rise, and that product by the length of the metal in inches. For example, if a 10 ft. aluminum rod is to be raised to a temperature of 1,200 degrees F. from a room temperature of 60 degrees F., the rod will expand 1.75 in.—0.00001280 (aluminum's coefficient of linear expansion) X 120 (length in inches) X 1140 (temperature rise).

Expansion and contraction have a tendency to buckle and warp thin sheet metal ⅛ in. or thinner. This is the result of having a large surface area that spreads heat rapidly and dissipates it soon after the source of heat is removed. The most effective method of alleviating this situation is to remove the heat from the metal near the weld, and thus prevent it from spreading across the whole surface area. This can be done by placing heavy pieces of metal, known as "chill bars," on either side of the weld; they absorb the heat and prevent it from spreading. Copper is most often used for chill bars because of its ability to absorb heat readily. Welding jigs sometimes use this same principle to remove heat from the base metal.

Expansion can also be controlled by tack welding at intervals along the joint.

The effect of welding a long seam (over 10 or 12 in.) is to draw the seam together as the weld progresses. If the edges of the seam are placed in contact with each other throughout their length before welding starts, the far ends of the seam will actually overlap before the weld is completed. This tendency can be overcome by setting the pieces to be welded with the seam spaced correctly at one end and increasing the space at the opposite end as shown in figure 5-16. The amount of space depends on the type of material, the thickness of the material, the welding process being used, and the shape and size of the pieces to be welded.

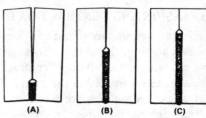

Figure 5-16. Allowance for a straight butt weld when welding a long seam.

(A)   (B)   (C)

The weld is started at the correctly spaced end and proceeds toward the end that has the increased gap. As the seam is welded, the space will close and should provide the correct gap at the point of welding. Sheet metal under 1/16 in. can be handled by flanging the edges, tack welding at intervals, and then by welding between the tacks.

There is less tendency for plate stock over ⅛ in. to warp and buckle when welded because the greater thickness limits the heat to a narrow area and dissipates it before it travels far on the plate.

Preheating the metal before welding is another method of controlling expansion and contraction. Preheating is especially important when welding tubular structures and castings. Great stress can be set up in tubular welds by contraction. When two members of a tee joint are welded, one tube tends to draw up because of the uneven contraction. If the metal is preheated before the welding operation begins, contraction still takes place in the weld, but the accompanying contraction in the rest of the structure is at almost the same rate, and internal stress is lessened.

CORRECT FORMING OF A WELD

The form of the weld metal has considerable bearing upon the strength and fatigue resistance of a joint. The strength of an improperly made weld is usually less than the strength for which the joint was designed. Low-strength welds are generally the result of insufficient penetration; undercutting of the base metal at the toe of the weld; poor fusion of the weld metal with the base metal; trapped oxides, slag, or gas pockets in the weld; overlap of the weld metal on the base metal; too much or too little reinforcement; and overheating of the weld.

VISUAL INSPECTION OF WELDED JOINTS

Although a clean, smooth weld is desirable, this characteristic does not necessarily mean that the weld is a good one; it may be dangerously weak inside. However, when a weld is rough, uneven, and pitted, it is almost always unsatisfactory inside. **Welds should never be filed to give them a better appearance, since filing deprives the weld of part of its strength. Welds should never be filled with solder, brazing material, or filler of any sort.**

Although the appearance of the completed weld is not a positive indication of quality, it gives a good clue to the care used in making it.

A properly designed joint weld is stronger than the base metal which it joins. The characteristics of a properly welded joint are discussed in the following paragraphs.

A good weld is uniform in width; the ripples are even and well feathered into the base metal, which shows no burn due to overheating. (See figure 5-17.) The weld has good penetration and is free of gas pockets, porosity, or inclusions. The edges of the bead illustrated in figure 5-17 (B) are not in a straight line, yet the weld is good, since penetration is excellent.

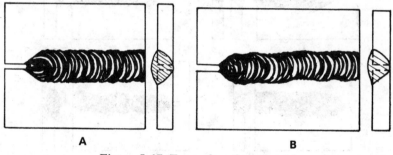

Figure 5-17. Examples of good welds.

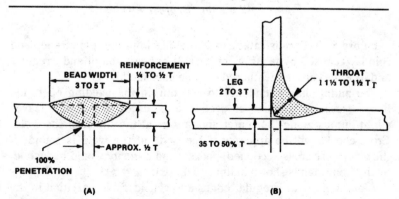

Figure 5-18. (A) Butt weld and (B) fillet weld, showing width and depth of bead.

135

Penetration is the depth of fusion in a weld. Thorough fusion is the most important characteristic which contributes to a sound weld. Penetration is affected by the thickness of the material to be joined, the size of the filler rod, and how it is added. In a butt weld the penetration should be 100 percent of the thickness of the base metal. On a fillet weld the penetration requirements are 25 to 50 percent of the thickness of the base metal. The width and depth of bead for a butt weld and fillet weld are shown in figure 5-18.

To assist further in determining the quality of a welded joint, several examples of incorrect welds are discussed in the following paragraphs.

The weld shown in figure 5-19 (A) was made too rapidly. The long and pointed appearance of the ripples was caused by an excessive amount of heat or an oxidizing flame. If the weld were cross-sectioned, it probably would disclose gas pockets, porosity, and slag inclusions.

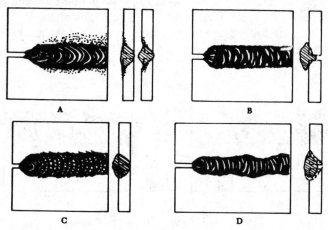

Figure 5-19. Examples of poor welds.

Figure 5-19 (B) illustrates a weld that has improper penetration and cold laps caused by insufficient heat. It appears rough and irregular and its edges are not feathered into the base metal.

The puddle has a tendency to boil during the welding operation if an excessive amount of acetylene is used. This often leaves slight bumps along the center and craters at the finish of the weld. Cross-checks will be apparent if the body of the weld is sound. If the weld were cross-sectioned, pockets and porosity would be visible. Such a condition is shown in figure 5-19 (C).

A bad weld with irregular edges and considerable variation in the depth of penetration is shown in D of figure 5-19. It often has the appearance of a cold weld.

When it is necessary to re-weld a joint, all old weld material must be removed before the operation is begun. It must be remembered, though, that reheating the area may cause the base metal to lose some of its strength and become brittle.

OXYACETYLENE WELDING OF FERROUS METALS
Steel

Low-carbon steel, low-alloy steel, cast steel, and wrought iron are easily welded with the oxyacetylene flame. Plain, low-carbon steel is the ferrous material that will be gas welded most frequently. As the carbon content of steel increases, it may be repaired by welding only under certain conditions. Factors involved are carbon content and hardenability. For corrosion- and heat-resistant nickel chromium steels, the allowed weldability depends upon their stability, carbon content, or re-heat treatment.

In order to make a good weld, the carbon content of the steel must not be altered, nor can other chemical constitutents be added to or subtracted from the base metal without seriously altering the properties of the metal. Molten steel has a great affinity for carbon, and oxygen and nitrogen combine with the molten puddle to form oxides and nitrates, both of which lower the strength of steel. When welding with an oxyacetylene flame, the inclusion of impurities can be minimized by observing the following precautions:

(1) Maintain an exact neutral flame for most steels, and a slight excess of acetylene when welding alloys with a high nickel or chromium content, such as stainless steel.
(2) Maintain a soft flame and control the puddle.
(3) Maintain a flame sufficient to penetrate the metal and manipulate it so that the molten metal is protected from the air by the outer envelope of flame.
(4) Keep the hot end of the welding rod in the weld pool or within the flame envelope.

Proper preparation for welding is an important factor in every welding operation. The edges of the parts must be prepared in accordance with the joint design chosen. The method chosen (bevel, groove, etc.) should allow for complete penetration of the base metal by the flame. The edges must be clean. Arrangements must be made for preheating, if this is required.

When preparing an aircraft part for welding, remove all dirt, grease or oil, and any protective coating such as cadmium plating, enamel, paint, or varnish. Such coatings not only hamper welding, but also mingle with the weld and prevent good fusion.

Cadmium plating can be chemically removed by dipping the edges to be welded in a mixture of 1 lb. of ammonium nitrate and 1 gal. of water.

Enamel, paint, or varnish may be removed from steel parts by a number of methods, such as a steel wire brush or emery cloth, by gritblasting, by using paint or varnish remover, or by treating the pieces with a hot, 10% caustic soda solution followed by a thorough washing with hot water to remove the solvent and residue. Gritblasting is the most effective method for removing rust or scale from steel parts. Grease or oil may be removed with a suitable grease solvent.

Enamel, paint, varnish, or heavy films of oxide on aluminum alloys can be removed using a hot 10% solution of either caustic soda or tri-sodium phosphate. After treatment, the parts should be immersed in a 10% nitric acid solution, followed with a hot water rinse to remove all traces of the chemicals. Paint and varnish can also be removed using paint and varnish remover.

The tip of the filler rod should be dipped below the surface of the weld puddle with a motion exactly opposite the motion of the torch. If the filler rod is held above the surface of the puddle, it will melt and fall into the puddle a drop at a time, ruining the weld.

Filler metal should be added until the surface of the joint is built up slightly above the edges of the parts being joined. The puddle of molten metal should be gradually advanced along the seam until the end of the material is reached.

As the end of the seam is approached, the torch should be raised slightly, chilling the molten steel to prevent it from spilling over the edge or melting through the work.

Chrome Molybdenum

The welding technique for chrome molybdenum is practically the same as that for carbon steels, except that the surrounding area must be preheated to a temperature between 300 degrees and 400 degrees F. before beginning to weld. If this is not done, the sudden application of heat causes cracks to form in the heated area.

A soft neutral flame should be used for welding; an oxidizing flame may cause the weld to crack when it cools, and a carburizing flame will make the metal brittle. The volume of the flame must be sufficient to melt the base metal, but not so hot as to weaken the grain structure of the surrounding area and set up strains in the metal. The filler rod should be the same as the base metal. If the weld requires high strength, a special chrome molybdenum rod is used and the piece is heat treated after welding.

Chrome molybdenum thicker than 0.093 in. is usually electric-arc welded, since for this thickness of metal, electric arc provides a narrow heat zone, fewer strains are developed, and a better weld is obtained, particularly when the part cannot be heat treated after welding.

Stainless Steel

The procedure for welding stainless steel is basically the same as that for carbon steels. There are, however, some special precautions that must be taken to obtain the best results.

Only stainless steel used for nonstructural members of aircraft can be welded satisfactorily; the stainless steel used for structural components is cold worked or cold rolled and, if heated, loses some of its strength. Nonstructural stainless steel is obtained in sheet and tubing form and is often used for exhaust collectors, stacks or manifolds. Oxygen combines very readily with this metal in the molten state, and extreme care must be taken to prevent this from occurring.

A slightly carburizing flame is recommended for welding stainless steel. The flame should be adjusted so that a feather of excess acetylene, about 1/16 in. long, forms around the inner cone. Too much acetylene, however, will add carbon to the metal and cause it to lose its resistance to corrosion. The torch tip size should be one or two sizes smaller than that prescribed for a similar gage of low carbon steel. The smaller tip lessens the chances of overheating and subsequent loss of the corrosion-resistant qualities of the metal.

To prevent the formation of chromium oxide, a flux should be spread on the underside of the joint and on the filler rod. Since oxidation is to be avoided as much as possible, sufficient flux should be used. Another method used to keep oxygen from reaching the metal is to surround the weld with a blanket of hydrogen gas.

Since the coefficient of expansion of stainless steel is high, thin sheets which are to be butt-welded should be tacked at intervals of 1¼ to 1½ inches, as shown in figure 5-20. This is one means of lessening warping and distortion during the welding process.

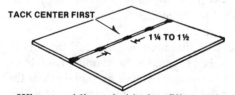

Figure 5-20. Tack welding method for stainless steel welding.

When welding, hold the filler rod within the envelope of the torch flame so that the rod is melted in place or melted at the same time as the base metal. Add the filler rod by allowing it to flow into the molten pool. If the weld pool is stirred, air will enter the weld and increase oxidation. Avoid rewelding any portion or welding on the reverse side of the weld. Such practices result in warping and overheating of the metal.

WELDING NONFERROUS METALS USING OXYACETYLENE

Nonferrous metals are those that contain no iron. Examples of nonferrous metals are lead, copper, silver, magnesium, and most important in aircraft construction, aluminum. Some of these metals are lighter than the ferrous metals, but in most cases they are not as strong. Aluminum manufacturers have compensated for the lack of strength of pure aluminum by alloying it with other metals or by cold working it. For still greater strength, some aluminum alloys are also heat treated.

Aluminum Welding

The weldable aluminum alloys used in aircraft construction are 1100, 3003, 4043, and 5052. Alloy numbers 6053, 6061, and 6151 can also be welded, but since these alloys are in the heat-treated condition, welding should not be done unless the parts can be re-heat treated.

The equipment and technique used for aluminum welding differ only slightly from those of methods discussed earlier. As in all welding, the first step is to clean the surface to be welded—steel wool or a wire brush may be used, or a solvent in the case of paint or grease. The welder should be careful not to scratch the surface of the metal beyond the area to be welded; these scratches provide entry points for corrosion. The piece should then be preheated to lessen the strains caused by the large coefficient of expansion of aluminum.

Never preheat aluminum alloys to a temperature higher than 800 degrees F. because the heat may melt some of the alloys and burn the metal. For thin sheet aluminum, merely passing the flame back and forth across the sheet three or four times should be sufficient.

Either of two types of filler rod can be used in welding aluminum alloys. Choosing the proper filler rod is important.

Aluminum and its alloys combine with air and form oxides very rapidly; oxides form doubly fast if the metal is hot. For this reason it is important to use a flux that will minimize or prevent oxides from forming.

Using the proper flux in welding aluminum is extremely important. Aluminum welding flux is designed to remove the aluminum oxide by chemically combining with it. Aluminum fluxes dissolve below the surface of the puddle and float the oxides to the top of the weld where they can be skimmed off. The flux can be painted directly on the top and bottom of the joint if no filler rod is required; if filler rod is used, it can be coated, and if the pieces to be welded are thick, both the metal and the rod should be coated with flux.

After welding is finished, it is important that all traces of flux be removed by using a brush and hot water. If aluminum flux is left on the weld, it will corrode the metal. A diluted solution of 10% sulfuric acid may be used if hot water is not available. The acid solution should be washed off with cold water.

Thickness of the aluminum alloy material determines the method

of edge preparation. On material up to 0.062 in., the edges are usually formed to a 90 degree flange about the same height as the thickness of the material (figure 5-21A). The flanges should be straight
and square. No filler rod is necessary when the edges are flanged in
this manner.

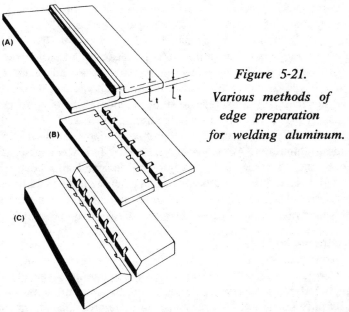

Figure 5-21.

*Various methods of
edge preparation
for welding aluminum.*

Unbeveled butt welds are usually made on aluminum alloy from
0.062 to 0.188 in. thick. It may also be necessary to notch the edges
with a saw or cold chisel in a manner similar to that shown in figure
5-21B. Edge notching is recommended in aluminum welding because
it aids in getting full penetration and also prevents local distortion.
All butt welds in material over 0.125 in. thick are generally notched
in some manner.

In welding aluminum over 0.188 in. thick, the edges are usually
beveled and notched as shown in figure 5-21C. The included angle
of bevel may be from 90 degrees to 120 degrees.

A neutral flame should generally be used to weld aluminum alloys.
In some cases a slightly carburizing flame can be used. However, the
excess of acetylene should not be too great, as it will be absorbed into
the molten metal, resulting in a weakened joint. The torch must
be adjusted to give the mildest flame that can be obtained without
popping. The use of a strong, harsh flame makes it difficult to control
the melting metal, and holes are often burned through the metal.

When starting to weld, the two joint edges should begin to melt before the filler rod is added. The work must be watched carefully for
signs of melting. The melting point of aluminum is low and heat

141

is conducted rapidly through the material. There is very little physical or color change to indicate that the metal is reaching the melting point. When the melting point is reached, the metal suddenly collapses and runs, leaving a hole in the aluminum.

A filler rod can be used to test the metal's condition. Aluminum begins to feel soft and plastic just before it reaches the melting point. Any tendency of the metal to collapse can be rectified by rapidly lifting the flame clear of the metal. With practice it is possible to develop enough skill to melt the metal surface without forming a hole.

The flame should be neutral and slanted at an approximate 45 degree angle to the metal. The inner cone should be about ⅛ in. from the metal. A constant and uniform movement of the torch is necessary to prevent burning a hole through the metal.

The correct integration of torch and rod action is important when welding aluminum. After heating the metal and when melting has begun, the filler rod is dipped into the pool and allowed to melt. The filler rod is lifted and the torch movement continues as the weld progresses. The rod is never lifted out of the outer envelope of flame, but is held there until almost melted and then added to the pool.

Magnesium Welding

Many aircraft parts are constructed of magnesium because of its light weight, strength, and excellent machinability. This metal is only two-thirds as heavy as aluminum and, like aluminum, is very soft in its pure state. For this reason, it is generally alloyed with zinc, manganese, tin, aluminum, or combinations of these metals. Repair of magnesium by welding is limited by two factors:

(1) If the magnesium is used as a structural member, it is usually heat treated and, like heat-treated aluminum, the welded section can never have the strength of the original metal. (As a rule, failures do not occur in the welded area, but in the areas adjacent to the weld, because the heat applied to the metal weakens the grain structure in those areas.)

(2) It is necessary to use flux in making all magnesium welds, and to remove all the flux from the metal after welding or severe corrosion will take place.

The type of joint is limited to those that provide no possibility of trapping the flux—therefore, only butt welds can be made. Magnesium cannot be welded to other metals, and magnesium alloy castings are not considered suitable for stressed welds. If varying thicknesses of magnesium are to be welded, the thicker part must be preheated. The filler rod should be of the same composition as the base metal and one prepared by the manufacturer to fuse with his alloy. The filler rod comes with a protective plating that must be cleaned off before using.

The method of preparing the butt joint depends on the thickness of the metal. See figure 5-22.

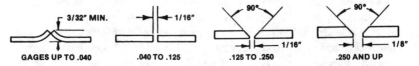

Figure 5-22. Preparation of edges for welding magnesium sheet.

Remove oil or grease with a suitable solvent, and then use a wire brush or abrasive cloth to clean and brighten the metal for a distance of ¾ in. back from the weld area. Select a filler rod of the same material as the base metal. The filler rod and both sides of the seam should be covered with flux. Use a neutral or slightly carburizing flame, and hold it at a flat angle to the work to avoid burning through.

Two rod techniques are recommended for the welding of magnesium. One method requires that the filler rod be kept in the puddle at all times; the other method is the same as that used in welding aluminum.

It is preferable to make the weld on one uninterrupted pass, but if oxidation occurs, the weld should be stopped and scraped out before continuing. The joint edges should be tack-welded at the ends at intervals of ½ to 3 in., depending upon the shape and thickness of the metal.

Welding should be accomplished as quickly and with as little heat as possible. Buckling and warping can be straightened while the metal is still hot by hammering with a soft-faced mallet. The metal should be allowed to cool slowly. When the weld is cool enough to handle, the accessible portions should be scrubbed lightly, using a bristle brush and hot water, to remove excess flux. The part should then be soaked in hot water (160 degrees to 200 degrees F.) to float off the flux adhering to any portions not reached by the scrub brush. When soaking is completed, the part should be immersed in a 1% solution of citric acid for approximately 10 min.

After the citric acid bath the part should be drained thoroughly and then rinsed clean in fresh water. The part must be dried quickly and completely to prevent oxidation.

BRAZING METHODS

Brazing has little direct application in aircraft fabrication or repair. Its principle use is in shop maintenance, making and repairing tools, jigs, and machinery.

Brazing refers to a group of metal-joining processes in which the bonding material is a nonferrous metal or alloy with a melting point higher than 800 degrees F., but is lower than that of the metals being joined. Brazing includes silver soldering, also called hard soldering, copper brazing, and aluminum brazing.

Brazing requires less heat than welding and can be used to join metals that are damaged by high heat. **However, because the strength of brazed joints is not so great as welded joints, brazing is not used for structural repairs on aircraft.** In deciding whether brazing of a joint is justified, it should be remembered that a metal which will be subjected to a sustained high temperature in use should not be brazed.

As the definition of brazing implies, the base metal parts are not melted. The brazing metal adheres to the base metal by molecular attraction and intergranular penetration; it does not fuse and amalgamate with them.

In brazing, the edges of the pieces to be joined are usually beveled as in welding steel. The surrounding surfaces must be cleaned of dirt and rust. Parts to be brazed must be securely fastened together to prevent any relative movement. The strongest brazed joint is one in which the molten filler metal is drawn in by capillary action, thus a close fit must be obtained.

A brazing flux is necessary to obtain a good union between the base metal and the filler metal. A good flux for brazing steel is a mixture containing two parts borax and one part boric acid. Application of the flux may be made in the powder form or dissolved in hot water to a highly saturated solution. A neutral torch flame should be used, moved with a slight semicircular motion.

The base metal should be preheated slowly with a mild flame. When it reaches a dull red heat (in the case of steel), the rod should be heated to a dark or purple color and dipped into the flux. Since enough flux adheres to the rod, it is not necessary to spread it over the surface of the metal.

A neutral flame is used for most brazing applications. However, a slightly oxidizing flame should be used when copper/zinc, copper/zinc/silicon, or copper/zinc/nickel/silicon filler alloys are used. When brazing aluminum and its alloys a neutral flame is preferred, but if difficulties are encountered, a slightly reducing flame is preferred to an oxidizing flame.

The filler rod can now be brought near the tip of the torch, causing the molten bronze to flow over a small area of the seam. The base metal must be at the flowing temperature of the filler metal before it will flow into the joint. The brazing metal melts when applied to the steel and runs into the joint by capillary attraction. The rod should continue to be added as the brazing progresses, with a rhythmic dipping action so that the bead will be built to a uniform width and height. The job should be completed rapidly and with as few passes as possible of the rod and torch.

When the job is finished, the weld should be allowed to cool slowly. After cooling, remove the flux from the parts by immersing them for 30 minutes in a lye solution.

Silver Solder

The principal use of silver solder in aircraft work is in the fabrication of high-pressure oxygen lines and other parts which must withstand vibration and high temperatures. Silver solder is used extensively to join copper and its alloys, nickel and silver, as well as various combinations of these metals, and thin steel parts. Silver soldering produces joints of higher strength than those produced by other brazing processes.

It is necessary to use flux in all silver soldering operations because of the necessity for having the base metal chemically clean without the slightest film of oxide to prevent the silver solder from coming into intimate contact with the base metal.

The joint must be physically clean, which means it must be free of all dirt, grease, oil, and/or paint, and also chemically clean. After removing the dirt, grease, and/or paint, any oxide should be removed by grinding or filing the piece until bright metal can be seen. During the soldering operation, the flux continues the process of keeping oxide away from the metal, and aids the flow of the solder.

In figure 5-23, three types of joints for silver soldering are shown. Flanged, lap, and edge joints, in which the metal may be formed to furnish a seam wider than the base metal thickness, furnish the type of joint which will bear up under all kinds of loads. If a lap joint is used, the amount of lap should be determined according to the strength needed in the joint. For strength equal to that of the base metal in the heated zone, the amount of lap should be four to six times the metal thickness for sheet metal and small-diameter tubing.

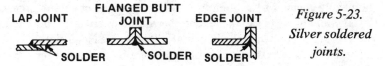

LAP JOINT   FLANGED BUTT JOINT   EDGE JOINT   *Figure 5-23.*
SOLDER   SOLDER   SOLDER   *Silver soldered*
                                              joints.

The oxyacetylene flame for silver soldering should be neutral, but may have a slight excess of acetylene. It must be soft, not harsh. During both preheating and application of the solder, the tip of the inner cone of the flame should be held about ½ in. from the work. The flame should be kept moving so that the metal will not become overheated.

When both parts of the base metal are at the right temperature (indicated by the flow of flux), solder can be applied to the surface of the under or inner part at the edge of the seam. It is necessary to simultaneously direct the flame over the seam and keep moving it so that the base metal remains at an even temperature.

SOFT SOLDERING

Soft soldering is used chiefly for copper, brass, and coated iron in combination with mechanical seams; that is, seams that are rivited, bolted, or folded. It is also used where a leakproof joint is desired, and sometimes for fitting joints to promote rigidity and prevent corrosion. Soft soldering is generally performed only in very minor repair jobs. This process is also used to join electrical connections. It forms a strong union with low electrical resistance.

Soft solder yields gradually under a steadily applied load and should not be used unless the transmitted loads are very low. **It should never be used as a means of joining structural members.**

A soldering copper (called a soldering iron if it is electrically heated) is the tool used in soldering. Its purpose is to act as a source of heat for the soldering operation. The bit, or working face, is made from copper, since this metal will readily take on heat and transmit it to the work. Figure 5-24 shows a correctly shaped bit.

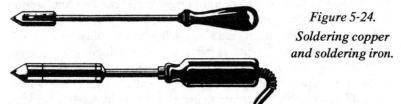

Figure 5-24.

Soldering copper and soldering iron.

To tin the copper, it is first heated to a bright red, then the point is cleaned by filing until it is smooth and bright. No dirt or pits should remain on its surface. After the copper has been mechanically cleaned, it should be re-heated sufficiently to melt solder, and chemically cleaned by rubbing it lightly on a block of sal ammoniac. (If sal ammoniac is not available, powdered resin may be used.) Then solder is applied to the joint and wiped with a clean cloth.

The last two operations may be combined by melting a few drops of solder on a block of sal ammoniac (cleaning compound) and then rubbing the soldering copper over the block until the tip is well coated with solder. A properly tinned copper has a thin unbroken film of solder over the entire surface of its point.

Soft solders are chiefly alloys of tin and lead. The percentages of tin and lead vary considerably in various solders, with a corresponding change in their melting points, ranging from 293 degrees to 592 degrees F. "half-and-half" (50-50) solder is a general purpose solder and is most frequently used. It contains equal proportions of tin and lead and melts at approximately 360 degrees F.

The application of the melted solder requires somewhat more care than is apparent. The parts should be locked together or held mechanically or manually while tacking. To tack the seam, the hot copper is touched to a bar of solder, then the drops of solder adhering to the copper are used to tack the seam at a number of points. The film of solder between the surfaces of a joint must be kept thin to make the strongest joint.

A hot, well-tinned soldering copper should be held so that its point lies flat on the metal at the seam, while the back of the copper extends over the seam proper at a 45 degree angle, and a bar of solder is touched to the point. As the solder melts, the copper is drawn slowly along the seam. As much solder as necessary is added without raising the soldering copper from the job. The melted solder should run between the surfaces of the two sheets and cover the full width of the seam. Work should progress along the seam only as fast as the solder will flow into the joint.

ELECTRIC ARC WELDING

Electric arc welding is a fusion process based on the principle of generating heat with an electric arc jumping an airgap to complete an electrical circuit. This process develops considerably more heat than an oxyacetylene flame. In some applications, it reaches a temperature of approximately 10,000 degrees F. Variations of the process are metallic arc welding, inert-gas (helium) welding, and multi-arc welding. The metallic arc and helium processes have the widest application in aircraft maintenance.

The welding circuit (figure 5-25) consists of a welding machine, (figure 5-26), two leads, an electrode holder, an electrode, and the work to be welded. The electrode, which is held in electrode holder (figure 5-27), is connected to one lead, and the work to be welded is connected to the other lead. When the electrode is touched to the metal to be welded, the electrical circuit is completed and the current flows. When the electrode is withdrawn from the metal, an airgap is formed between the metal and the electrode. If this gap is of the proper length, the electric current will bridge this gap to form a sustained electric spark, called the electric arc.

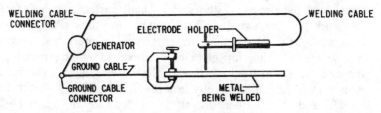

Figure 5-25. Typical arc-welding circuit.

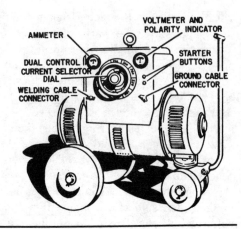

Figure 5-26.

Dual control direct current welding machine.

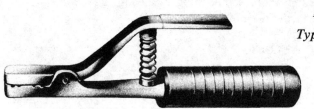

Figure 5-27.

Typical electrode holders.

METALLIC ARC WELDING

Metallic arc welding is used mainly for welding low-carbon and low-alloy steels. However, many nonferrous materials, such as aluminum and nickel alloys, can be welded using this method.

To form an arc between the electrode and the work, the electrode is applied to the work and immediately withdrawn. This initiates an arc of intense heat. To maintain the arc between the electrode and the work, the metal electrode must be fed at a uniform rate or maintained at a constant distance from the work as it melts.

Metallic arc welding is a nonpressure fusion welding process which develops welding heat through an arc produced between a metal electrode and the work to be welded. Under the intense heat developed by the arc, a small part of the base metal or work to be welded is brought to the melting point instantaneously. At the same time, the end of the metal electrode is also melted, and tiny globules or drops of molten metal pass through the arc to the base metal. The force of the arc carries the molten metal globules directly into the puddle formed on the base metal, and thus filler metal is added to the part being welded. By moving the metal electrode along the joint and down to the work, a controlled amount of filler metal can be deposited on the base metal to form a weld bead.

The instant the arc is formed, the temperature of the work at the point of welding and the welding electrode increases to approximately 6,500 degrees F. This tremendous heat is concentrated at the point of welding and in the end of the electrode, and simultaneously melts the end of the electrode and a small part of the work to form a small pool of molten metal, commonly called the crater.

The heat developed is concentrated and causes less buckling and warping of work than gas welding. This localization of the heat is advantageous when welding cracks in heat-treated parts and when welding in close places.

ATOMIC HYDROGEN ARC WELDING

This system employs two tungsten electrodes. An arc is maintained between the ends, and a stream of hydrogen gas is passed into the arc and around the electrodes. The heat of the arc breaks up the molecules of hydrogen into atoms, which re-combine outside the arc to form molecular hydrogen again. The intense heat liberated by the hydrogen as it re-combines is used to fuse the metal.

Atomic hydrogen welding is frequently used in welding aluminum and its alloys, and corrosion-and heat-resistant steels.

INERT-GAS WELDING

In the inert-gas welding process a tungsten or carbon electrode surrounded by helium or argon gas is used. The helium or argon gas are inert and exclude the oxygen and hydrogen present in air from the area being welded. This process is particularly adaptable to the welding of magnesium. It can also be used for welding aluminum, and if argon is used as the shielding gas, no flux is required.

WELDING PROCEDURES AND TECHNIQUES

Due to the limited use of electric arc welding by the field mechanic, detailed welding procedures and techniques will not be discussed.

Chapter 6

Aircraft Structural Repairs

Repair or Replace?

Although this chapter outlines structural repairs of the aircraft, the decision of whether to repair or replace a major unit of structure should be influenced by a comparison of labor costs with the price of replacement components. Experience indicates that replacement, in many cases, is less costly than major repairs, especially considering the ready availability of parts from the manufacturer of the modern airplane. When the aircraft must be restored to its airworthy condition in a limited length of time, replacement is preferable. Restoration of a damaged aircraft to its original design strength, shape and alignment involves careful evaluation of the damage, followed by exacting workmanship in performing the repairs.

Methods of repairing structural portions of an aircraft are numerous and varied, and no set of specific repair patterns has been found which will apply in all cases. Since design loads acting in various structural parts of an aircraft are not always available, the problem of repairing a damaged section must usually be solved by duplicating the original part in strength, kind of material, and dimensions. Some general rules concerning the selection of material and the forming of parts which may be applied universally by the airframe mechanic will be considered in this chapter.

The repairs discussed are typical of those used in aircraft maintenance and are included to introduce some of the operations involved. **For exact information about specific repairs, consult the manufacturer's maintenance or service manuals.** The major aircraft manufacturers maintain large customer service departments. Consult the factory when in doubt about a repair for which no clear-cut procedure exists. Also, Federal Aviation Regulation, Part 43 "Aircraft Inspection and Repair," should be referred to.

150

USE OF REPAIR JIGS

The semi-monocoque construction of major assemblies and the cantelever wing design of the modern aircraft provides little or no means for adjusting the alignment of flight critical surfaces such as angle of incidence or wing dihedral angle. The alignment of the wings, tail surfaces and engine thrust line are all dependent on exactingly located attach points.

Whenever a repair is to be made which could affect structural alignment, suitable jigs must be used to assure correct alignment of major attach points. These jigs are normally available from the manufacturers of the aircraft.

BASIC PRINCIPLES OF SHEET METAL REPAIR

The first and one of the most important steps in repairing structural damage is "sizing up" the job and making an accurate estimate of what is to be done. This sizing up includes an estimate of the best type and shape of patch to use; the type, size, and number of rivets needed; and the strength, thickness, and kind of material required to make the repaired member no heavier (or only slightly heavier) and just as strong as the original. Also inspect the surrounding members for evidence of corrosion and load damage so that the required extent of the "cleanout" of the old damage can be estimated accurately. After completing the cleanout, first make the layout of the patch on paper, then transfer it to the sheet stock selected. Then, cut and chamfer the patch, form it so that it matches the contour of that particular area, and apply it.

Maintaining Original Strength

In making any repair, certain fundamental rules must be observed if the original strength of the structure is to be maintained. The patch plate should have a cross-sectional area equal to, or greater than, that of the original damaged section. If the member is subjected to compression or to bending loads, place the splice on the outside of the member to secure a higher resistance to such loads. If the splice cannot be placed on the outside of the member, use material that is stronger than the material used in the original member.

To reduce the possibility of cracks starting from the corners of cutouts, try to make cutouts either circular or oval in shape. Where it is necessary to use a rectangular cutout, make the radius of curvature at each corner no smaller than ½ in. Either replace buckled or bent members or reinforce them by attaching a splice over the affected area.

Be sure the material used in all replacements or reinforcements is similar to the material used in the original structure. If it is necessary to substitute an alloy weaker than the original, use material of a heavier gage to give equivalent cross-sectional strength. But never practice the reverse; that is, never substitute a lighter gage stronger material for the original. This apparent inconsistency is because one material can have greater tensile strength than another, but less compressive strength, or vice versa. As an example, the mechanical properties of alloys 2024-T and 2024-T80 are compared in the following paragraph.

If alloy 2024-T were substituted for alloy 2024-T80, the substitute material would have to be thicker unless the reduction in compressive strength was known to be acceptable. On the other hand, if 2024-T80 material were substituted for 2024-T stock, the substitute material would have to be thicker unless the reduction in tensile strength was known to be acceptable. Similarly, the buckling and torsional strength of many sheet-metal and tubular parts are dependent primarily upon the thickness rather than the allowable compressive and shear strengths.

When forming is necessary, be particularly careful, for heat-treated and cold-worked alloys will stand very little bending without cracking. Soft alloys, on the other hand, are easily formed but are not strong enough for primary structures. Strong alloys can be formed in their annealed condition and heat treated to develop their strength before assembling.

In some cases, if the annealed metal is not available, heat the metal, quench it according to regular heat-treating practices, and form it before age-hardening sets in. The forming should be completed in about half an hour after quenching, or the material will become too hard to work.

The size of rivets for any repair can be determined by referring to the rivets used by the manufacturer in the next parallel rivet row inboard on the wing, or forward on the fuselage. Another method of determining the size of rivets to be used is to multiply the thickness of the skin by three and use the next larger size rivet corresponding to that figure. For example, if the skin thickness is 0.040-in., multiply 0.040 by 3, which equals 0.120; use the next larger size rivet, ⅛ in.(0.125 in.).

All repairs made on structural parts of aircraft require a definite number of rivets on each side of the break to restore the original strength. This number varies according to the thickness of the material being repaired and the size of the damage. The number of rivets or bolts required can be determined by referring to a similar splice made by the manufacturer, or by using the following rivet formula:

$$\frac{\text{Number of rivets required}}{\text{on each side of the break}} = \frac{\text{L x T x 75,000}}{\text{S or B}}$$

The number of rivets to be used on each side of the break is equal to the length of the break (L) times the thickness of the material (T) times 75,000, divided by the shear strength or bearing strength (S or B) of the material being repaired, whichever is the smaller of the two.

The length of the break is measured perpendicular to the direction of the general stress running through the damaged area.

The thickness of the material is the actual thickness of the piece of material being repaired and is measured in thousandths of an inch.

The 75,000 used in the formula is an assumed stress load value of 60,000 p.s.i. increased by a safety factor of 25%. It is a constant value.

Shear strength is taken from the charts shown in figure 6-1. It is the amount of force required to cut a rivet holding together two or more sheets of material. If the rivet is holding two parts, it is under single shear; if it is holding three sheets or parts, it is under double shear. To determine the shear strength, the diameter of the rivet to be used must be known. This is determined by multiplying the thickness of the material by three. For example, material thickness 0.040 multiplied by 3 equals 0.120; the rivet selected would be ⅛ in. (0.125 in.) in diameter.

*Single-Shear Strength of Aluminum-Alloy Rivets (Pounds)									
Composition of Rivet (Alloy)	Ultimate Strength of Rivet Metal (Pounds Per Square Inch)	Diameter of Rivet (Inches)							
		1/16	3/32	1/8	5/32	3/16	1/4	5/16	3/8
2117 T	27,000	83	186	331	518	745	1,325	2,071	2,981
2017 T	30,000	92	206	368	573	828	1,472	2,300	3,313
2024 T	35,000	107	241	429	670	966	1,718	2,684	3,865
*Double-shear strength is found by multiplying the above values by 2.									

Figure 6-1. Single shear strength chart for rivets.

Bearing strength is a value taken from the chart shown in figure 6-2 and is the amount of tension required to pull a rivet through the edge of two sheets riveted together, or to elongate the hole. The diameter of the rivet to be used and the thickness of material being riveted must be known to use the bearing strength chart. The diameter of the rivet would be the same as that used when determining the shear strength value. Thickness of material would be that of the material being repaired.

Example:

Using the formula, determine the number of 2117-T rivets needed to repair a break 2¼ in. long in material 0.040-in. thick:

$$\text{Number rivets per side} = \frac{L \times T \times 75{,}000}{S \text{ or } B}$$

Given:

L = 2¼ (2.25) in.

T = 0.040 in.

Size of rivet: 0.040 x 3 = 0.120, so rivet must be ⅛ in. or 0.125.

S = 331 (from the shear strength chart).

B = 410 (from the bearing strength chart).

(Use S to find number of rivets per side as it is smaller than B.)

Substituting in the formula:

$$\frac{2.25 \times 0.040 \times 75{,}000}{331} = \frac{6{,}750}{331}$$
$$= 20.39 \text{ (or 21)}$$
$$\text{rivets/side.}$$

Since any fraction must be considered as a whole number, the actual number of rivets required would be 21 for each side, or 42 rivets for the entire repair.

Thickness of Sheet (Inches)	Diameter of Rivet (Inches)							
	1/16	3/32	1/8	5/32	3/16	1/4	5/16	3/8
0.014	71	107	143	179	215	287	358	430
.016	82	123	164	204	246	328	410	492
.018	92	138	184	230	276	369	461	553
.020	102	153	205	256	307	410	412	615
.025	128	192	256	320	284	512	640	768
.032	164	245	328	409	492	656	820	984
.036	184	276	369	461	553	738	922	1,107
.040	205	307	410	512	615	820	1,025	1,230
.045	230	345	461	576	691	922	1,153	1,383
.051	261	391	522	653	784	1,045	1,306	1,568
.064		492	656	820	984	1,312	1,640	1,968
.072		553	738	922	1,107	1,476	1,845	2,214
.081		622	830	1,037	1,245	1,660	2,075	2,490
.091		699	932	1,167	1,398	1,864	2,330	2,796
.102		784	1,046	1,307	1,569	2,092	2,615	3,138
.125		961	1,281	1,602	1,922	2,563	3,203	3,844
.156		1,198	1,598	1,997	2,397	3,196	3,995	4,794
.188		1,445	1,927	2,409	2,891	3,854	4,818	5,781
.250		1,921	2,562	3,202	3,843	5,125	6,405	7,686
.313		2,405	3,208	4,009	4,811	6,417	7,568	9,623
.375		2,882	3,843	4,803	5,765	7,688	9,068	11,529
.500		3,842	5,124	6,404	7,686	10,250	12,090	15,372

Figure 6-2. Bearing strength chart (pounds) for rivets.

Maintaining Original Contour

Form all repairs in such a manner that they will fit the original contour perfectly. A smooth contour is especially desirable when making patches on the smooth external skin of high-speed aircraft.

Keeping Weight to a Minimum

Keep the weight of all repairs to a minimum. Make the size of the patches as small as practicable and use no more rivets than are necessary. In many cases, repairs disturb the original balance of the structure. The addition of excessive weight in each repair may unbalance the aircraft so much that it will require adjustment of the trim-and-balance tabs. In areas such as the spinner on the propeller, a repair will require application of balancing patches so that a perfect balance of the propeller assembly can be maintained.

GENERAL STRUCTURAL REPAIR

Aircraft structural members are designed to perform a specific function or to serve a definite purpose. The prime objective of aircraft repair is to restore damaged parts to their original condition. **Very often, replacement is the only way in which this can be done effectively.** When repair of a damaged part is possible, first study the part carefully so that its purpose or function is fully understood.

Strength may be the principal requirement in the repair of certain structures, while others may need entirely different qualities. For example, fuel tanks and floats must be protected against leakage; but cowlings, fairings, and similar parts must have such properties as neat appearance, streamlined shape, and accessibility. The function of any damaged part must be carefully determined so that the repair will meet the requirements.

INSPECTION OF DAMAGE

When visually inspecting damage, remember that there may be other kinds of damage than that caused by impact from foreign objects or collision. A rough landing may overload one of the landing gear, causing it to become sprung; this would be classified as load damage. During inspection and "sizing up of the repair job," consider how far the damage caused by the sprung shock strut extends to supporting structural members.

A shock occurring at one end of a member will be transmitted throughout its length; therefore, inspect closely all rivets, bolts, and attaching structures along the complete member for any evidence of damage. Make a close examination for rivets that have partially failed and for holes which have been elongated.

Another kind of damage to watch for is that caused by weathering or corrosion. This is known as corrosion damage. Corrosion damage of aluminum material is usually detected by the white crystalline deposits that form around loose rivets, scratches, or any portion of the structure that may be a natural spot for moisture to settle.

CLASSIFICATION OF DAMAGE

Damages may be grouped into four general classes. In many cases, the availability or lack of repair materials and time are the most important factors in determining whether a part should be repaired or replaced.

Negligible Damage

Damage which does not affect the structural integrity of the member involved, or damage which can be corrected by a simple procedure without placing flight restrictions on the aircraft, is classified as negligible damage. Small dents, scratches, cracks, or holes that can be repaired by smoothing, sanding, stop drilling, or hammering out, or otherwise repaired without the use of additional materials, fall in this classification.

Damage Repairable by Patching

Damage repairable by patching is any damage exceeding negligible damage limits which can be repaired by bridging the damaged area of a component with a material splice. The splice or patch material used in internal riveted and bolted repairs is normally the same type of material as the damaged part, but one gage heavier. In a patch repair, filler plates of the same gage and type of material as that in the damaged component may be used for bearing purposes or to return the damaged part to its original contour.

Damage Repairable by Insertion

Damage which can be repaired by cutting away the damaged section and replacing it with a like section, then securing the insertion with splices at each end is classified as damage repairable by insertion.

Damage Necessitating Replacement of Parts

Replacement of an entire part is considered when one or more of the following conditions exist:
(1) When a complicated part has been extensively damaged.
(2) When surrounding structure or inaccessiblity makes repair impractical.
(3) When damaged part is relatively easy to replace.
(4) When forged or cast fittings are damaged beyond the negligible limits.

SPECIAL TOOLS AND DEVICES FOR SHEET METAL

The airframe mechanic does a lot of work with special tools and devices that have been developed to make his work faster, simpler, and better. These special tools and devices include dollies and stakes and various types of blocks and sandbags used as support in the bumping process.

Dollies and Stakes

Sheet metal is often formed or finished (planished) over variously shaped anvils called dollies and stakes. These are used for forming small, oddshaped parts, or for putting on finishing touches for which a large machine may not be suited. Dollies are meant to be held in the hand, whereas stakes are designed to be supported by a flat cast iron bench plate fastened to the workbench (figure 6-3).

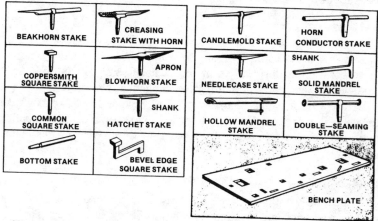

Figure 6-3. Bench plate and stakes used in forming sheet metal.

Most stakes have machined, polished surfaces which have been hardened. Do not use stakes to back up material when chiseling, or when using any similar cutting tool because this will deface the surface of the stake and make it useless for finish work.

V-Blocks

V-blocks made of hardwood are widely used in airframe metalwork for shrinking and stretching metal, particularly angles and flanges. The size of the block depends on the work being done and on personal preference. Although any type of hardwood is suitable, maple and ash are recommended for best results when working with aluminum alloys.

Hardwood Form Blocks

Hardwood form blocks can be constructed to duplicate practically any aircraft structural or nonstructural part. The wooden block or form is shaped to the exact dimensions and contour of the part to be formed.

157

Shrinking Blocks

A shrinking block consists of two metal blocks and some device for clamping them together. One block forms the base, and the other is cut away to provide space where the crimped material can be hammered. The legs of the upper jaw clamp the material to the base block on each side of the crimp so that the material will not creep away but will remain stationary while the crimp is hammered flat (being shrunk). This type of crimping block is designed to be held in a bench vise.

Shrinking blocks can be made to fit any specific need. The basic form and principle remain the same, even though the blocks may vary considerably in size and shape.

Sandbags

A sandbag is generally used as a support during the bumping process. A serviceable bag can be made by sewing heavy canvas or soft leather to form a bag of the desired size, and filling it with sand which has been sifted through a fine mesh screen.

Before filling canvas bags with sand, use a brush to coat the inside of it with softened paraffin or beeswax, which forms a sealing layer and prevents the sand from working through the pores of the canvas.

Holding Devices

Vises and clamps are tools used for holding materials of various kinds on which some types of operation is being performed. The type of operation being performed and the type of metal being used determine the holding device to be used.

The most commonly used vises are shown in figure 6-4; the machinist's vise has flat jaws and usually a swivel base, whereas the utility bench vise has scored, removable jaws and an anvil-faced back jaw. This vise will hold heavier material than the machinist's vise and will also grip pipe or rod firmly. The back jaw can be used for an anvil if the work being done is light.

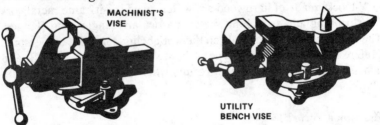

Figure 6-4. Vises.

The carriage clamp, or C-clamp, as it is commonly called, is shaped like a large C and has three main parts: (1) The threaded screw, (2) the jaw, and (3) the swivel head. The swivel plate, which is at the bottom of the screw, prevents the end from turning directly against the material being clamped. Although C-clamps vary in size from 2 in. upward, their function is always that of clamping or holding.

The shape of the C-clamp allows it to span obstructions near the edge of a piece of work. The greatest limitation in the use of the carriage clamp is its tendency to spring out of shape. It should never be tightened more than hand-tight.

The most commonly used sheet-metal holder is the Cleco fastener (figure 6-5). It is used to keep drilled parts made from sheet stock pressed tightly together. Unless parts are held tightly together they will separate while being riveted.

Figure 6-5.

Cleco fasteners are used to temporarily hold parts together while riveting.

This type of fastener is available in six different sizes: 3/32-, 1/8-, 5/32, 3/16, 1/4-, and 3/8-in. The size is stamped on the fastener. Special pliers are used to insert the fastener in a drilled hole. One pair of pliers will fit the six different sizes.

Sheet-metal screws are sometimes used as temporary holders. The metal sheets must be held tightly together before installing these screws, since the self-tapping action of the threads tends to force the sheets apart. Washers placed under the heads of the screws keep them from marring or scratching the metal.

METALWORKING MACHINES

Without metalworking machines a job would be more difficult and tiresome, and the time required to finish a task would be much longer. Some of the machines used are discussed here; these include the powered and nonpowered metal-cutting machines, such as the various types of saws, powered and nonpowered shears, and nibblers. Also included is the forming equipment (both power driven and nonpowered), such as brakes and forming rolls, the bar folder, and shrinking and stretching machines.

Squaring shears (figure 6-6) provide a convenient means of cutting and squaring metal. Three distinctly different operations can be performed on the squaring shears: (1) Cutting to a line, (2) squaring, and (3) multiple cutting to a specific size.

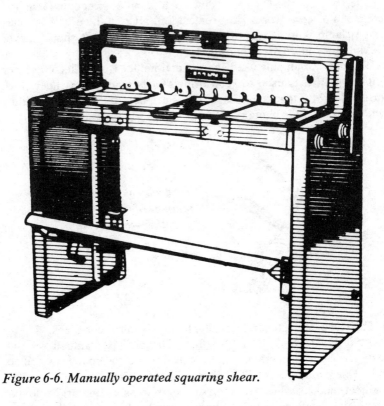

Figure 6-6. Manually operated squaring shear.

Scroll shears (figure 6-7) are used for cutting irregular lines on the inside of a sheet without cutting through to the edge. The upper cutting blade is stationary while the lower blade is movable. The machine is operated by a handle connected to the lower blade.

Throatless shears (figure 6-8) are best used to cut 10-gage mild carbon sheet metal and 12-gage stainless steel. The shear gets its name from its construction; it actually has no throat. There are no obstructions during cutting since the frame is throatless. A sheet of any length can be cut, and the metal can be turned in any direction to allow for cutting irregular shapes. The cutting blade (top blade) is operated by a hand lever.

The rotary punch (figure 6-9) is used in the airframe repair shop to punch holes in metal parts. This machine can be used for cutting radii in corners, for making washers, and for many other jobs where holes are required.

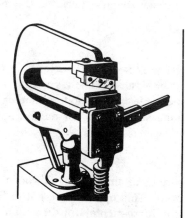

Figure 6-7. Scroll shears.

Figure 6-8. Throatless shears.

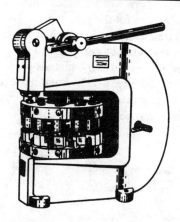

Figure 6-9. Rotary punch.

Metal-Cutting Power-Operated Tools

The portable, air powered reciprocating saw (figure 6-10) has a gun-type shape for balancing and ease of handling and operates most effectively at an air pressure of from 85 to 100 p.s.i. The reciprocating saw uses a standard hacksaw blade and can cut a 360 degree circle or a square or rectangular hole. This saw is easy to handle and safe to use.

Figure 6-10. Reciprocating saw.

161

A reciprocating saw should be used in such a way that at least two teeth of the saw blade are cutting at all times. Avoid applying too much downward pressure on the saw handle because the blade may break.

Nibblers

Stationary and portable nibblers are used to cut metal by a high-speed blanking action. The cutting or blanking action is caused by the lower die moving up and down and meeting the upper stationary die. The shape of the lower die permits small pieces of metal approximately 1/16-in. wide to be cut out.

Portable Power Drills

One of the most common operations in airframe metalwork is that of drilling holes for rivets and bolts. This operation is not difficult, especially on light metal. Once the fundamentals of drills and their uses are learned, a small portable power drill is usually the most practical machine to use. However, there will be times when a drill press may prove to be the better machine for the job.

Some portable power drills will be encountered which are operated by electricity and others which are operated by compressed air.

Portable power drills are available in various shapes and sizes to satisfy almost any requirement (figure 6-11). Pneumatic drills are recommended for use on projects around flammable materials where sparks from an electric drill might become a fire hazard.

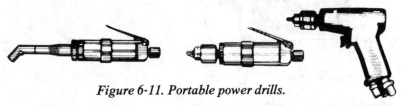

Figure 6-11. Portable power drills.

When access to a place where a hole is to be drilled is difficult or impossible with a straight drill, various types of drill extensions and adapters are used. A straight extension can be made from an ordinary piece of drill rod. The twist drill is attached to the drill rod by shrink fit, brazing, or silver soldering. Angle adapters can be attached to either an electric or pneumatic drill when the location of the hole is inaccessible to a straight drill. Angle adapters have an extended shank fastened to the chuck of the drill. In use, the drill is held in one hand and the adapter in the other to prevent the adapter from spinning around the drill chuck.

A flexible extension can be used for drilling inplaces which are inaccessible to ordinary drills. Its flexibility permits drilling around obstructions with a minimum of effort.

When using the portable power drill, hold it firmly with both hands. Before drilling, be sure to place a backup block of wood under the hole to be drilled to add support to the metal.

The twist drill should be inserted in the chuck and tested for trueness or vibration. This may be visibly checked by running the motor freely. A drill that wobbles or is slightly bent should not be used since such a condition will cause enlarged holes.

The drill should always be held at right angles to the work regardless of the position or curvatures. Tilting the drill at any time when drilling into or withdrawing from the material may cause elongation (egg shape) of the hole.

Always wear safety goggles while drilling.

When drilling through sheet metal, small burrs are formed around the edge of the hole. Burrs must be removed to allow rivets or bolts to fit snugly and to prevent scratching. Burrs may be removed with a bearing scraper, a countersink, or a twist drill larger than the hole. If a drill or countersink is used, it should be rotated by hand.

The drill press (figure 6-12) is a precision machine used for drilling holes that require a high degree of accuracy. It serves as an accurate means of locating and maintaining the direction of a hole that is to be drilled and provides the operator with a feed lever that makes the task of feeding the drill into the work an easy one.

Figure 6-12. A drill press.

Grinders

A grinding wheel is a cutting tool with a large number of cutting edges arranged so that when they become dull they break off and new cutting edges take their place.

Silicon carbide and aluminum oxide are the kinds of abrasives used in most grinding wheels. Silicon carbide is the cutting agent for grinding hard, brittle material, such as cast iron. It is also used in grinding aluminum, brass, bronze, and copper. Aluminum oxide is the cutting agent for grinding steel and other metals of high tensile strength.

The size of the abrasive particles used in grinding wheels is indicated by a number which corresponds to the number of meshes per linear inch in the screen through which the particles will pass. As an example, a number 30 abrasive will pass through a screen having 30 holes per linear inch, but will be retained by a smaller screen having more than 30 holes per linear inch.

A common type bench grinder found in most metalworking shops is shown in figure 6-13. This grinder can be used to dress mushroomed heads on chisels, and points on chisels, screwdrivers, and drills. It can be used for removing excess metal from work and smoothing metal surfaces.

Figure 6-13.

Bench grinder.

As a rule, it is not good practice to grind work on the side of an abrasive wheel. When an abrasive wheel becomes worn, its cutting efficiency is reduced because of a decrease in surface speed. When a wheel becomes worn in this manner, it should be discarded and a new one installed.

Before using a bench grinder, make sure the abrasive wheels are firmly held on the spindles by the flange nuts. If an abrasive wheel should come off or become loose, it could seriously injure the operator in addition to ruining the grinder.

Another hazard is loose tool rests. A loose tool rest could cause the tool or piece of work to be "grabbed" by the abrasive wheel and cause the operator's hand to come in contact with the wheel.

Always wear goggles when using a grinder, even if eyeshields are attached to the grinder. Goggles should fit firmly against your face and nose. This is the only way to protect your eyes from the fine pieces of steel.

Be sure to check the abrasive wheel for cracks before using the grinder. A cracked abrasive wheel is likely to fly apart when turning at high speeds. Never use a grinder unless it is equipped with wheel guards.

FORMING MACHINES

Forming machines can be either hand operated or power driven. Small machines are usually hand operated, whereas the larger ones are power driven. Straight line machines include such equipment as the bar folder, cornice brake, and box and pan brake. Rotary machines include the slip roll former and combination machine. Power-driven machines are those that require a motor of some description for power. These include such equipment as the power-driven slip roll former, and power flanging machine.

Bar Folder

The bar folder (figure 6-14) is designed for use in making bends or folds along edges of sheets. This machine is best suited for folding small hems, flanges, seams, and edges to be wired. Most bar folders have a capacity for metal up to 22 gage in thickness and 42 inches in length.

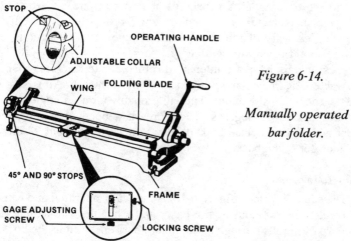

Figure 6-14.

Manually operated bar folder.

Before using the bar folder, several adjustments must be made for thickness of material, width of fold, sharpness of fold, and angle of fold.

To make the fold, adjust the machine correctly and then insert the metal. The metal goes between the folding blade and the jaw. Hold the metal firmly against the gage and pull the operating handle toward the body. As the handle is brought forward, the jaw automatically raises and holds the metal until the desired fold is made. When the handle is returned to its original position, the jaw and blade will return to their original positions and release the metal.

Cornice Brake

The cornice brake (figure 6-15) has a much greater range of usefulness than the bar folder. Any bend formed on a bar folder can be made on the cornice brake. The bar folder can form a bend or edge only as wide as the depth of the jaws. In comparison, the cornice brake allows the sheet that is to be folded or formed to pass through the jaws from front to rear without obstruction.

Figure 6-15.

The cornice brake has a much greater range of usefulness than the bar folder.

The bending capacity of a cornice brake is determined by the manufacturer. Standard capacities of this machine are from 12- to 22-gage sheet metal, and bending lengths are from 3 to 12 ft. The bending capacity of the brake is determined by the bending edge thickness of the various bending leaf bars.

Most metals have a tendency to return to their normal shape—a characteristic known as springback. If the cornice brake is set for a 90 degree bend, the metal bent will probably form an angle of about 87 degrees to 88 degrees. Therefore, if a bend of 90 degrees is desired, set the cornice brake to bend an angle of about 93 degrees to allow for springback.

Slip Roll Former

The slip roll former (figure 6-16) is manually operated and consists of three rolls, two housings, a base, and a handle. The handle turns the two front rolls through a system of gears enclosed in the housing. By properly adjusting the roller spacing, metal can be formed into a curve.

Forming Processes

Before a part is attached to the aircraft during either manufacture or repair, it has to be shaped to fit into place. This shaping process is called forming. Forming may be a very simple process, such as making one or two holes for attaching, or it may be exceedingly complex, requiring shapes with complex curvatures.

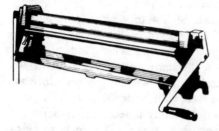

Figure 6-16. Slip roll folder.

Parts are formed at the factory on large presses or by drop hammers equipped with dies of the correct shape. Every part is planned by factory engineers, who set up specifications for the materials to be used so that the finished part will have the correct temper when it leaves the machines. A layout for each part is prepared by factory draftsmen.

Forming processes used on the flight line and those practiced in the maintenance or repair shop are almost directly opposite in the method of procedure. They have much in common, however, and many of the facts and techniques learned in the one process can be applied to the other.

Forming is of major concern to the airframe mechanic and requires the best of his knowledge and skill. This is especially true since forming usually involves the use of extremely light-gage alloys of a delicate nature which can be readily made useless by coarse and careless workmanship. A formed part may seem outwardly perfect, yet a wrong step in the forming procedure may leave the part in a strained condition. Such a defect may hasten fatigue or may cause sudden structural failure.

Of all the aircraft metals, pure aluminum is the most easily formed. In aluminum alloys, ease of forming varies with the temper condition. Since modern aircraft are constructed chiefly of aluminum and aluminum alloys, this section will deal with the procedures for forming aluminum or aluminum alloy parts.

Most parts can be formed without annealing the metal, but if extensive forming operations, such as deep draws (large folds) or complex curves are planned, the metal should be in the dead soft or annealed condition. During the forming of some complex parts, operations may have to be stopped and the metal annealed before the process can be continued or completed. Alloy 2024 in the "O" condition can be formed into almost any shape by the common forming operations, but it must be heattreated afterward.

When forming, use hammers and mallets as sparingly as practicable, and make straight bends on bar folders or cornice brakes. Use rotary machines whenever possible. If a part fits poorly or not at all, do not straighten a bend or a curve and try to re-form it, discard the piece of metal and start with a new one.

When making layouts, be careful not to scratch aluminum or aluminum alloys. A pencil, if kept sharp, will be satisfactory for marking purposes. Scribers make scratches which induce fatigue failure; but they may be used if the marking lines fall outside the finished part, that is, if the scribed line will be part of the waste material. Keep bench tops covered with material hard enough to prevent chips and other foreign material from becoming imbedded in them. Be sure also to keep bench tops clean and free from chips, filings, and the like. For the protection of the metals being worked, keep vise jaws covered with soft metal jaw caps.

Stainless steel can be formed by any of the usual methods but requires considerably more skill than is required for forming aluminum or aluminum alloys. Since stainless steel work-hardens very readily, it requires frequent annealing during the forming operations. Always try to press out stainless steel parts in one operation. Use dies, if possible.

FORMING OPERATIONS AND TERMS

The methods used in forming operations include such sheetmetal work processes as shrinking, stretching, bumping, crimping, and folding.

Bumping

Shaping or forming malleable metal by hammering or pounding is called bumping. During this process, the metal is supported by a dolly, a sandbag, or a die. Each contains a depression into which hammered portions of the metal can sink. Bumping can be done by hand or by machine.

Crimping

Folding, pleating, or corrugating a piece of sheet metal in a way that shortens it is called crimping. Crimping is often used to make one end of a piece of stovepipe slightly smaller so that one section may be slipped into another. Turning down a flange on a seam is also called crimping. Crimping one side of a straight piece of angle with crimping pliers will cause it to curve, as shown in figure 6-17.

Stretching

Hammering a flat piece of metal in an area such as that indicated in figure 6-17 will cause the material in that area to become thinner. However, since the amount of metal will not have been decreased, it will cover a greater area because the metal will have been stretched.

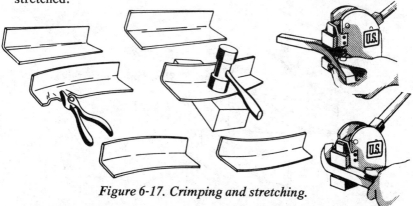

Figure 6-17. Crimping and stretching.

Stretching one portion of a piece of metal affects the surrounding material, especially in the case of formed and extruded angles. For example, hammering the metal in the horizontal flange of the angle strip over a metal block, as shown in figure 6-17, would cause its length to be increased (stretched); therefore, that section would become longer than the section near the bend. To allow for this difference in length, the vertical flange, which tends to keep the material near the bend from stretching, would be forced to curve away from the greater length.

Shrinking

During the shrinking process, material is forced or compressed into a smaller area. The shrinking process is used when the length of a piece of metal, especially on the inside of a bend, is to be reduced. Sheet metal can be shrunk in two ways: (1) By hammering on a V-block (figure 6-18), or (2) by crimping and then shrinking on a shrinking block.

To curve the formed angle by the V-block method, place the angle on the V-block and gently hammer downward against the upper edge directly over the "V" (figure 6-18). While hammering, move the angle back and forth across the V-block to compress the material along the upper edge. Compression of the material along the upper edge of the vertical flange will cause the formed angle to take on a curved shape. The material in the horizontal flange will merely bend down at the center, and the length of that flange will remain the same.

To make a sharp curve or a sharply bent flanged angle, crimping and a shrinking block can be used. In this process, crimps are placed in the one flange, and then by hammering the metal on a shrinking block, the crimps will be driven out (shrunk out) one at a time.

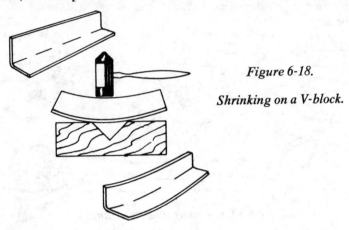

Figure 6-18.

Shrinking on a V-block.

Folding

Making bends in sheets, plates, or leaves is called folding. Folds are usually thought of as sharp, angular bends; they are generally made on folding machines.

MAKING STRAIGHT LINE BENDS

When forming straight bends, the thickness of the material, its alloy composition, and its temper condition must be considered. Generally speaking, the thinner the material, the sharper it can be bent (the smaller the radius of bend), and the softer the material, the sharper the bend. Other factors that must be considered when making straight line bends are bend allowance, setback, and brake or sight line.

The radius of bend of a sheet of material is the radius of the bend as measured on the inside of the curved materials. The minimum radius of bend of a sheet of material is the sharpest curve, or bend, to which the sheet can be bent without critically weakening the metal at the bend. If the radius of bend is too small, stresses and strains will weaken the metal and may result in cracking.

A minimum radius of bend is specified for each type of aircraft sheet metal. The kind of material, thickness, and temper condition of the sheet are factors affecting it. Annealed sheet can be bent to a radius approximately equal to its thickness. Stainless steel and 2024-T aluminum alloy require a fairly large bend radius.

Bend Allowance

When making a bend or fold in a sheet of metal, the bend allowance must be calculated. Bend allowance is the length of material required for the bend. This amount of metal must be added to the overall length of the layout pattern to assure adequate metal for the bend.

Bend allowance depends on four factors: (1) The degree of bend, (2) the radius of the bend, (3) the thickness of the metal, and (4) the type of metal used. The radius of the bend is generally proportional to the thickness of the material. Furthermore, the sharper the radius of bend, the less the material that will be needed for the bend. The type of material is also important. If the material is soft it can be bent very sharply; but if it is hard, the radius of bend will be greater, and the bend allowance will be greater. The degree of bend will affect the overall length of the metal, whereas the thickness influences the radius of bend.

Bending a strip compresses the material on the inside of the curve and stretches the material on the outside of the curve. However, at some distance between these two extremes lies a space which is not affected by either force. This is known as the neutral line or neutral axis and occurs at a distance approximately 0.445 times the metal thickness (0.455 × T) from the inside of the radius of the bend (figure 6-19).

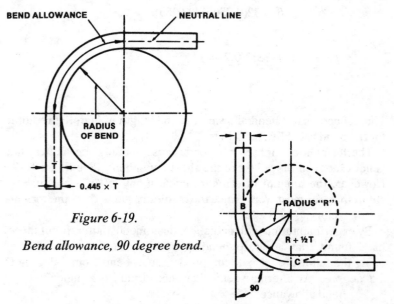

Figure 6-19.

Bend allowance, 90 degree bend.

When bending metal to exact dimensions, the length of the neutral line must be determined so that sufficient material can be allowed for the bend. To save time in calculation of the bend allowance, formulas and charts for various angles, radii of bends, material thicknesses, and other factors have been established. The bend allowance formula for a 90 degree bend is discussed in the following paragraphs.

Compute the circumference of this circle by multiplying the radius of curvature of the neutral line (R + ½ T in figure 6-19) by 2π :

$$2\pi (R + \tfrac{1}{2} T).$$

Note: $\pi = 3.1416$.

Since a 90 degree bend is a quarter of the circle, divide the circumference by 4. This gives:

$$\frac{2\pi (R + \tfrac{1}{2} T).}{4}.$$

Therefore, bend allowance for a 90 degree bend is

$$\frac{2\pi (R + \tfrac{1}{2} T).}{4}.$$

To use the formula in finding the bend allowance for a 90 degree bend having a radius of ¼ in. for material 0.051-in. thick, substitute in the formula as follows:

Bend allowance

$$= \frac{2 \times 3.1416(0.250 + \tfrac{1}{2} \times 0.051)}{4}$$

$$= \frac{6.2832(0.250 + 0.0255)}{4}$$

$$= \frac{6.2832(0.2755)}{4}$$

$$= 0.4323.$$

Thus, if necessary, bend allowance or the length of material required for the bend is 0.4323, or 7/16 in.

The formula is slightly in error because actually the neutral line is not exactly in the center of the sheet being bent. (See figure 6-19.) However, the amount of error incurred in any given problem is so slight that, for most work, since the material used is thin, the formula is satisfactory.

By experimentation with actual bends in metals, aircraft engineers have found that accurate bending results could be obtained by using the following formula for any degree of bend from 1 degree to 180 degrees. An alternate bend allowance formula is as follows:

Bend allowance

$$= (0.01743 \times R + 0.0078 \times T) \times N$$

where:

R = The desired bend radius,

T = Thickness of the material, and

N = Number of degrees of bend.

Either formula may be used in the absence of a bend allowance chart. To determine bend allowance for any degree of bend by use of the chart (figure 6-20), find the allowance per degree for the number of degrees in the bend.

RADIUS GAGE	° OF BEND IN INCHES													
	.031	.063	.094	.125	.156	.188	.219	.250	.281	.313	.344	.375	.438	.500
.020	.062 .000693	.113 .001251	.161 .001792	.210 .002333	.259 .002874	.309 .003433	.358 .003974	.406 .004515	.455 .005056	.505 .005614	.554 .006155	.603 .006695	.702 .007795	.799 .008877
.025	.066 .000736	.116 .001294	.165 .001835	.214 .002376	.263 .002917	.313 .003476	.362 .004017	.410 .004558	.459 .005098	.509 .005657	.558 .006198	.607 .006739	.705 .007838	.803 .008920
.028	.068 .000759	.119 .001318	.167 .001859	.216 .002400	.265 .002941	.315 .003499	.364 .004040	.412 .004581	.461 .005122	.511 .005680	.560 .006221	.609 .006762	.708 .007862	.805 .008943
.032	.071 .000787	.121 .001345	.170 .001886	.218 .002427	.267 .002968	.317 .003526	.366 .004067	.415 .004608	.463 .005149	.514 .005708	.562 .006249	.611 .006789	.710 .007889	.807 .008971
.038	.075 .000837	.126 .001396	.174 .001937	.223 .002478	.272 .003019	.322 .003577	.371 .004118	.419 .004659	.468 .005200	.518 .005758	.567 .006299	.616 .006840	.715 .007940	.812 .009021
.040	.077 .000853	.127 .001411	.176 .001952	.224 .002493	.273 .003034	.323 .003593	.372 .004134	.421 .004675	.469 .005215	.520 .005774	.568 .006315	.617 .006856	.716 .007955	.813 .009037
.051		.134 .001413	.183 .002034	.232 .002575	.280 .003116	.331 .003675	.379 .004215	.428 .004756	.477 .005297	.527 .005855	.576 .006397	.624 .006934	.723 .008037	.821 .009119
.064		.144 .001595	.192 .002136	.241 .002676	.290 .003218	.340 .003776	.389 .004317	.437 .004858	.486 .005399	.536 .005957	.585 .006498	.634 .007039	.732 .008138	.830 .009220
.072			.198 .002202	.247 .002743	.296 .003284	.345 .003842	.394 .004283	.443 .004924	.492 .005465	.542 .006023	.591 .006564	.639 .007105	.738 .008205	.836 .009287
.078			.202 .002249	.251 .002790	.300 .003331	.350 .003889	.399 .004430	.447 .004963	.496 .005512	.546 .006070	.595 .006611	.644 .007152	.745 .008252	.840 .009333
.081			.204 .002272	.253 .002813	.302 .003354	.352 .003912	.401 .004453	.449 .004969	.498 .005535	.548 .006094	.598 .006635	.646 .007176	.745 .008275	.842 .009357
.091			.212 .002350	.260 .002891	.309 .003432	.359 .003990	.408 .004531	.456 .005072	.505 .005613	.555 .006172	.604 .006713	.653 .007254	.752 .008353	.849 .009435
.094			.214 .002374	.262 .002914	.311 .003455	.361 .004014	.410 .004555	.459 .005096	.507 .005637	.558 .006195	.606 .006736	.655 .007277	.754 .008376	.851 .009458
.102				.268 .002977	.317 .003518	.367 .004076	.416 .004617	.464 .005158	.513 .005699	.563 .006257	.612 .006798	.661 .007339	.760 .008439	.857 .009521
.109				.273 .003031	.321 .003572	.372 .004131	.420 .004672	.469 .005213	.518 .005754	.568 .006312	.617 .006853	.665 .007394	.764 .008493	.862 .009575
.125				.284 .003156	.333 .003697	.383 .004256	.432 .004797	.480 .005338	.529 .005878	.579 .006437	.628 .006978	.677 .007519	.776 .008618	.873 .009575
.156					.355 .003939	.405 .004497	.453 .005038	.502 .005579	.551 .006120	.601 .006679	.650 .007220	.698 .007761	.797 .008860	.895 .009942
.188						.417 .004747	.476 .005288	.525 .005829	.573 .006370	.624 .006928	.672 .007469	.721 .008010	.820 .009109	.917 .010191
.250								.568 .006313	.617 .006853	.667 .007412	.716 .007953	.764 .008494	.863 .009593	.961 .010675

Figure 6-20. Bend allowance chart.

Radius of bend is given as a decimal fraction on the top line of the chart. Bend allowance is given directly below the radius figures. The top number in each case is the bend allowance for a 90 degree angle, whereas the lower placed number is for a 1 degree angle. Material thickness is given in the left column of the chart.

To find the bend allowance when the sheet thickness is 0.051 in., the radius of bend is ¼ in. (0.250 in.), and the bend is to be 90 degrees. Reading across the top of the bend allowance chart, find the column for a radius of bend of 0.250 in. Now find the block in this column that is opposite the gage of 0.051 in the column at left. The upper number in the block is 0.428, the correct bend allowance in inches for a 90 degree bend.

If the bend is to be other than 90 degrees, use the lower number in the block (the bend allowance for 1 degree) and compute the bend allowance. The lower number in this case is 0.004756. Therefore, if the bend is to be 120 degrees, the total bend allowance in inches will be 120 × 0.004756, or 0.5707 in.

When bending a piece of sheet stock, it is necessary to know the starting and ending points of the bend so that the length of the "flat"

173

of the stock can be determined. Two factors are important in determining this, the radius of bend and the thickness of the material.

In figure 6-21, note that **setback is the distance from the bend tangent line to the mold point.** The mold point is the point of intersection of the lines extending from the outside surfaces, whereas the bend tangent lines are the starting and end points of the bend. Also note that setback is the same for the vertical flat and the horizontal flat.

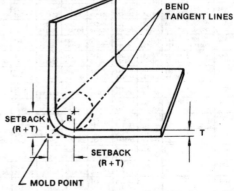

Figure 6-21.

Setback, 90 degree bend.

To calculate the setback for a 90 degree bend, merely add the inside radius of the bend to the thickness of the sheet stock, i.e.,

Setback $= R + T$.

To calculate setback for angles larger or smaller than 90 degrees, consult standard setback charts (figure 6-22), or K chart, for a value called K, and then substitute this value in the formula,

Setback $= K (R + T)$.

The value for K varies with the number of degrees in the bend.

Example:

Calculate the setback for a 90 degree bend, if the material is 0.051-in. thick and the radius of bend is specified to be ⅛ in. (0.125).

Setback $= R + T$
$= 0.125 + 0.051$
$= 0.176$ in.

Example:

Calculate the setback for a 120 degree bend with a radius of bend of 0.125 in. in a sheet 0.032-in. thick.

Setback $= K (R + T)$
$= 1.7320 (0.125 + 0.032)$
$= 0.272$ in.

Brake or Sight Line

The brake or sight line is the mark on a flat sheet which is set even with the nose of the radius bar of the cornice brake and serves as a guide in bending. The brake line can be located by measuring out one radius from the bend tangent line closest to the end which is to be inserted under the nose of the brake or against the radius form block. The nose of the brake or radius bar should fall directly over the brake or sight line as shown in figure 6-23.

A	K	A	K	A	K
1°	.00873	61°	.58904	121°	1.7675
2°	.01745	62°	.60086	122°	1.8040
3°	.02618	63°	.61280	123°	1.8418
4°	.03492	64°	.62487	124°	1.8807
5°	.04366	65°	.63707	125°	1.9210
6°	.05241	66°	.64941	126°	1.9626
7°	.06116	67°	.66188	127°	2.0057
8°	.06993	68°	.67451	128°	2.0503
9°	.07870	69°	.68728	129°	2.0965
10°	.08749	70°	.70021	130°	2.1445
11°	.09629	71°	.71329	131°	2.1943
12°	.10510	72°	.72654	132°	2.2460
13°	.11393	73°	.73996	133°	2.2998
14°	.12278	74°	.75355	134°	2.3558
15°	.13165	75°	.76733	135°	2.4142
16°	.14054	76°	.78128	136°	2.4751
17°	.14945	77°	.79543	137°	2.5386
18°	.15838	78°	.80978	138°	2.6051
19°	.16734	79°	.82434	139°	2.6746
20°	.17633	80°	.83910	140°	2.7475
21°	.18534	81°	.85408	141°	2.8239
22°	.19438	82°	.86929	142°	2.9042
23°	.20345	83°	.88472	143°	2.9887
24°	.21256	84°	.90040	144°	3.0777
25°	.22169	85°	.91633	145°	3.1716
26°	.23087	86°	.93251	146°	3.2708
27°	.24008	87°	.80978	147°	3.3759
28°	.24933	88°	.96569	148°	3.4874
29°	.25862	89°	.98270	149°	3.6059
30°	.26795	90°	1.0000C	150°	3.7320

A	K	A	K	A	K
31°	.27732	91°	1.0176	151°	3.8667
32°	.28674	92°	1.0355	152°	4.0108
33°	.29621	93°	1.0538	153°	4.1653
34°	.30573	94°	1.0724	154°	4.3315
35°	.31530	95°	1.0913	155°	4.5107
36°	.32492	96°	1.1106	156°	4.7046
37°	.33459	97°	1.1303	157°	4.9151
38°	.34433	98°	1.1504	158°	5.1455
39°	.35412	99°	1.1708	159°	5.3995
40°	.36397	100°	1.1917	160°	5.6713
41°	.37388	101°	1.2131	161°	5.9758
42°	.38386	102°	1.2349	162°	6.3137
43°	.39391	103°	1.2572	163°	6.6911
44°	.40403	104°	1.2799	164°	7.1154
45°	.41421	105°	1.3032	165°	7.5957
46°	.42447	106°	1.3270	166°	8.1443
47°	.43481	107°	1.3514	167°	8.7769
48°	.44523	108°	1.3764	168°	9.5144
49°	.45573	109°	1.4019	169°	10.385
50°	.46631	110°	1.4281	170°	11.430
51°	.47697	111°	1.4550	171°	12.706
52°	.48773	112°	1.4826	172°	14.301
53°	.49858	113°	1.5108	173°	16.350
54°	.50952	114°	1.5399	174°	19.081
55°	.52057	115°	1.5697	175°	22.904
56°	.53171	116°	1.6003	176°	26.636
57°	.54295	117°	1.6318	177°	38.188
58°	.55431	118°	1.6643	178°	57.290
59°	.56577	119°	1.6977	179°	114.590
60°	.57735	120°	1.7320	180°	Infinite

Figure 6-22. Setback (K) chart.

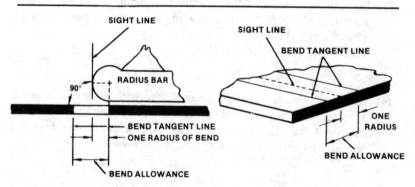

Figure 6-23. Brake or sight line.

MAKING LAYOUTS

It is wise to make a layout or pattern of the part before forming it to prevent any waste of material and to get a greater degree of accuracy in the finished part. Where straight angle bends are concerned, correct allowances must be made for setback and bend allowance. If the shrinking or stretching processes are to be used, allowances must be made so that the part can be turned out with a minimum

175

amount of forming.

The layout procedures can be put into three general groups: (1) Flat layout, (2) duplication of pattern, and (3) projection through a set of points. All three processes require a good working knowledge of arithmetic and geometry. This presentation will discuss only two processes, flat layout and duplication of pattern.

Flat Layout

Assume that it is necessary to lay out a flat pattern of a channel (figure 6-24) in which the left-hand, A, is to be 1 in. high, the right-hand flat, C, is to be 1¼ in. high, and the distance between the outside surface of the two flats, B, is to be 2 in. The material is 0.051-in. thick, and the radius of bend is to be 3/16 in. (0.188). The angles are to be 90 degrees. Proceed as follows:

(1) Determine the setback to establish the distance of the flats.

(a) The setback for the first bend:

Setback = R + T
= 0.188 + 0.051
= 0.239.

(b) The first flat A is equal to the overall dimension less setback:

Flat A = 1.000 — 0.239
= 0.761 in.

(2) Calculate the bend allowance for the first bend by using the bend allowance chart (figure 6-20). (BA = 0.3307 or 0.331.)

(3) Now lay off the second flat, B. This is equal to the overall dimension less the setback at each end, or B minus two setbacks: (See figure 6-24).

Flat B = 2.00—(0.239+0.239)
= 2.000 — .478
= 1.522 in.

(4) The bend allowance for the second bend is the same as that for the first bend (0.331). Mark off this distance. (See figure 6-24.)

(5) The third flat, C, is equal to the overall dimension less the setback. Lay off this distance. (See figure 6-24.)

Flat C = 1.250 — 0.239
= 1.011 in.

(6) Adding the measurements of flats A, B, and C, and both bend allowances, (0.761 + 0.331 + 1.522 + 0.331 + 1.011), the sum is 3.956, or approximately 4.00 inches. Totaling the three flats, A, B, and C, 1 in., 2 in., and 1¼ in., respectively, the sum is 4.250 in. of material length. This illustrates how setback and bend allowance affect material lengths in forming straight line bends. In this case, the reduction is approximately ¼ in.

After all measurements are calculated, cut the material and mark off the brake or sight lines, as shown in figure 6-24.

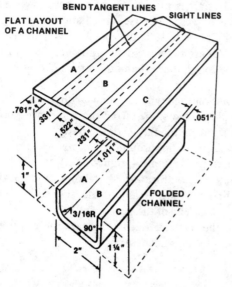

Figure 6-24.

Flat layout of a channel.

Duplication of Pattern

When it is necessary to duplicate an aircraft part and blueprints are not available, take measurements directly from the original or from a duplicate part. In studying the following steps for laying out a part to be duplicated, refer to the illustrations in figure 6-25.

Draw a reference (datum) line, AB, on the sample part and a corresponding line on the template material (example 1, figure 6-25).

Next, with point A on the sample part as a center, draw an arc having a radius of approximately ½ in. and extending to the flanges (example 2, figure 6-25).

Figure 6-25.

Duplicating a pattern.

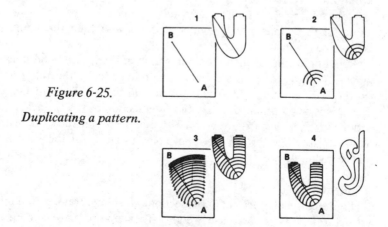

Draw similar arcs each with a radius ½ in. greater than the previous one until the entire part is marked. In case there is an extremely sharp curve in the object, decrease the distance between the arcs to increase the number of arcs. This procedure will increase the accuracy of the layout. An arc must pass through every corner of the part; one arc may pass through more than one corner (example 3, figure 6-25).

Locate the coordinate point on the layout by measuring on the part with dividers. Always measure the distance from the reference point to the beginning of the bend line on the flange of the part.

After locating all points, draw a line through them, using a French curve to ensure a smooth pattern (example 4, figure 6-25).

Allow for additional material for forming the flange and locate the inside bend tangent line by measuring, inside the sight line, a distance equal to the radius of bend of the part.

Using the intersection of the lines as a center, locate the required relief holes. Then cut out and form as necessary.

Relief Holes

Wherever two bends intersect, material must be removed to make room for the material contained in the flanges. Holes are therefore drilled at the intersection. These holes, called relief holes, prevent strains from being set up at the intersection of the inside bend tangent lines which would cause the metal to crack. Relief holes also provide a neatly trimmed corner from which excess material may be trimmed.

The size of relief holes varies with thickness of the material. They should be not less than ⅛ in. in diameter for aluminum alloy sheet stock up to and including 0.064-in. thick, or 3/16 in. for stock ranging from 0.072 in. to 0.128 in. in thickness. The most common method of determining the diameter of a relief hole is to use the radius of bend for this dimension, provided it is not less than the minimum allowance (⅛ in.).

Relief holes must touch the intersection of the inside bend tangent lines. To allow for possible error in bending, make the relief holes so they will extend 1/32 to 1/16 in. behind the inside bend tangent lines. It is good practice to use the intersection of these lines as the center for the holes (figure 6-26). The line on the inside of the curve is cut at an angle toward the relief holes to allow for the stretching of the inside flange.

Lightening Holes

Lightening holes are cut in rib sections, fuselage frames, and other structural parts to decrease weight. To keep from weakening the member by removal of the material, flanges are often pressed around the holes to strengthen the area from which the material was removed.

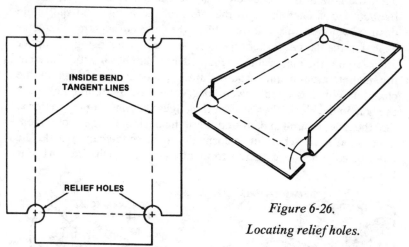

INSIDE BEND
TANGENT LINES

RELIEF HOLES

Figure 6-26.
Locating relief holes.

Lightening holes should never be cut in any structural part unless authorized. The size of the lightening hole and the width of the flange formed around the hole are determined by design specifications. Margins of safety are considered in the specifications so that the weight of the part can be decreased and still retain the necessary strength. Lightening holes may be cut by any one of the following methods:

(1) Punching out, if the correct size punch die is available.
(2) Cutting out with a fly cutter mounted on a drill.
(3) Scribing the circumference of a hole with dividers and drilling around the entire circumference with a small drill, allowing enough clearance to file smooth.
(4) Scribing the circumference of the hole with dividers, drilling the hole inside the circumference large enough to insert aviation snips, cutting out excess metal, and filing smooth.

Form the flange by using a flanging die, or hardwood or metal form blocks. Flanging dies consist of two matching parts, a female and a male die. For flanging soft metal, dies can be of hardwood, such as maple. For hard metal or for more permanent use, they should be made of steel. The pilot guide should be the same size as the hole to be flanged, and the shoulder should be the same width and angle as the desired flange.

When flanging lightening holes, place the material between the mating parts of the die and form it by hammering or squeezing the dies together in a vise or in an arbor press. The dies will work more smoothly if they are coated with light machine oil.

Note that in the two form blocks shown on the left side of figure 6-27, the hole in the upper block is the same size as the hole to be flanged and is chamfered to the width of the flange and the angle desired, whereas in the lower block, the hole is the same diameter as that of the flange. Either type may be used. When using the upper block, center the material to be flanged and hammer it with a stretching mallet, around and around, until the flange conforms to the chamfer. When using the lower block, center the lightening hole over the hole in the block, then stretch the edges, hammering the material into the hole, around and around, until the desired flange is obtained. Occasionally, the chamfer is formed with a cone-shaped male die used in conjunction with the form block with which the part was formed.

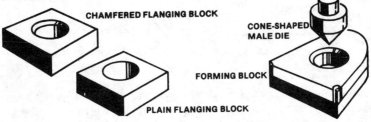

Figure 6-27. Flanging form blocks.

HAND FORMING

Hand forming of detail parts such as a wing rib or fuselage bulkhead is a time-consuming operation requiring considerable skill and will not be discussed in detail in this chapter. Practically every detail part is available from the manufacturer for most aircraft produced since World War II.

All forming revolves around the process of shrinking and stretching, and hand forming processes are no exception. If a formed or extruded angle is to be curved, either stretch one leg or shrink the other, whichever will make the part fit. In bumping, the material is stretched in the bulge to make it "balloon," and in joggling, the material is stretched between the joggles. Material in the edge of lightening holes is often stretched to form a beveled reinforcing ridge around them.

Working Stainless Steel

When working with stainless steel, make sure that the metal does not become unduly scratched or marred. Also take special precautions when shearing, punching, or drilling this metal. It takes about twice as much pressure to shear or punch stainless steel as it does mild steel. Keep the shear or punch and die adjusted very closely. Too much clearance will permit the metal to be drawn over the edge of the die and cause it to become work-hardened, resulting in excessive strain on the machine.

When drilling stainless steel, use a high-speed drill ground to an included angle of 140 degrees. Some special drills have an offset point, whereas others have a chip curler in the flutes. When using an ordinary twist drill, grind its point to a stubbier angle than the standard drill point. Keep the drill speed about one-half that required for drilling mild steel, but never exceed 750 r.p.m. Keep a uniform pressure on the drill so the feed is constant at all times. Drill the material on a backing plate, such as cast iron, which is hard enough to permit the drill to cut all the way through the stock without pushing the metal away from the drill point. Spot the drill before turning on the power and also make sure that when the power is turned on, pressure is being exerted.

To avoid overheating, dip the drill in water after drilling each hole. When it is necessary to drill several deep holes in stainless steel, use a liquid coolant. A compound made up of 1 lb. of sulfur added to 1 gal. of lard oil will serve the purpose. Apply the coolant to the material immediately upon starting the drill. High-speed portable hand drills have a tendency to burn the drill points and excessively work-harden the material at the point of contact; thus high-speed portable hand drills should not be used because of the temperatures developed. A drill press adjustable to speeds under 750 r.p.m. is recommended.

SPECIFIC REPAIR TYPES

Before discussing any type of a specific repair that could be made on an aircraft, remember that the methods, procedures, and materials mentioned in the following paragraphs are only typical and should not be used as the authority for the repair. When repairing a damaged component or part, consult the applicable section of the manufacturer's structural repair manual for the aircraft. Normally, a similar repair will be illustrated, and the types of material, rivets, and rivet spacing and the methods and procedures to be used will be listed. Any additional knowledge needed to make a repair will also be detailed.

If the necessary information is not found in the structural repair manual, attempt to find a similar repair or assembly installed by the manufacturer of the aircraft.

Smooth Skin Repair

Minor damage to the outside skin of an aircraft can be repaired by applying a patch to the inside of the damaged sheet. A filler plug must be installed in the hole made by the removal of the damaged skin area. It plugs the hole and forms a smooth outside surface necessary for aerodynamic smoothness of modern day aircraft.

The size and shape of the patch is determined in general by the number of rivets required in the repair. If not otherwise specified, calculate the required number of rivets by using the rivet formula. Make the patch plate of the same material as the original skin and of the same thickness or of the next greater thickness.

Elongated Octagonal Patch

Whenever possible, use an elongated octagonal patch for repairing the smooth skin. This type of patch provides a good concentration of rivets within the critical stress area, eliminates dangerous stress concentrations, and is very simple to lay out. This patch may vary in length according to the condition of the repair.

Follow the steps shown in the paper layout of this patch (figure 6-28). First, draw the outline of the trimmed-out damage. Then, using a spacing of three to four diameters of the rivet to be used, draw lines running parallel to the line of stress. Locate the lines for perpendicular rows two and one-half rivet diameters from each side of the cutout, and space the remaining lines three-fourths of the rivet pitch apart.

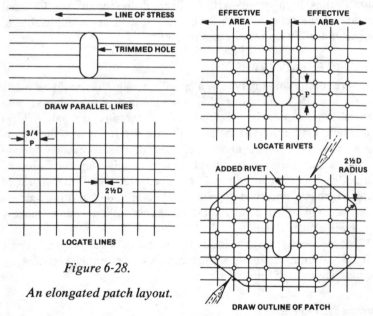

Figure 6-28.

An elongated patch layout.

Locate the rivet spots on alternate lines perpendicular to the stress lines to produce a stagger between the rows and to establish a distance between rivets (in the same row) of about six to eight rivet diameters. After locating the proper number of rivets on each side of the cutout, add a few more if necessary so that the rivet distribution will be uniform. At each of the eight corners, swing an arc of two and one-half rivet diameters from each corner rivet. This locates the edge of the patch. Using straight lines, connect these arcs to complete the layout.

Round Patch

Use the round patch for flush repairs of small holes in smooth sheet sections. The uniform distribution of rivets around its circumference makes it an ideal patch for places where the direction of the stress is unknown or where it is known to change frequently.

If a two-row round patch is used (figure 6-29), first draw the outline of the trimmed area on paper. Draw two circles, one with a radius equal to the radius of the trimmed area plus the edge distance, and the other with a radius ¾-in. larger. Determine the number of rivets to be used and space two-thirds of them equally along the outer row. Using any two adjacent rivet marks as centers, draw intersecting arcs; then draw a line from the point of intersection of the arcs to the center of the patch. Do the same with each of the other pairs of rivet marks. This will give half as many lines as there are rivets in the outer row. Locate rivets where these lines intersect the inner circle. Then transfer the layout to the patch material, adding regular outer edge material of two and one-half rivet diameters to the patch.

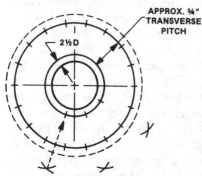

Figure 6-29. Layout of a round patch with two rows of rivets.

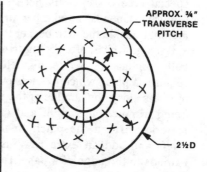

Figure 6-30. Layout of a round patch with three rows of rivets.

Use a three-row round patch (figure 6-30) if the total number of rivets is large enough to cause a pitch distance smaller than the minimum for a two-row patch. Draw the outline of the area on paper; then draw a circle with a radius equal to that of the trimmed area plus the edge distance. Equally space one-third of the required number of rivets in this row. Using each of these rivet locations as a center, draw arcs having a ¾-in. radius. Where they intersect, locate the second row rivets. Locate the third row in a similar manner. Then allow extra material of two and one-half rivet diameters around the outside rivet row. Transfer the layout to the patch material.

After laying out and cutting the patch, remove the burrs from all edges. Chamfer the edges of all external patches to a 45 degree angle and turn them slightly downward so that they will fit close to the surface (figure 6-31).

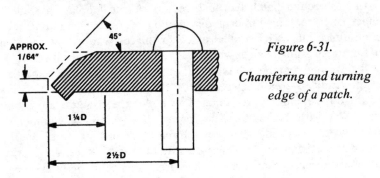

Figure 6-31.

Chamfering and turning edge of a patch.

Panel Repair

In aircraft construction, a panel is any single sheet of metal covering. A panel section is the part of a panel between adjacent stringers and bulkheads. Where a section of skin is damaged to such an extent that it is impossible to install a standard skin repair, a special type of repair is necessary. The particular type of repair required depends on whether the damage is reparable outside the member, inside the member, or to the edges of the panel.

Damage which, after being trimmed, has less than eight and one-half manufacturer's rivet diameters of material inside the members requires a patch which extends over the members, plus an extra row of rivets along the outside of the members. For damage which, after being trimmed, has eight and one-half rivet diameters or more of material, extend the patch to include the manufacturer's row of rivets and add an extra row inside the members. Damage which extends to the edge of a panel requires only one row of rivets along the panel edge, unless the manufacturer used more than one row. The repair procedure for the other edges of the damage follows the previously explained methods.

The procedures for making all three types of panel repairs are similar. Trim out the damaged portion to the allowances mentioned in the preceding paragraph. For relief of stresses at the corners of the trim-out, round them to a minimum radius of ½ in. Lay out the new rivet row with a transverse pitch of approximately five rivet diameters and stagger the rivets with those put in by the manufacturer.

Cut the patch plate from material of the same thickness as the original or the next greater thickness, allowing an edge distance of two and one-half rivet diameters. At the corners, strike arcs having the radius equal to the edge distance. Chamfer the edges of the patch plate for a 45 degree angle and form the plate to fit the contour of the original structure. Turn the edges downward slightly so that the edges fit closely.

Place the patch plate in its correct position, drill one rivet hole, and temporarily fasten the plate in place with a fastener. Using a hole finder, locate the position of a second hole, drill it, and insert a second fastener. Then, from the back side and through the original holes, locate and drill the remaining holes. Remove the burrs from the rivet holes and apply corrosion protective material to the contacting surfaces before riveting the patch into place.

In many cases it may be preferrable to replace complete skin panels. Figure 6-32 shows an illustration from a manufacturers service manual indicating skin materials and thickness.

Stringer Repair

The fuselage stringers extend from the nose of the aircraft to the tail, and the wing stringers extend from the fuselage to the wing tip. Surface control stringers usually extend the length of the control surface. The skin of the fuselage, wing, or control surface is riveted to stringers.

Stringers may be damaged by vibration, corrosion, or collision. Damages are classified as negligible, damage reparable by patching, and damage necessitating replacement of parts. Usually the damage involves the skin and sometimes the bulkhead or formers. Such damage requires a combination of repairs involving each damaged member.

Because stringers are made in many different shapes repair procedures differ. The repair may require the use of preformed or extruded repair material, or it may require material formed by the airframe mechanic. Some repairs may need both kinds of repair material.

When repairing a stringer, first determine the extent of the damage and remove the rivets from the surrounding area. Then remove the damaged area by using a hacksaw, keyhole saw, drill, or file.

In most cases, a stringer repair will require the use of an insert and splice angle. When locating the splice angle on the stringer during repair, be sure to consult the applicable structural repair manual for the repair piece's position. Some stringers are repaired

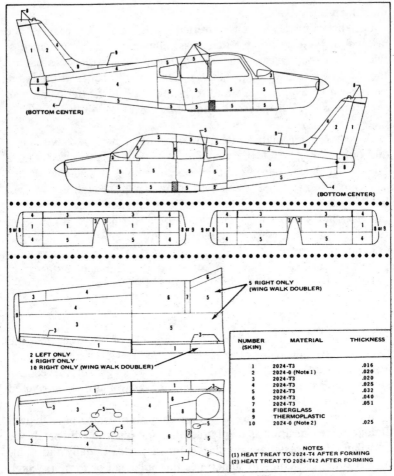

NUMBER (SKIN)	MATERIAL	THICKNESS
1	2024-T3	.016
2	2024-0 (Note 1)	.020
3	2024-T3	.020
4	2024-T3	.025
5	2024-T3	.032
6	2024-T3	.040
7	2024-T3	.051
8	FIBERGLASS	
9	THERMOPLASTIC	
10	2024-0 (Note 2)	.025

NOTES
(1) HEAT TREAT TO 2024-T4 AFTER FORMING
(2) HEAT TREAT TO 2024-T42 AFTER FORMING

Figure 6-32. Typical drawing from a manufacturer's maintenance manual showing skin materials and thickness.

by placing the splice angle on the inside, whereas others are repaired by placing it on the outside.

Extrusions and preformed materials are commonly used to repair angles and insertions or fillers. If repair angles and fillers must be formed from flat sheet stock, use the brake. It may be necessary to use bend allowance and sight lines when making the layout and bends for these formed parts. For repairs to curved stringers, make the repair parts so that they will fit the original contour.

When calculating the number of rivets to be used in the repair, first determine the length of the break. In bulb-angle stringers, the length of the break is equal to the cross sectional length plus three times the thickness of the material in the standing leg (to allow for the bulb), plus the actual cross sectional length for the formed stringers and straight angles.

Substitute the value obtained, using the procedure above as the length of the break in the rivet formula, and calculate the number of rivets required. The rivet pitch should be the same as that used by the manufacturer for attaching the skin to the stringer. In case this pitch exceeds the maximum of 10 rivet diameters, locate additional rivets between the original rivets. Never make the spacing less than four rivet diameters.

When laying out this spacing, allow two and one-half rivet diameters for edge distance on each side of the break until all required rivets are located. At least five rivets must be inserted on each end of the splice section. If the stringer damage requires the use of an insertion or filler of a length great enough to justify more than 10 rivets, two splice angles should usually be used.

If the stringer damage occurs close to a bulkhead, cut the damaged stringer so that only the filler extends through the opening in the bulkhead. The bulkhead is weakened if the opening is enlarged to accommodate both the stringer and the splice angle. Two splice angles must be used to make such a repair.

Because the skin is fastened to the stringers, it is often impossible to drill the rivet holes for the repair splices with the common air drill. These holes can be drilled with an angle drill. When riveting a stringer, it may be necessary to use an offset rivet set and various shaped bucking bars.

Former or Bulkhead Repairs

Bulkheads are the oval-shaped members of the fuselage which give form to and maintain the shape of the structure. Bulkheads or formers are often called forming rings, body frames, circumferential rings, belt frames, and other similar names. They are designed to carry concentrated stressed loads.

There are various types of bulkheads. The most common type is a curved channel formed from sheet stock with stiffeners added. Others have a web made from sheet stock with extruded angles riveted in place as stiffeners and flanges. Most of these members are made from aluminum alloy. Corrosion-resistant steel formers are used in areas which are exposed to high temperatures.

Bulkhead damages are classified in the same manner as other damages. Specifications for each type of damage are established by the manufacturer and specific information is given in the maintenance manual or structural repair manual for the aircraft. Bulkheads, are identified with station numbers, which are very helpful in locating repair information.

Repairs to these members are generally placed in one of two cat-

187

egories: (1) One-third or less of the cross sectional area damaged, or (2) more than one-third of the cross sectional area damaged. If one-third or less of the cross sectional area has been damaged, a patch plate, reinforcing angle, or both, may be used. First, clean out the damage and then use the rivet formula to determine the number of rivets required in order to establish the size of the patch plate. For the length of the break, use the depth of the cutout area plus the length of the flange.

If more than one-third of the cross sectional area is damaged, remove the entire section and make a splice repair (figure 6-33). When removing the damaged section, be careful not to damage the surrounding equipment, such as electrical lines, plumbing, instruments, and so forth. Use a hand file, rotary file, snips, or a drill to remove larger damages. To remove a complete section, use a hacksaw, keyhole saw, drill, or snips.

Measure the length of break as shown in figure 6-33 and determine the number of rivets required by substituting this value in the rivet formula. Use the double shear value of the rivet in the calculations. The result represents the number of rivets to be used in each end of the splice plate.

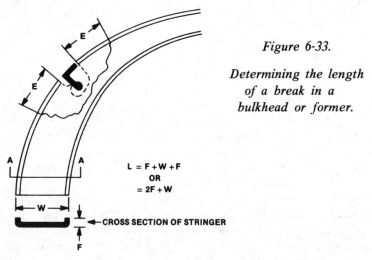

Figure 6-33.

Determining the length of a break in a bulkhead or former.

$$L = F + W + F$$
$$\text{OR}$$
$$= 2F + W$$

← CROSS SECTION OF STRINGER

Most repairs to bulkheads are made from flat sheet stock if spare parts are not available. When fabricating the repair from flat sheet, remember that the substitute material must provide cross sectional tensile, compressive, shear, and bearing strength equal to the original material. Never substitute material which is thinner or has a cross sectional area less than the original material. Curved repair parts made from flat sheet must be in the "O" condition before forming, and then must be heat treated before installation.

Longeron Repair

Generally, longerons are comparatively heavy members which serve approximately the same function as stringers. Consequently, longeron repair is similar to stringer repair. Because the longeron is a heavy member and more strength is needed than with a stringer, heavy rivets will be used in the repair. Sometimes bolts are used to install a longeron repair; but, because of the greater accuracy required, they are not as suitable as rivets. Also, bolts require more time for installation.

If the longeron consists of a formed section and an extruded angle section, consider each section separately. Make the longeron repair as you would a stringer repair. However, keep the rivet pitch between four- and six-rivet diameters. If bolts are used, drill the bolt holes for a light drive fit.

Spar Repair

The spar is the main supporting member of the wing. Other components may also have supporting members called spars which serve the same function as the spar does in the wing. Think of spars as the "hub" or "base" of the section in which they are located, even though they are not in the center. The spar is usually the first member located during the construction of the section, and the other components are fastened directly or indirectly to it.

Because of the load the spar carries, it is very important that particular care be taken when repairing this member to ensure that the original strength of the structure is not impaired. The spar is so constructed that two general classes of repairs, web repairs and cap strip repairs, are usually necessary.

For a spar web butt splice, first clean out the damage; then measure the fill width of the web section. Determine the number of rivets to be placed in each side of the splice plate by substituting this value for the length of break in the rivet formula. Prepare an insert section of the same type material and thickness as that used in the original web. Make a paper pattern of the rivet layout for the splice plate using the same pitch as that used in the attachment of the web to the cap strip. Cut the splice plates from sheet stock having the same weight as that in the web, or one thickness heavier, and transfer the rivet layout from the paper pattern to the splice plates.

Give all contacting surfaces a corrosion-resistant treatment and rivet the component parts of the repair into place. The rivets used in attaching the insert section to the cap strips are in addition to those calculated for attaching the splice plates. Replace all web stiffeners removed during the repair. An exploded view of a spar web butt splice is shown in figure 6-34.

189

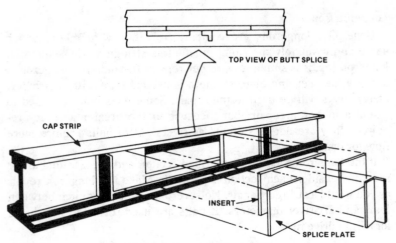

TOP VIEW OF BUTT SPLICE

CAP STRIP

INSERT

SPLICE PLATE

Figure 6-34. Spar web butt splice.

When making a spar web joggle splice, no splice plates are needed. Instead, form the web repair section so that it overlaps the original web sufficiently to accommodate the required number of rivets. Make a joggle in each end of the repair section so that the repair piece contacts the cap strips to which it is riveted. Rivet calculation for this repair is similar to that described for butt splicing.

Many forms of cap strips are used in aircraft manufacturing, and each requires a distinct type of repair. In calculating the number of rivets required in an extruded T-spar cap strip repair, take the width of the base of the T, plus the length of the leg as the length of the break, and use double shear values.

Place one-fourth of the required number of rivets in each row of original rivets in the base of the T-section. Locate them midway between each pair of the original rivets. Locate the remainder of the rivets along the leg of the T-section in two rows. Consider all original rivets within the area of the splice as part of the required rivets.

Make the filler piece of a similar piece of T-section extrusion or of two pieces of flat stock. It is possible to make the splice pieces of extruded angle material or to form them from sheet stock; in either case, they must be the same thickness as the cap strip. Figure 6-35 shows an exploded view of a T-spar cap strip repair. The rivets used in the leg of the cap strip may be either the round-, flat-, or brazier-head type; but the rivets used in the base must be the same type as those used in the skin.

The repair of milled cap strips is limited to damages occuring to flanges. Damages beyond flange areas require replacement of the entire cap strip. To make a typical flange repair, substitute the depth of the trimmed-out area as the length of break in the rivet formula and calculate the number of rivets required. Form a splice plate of the required length and drill it to match the original rivet layout. Cut an insert to fit the trimmed-out area and rivet the repair in place. If the trimmed-out area is more than 4 in. in length, use an angle splice plate to provide added strength.

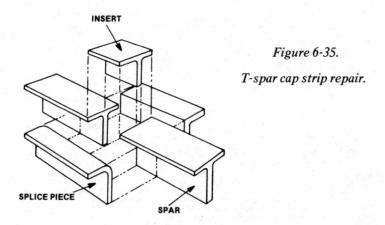

Figure 6-35.

T-spar cap strip repair.

Rib and Web Repair

Web repairs can be generally classified into two types: (1) Those made to web sections considered critical, such as those in the wing ribs, and (2) those considered less critical, such as those in elevators, rudders, flaps, and the like. Web sections must be repaired in such a way that the original strength of the member is restored.

In the construction of a member using a web, the web member is usually a light gage aluminum alloy sheet forming the principal depth of the member. The web is bounded by heavy aluminum alloy extrusions known as cap strips. These extrusions carry the loads caused by bending and also provide a foundation for attaching the skin. The web may be stiffened by stamped beads, formed angles, or extruded sections riveted at regular intervals along the web.

The stamped beads are a part of the web itself and are stamped in when the web is made. Stiffeners help to withstand the compressive loads exerted upon the critically stressed web members.

Often ribs are formed by stamping the entire piece from sheet stock. That is, the rib lacks a cap strip, but does have a flange around the entire piece, plus lightening holes in the web of the rib. Ribs may be formed with stamped beads for stiffeners, or they may have extruded angles riveted on the web for stiffeners.

Most damages involve two or more members; however, it may be that only one member is damaged and needs repairing. Generally, if the web is damaged, all that is required is cleaning out the damaged area and installing a patch plate.

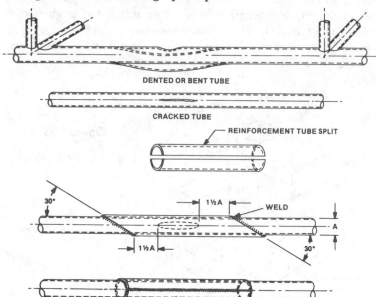

Figure 6-36. Repair of tubing structure using a welded sleeve.

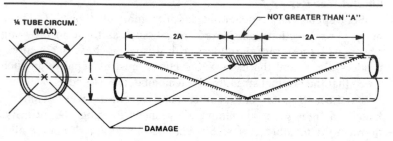

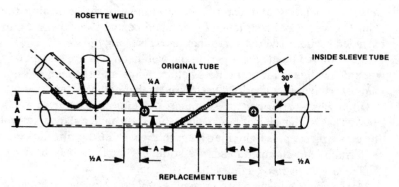

Figure 6-37. Splicing by inner-sleeve method.

192

The patch plate should be of sufficient size to ensure room for at least two rows of rivets around the perimeter of the damage; this will include proper edge distance, pitch, and transverse pitch for the rivets. The patch plate should be of material having the same thickness and composition as the original member. If any forming is necessary when making the patch plate, such as fitting the contour of a lightening hole, use material in the "O" condition and then heat treat it after forming.

Damage to ribs and webs which require a repair larger than a simple plate will probably need a patch plate, splice plates, or angles and an insertion. To repair such a damage by forming the necessary parts may take a great deal of time; therefore, if damaged parts which have the necessary areas intact are available from salvage, use them.

For example, if an identical rib can be located in salvage and it has a cracked web but the area in question is intact, clean out the damaged area; then cut the repair piece from the rib obtained from salvage. Be sure to allow plenty of material for correct rivet installation. Using a part from salvage will eliminate a great deal of hard work plus the heat-treating operation needed by a new repair piece.

Leading Edge Repair

The leading edge is the front section of a wing, stabilizer, or other airfoil. The purpose of the leading edge is to streamline the forward section of the wings or control surfaces so that the airflow is effective. The space within the leading edge is sometimes used to store fuel. This space may also house extra equipment such as landing lights, plumbing lines, or thermal anti-icing systems.

The construction of the leading edge section varies with the type of aircraft. Generally, it will consist of cap strips, nose ribs, stringers and skin. The cap strips are the main lengthwise extrusions, and they stiffen the leading edges and furnish a base for the nose ribs and skin. They also fasten the leading edge to the front spar.

The nose ribs are stamped from aluminum alloy sheet. These ribs are U-shaped and may have their web sections stiffened. Regardless of their design, their purpose is to give contour to the leading edge.

Stiffeners are used to stiffen the leading edge and supply a base for fastening the nose skin. When fastening the nose skin, use only flush rivets.

Leading edges constructed with thermal anti-icing systems consist of two layers of skin separated by a thin air space. The inner skin, sometimes corrugated for strength, is perforated to conduct the hot air to the nose skin for anti-icing purposes.

Damage to leading edges are also classified in the same manner as other damages. Damage can be caused by contact with other objects, namely, pebbles, birds in flight, and hail. However, the major cause of damage is carelessness while the aircraft is on the ground.

A damaged leading edge will usually involve several structural parts. Flying-object damage will probably involve the nose skin, nose ribs, stringers, and possibly the cap strip. Damage involving all of these members will necessitate installing an access door to make the repair possible. First, the damaged area will have to be removed and repair procedures established. The repair will need insertions and splice pieces. If the damage is serious enough, it may require repair of the cap strip and stringer, a new nose rib, and a skin panel. When repairing a leading edge, follow the procedures prescribed in the appropriate repair manual for this type of repair.

WELDING OF AIRCRAFT STEEL STRUCTURES

The techniques and procedures for welding are presented in Chapter 5.

Oxyacetylene or electric arc welding may be utilized for repair of some aircraft structures, since most aircraft structures are fabricated from one of the weldable alloys; however, careful consideration should be given to the alloy being welded since all alloys are not readily weldable. Also, certain structural parts may be heat treated and therefore could require special handling. In general, the more responsive an alloy steel is to heat treatment, the less suitable it is for welding because of its tendency to become brittle and lose its ductility in the welded area. The following steels are readily weldable: (1) Plain carbon of the 1000 series, (2) nickel steel of the SAE 2300 series, (3) chrome/nickel alloys of the SAE 3100 series, (4) chrome/molybdenum steels of the SAE 4100 series, and (5) low-chrome/molybdenum steel of the SAE 8600 series.

Aircraft Steel Parts Not To Be Welded

Welding repairs should not be performed on aircraft parts whose proper function depends on strength properties developed by cold working, such as streamlined wires and cables.

Brazed or soldered parts should never be repaired by welding, since the brazing mixture or solder can penetrate the hot steel and weaken it.

Aircraft parts such as turnbuckle ends and aircraft bolts which have been heat treated to improve their mechanical properties should not be welded.

Repair of a dented or bent tube using a welded sleeve is illustrated in figure 6-36. The repair material selected should be a length of steel tube sleeving having an inside diameter approximately equal to the outside diameter of the damaged tube and of the same material and wall thickness. This sleeve reinforcement should be cut at a 30 degree angle on both ends so that the minimum distance of the sleeve from the edge of the crack or dent is not less than one and one-half times the diameter of the damaged tube.

After the angle cuts have been made to the ends, the entire length of the reinforcement sleeve should be cut, separating the sleeve into half-sections (figure 6-36). The two sleeve sections are then clamped to the proper positions on the affected areas of the original tube. The sleeve is welded along the length of the two sides, and both ends are welded to the damaged tube, as shown in figure 6-36.

Welded-Patch Repair

Dents or holes in tubing can be safely repaired by a welded patch of the same material but one gage thicker, as illustrated in figure 6-36.

Splicing Tubing by Inner Sleeve Method

If the damage to a structural tube is such that a partial replacement of the tube is necessary, the inner sleeve splice shown in figure 6-37 is recommended, especially where a smooth tube surface is desired. A diagonal cut is made to remove the damaged portion of the tube, and the burrs are removed from the edges of the cut by filing or similar means. A replacement steel tube of the same material and diameter, and at least the same wall thickness is then cut to match the length of the removed portion of the damaged tube. At each end of the replacement tube a ⅛-in. gap should be allowed from the diagonal cuts to the stubs of the original tube.

A length of steel tubing should next be selected of at least the same wall thickness and of an outside diameter equal to to the inside diameter of the damaged tube. This inner tube material should be fitted snugly within the original tube. Cut two sections of tubing from this inner-sleeve tube material, each of such a length that the ends of the inner sleeve will be a minimum distance of one and one-half tube diameters from the nearest end of the diagonal cut.

If the inner sleeve fits very tightly in the replacement tube, the sleeve can be chilled with dry ice or in cold water. If this procedure is inadequate, the diameter of the sleeve can be polished down with emery cloth. The inner sleeve can be welded to the tube stubs through the ⅛-in. gap, forming a weld bead over the gap.

Engine Mount Repairs

All welding on an engine mount should be of the highest quality, since vibration tends to accentuate any minor defect. Engine-mount members should preferably be repaired by using a larger diameter replacement tube telescoped over the stub of the original member using fishmouth and rosette welds. However, 30 degree scarf welds in place of the fishmouth welds are usually considered acceptable for engine mount repair work.

Repaired engine mounts must be checked for accurate alignment. When tubes are used to replace bent or damaged ones, the original alignment of the structure must be maintained. This can be done by measuring the distance between points of corresponding members that have not been distorted, and by reference to the manufacturer's drawings.

Minor damage, such as a crack adjacent to an engine attachment lug, can be repaired by re-welding the ring and extending a gusset or a mounting lug past the damaged area. Engine mount rings which are extensively damaged must not be repaired, unless the method of repair is specifically approved by an authorized representative of the Federal Aviation Administration, or is accomplished using instructions furnished by the aircraft manufacturer.

Repair at Built-In Fuselage Fittings

An example of a recommended repair at built-in fuselage fittings is illustrated in figure 6-38. There are several acceptable methods for effecting this type of repair. The method illustrated in figure 6-38 utilizes a tube (sleeve) of larger diameter than the original. This necessitates reaming the fitting holes in the longeron to a larger diameter. The forward splice is a 30 degrees scarf splice. The rear longeron is cut approximately 4 in. from the center line of the joint, and a spacer 1 in. long is fitted over the longeron. The spacer and longeron are edgewelded. A tapered "V" cut approximately 2 in. long is made in the aft end of the outer sleeve, and the end of the outer sleeve is swaged to fit the longeron and then welded.

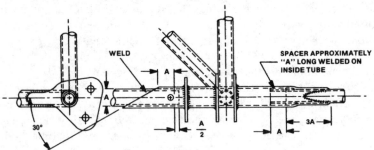

Figure 6-38. Repair at built-in fuselage fitting.

Landing Gear Repair

Landing gear made of round tubing is generally repaired using repairs and splices illustrated in figures 6-35 and 6-38.

Representative types of repairable and nonrepairable landing gear axle assemblies are shown in figure 6-39. The type shown in A of this figure are formed from steel tubing and may be repaired by any of the methods described in this section. However, it will always be necessary to ascertain whether or not the members are heat treated. Assemblies originally heat treated must be re-heat treated after welding.

The axle assembly shown in B of figure 6-39 is, in general, of a nonrepairable type for the following reasons:

(1) The axle stub is usually made from a highly heat treated nickel alloy steel and carefully machined to close tolerances. These stubs are usually replaced when damaged.

(2) The oelo portion of the structure is generally heat treated after welding and is perfectly machined to assure proper functioning of the shock absorber. These parts would be distorted by welding after the machining process.

A spring-steel leaf, shown in C of figure 6-39, supports each main landing gear wheel assembly on many light aircraft. These springs are, in general, nonrepairable and should be replaced when they become excessively sprung or are otherwise damaged.

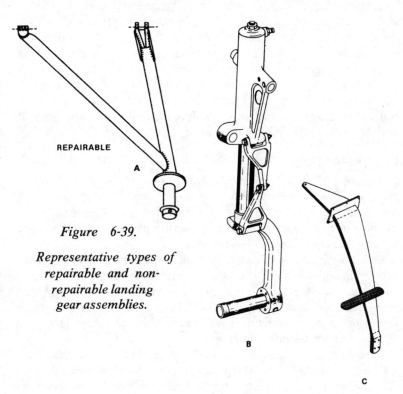

REPAIRABLE

A

Figure 6-39.

Representative types of repairable and non-repairable landing gear assemblies.

B

C

NON-REPAIRABLE

Chapter 7

Fluid Lines
and Fittings

The term "aircraft plumbing" refers not only to the hose, tubing, fittings, and connectors used in the aircraft, but also to the processes of forming and installing them.

Occasionally it may be necessary to repair or replace damaged aircraft plumbing lines. Very often the repair can be made simply by replacing the tubing. However, if replacements are not available, the needed parts may have to be fabricated. Replacement tubing should be of the same size and material as the original line. All tubing is pressure tested prior to initial installation, and is designed to withstand several times the normal operating pressure to which it will be subjected. If a tube bursts or cracks, it is generally the result of excessive vibration, improper installation, or damage caused by collision with an object. All tubing failures should be carefully studied and the cause of the failure determined.

PLUMBING LINES

Aircraft plumbing lines usually are made of metal tubing and fittings or of flexible hose. Metal tubing is widely used in aircraft for fuel, oil, coolant, oxygen, instrument, and hydraulic lines. Flexible hose is generally used with moving parts or where the hose is subject to considerable vibration.

Generally, aluminum alloy or corrosion-resistant steel tubing have replaced copper tubing. The high fatigue factor of copper tubing is the chief reason for its replacement. It becomes hard and brittle from vibration and finally breaks. The workability, resistance to corrosion, and lightweight of aluminum alloy are major factors in its adoption for aircraft plumbing.

In some special high-pressure (3,000 p.s.i.) hydraulic installations, corrosion-resistant steel tubing, either annealed or ¼-hard, is used. Corrosion-resistant steel tubing does not have to be annealed for flaring or forming; in fact, the flared section is somewhat strengthened by the cold working and strain hardening during the flaring process. Its higher tensile strength permits the use of tubing with thinner walls; consequently, the final installation weight is not much greater than that of the thicker-wall aluminum alloy tubing.

Identification of Materials

Before making repairs to any aircraft plumbing, it is important to make accurate identification of plumbing materials. Aluminum alloy or steel tubing can be identified readily by sight where it is used as the basic plumbing material. However, it is difficult to determine whether a material is carbon steel or stainless steel, or whether it is 1100, 3003, 5052-O, or 2024-T aluminum alloy.

It may be necessary to test samples of the material for hardness by filing or scratching with a scriber. The magnet test is the simplest method for distinguishing between the annealed austenitic types the ferritic stainless steels. The austenitic types are nonmagnetic unless heavily cold worked, whereas the straight chromium carbon and low alloy steels are strongly magnetic. Figure 7-1 gives the methods for identifying five common metallic materials by using the magnet and concentrated nitric acid tests.

Material	Magnet test	Nitric acid test
Carbon steel_ _	Strongly magnetic.	Slow chemical action, brown.
18-8_ _ _ _ _ _ _ _	Nonmagnetic.	No action.
Pure nickel_ _ _ _	Strongly magnetic.	Slow action, pale green.
Monel_ _ _ _ _ _ _ _	Slightly magnetic.	Rapid action, greenish blue.
Nickel steel_ _ _	Nonmagnetic.	Rapid action, greenish blue.

Figure 7-1. Various tests used to identify metallic materials.

By comparing code markings of the replacement tubing with the original markings on the tubing being replaced, it is possible to identify definitely the material used in the original installation.

The alloy designation is stamped on the surface of large aluminum alloy tubing. On small aluminum alloy tubing, the designation may be stamped on the surface, but more often it is shown by a color code. Bands of the color code, not more than 4 inches in width, are painted at the two ends and approximately midway between the ends of some tubing. When the band consists of two colors, one-half the width is used for each color.

199

Painted color codes used to identify aluminum alloy tubing are:

Aluminum alloy number	Color of band
1100	White
3003	Green
2014	Gray
2024	Red
5052	Purple
6053	Black
6061	Blue and Yellow
7075	Brown and Yellow

Aluminum alloy tubing, 1100 (½-hard) or 3003 (½-hard), is use for general purpose lines of low or negligible fluid pressures, such as instrument lines and ventilating conduits. The 2024-T and 5052-O aluminum alloy materials are used in general purpose systems of low and medium pressures, such as hydraulic and pneumatic 1,000 to 1,500 p.s.i. systems and fuel and oil lines. Occasionally, these materials are used in high pressure (3,000 p.s.i.) systems.

Tubing made from 2024-T and 5052-O materials will withstand a fairly high pressure before bursting. These materials are easily flared and are soft enough to be formed with handtools. They must be handled with care to prevent scratches, dents, and nicks.

Corrosion-resistant steel tubing, annealed ¼-hard, is used extensively in high-pressure hydraulic systems for the operation of landing gear, flaps, brakes, and the like. External brake lines should always be made of corrosion-resistant steel to minimize damage from rocks thrown by the tires during takeoff and landing, and from careless ground handling. Although identification markings for steel tubing differ, each usually includes the manufacturer's name or trademark, the SAE number, and the physical condition of the metal.

Metal tubing is sized by outside diameter, which is measured fractionally in sixteenths of an inch. Thus, Number 6 tubing is 6/16 (or ⅜ inch) and Number 8 tubing is 8/16 (or ½ inch), etc.

In addition to other classifications or means of identification, tubing is manufactured in various wall thicknesses. Thus, it is important when installing tubing to know not only the material and outside diameter, but also the thickness of the wall.

FLEXIBLE HOSE

Flexible hose is used in aircraft plumbing to connect moving parts with stationary parts in locations subject to vibration or where a great amount of flexibility is needed. It can also serve as a connector in metal tubing systems.

Synthetics

Synthetic materials most commonly used in the manufacture of flexible hose are: Buna-N, Neoprene, Butyl and Teflon (trademark of DuPont Corp.). **Buna-N** is a synthetic rubber compound which has excellent resistance to petroleum products. Do not confuse with Buna-S. Do not use for phosphate ester base hydraulic fluid (Skyrol®). **Neoprene** is a synthetic rubber compound which has an acetylene base. Its resistance to petroleum products is not as good as Buna-N but has better abrasive resistance. Do not use for phosphate ester base hydraulic fluid (Skydrol®). **Butyl** is a synthetic rubber compound made from petroleum raw materials. It is an excellent material to use with phosphate ester based hydraulic fluid (Skydrol®). Do not use with petroleum products. **Teflon** is the Du-Pont trade name for tetrafluoroethylene resin. It has a broad operating temperature range (-65 degrees F. to $+450$ degrees F.). It is compatible with nearly every substance or agent used. It offers little resistance to flow; sticky viscous materials will not adhere to it. It has less volumetric expansion than rubber and the shelf and service life is practically limitless.

Rubber Hose

Flexible rubber hose consists of a seamless synthetic rubber inner tube covered with layers of cotton braid and wire braid, and an outer layer of rubber-impregnated cotton braid. This type of hose is suitable for use in fuel, oil, coolant, and hydraulic systems. The types of hose are normally classified by the amount of pressure they are designed to withstand under normal operating conditions.

1. Low pressure, any pressure below 250 p.s.i. Fabric braid reinforcement.
2. Medium pressure, pressures up to 3,000 p.s.i.
   One wire braid reinforcement.
   Smaller sizes carry pressure up to 3,000 p.s.i.
   Larger sizes carry pressure up to 1,500 p.s.i.
3. High pressure (all sizes up to 3,000 p.s.i. operating pressures).

Identification markings consisting of lines, letters, and numbers are printed on the hose. (See figure 7-2.) These code markings show such information as hose size, manufacturer, date of manufacture, and pressure and temperature limits. Code markings assist in replacing a hose with one of the same specification or a recommended substitute. Hose suitable for use with phosphate ester base hydraulic fluid will be marked "Skydrol® use". In some instances several types of hose may be suitable for the same use. Therefore, in order to make the correct hose selection, always refer to the maintenance or parts manual for the particular airplane.

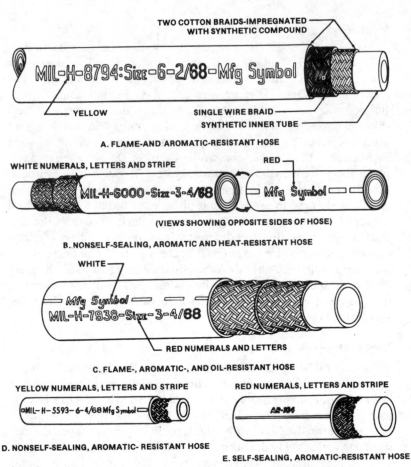

Figure 7-2. Hose identification markings.

Teflon Hose

Teflon hose is a flexible hose designed to meet the requirements of higher operating temperatures and pressures in present aircraft systems. It can generally be used in the same manner as rubber hose. Teflon hose is processed and extruded into tube shape to a desired size. It is covered with stainless steel wire, which is braided over the tube for strength and protection.

Teflon hose is unaffected by any known fuel, petroleum, or synthetic base oils, alcohol, coolants, or solvents commonly used in aircraft. Although it is highly resistant to vibration and fatigue, the principle advantage of this hose is its operating strength.

Size Designation

The size of flexible hose is determined by its inside diameter. Sizes are in one-sixteenth-inch increments and are identical to corresponding sizes of rigid tubing, with which it can be used.

Identification of Fluid Lines

Fluid lines in aircraft are often identified by markers made up of color codes, words, and geometric symbols. These markers identify each line's function, content, and primary hazard, as well as the direction of fluid flow. Figure 7-3 illustrates the various color codes and symbols used to designate the type of system and its contents.

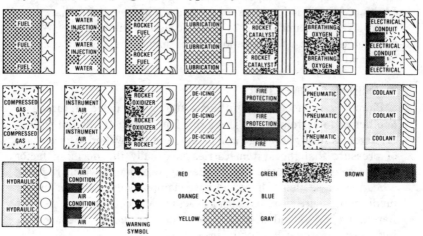

Figure 7-3. Identification of aircraft fluid lines.

In most instances, fluid lines are marked with 1-inch tape or decals, as shown in figure 7-4 (A). On lines 4 inches in diameter (or larger), lines in oily environment, hot lines, and on some cold lines, steel tags may be used in place of tape or decals, as shown in figure 7-4 (B). Paint is used on lines in engine compartments, where there is the possibility of tapes, decals, or tags being drawn into the engine induction system.

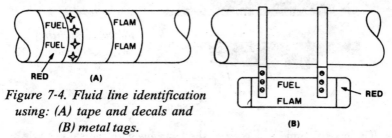

Figure 7-4. Fluid line identification using: (A) tape and decals and (B) metal tags.

In addition to the above-mentioned markings, certain lines may be further identified as to specific function within a system; for example, DRAIN, VENT, PRESSURE, or RETURN.

Lines conveying fuel may be marked FLAM; lines containing toxic materials are marked TOXIC in place of FLAM. Lines containing physically dangerous materials, such as oxygen, nitrogen, or freon, are marked PHDAN.

The aircraft and engine manufacturers are responsible for the original installation of identification markers, but the aviation mechanic is responsible for their replacement when it becomes necessary.

Generally, tapes and decals are placed on both ends of a line and at least once in each compartment through which the line runs. In addition, identification markers are placed immediately adjacent to each valve, regulator, filter, or other accessory within a line. Where paint or tags are used, location requirements are the same as for tapes and decals.

PLUMBING CONNECTORS

Plumbing connectors, or fittings, attach one piece of tubing to another or to system units. There are four types: (1) Flared fitting, (2) flareless fitting, (3) bead and clamp, and (4) swaged. The amount of pressure that the system carries is usually the deciding factor in selecting a connector. The beaded type of joint, which requires a bead and a section of hose and hose clamps, is used only in low- or medium-pressure systems, such as vacuum and coolant systems. The flared, flareless, and swaged types may be used as connectors in all systems, regardless of the pressure.

Flared-Tube Fittings

A flared-tube fitting consists of a sleeve and a nut, as shown in figure 7-5. The nut fits over the sleeve and, when tightened, draws the sleeve and tubing flare tightly against a male fitting to form a seal. Tubing used with this type of fitting must be flared before installation.

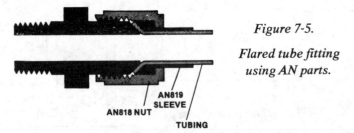

Figure 7-5.

Flared tube fitting using AN parts.

AN819 SLEEVE

AN818 NUT

TUBING

The male fitting has a cone-shaped surface with the same angle as the inside of the flare. The sleeve supports the tube so that vibration does not concentrate at the edge of the flare, and distributes the shearing action over a wider area for added strength. Tube flaring and the installation of flared-tube fittings are discussed in detail later in this chapter.

The AC (Air Corps) flared-tube fittings have been replaced by the AN (Army/Navy) Standard and MS (Military Standard) fittings. However, since AC fittings are still in use in some of the older aircraft, it is important to be able to identify them. The AN fitting has a shoulder between the end of the threads and the flare cone. (See figure 7-6.) The AC fitting does not have this shoulder.

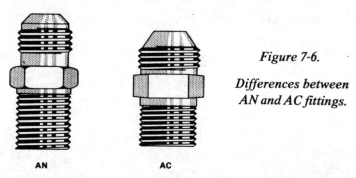

Figure 7-6.

Differences between AN and AC fittings.

AN   AC

Other differences between the AC and AN fittings include the sleeve design, the AC sleeve being noticeably longer than the AN sleeve of the same size. Although certain flared-tube fittings are interchangeable, the pitch of the threads is different in most cases.

The AN standard fitting is the most commonly used flared-tubing assembly for attaching the tubing to the various fittings required in aircraft plumbing systems. The AN standard fittings include the AN818 nut and AN819 sleeve. (See figure 7-5, 7-7 and Appendix I). The AN819 sleeve is used with the AN818 coupling nut. All these fittings have straight threads, but they have different pitch for the various types.

Flared-tube fittings are made of aluminum alloy, steel, or copper base alloys. For identification purposes, all AN steel fittings are colored black, and all AN aluminum alloy fittings are colored blue. The AN 819 aluminum bronze sleeves are cadmium plated and are not colored. The size of these fittings is given in dash numbers, which equal the nominal tube outside diameter (O.D.) in sixteenths of an inch.

Threaded flared-tube fittings have two types of ends, referred to as male and female. The male end of a fitting is externally threaded, whereas the female end of a fitting is internally threaded.

Flareless-tube Fittings

The MS (Military Standard) flareless-tube fittings are finding wide application in aircraft plumbing systems. Using this type fitting eliminates all tube flaring, yet provides a safe, strong, dependable tube connection. The fitting consists of three parts: a body, a sleeve, and a nut. The body has a counterbored shoulder, against which the end of the tube rests. (See figure 7-8.) The angle of the counterbore causes the cutting edge of the sleeve to cut into the outside of the tube when the two are joined. Installation of flareless-tube fittings is discussed later in this chapter.

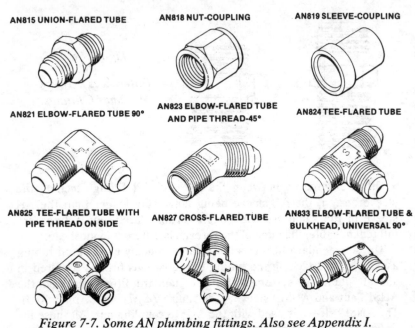

Figure 7-7. Some AN plumbing fittings. Also see Appendix I.

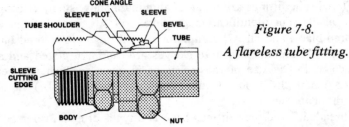

Figure 7-8.
A flareless tube fitting.

Quick-disconnect Couplings

Quick-disconnect couplings of the self-sealing type are used at various points in many fluid systems. The couplings are installed at locations where frequent uncoupling of the lines is required for inspection and maintenance.

Quick-disconnect couplings provide a means of quickly disconnecting a line without loss of fluid or entrance of air into the system. Each coupling assembly consists of two halves, held together by a union nut. Each half contains a valve that is held open when the coupling is connected, allowing fluid to flow through the coupling in either direction. When the coupling is disconnected, a spring in each half closes the valve, preventing the loss of fluid and entrance of air.

The union nut has a quick-lead thread which permits connecting or disconnecting the coupling by turning the nut. The amount the nut must be turned varies with different style couplings. One style requires a quarter turn of the union nut to lock or unlock the coupling while another style requires a full turn.

Some couplings require wrench tightening; others are connected and disconnected by hand. The design of some couplings is such that they must be safetied with safety wire. Others do not require lock wiring, the positive locking being assured by the teeth on the locking spring, which engage ratchet teeth on the union nut when the coupling is fully engaged. The lock spring automatically disengages when the union nut is unscrewed. Because of individual differences, all quick disconnects should be installed according to instructions in the aircraft maintenance manual.

Flexible Connectors

Flexible connectors may be equipped with either swaged fittings or detachable fittings, or they may be used with beads and hose clamps. Those equipped with swaged fittings are ordered by correct length from the manufacturer and ordinarily cannot be assembled by the mechanic. They are swaged and tested at the factory and are equipped with standard fittings.

The fittings on detachable connectors can be detached and reused if they are not damaged; otherwise new fittings must be used.

The bead and hose clamp connector is often used for connecting oil, coolant, and low-pressure fuel system tubing. The bead, a slightly raised ridge around the tubing or the fitting, gives a good gripping edge that aids in holding the clamp and hose in place. The bead may appear near the end of the metal tubing or on one end of a fitting.

TUBE FORMING PROCESSES

Damaged tubing and fluid lines should be replaced with new parts whenever possible. Sometimes replacement is impractical and repair is necessary. Scratches, abrasions, and minor corrosion on the outside of fluid lines may be considered negligible and can be smoothed out with a burnishing tool or aluminum wool. Limitations on the amount of damage that can be repaired in this manner are discussed later in this chapter under "Repair of Metal Tube Lines." If a fluid line assembly is to be replaced, the fittings can often be salvaged; then the repair will involve only tube forming and replacement.

Tube forming consists of four processes: (1) Cutting, (2) bending, (3) flaring, and (4) beading. If the tubing is small and of soft material, the assembly can be formed by hand bending during installation. If the tubing is ¼-inch diameter, or larger, hand bending without the aid of tools is impractical.

Tube-Cutting

When cutting tubing, it is important to produce a square end, free of burrs. Tubing may be cut with a tube cutter or a hacksaw. The cutter can be used with any soft metal tubing, such as copper, aluminum, or aluminum alloy. Correct use of the tube cutter is shown in figure 7-9.

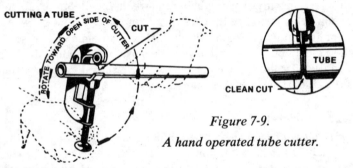

Figure 7-9.
A hand operated tube cutter.

A new piece of tubing should be cut approximately 10 percent longer than the tube to be replaced, to provide for minor variations in bending. Place the tubing in the cutting tool, with the cutting wheel at the point where the cut is to be made. Rotate the cutter around the tubing, applying a light pressure to the cutting wheel by intermittently twisting the thumbscrew. Too much pressure on the cutting wheel at one time could deform the tubing or cause excessive burring. After cutting the tubing, carefully remove any burrs from inside and outside the tube. Use a knife or the burring edge attached to the tube cutter.

When performing the deburring operation use extreme care that the wall thickness of the end of the tubing is not reduced or fractured. Very slight damage of this type can lead to fractured flares or defective flares which will not seal properly. A fine tooth file can be used to file the end square and smooth.

If a tube cutter is not available, or if tubing of hard material is to be cut, use a fine-tooth hacksaw, preferably one having 32 teeth per inch. After sawing, file the end of the tube square and smooth, removing all burrs.

An easy way to hold small-diameter tubing, when cutting it, is to place the tube in a combination flaring tool and clamp the tool in a vise. Make the cut about one-half inch from the flaring tool. This procedure keeps sawing vibrations to a minimum and prevents damage to the tubing if it is accidentally hit with the hacksaw frame or file handle while cutting. Be sure all filings and cuttings are removed from the tube.

Tube Bending

The objective in tube bending is to obtain a smooth bend without flattening the tube. Tubing under one-fourth inch in diameter usually can be bent without the use of a bending tool. For larger sizes, a hand tube bender similar to that shown in figure 7-10 is usually used.

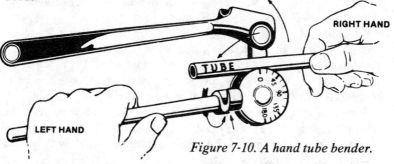

Figure 7-10. A hand tube bender.

To bend tubing with the hand tube bender, insert the tubing by raising the slide bar handle as far as it will go. Adjust the handle so that the full length of the groove in the slide bar is in contact with the tubing. The zero mark on the radius block and the mark on the slide bar must align. Make the bend by rotating the handle until the desired angle of bend is obtained, as indicated on the radius block.

Bend the tubing carefully to avoid excessive flattening, kinking, or wrinkling. A small amount of flattening in bends is acceptable, but the small diameter of the flattened portion must not be less than 75 percent of the original outside diameter. Tubing with flattened, wrinkled or irregular bends should not be installed. Wrinkled bends usually result from trying to bend thin-wall tubing without using a tube bender. Examples of correct and incorrect tubing bends are shown in figure 7-11.

Tube bending machines for all types of tubing are generally used in repair stations and large maintenance shops. With such equipment, proper bends can be made on large diameter tubing and on tubing made from hard material. The production tube bender is an example of this type of machine.

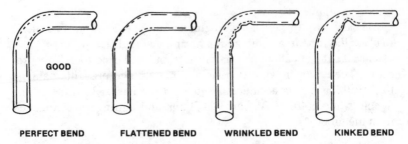

PERFECT BEND	**FLATTENED BEND**	**WRINKLED BEND**	**KINKED BEND**

Figure 7-11. Correct and incorrect tubing bends.

The ordinary production tube bender will accommodate tubing ranging from ½-inch to 1½-inch outside diameter. Benders for larger sizes are available, and the principle of their operation is similar to that of the hand tube bender. The radius blocks are so constructed that the radius of bend will vary with the tubing diameter. The radius of bend is usually stamped on the block.

When hand or production tube benders are not available or are not suitable for a particular bending operation, a filler of metallic composition or of dry sand may be used to facilitate bending. When using this method, cut the tube slightly longer than is required. The extra length is for inserting a plug (which may be wooden) in each end.

After plugging one end, fill and pack the tube with fine, dry sand and plug tightly. Both plugs must be tight so they will not be forced out when the bend is made. The tube can also be closed by flattening the ends or by soldering metal disks in them. After the ends are closed, bend the tubing over a forming block shaped to the specified radius.

In a modified version of the filler method, a fusible alloy is used instead of sand. In this method, the tube is filled under hot water with a fusible alloy that melts at 160 degrees F. The alloy-filled tubing is then removed from the water, allowed to cool, and bend slowly by hand around a forming block or with a tube bender. After the bend is made, the alloy is again melted under hot water and removed from the tubing.

When using either filler method, make certain that all particles of the filler are removed so that none will be carried into the system in which the tubing is installed. Store the fusible alloy filler where it will be free from dust or dirt. It can be re-melted and re-used as often as desired. Never heat this filler in any other than the prescribed method, as the alloy will stick to the inside of the tubing, making them both unusable.

Tube Flaring

Two kinds of flares are generally used in aircraft plumbing systems, the single flare and the double flare. Flares are frequently subjected to extremely high pressures; therefore, the flare on the tubing must be properly shaped or the connection will leak or fail.

A flare made too small produces a weak joint, which may leak or pull apart; if made too large it interferes with the proper engagement of the screw thread on the fittings and will cause leakage. A crooked flare is the result of the tubing not being cut squarely. If a flare is not made properly, flaws cannot be corrected by applying additional torque when tightening the fitting. The flare and tubing must be free from cracks, dents, nicks, scratches, or any other defects.

The flaring tool used for aircraft tubing has male and female dies ground to produce a flare of 35 degrees to 37 degrees. Under no circumstances is it permissible to use an automotive type flaring tool which produces a flare of 45 degrees.

Single Flare

A hand flaring tool similar to that shown in figure 7-12 is used for flaring tubing. The tool consists of a flaring block or grip die, a yoke, and a flaring pin. The flaring block is a hinged double bar with holes corresponding to various sizes of tubing. These holes are countersunk on one end to form the outside support against which the flare is formed. The yoke is used to center the flaring pin over the end of the tube to be flared.

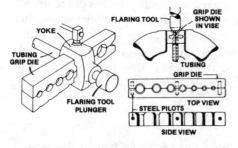

Figure 7-12.

A hand tool for flaring tubing (single flare).

To prepare a tube for flaring, cut the tube squarely and remove all burrs. Slip the fitting nut and sleeve on the tube and place the tube in the proper size hole in the flaring tool. Center the plunger or flaring pin over the end of the tube. Then project the end of the tubing slightly from the top of the flaring tool, about the thickness of a dime, and tighten the clamp bar securely to prevent slippage.

Make the flare by striking the plunger several light blows with a lightweight hammer or mallet. Turn the plunger a half turn after each blow and be sure it seats properly before removing the tube from the flaring tool. Check the flare by sliding the sleeve into position over the flare. The outside diameter of the flare should extend approximately one-sixteenth inch beyond the end of the sleeve, but should not be larger than the major outside diameter of the sleeve.

Double Flare

A double flare should be used on 5052-O and 6061-T aluminum alloy tubing for all sizes from ⅛- to ⅜-inch outside diameter. This is necessary to prevent cutting off the flare and failure of the tube assembly under operating pressures. Double flaring is not necessary on steel tubing. See figure 7-13 for an illustration of single- and double-flared tubing. The double flare is smoother and more concentric than the single flare and, therefore, seals better. It is also more resistant to the shearing effect of torque.

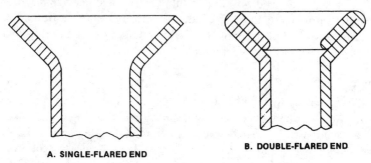

A. SINGLE-FLARED END   B. DOUBLE-FLARED END

Figure 7-13. Cross-sectional views of single and double flared tube ends.

To make the double flare, separate the clamp blocks of the double-flaring tool and insert and clamp the tubing with the burred end flush with the top of the clamp. Insert the starting pin into the flaring pin guide and strike the pin sharply with a hammer until the shoulder of the pin stops against the clamp blocks. Remove the starting pin and insert the finishing pin; hammer it until its shoulder rests on the clamp block.

Beading

Tubing may be beaded with a hand-beading tool, with machine-beading rolls, or with grip dies. The method to be used depends on the diameter and wall thickness of the tube and the material from which it was made.

The hand-beading tool is used with tubing having ¼- to 1-inch outside diameter. The bead is formed by using the beader frame with the proper rollers attached. The inside and outside of the tube is lubricated with light oil to reduce the friction between the rollers during beading. The sizes, marked in sixteenths of an inch on the rollers, are for the outside diameter of the tubing that can be beaded with the rollers.

Separate rollers are required for the inside of each tubing size, and care must be taken to use the correct parts when beading. The hand-beading tool works somewhat like the tube cutter in that the roller is screwed down intermittently while rotating the beading tool around the tubing. In addition, a small vise (tube holder) is furnished with the kit.

Other methods and types of beading tools and machines are available, but the hand-beading tool is used most often. As a rule, beading machines are limited to use with large-diameter tubing, over 1 15/16 inch, unless special rollers are supplied. The grip-die method of beading is confined to small tubing.

Flareless-Tube Assemblies

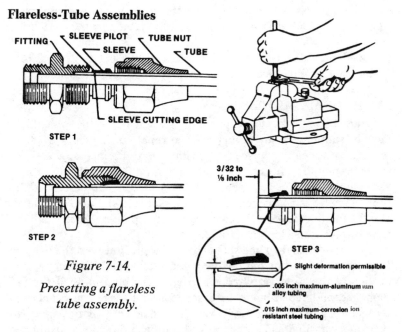

Figure 7-14.

Presetting a flareless tube assembly.

Although the use of flareless-tube fittings eliminates all tube flaring, another operation, referred to as presetting, is necessary prior to installation of a new flareless-tube assembly. Figure 7-14 (steps 1, 2, and 3) illustrates the presetting operation, which is performed as follows:

(a.) Cut the tube to the correct length, with the ends perfectly square. Deburr the inside and outside of the tube. Slip the nut, then the sleeve, over the tube (step 1).

(b.) Lubricate the threads of the fitting and nut with hydraulic fluid. Place the fitting in a vise (step 2), and hold the tubing firmly and squarely on the seat in the fitting. (Tube must bottom firmly in the fitting.) Tighten the nut until the cutting edge of the sleeve grips the tube. This point is determined by slowly turning the tube back and forth while tightening the nut. When the tube no longer turns, the nut is ready for final tightening.

(c.) Final tightening depends upon the tubing. For aluminum alloy tubing up to and including ½-inch outside diameter, tighten the nut from one to one and one-sixth turns. For steel tubing and aluminum alloy tubing over ½-inch outside diameter, tighten from one and one-sixth to one and one-half turns.

After presetting the sleeve, disconnect the tubing from the fitting and check the following points (illustrated in step 3):

(a.) The tube should extend 3/32 to ⅛ inch beyond the sleeve pilot; otherwise blowoff may occur.

(b.) The sleeve pilot should contact the tube or have a maximum clearance of 0.005 inch for aluminum alloy tubing or 0.015 inch for steel tubing.

(c.) A slight collaspe of the tube at the sleeve cut is permissible. No movement of the sleeve pilot, except rotation, is permissible.

REPAIR OF METAL TUBE LINES

Scratches or nicks no deeper than 10 percent of the wall thickness in aluminum alloy tubing may be repaired, if they are not in the heel of a bend. Replace lines with severe die marks, seams, or splits in the tube. Any crack or deformity in a flare is also unacceptable and is cause for rejection. A dent of less than 20 percent of the tube diameter is not objectionable, unless it is in the heel of a bend. Dents can be removed by drawing a bullet of proper size through the tube by means of a length of cable.

A severely damaged line should be replaced. However, the line can be repaired by cutting out the damaged section and inserting a tube section of the same size and material. Flare both ends of the undamaged and replacement tube sections and make the connection by using standard unions, sleeves, and tube nuts. If the damaged portion is short enough, omit the insert tube and repair by using one union and two sets of connecting fittings.

When repairing a damaged line, be very careful to remove all chips and burrs. Any open line that is to be left unattended for some time should be sealed, using metal, wood, rubber, or plastic plugs or caps.

When repairing a low-pressure line using a flexible fluid connection assembly, position the hose clamps carefully in order to prevent overhang of the clamp bands or chafing of the tightening screws on adjacent parts. If chafing can occur, the hose clamps should be repositioned on the hose. Figure 7-15 illustrates the design of a flexible fluid connection assembly and gives the maximum allowable angular and dimensional offset.

Layout of Lines

Remove the damaged or worn assembly, taking care not to further damage or distort it, and use it as a forming template for the new part. If the old length of tubing cannot be used as a pattern, make a wire template, bending the pattern by hand as required for the new assembly. Then bend the tubing to match the wire pattern.

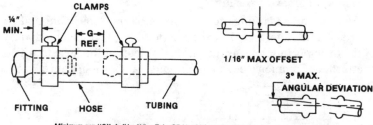

Minimum gap "G" shall be ½" or Tube OD/4, whichever is greater.
Maximum gap "G" is not limited except on suction lines using other than self-sealing hose. On such suction lines, maximum G shall be 1-½ inch or one tube diameter, whichever is greater.

Figure 7-15. Flexible fluid connection assembly for low pressure lines.

Never select a path that does not require bends in the tubing. A tube cannot be cut or flared accurately enough so that it can be installed without bending and still be free from mechanical strain. Bends are also necessary to permit the tubing to expand or contract under temperature changes and to absorb vibration. If the tube is small (under one-fourth inch) and can be hand formed, casual bends may be made to allow for this. If the tube must be machine formed, definite bends must be made to avoid a straight assembly.

Start all bends a reasonable distance from the fittings, because the sleeves and nuts must be slipped back during the fabrication of flares and during inspections. In all cases the new tube assembly should be so formed prior to installation that it will not be necessary to pull or deflect the assembly into alignment by means of the coupling nuts.

FABRICATION AND REPLACEMENT OF FLEXIBLE HOSE

Hose and hose assemblies should be checked for deterioration at each inspection period. Leakage, separation of the cover or braid from the inner tube, cracks, hardening, lack of flexibility, and excessive "cold flow" are apparent signs of deterioration and reason for replacement. The term "cold flow" describes the deep, permanent impressions in the hose produced by the pressure of hose clamps or supports.

When failure occurs in a flexible hose equipped with swaged end fittings, the entire assembly must be replaced. Obtain a new hose assembly of the correct size and length, complete with factory installed end fittings.

When failure occurs in hose equipped with reusable end fittings, a replacement line can be fabricated with the use of such tooling as may be necessary to comply with the assembly instructions of the manufacturer.

Assembly of Sleeve-Type Fittings

Sleeve-type end fittings for flexible hose are detachable and may be reused if determined to be serviceable. The inside diameter of the fitting is the same as the inside diameter of the hose to which it is attached. Common sleeve-type fittings are shown in figure 7-16.

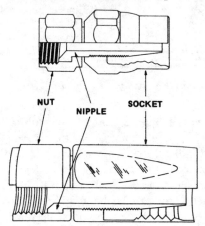

NUT **NIPPLE** **SOCKET**

Figure 7-16.

A sleeve type end fitting for flexible hose.

To make a hose assembly, select the proper size hose and end fittings. Cut the hose to the correct length using a fine-tooth hacksaw. Place the socket in a vise. Screw the hose into the socket counterclockwise until the hose bottoms on the shoulder of the socket (figure 7-17); then back off one-quarter turn. Lubricate inside of hose and nipple threads liberally. Mark the hose position around the hose at the rear of the socket using a grease pencil or painted line. Insert the nipple into the nut and tighten the nipple and nut on the assembly tool. If an assembly tool is not available, a mating AN815 adapter may be used. Using a wrench on the assembly tool, screw the nipple into the socket and hose. A 1/32- to 1/16-inch clearance between the nut and sleeve is required so that the nut will swivel freely when the assembly tool is removed. After assembly, always make sure all foreign matter is removed from inside the hose by blowing out with compressed air.

Proof-test After Assembly

All flexible hose must be proof-tested after assembly by plugging or capping one end of the hose and applying pressure to the inside of the hose assembly. The proof-test medium may be a liquid or a gas. For example, hydraulic, fuel, and oil lines are generally tested using hydraulic oil or water, whereas air or instrument lines are tested with dry, oil-free air or nitrogen. When testing with a liquid, all trapped air is bled from the assembly prior to tightening the cap or plug. Hose tests, using a gas, are conducted underwater. In all cases follow the hose manufacturer's instructions for proof-test pressure and fluid to be used when testing a specific hose assembly.

Place the hose assembly in a horizontal position and observe for leakage while maintaining the test pressure. Proof-test pressures should be maintained for at least 30 seconds.

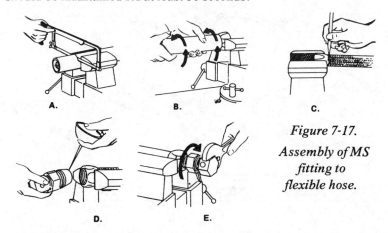

Figure 7-17.

Assembly of MS fitting to flexible hose.

Installation of Flexible Hose Assemblies

Flexible hose must not be twisted on installation, since this reduces the life of the hose considerably and may also loosen the fittings. Twisting of the hose can be determined from the identification stripe running along its length. This stripe should not spiral around the hose.

Flexible hose should be protected from chafing by wrapping it with tape, but only where necessary.

The minimum bend radius for flexible hose varies according to size and construction of the hose and the pressure under which the hose is to operate. Bends that are too sharp will reduce the bursting pressure of flexible hose considerably below its rated value (figure 7-18).

Flexible hose should be installed so that it will be subject to a minimum of flexing during operation. Although hose must be supported at least every 24 inches, closer supports are desirable. A flexible hose must never be stretched tightly between two fittings. From 5 percent to 8 percent of its total length must be allowed for freedom of movement under pressure. When under pressure, flexible hose contracts in length and expands in diameter.

Protect all flexible hose from excessive temperatures, either by locating the lines so they will not be affected or by installing shrouds around them.

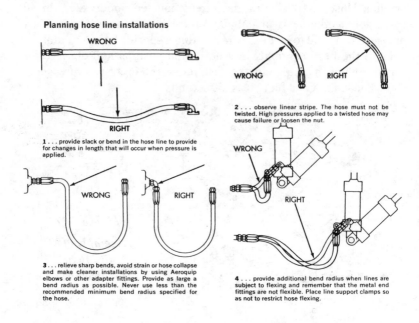

Figure 7-18. Proper (and improper) hose installations.

INSTALLATION OF RIGID TUBING

Before installing a line assembly in an aircraft, inspect the line carefully. Remove dents and scratches, and be sure all nuts and sleeves are snugly mated and securely fitted by proper flaring of the tubing. The line assembly should be clean and free of all foreign matter.

Never apply compound to the faces of the fitting or the flare, for it will destroy the metal-to-metal contact between the fitting and flare, a contact which is necessary to produce the seal. Be sure that the line assembly is properly aligned before tightening the fittings. Do not pull the installation into place with torque on the nut. Correct and incorrect methods of installing flared-tube assemblies are illustrated in figure 7-19. Proper torque values are given in figure 7-20. It must be remembered that these torque values are for flared-type fittings only. Always tighten fittings to the correct torque value when installing a tube assembly. Overtightening a fitting may badly damage or completely cut off the tube flare, or it may ruin the sleeve or fitting nut. Failure to tighten sufficiently also can be serious, as this condition may allow the line to blow out of the assembly or to leak under system pressure.

The use of torque wrenches and the prescribed torque values prevents overtightening or undertightening. If a tube fitting assembly is tightened properly, it can be removed and re-tightened many times before re-flaring is necessary.

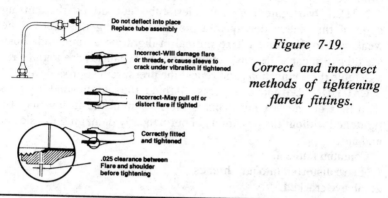

Figure 7-19.

Correct and incorrect methods of tightening flared fittings.

Tubing O.D.	Fitting Bolt or Nut Size	Aluminum Alloy Tubing, Bolt, Fitting or Nut Torque inch–lbs.	Steel Tubing, Bolt Fitting or Nut Torque inch–lbs.	Hose End Fittings and Hose Assemblies MS28740 or Equivalent End Fitting		Minimum bend radii (inches) Alum. alloy 1100-H14 5052-0		
				Minimum	Maximum		Steel
1/8	–2						
3/16	–3	20 – 30				3/8	
1/4	–4	30 – 40	90 – 100	70	120	7/16	21/32
5/16	–5	40 – 65	135 – 150	100	250	9/16	7/8
3/8	–6	60 – 85	180 – 200	210	420	3/4	1 1/8
1/2	–8	75 – 125	270 – 300	300	480	15/16	1 5/16
5/8	–10	150 – 250	450 – 500	500	850	1 1/4	1 3/4
3/4	–12	200 – 350	650 – 700	700	1150	1 1/2	2 3/16
7/8	–14	300 – 500	900 – 1000			1 3/4	2 5/8
1	–16	500 – 600	1000 – 1100				
1–1/4	–20	500 – 700	1200 – 1400			3	3 1/2
1–1/2	–24	600 – 900	1200 – 1400			3 3/4	4 3/8
1–3/4	–28	600 – 900	1500 – 1800			5	5 1/4
2	–32	850 – 1050				7	6 1/8
		950 – 1150				8	7

Figure 7-20. Torque values for tightening flared tube fittings.

Flareless Tube Installation

Tighten the nut by hand until an increase in resistance to turning is encountered. Should it be impossible to run the nut down with the fingers, use a wrench, but be alert for the first signs of bottoming. It is important that the final tightening commence at the point where the nut just begins to bottom.

With a wrench, turn the nut 1/6 turn (one flat on a hex nut). Use a wrench on the connector to prevent it from turning while tightening the nut. After the tube assembly is installed, the system should be pressure tested. Should a connection leak, it is permissible to tighten the nut an additional 1/6 turn (making a total of ⅓ turn). If, after tightening the nut a total of ⅓ turn, leakage still exists, the assembly should be removed and the components of the assembly inspected for scores, cracks, presence of foreign material, or damage from overtightening.

NOTE: Overtightening a flareless-tube nut drives the cutting edge of the sleeve deeply into the tube, causing the tube to be weakened to the point where normal in-flight vibration could cause the tube to shear. After inspection (if no discrepancies are found), re-assemble the connections and repeat the pressure test procedures.

CAUTION: Do not in any case tighten the nut beyond ⅓ turn (two flats on the hex nut); this is the maximum the fitting may be tightened without the possibility of permanently damaging the sleeve and nut.

Common faults are:

1. Flare distorted into nut threads.
2. Sleeve cracked.
3. Flare cracked or split.
4. Flare out of round.
5. Inside of flare rough or scratched.
6. Fitting cone rough or scratched.
7. Threads of nut or union dirty, damaged or broken.

Some manufacturers service instructions will specify wrench torque values for flareless tubing installations (e.g., see figure 7-21).

PLUMBING ASSEMBLY PRECAUTIONS

Make certain that the material in the fittings used is similar to that of the tubing; for example, use steel fittings with steel tubing and aluminum alloy fittings with aluminum alloy tubing. Brass fittings plated with cadmium may be used with aluminum alloy tubing.

For corrosion prevention, aluminum alloy lines and fittings are usually anodized. Steel lines and fittings, if not stainless steel, are plated to prevent rusting or corroding. Brass and steel fittings are usually cadmium plated, although some may come plated with nickel, chromium, or tin.

To ensure proper sealing of hose connections and to prevent breaking hose clamps or damaging the hose, follow the hose clamp tightening instructions carefully. When available, use the hose clamp torque-limiting wrench. These wrenches are available in calibrations of 15 and 25-inch pounds. In the absence of torque-limiting wrenches, the fingertight-plus-turns method should be followed. Because of the variations in hose clamp design and hose structure, the values

WRENCH TORQUE FOR 304 1/8 H STEEL TUBES

Tube Outside Diameter	Wall Thickness	Wrench Torque Inch—Pounds
3/16	0.016	90 – 110
3/16	0.020	90 – 110
1/4	0.016	110 – 140
1/4	0.020	110 – 140
5/16	0.020	100 – 120
3/8	0.020	170 – 230
3/8	0.028	200 – 250
1/2	0.020	300 – 400
1/2	0.028	400 – 500
1/2	0.035	500 – 600
5/8	0.020	300 – 400
5/8	0.035	600 – 700
5/8	0.042	700 – 850
3/4	0.028	650 – 800
3/4	0.049	800 – 960
1	0.020	800 – 950
1	0.065	1600 – 1750

WRENCH TORQUE FOR 304-1A or 3471A STEEL TUBES

Tube Outside Diameter	Wall Thickness	Wrench Torque Inch—Pounds
3/8	0.042	145 – 175
1/2	0.028	300 – 400
1/2	0.049	500 – 600
1	0.035	750 – 900

WRENCH TORQUE FOR 6061-T6 OR T4 TUBES

Tube Outside Diameter	Wall Thickness	Wrench Torque Inch—Pounds
1/4	0.035	110 – 140
3/8	0.035	145 – 175
1/2	0.035	270 – 330
1/2	0.049	320 – 380
5/8	0.035	360 – 440
5/8	0.049	425 – 525
3/4	0.035	380 – 470
1	0.035	750 – 900
1 1/4	0.035	900 – 1100

Figure 7-21. Torque values for flareless fittings.

given in figure 7-22 are approximate. Therefore, use good judgment when tightening hose clamps by this method. Since hose connections are subject to "cold flow" or a setting process, a followup tightening check should be made for several days after installation.

SUPPORT CLAMPS

Support clamps are used to secure the various lines to the airframe or powerplant assemblies. Several types of support clamps are used for this purpose. The rubber-cushioned and plain are the most commonly used clamps. The rubber-cushioned clamp is used to secure lines subject to vibration; the cushioning prevents chafing of the tubing. The plain clamp is used to secure lines in areas not subject to vibration.

A Teflon-cushioned clamp is used in areas where the deteriorating effect of Skydrol ® 500, hydraulic fluid (MIL-0-5606), or fuel is expected. However, because it is less resilient, it does not provide as good a vibration-damping effect as other cushion materials.

Hose clamp tightening, finger-tight-plus turns method		
Initial installation only	Worm screw type clamp 10 threads per inch	Clamps—radial and other type—28 threads per inch
Self sealing hose approximately 15 inch-pounds	Finger-tight-plus 2 complete turns	Finger-tight-plus 2½ complete turns
All other aircraft hose approximately 25 inch-pounds	Finger-tight Plus 1¼ complete turns	Finger-tight Plus 2 complete turns
Retightening of Hose Clamps If clamps do not seal at specified tightening, examine hose connections and replace parts as necessary The above is for initial installation and should not be used for loose clamps. For re-tightening loose hose clamps in service proceed as follows: 1. Non-self-sealing hose—If the clamp screw cannot be tightened with the fingers do not disturb unless leakage is evident. If leakage is present tighten ¼ turn. 2. Self-sealing hose—If looser than finger-tight, tighten to finger tight and add ¼ turn.		

Figure 7-22.
Hose clamp tightening data.

Use bonded clamps to secure metal hydraulic, fuel, and oil lines in place. Unbonded clamps should be used only for securing wiring. Remove any paint or anodizing from the portion of the tube at the bonding clamp location. Make certain that clamps are of the correct size. Clamps or supporting clips smaller than the outside diameter of the hose may restrict the flow of fluid through the hose.

All plumbing lines must be secured at specified intervals. The maximum distance between supports for rigid fluid tubing is shown in figure 7-23.

Tube OD (in.)	Distance between supports (in.)	
	Aluminum Alloy	Steel
⅛	9½	11½
3/16	12	14
¼	13½	16
5/16	15	18
⅜	16½	20
½	19	23
⅝	22	25½
¾	24	27½
1	26½	30

Figure 7-23. Maximum distance between supports for fluid lines.

Chapter 8
Electrical Wiring and Installation

The satisfactory performance of any modern aircraft depends to a very great degree on the continuing reliability of electrical systems and subsystems. Improperly or carelessly installed wiring or improperly or carelessly maintained wiring can be a source of both immediate and potential danger. The continued proper performance of electrical systems depends on the knowledge and techniques of the mechanic who installs, inspects, and maintains the electrical system wires and cables.

Procedures and practices outlined in this section are general reccommendations and are not intended to replace the manufacturer's instructions and approved practices.

For the purpose of this discussion, a wire is described as a single, solid conductor, or as a stranded conductor covered with an insulating material. Figure 8-1 illustrates these two definitions of a wire.

The term cable, as used in aircraft electrical installations, includes:
(1) Two or more separately insulated conductors in the same jacket (multi-conductor cable).
(2) Two or more separately insulated conductors twisted together (twisted pair).

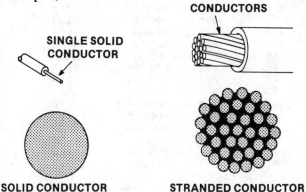

Figure 8-1. Single solid conductor and a conductor consisting of many strands.

		Cross section		Ohms per 1,000 ft.	
Gage number	Diameter (mils)	Circular mils	Square inches	25°C. (=77•F.)	65°C. (=149•F.)
0000	460.0	212,000.0	0.166	0.0500	0.0577
000	410.0	168,000.0	.132	.0630	.0727
00	365.0	133,000.0	.105	.0795	.0917
0	325.0	106,000.0	.0829	.100	.116
1	289.0	83,700.0	.0657	.126	.146
2	258.0	66,400.0	.0521	.159	.184
3	229.0	52,600.0	.0413	.201	.232
4	204.0	41,700.0	.0328	253	.292
5	182.0	33,100.0	.0260	.319	.369
6	162.0	26,300.0	.0206	.403	.465
7	144.0	20,800.0	.0164	.508	.586
8	128.0	16,500.0	.0130	.641	.739
9	114.0	13,100.0	.0103	.808	.932
10	102.0	10,400.0	.00815	1.02	1.18
11	91.0	8,230.0	.00647	1.28	1.48
12	81.0	6,530.0	.00513	1.62	1.87
13	72.0	5,180.0	.00407	2.04	2.36
14	64.0	4,110.0	.00323	2.58	2.97
15	57.0	3,260.0	.00256	3.25	3.75
16	51.0	2,580.0	.00203	4.09	4.73
17	45.0	2,050.0	.00161	5.16	5.96
18	40.0	1,620.0	.00128	6.51	7.51
19	36.0	1,290.0	.00101	8.21	9.48
20	32.0	1,020.0	.000802	10.4	11.9
21	28.5	810.0	.000636	13.1	15.1
22	25.3	642.0	.000505	16.5	19.0
23	22.6	509.0	.000400	20.8	24.0
24	20.1	404.0	.000317	26.2	30.2
25	17.9	320.0	.000252	33.0	38.1
26	15.9	254.0	.000200	41.6	48.0
27	14.2	202.0	.000158	52.5	60.6
28	12.6	160.0	.000126	66.2	76.4
29	11.3	127.0	.0000995	83.4	96.3
30	10.0	101.0	.0000789	105.0	121.0
31	8.9	79.7	.0000626	133.0	153.0
32	8.0	63.2	.0000496	167.0	193.0
33	7.1	50.1	.0000394	211.0	243.0
34	6.3	39.8	.0000312	266.0	307.0
35	5.6	31.5	.0000248	335.0	387.0
36	5.0	25.0	.0000196	423.0	488.0
37	4.5	19.8	.0000156	533.0	616.0
38	4.0	15.7	.0000123	673.0	776.0
39	3.5	12.5	.0000098	848.0	979.0
40	3.1	9.9	.0000078	1,070.0	1,230.0

Figure 8-2. Resistance values for American Wire Gage (AWG) standard annealed copper wire.

(3) One or more insulated conductors, covered with a metallic braided shield (shielded cable).

(4) A single insulated center conductor with a metallic braided outer conductor (radio frequency cable). The concentricity of the center conductor and the outer conductor is carefully controlled during manufacture to ensure that they are coaxial.

Wire Size

Wire is manufactured in sizes according to a standard known as the AWG (American wire gage). As shown in figure 8-2, the wire diameters become smaller as the gage numbers become larger. The largest wire size shown in figure 8-2 is number 0000, and the smallest is number 40. Larger and smaller sizes are manufactured but are not commonly used.

Figure 8-3. An AWG wire gage.

A wire gage is shown in figure 8-3. This type of gage will measure wires ranging in size from number zero to number 36. The wire to be measured is inserted in the smallest slot that will just accommodate the bare wire. The gage number corresponding to that slot indicates the wire size. The slot has parallel sides and should not be confused with the semicircular opening at the end of the slot. The opening simply permits the free movement of the wire all the way through the slot.

Gage numbers are useful in comparing the diameter of wires, but not all types of wire or cable can be accurately measured with a gage. Large wires are usually stranded to increase their flexibility. In such cases, the total area can be determined by multiplying the area of one strand (usually computed in circular mils when diameter or gage number is known) by the number of strands in the wire or cable.

Factors Affecting the Selection of Wire Size

Several factors must be considered in selecting the size of wire for transmitting and distributing electric power.

One factor is the allowable power loss (I^2R loss) in the line. This loss represents electrical energy converted into heat. The use of large conductors will reduce the resistance and therefore the I^2R loss However, large conductors are more expensive initially than small ones; they are heavier and require more substantial supports.

A second factor is the permissible voltage drop (IR drop) in the line. If the source maintains a constant voltage at the input to the lines, any variation in the load on the line will cause a variation in line current and a consequent variation in the IR drop in the line. A wide variation in the IR drop in the line causes poor voltage regulation at the load. The obvious remedy is to reduce either current or resistance. A reduction in load current lowers the amount of power being transmitted, whereas a reduction in line resistance increases the size and weight of conductors required. A compromise is generally reached whereby the voltage variation at the load is within tolerable limits and the weight of line conductors is not excessive.

A third factor is the current-carrying ability of the conductor. When current is drawn through the conductor, heat is generated. The temperature of the wire will rise until the heat radiated, or otherwise dissipated, is equal to the heat generated by the passage of current through the line. If the conductor is insulated, the heat generated in the conductor is not so readily removed as it would be if the conductor were not insulated. Thus, to protect the insulation from too much heat, the current through the conductor must be maintained below a certain value.

When electrical conductors are installed in locations where the ambient temperature is relatively high, the heat generated by external sources constitutes an appreciable part of the total conductor heating. Allowance must be made for the influence of external heating on the allowable conductor current, and each case has its own specific limitations. The maximum allowable operating temperature of insulated conductors varies with the type of conductor insulation being used.

Tables are available that list the safe current ratings for various sizes and types of conductors covered with various types of insulation. Figure 8-4 shows the current-carrying capacity, in amperes, of single copper conductors at an ambient temperature of below 30 degrees C. This example provides measurements for only a limited range of wire sizes.

Factors Affecting Selection of Conductor Material

Although silver is the best conductor, its cost limits its use to special circuits where a substance with high conductivity is needed.

The two most generally used conductors are copper and aluminum. Each has characteristics that make its use advantageous under certain circumstances. Also, each has certain disadvantages.

226

Size	Rubber or thermoplastic	Thermoplastic asbestos, var-cam, or asbestos var-cam	Impregnated asbestos	Asbestos	Slow-burning or weather-proof
0000	300	385	475	510	370
000	260	330	410	430	320
00	225	285	355	370	275
0	195	245	305	325	235
1	165	210	265	280	205
2	140	180	225	240	175
3	120	155	195	210	150
4	105	135	170	180	130
6	80	100	125	135	100
8	55	70	90	100	70
10	40	55	70	75	55
12	25	40	50	55	40
14	20	30	40	45	30

Figure 8-4. Current carrying capacity of wire in amperes for various wire sizes and insulation.

Characteristic	Copper	Aluminum
Tensile strength (lb./in.^{2})	55,000	25,000
Tensile strength for same conductivity (lb.)	55,000	40,000
Weight for same conductivity (lb.)	100	48
Cross section for same conductivity (C. M.)	100	160
Specific resistance (Ω/mil ft.)	10.6	17

Figure 8-5. Characteristics of copper and aluminum wire.

Nominal system voltage	Allowable voltage drop	
	Continuous operation	Intermittent operation
14	0.5	1
28	1	2
115	4	8
200	7	14

Figure 8-6. Recommended maximum voltage drop in load circuits.

Copper has a higher conductivity; it is more ductile (can be drawn), has relatively high tensile strength, and can be easily soldered. It is more expensive and heavier than aluminum.

Although aluminum has only about 60% of the conductivity of copper, it is used extensively. Its lightness makes possible long spans, and its relatively large diameter for a given conductivity reduces corona (the discharge of electricity from the wire when it has a high potential). The discharge is greater when small diameter wire is used than when large diameter wire is used. Some bus bars are made of aluminum instead of copper where there is a greater radiating surface for the same conductance. The characteristics of copper and aluminum are compared in figure 8-5.

Voltage Drop in Aircraft Wire and Cable

It is recommended that the voltage drop in the main power cables from the aircraft generation source or the battery to the bus should not exceed 2% of the regulated voltage when the generator is carrying rated current or the battery is being discharged at a 5-min. rate. The tabulation in table 8-6 shows the recommended maximum voltage drop in the load circuits between the bus and the utilization equipment.

The resistance of the current return path through the aircraft structure is always considered negligible. However, this is based on the assumption that adequate bonding of the structure or a special electric current return path has been provided and is capable of carrying the required electric current with a negligible voltage drop. A resistance measurement of 0.005 ohm from the ground terminal of any electrical device is considered satisfactory. Another satisfactory method of determining circuit resistance is to check the voltage drop across the circuit. If the voltage drop does not exceed the limit established by the aircraft or product manufacturer, the resistance value for the circuit is considered satisfactory. When using the voltage drop method of checking a circuit, the input voltage must be maintained at a constant value.

Instructions For Use of Electric Wire Chart

The chart in figures 8-7 and 8-8 apply to copper conductors carrying direct current. Curves 1, 2, and 3 are plotted to show the maximum ampere rating for the specified conductor under the specified conditions shown. To select the correct size of conductor, two major requirements must be met. First, the size must be sufficient to prevent an excessive voltage drop while carrying the required current over the required distance. Secondly, the size must be sufficient to prevent overheating of the cable while carrying the required current. The charts in figures 8-7 and 8-8 can simplify these determinations. To use these charts to select the proper size of conductor, the following must be known:
(1) The conductor length in feet.
(2) The number of amperes of current to be carried.
(3) The amount of voltage drop permitted.

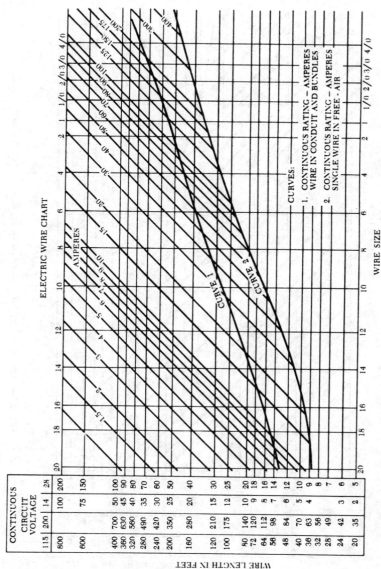

Figure 8-7. Wire selection chart for continuous flow. (For copper wire.)

229

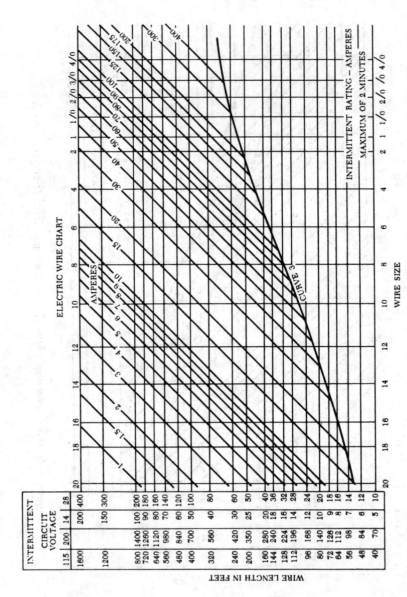

Figure 8-8. Wire selection chart for intermittant flow (For copper wire.)

230

(4) Whether the current to be carried will be intermittent or continuous, and if continuous, whether it is a single conductor in free air, in a conduit, or in a bundle.

Assume that it is desired to install a 50-ft. conductor from the aircraft bus to the equipment in a 28-volt system. For this length, a 1-volt drop is permissible for continuous operation. By referring to the chart in figure 8-7, the maximum number of feet a conductor may be run carrying a specified current with a 1-volt drop can be determined. In this example the number 50 is selected.

Assuming the current required by the equipment is 20 amperes, the line indicating the value of 20 amperes should be selected from the diagonal lines. Follow this diagonal line downward until it intersects the horizontal line number 50. From this point, drop straight downward to the bottom of the chart to find that a conductor between size No. 8 and No. 10 is required to prevent a greater drop than 1 volt. Since the indicated value is between two numbers, the larger size, No. 8, should be selected. This is the smallest size conductor which should be used to avoid an excessive voltage drop.

To determine that the conductor size is sufficient to preclude overheating, disregard both the numbers along the left side of the chart and the horizontal lines. Assume that the conductor is to be a single wire in free air carrying continuous current. Place a pointer at the top of the chart on the diagonal line numbered 20 amperes. Follow this line until the pointer intersects the diagonal line marked "curve 2." Drop the pointer straight downward to the bottom of the chart. This point is between numbers 16 and 18. The larger size, No. 16, should be selected. This is the smallest size conductor acceptable for carrying 20-ampere current in a single wire in free air without overheating.

If the installation is for equipment having only an intermittent (max. 2 min.) requirement for power, the chart in figure 8-8 is used in the same manner.

Conductor Insulation

Two fundamental properties of insulation materials (for example, rubber, glass, asbestos, or plastic) are insulation resistance and dielectric strength. These are entirely different and distinct properties.

Insulation resistance is the resistance to current leakage through and over the surface of insulation materials. Insulation resistance can be measured with a megger without damaging the insulation, and data so obtained serves as a useful guide in determining the general condition of the insulation. However, the data obtained in this manner may not give a true picture of the condition of the insulation. Clean, dry insulation having cracks or other faults might show a high value of insulation resistance but would not be suitable for use.

Dielectric strength is the ability of the insulator to withstand potential difference and is usually expressed in terms of the voltage at which the insulation fails because of the electrostatic stress. Maximum dielectric strength values can be measured by raising the voltage of a test sample until the insulation breaks down.

Because of the expense of insulation and its stiffening effect, together with the great variety of physical and electrical conditions under which the conductors are operated, only the necessary minimum insulation is applied for any particular type of cable designed to do a specific job.

The type of conductor insulation material varies with the type of installation. Such types of insulation as rubber, silk, and paper are no longer used extensively in aircraft systems. More common today are such materials as vinyl, cotton, nylon, Teflon, and Rockbestos.

Identifying Wire and Cable

Aircraft electrical system wiring and cable may be marked with a combination of letters and numbers to identify the wire, the circuit it belongs to, the gage number, and other information necessary to relate the wire or cable to a wiring diagram. Such markings are called the identification code.

There is no standard procedure for marking and identifying wiring; each manufacturer normally develops his own identification code. One identification system (figure 8-9) shows the usual spacing in marking a wire. The number 22 in the code refers to the system in which the wire is installed, **e.g.,** the VHF system. The next set of numbers, .013, is the wire number, and the 18 indicates the wire size.

Figure 8-9. One method of marking and identifying wire.

Some system components, especially plugs and jacks, are identified by a letter or group of letters and numbers added to the basic identification number. These letters and numbers may indicate the location of the component in the system. Interconnected cables are also marked in some systems to indicate location, proper termination, and use.

In any system, the marking should be legible, and the stamping color should contrast with the color of the wire insulation. For example, black stamping should be used with light-colored backgrounds, or white stamping on dark-colored backgrounds.

Wires are usually marked at intervals of not more than 15 in. lengthwise and within 3 in. of each junction or terminating point. Figure 8-10 shows wire identification at a terminal block.

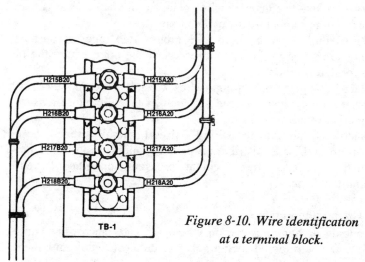

Figure 8-10. Wire identification at a terminal block.

Coaxial cable and wires at terminal blocks and junction boxes are often identified by marking or stamping a wiring sleeve rather than the wire itself. For general purpose wiring, a flexible vinyl sleeving, either clear or white opaque, is commonly used. For high-temperature applications, silicone rubber or silicone fiber glass sleeving is recommended. Where resistance to synthetic hydraulic fluids or other solvents is necessary, either clear or white opaque nylon sleeving can be used.

Figure 8-11. Alternate methods of identifying wire bundles.

While the preferred method is to stamp the identification marking directly on the wire or on the sleeving, other methods are often employed. Figure 8-11 shows two alternate methods: one method uses a marked sleeve tied in place; the other uses a pressure-sensitive tape.

Electrical Wiring Installation

The following recommended procedures for installing aircraft electrical wiring are typical of those used on most aircraft. For purposes of this discussion, the following definitions are applicable:

(1) Open wiring—any wire, wire group, or wire bundle not enclosed in conduit.

(2) Wire group—two or more wires going to the same location tied together to retain identity of the group.

(3) Wire bundle—two or more wire groups tied together because they are going in the same direction at the point where the tie is located.

(4) Electrically protected wiring—wires which include (in the circuit) protection against overloading, such as fuses, circuit breakers, or other limiting devices.

(5) Electrically unprotected wiring—wires (generally from generators to main bus distribution points) which do not have protection, such as fuses, circuit breakers, or other current-limiting devices.

Wire Groups and Bundles

Grouping or bundling certain wires, such as electrically unprotected power wiring and wiring going to duplicate vital equipment, should be avoided.

Wire bundles should generally be less than 75 wires, or 1½ to 2 in. in diameter where practicable. When several wires are grouped at junction boxes, terminal blocks, panels, etc., identity of the group within a bundle (figure 8-12) can be retained.

Figure 8-12. Groups and bundle ties.

Twisting Wires

When specified on the engineering drawing, or when accomplished as a local practice, parallel wires must sometimes be twisted. The following are the most common examples:

(1) Wiring in the vicinity of magnetic compass or flux valve.

(2) Three-phase distribution wiring.

(3) Certain other wires (usually radio wiring) as specified on engineering drawings.

Twist the wires so that they will lie snugly against each other, making approximately the number of twists per foot as shown in figure 8-13. Always check wire insulation for damage after twisting. If the insulation is torn or frayed, replace the wire.

	Wire Size									
	#22	#20	#18	#16	#14	#12	#10	#8	#6	#4
2 Wires	10	10	9	8	7½	7	6½	6	5	4
3 Wires	10	10	8½	7	6½	6	5½	5	4	3

Figure 8-13. Recommended number of twists per foot.

Spliced Connections in Wire Bundles

Spliced connections in wire groups or bundles should be located so that they can be easily inspected. Splices should also be staggered (figure 8-14) so that the bundle does not become excessively enlarged. All noninsulated splices should be covered with plastic, securely tied at both ends.

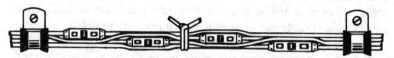

Figure 8-14. Staggered splices in a wire bundle.

Slack in Wiring Bundles

Single wires or wire bundles should not be installed with excessive slack. Slack between supports should normally not exceed a maximum of ½ in. deflection with normal hand force (figure 8-15). However, this may be exceeded if the wire bundle is thin and the clamps are far apart. Slack should never be so great that the wire bundle could abrade against any surface. A sufficient amount of slack should be allowed near each end of a bundle to:

(1) Permit easy maintenance.
(2) Allow replacement of terminals.
(3) Prevent mechanical strain on the wires, wire junctions, and supports.
(4) Permit free movement of shock and vibration-mounted equipment.
(5) Permit shifting of equipment for purposes of maintenance.

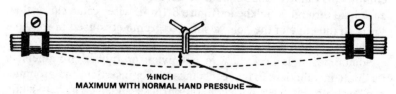

½INCH
MAXIMUM WITH NORMAL HAND PRESSURE

Figure 8-15. Maximum recommended slack in wire bundles between supports.

Bend Radii

Bends in wire groups or bundles should be not less than 10 times the outside diameter of the wire group or bundle. However, at terminal strips, where wire is suitably supported at each end of the bend, a minimum radius of three times the outside diameter of the wire, or wire bundle, is normally acceptable. There are, of course, exceptions to these guidelines in the case of certain types of cable; for example, coaxial cable should never be bent to a smaller radius than six times the outside diameter.

Routing and Installations

All wiring should be installed so that it is mechanically and electrically sound and neat in appearance. Whenever practicable, wires and bundles should be routed parallel with, or at right angles to, the stringers or ribs of the area involved. An exception to this general rule is coaxial cable, which is routed as directly as possible.

The wiring must be adequately supported throughout its length. A sufficient number of supports must be provided to prevent undue vibration of the unsupported lengths. All wires and wire groups should be routed and installed to protect them from:

(1) Chafing or abrasion.
(2) High temperature.
(3) Being used as handholds, or as support for personal belongings and equipment.
(4) Damage by personnel moving within the aircraft.
(5) Damage from cargo stowage or shifting.
(6) Damage from battery acid fumes, spray, or spillage.
(7) Damage from solvents and fluids.

Protection Against Chafing

Wires and wire groups should be protected against chafing or abrasion in those locations where contact with sharp surfaces or other wires would damage the insulation. Damage to the insulation can cause short circuits, malfunction, or inadvertent operation of equipment. Cable clamps should be used to support wire bundles at each hole through a bulkhead (figure 8-16). If wires come closer than ¼ in. to the edge of the hole, a suitable grommet is used in the hole as shown in figure 8-17.

Sometimes it is necessary to cut nylon or rubber grommets to facilitate installation. In these instances, after insertion, the grommet can be secured in place with general-purpose cement. The cut should be at the top of the hole, and made at an angle of 45 degrees to the axis of the wire bundle hole.

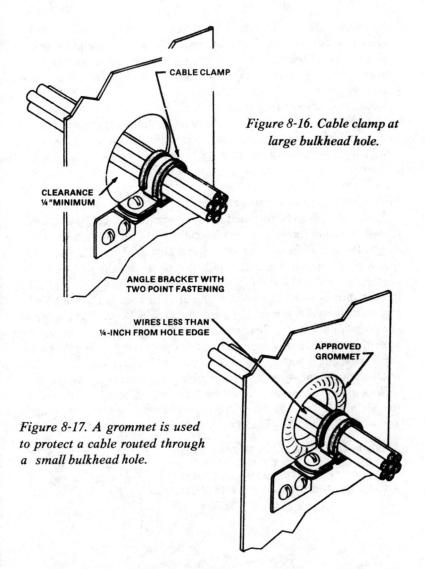

Figure 8-16. Cable clamp at large bulkhead hole.

CABLE CLAMP

CLEARANCE ¼"MINIMUM

ANGLE BRACKET WITH TWO POINT FASTENING

WIRES LESS THAN ¼-INCH FROM HOLE EDGE

APPROVED GROMMET

Figure 8-17. A grommet is used to protect a cable routed through a small bulkhead hole.

Protection against High Temperature

To prevent insulation deterioration, wires should be kept separate from high-temperature equipment, such as resistors, exhaust stacks, or heating ducts. The amount of separation is normally specified by engineering drawings. Some wires must invariably be run through hot areas. These wires must be insulated with high-temperature material such as asbestos, fiber glass, or Teflon. Additional protection is also often requred in the form of conduits. A low-temperature insulation wire should never be used to replace a high-temperature insulation wire.

237

Many coaxial cables have soft plastic insulation, such as poly-ethylene, which is especially subject to deformation and deterior-ation at elevated temperatures. All high-temperature areas should be avoided when installing these cables insulated with plastic or polyethylene.

Additional abrasion protection should be given to asbestos wires enclosed in conduit. Either conduit with a high-temperature rubber liner should be used, or asbestos wires can be enclosed individu-ally in high-temperature plastic tubes before being installed in the conduit.

Protection Against Solvents and Fluids

Wires should not be installed in areas where they will be subjected to damage from fluids or in the lowest 4 in. of an aircraft fuselage, except those that must terminate in that area. If there is a possibility that wire may be soaked with fluids, plastic tubing should be used to protect the wire. This tubing should extend past the exposure area in both directions and should be tied at each end. If the wire has a low point between the tubing ends, provide a ⅛-in. drain hole, as shown in figure 8-18. This hole should be punched into the tubing after the installation is complete and the low point definitely estab-lished by using a hole punch to cut a half circle. Care should be taken not to damage any wires inside the tubing when using the punch.

Wire should never be routed below an aircraft battery. All wires in the vicinity of an aircraft battery should be inspected frequently and wires discolored by battery fumes should be replaced.

DRAINAGE HOLE 1/8-INCH DIAMETER AT LOWEST POINT IN TUBING. MAKE THE HOLE AFTER INSTALLATION IS COMPLETE AND LOWEST POINT IS FIRMLY ESTABLISHED.

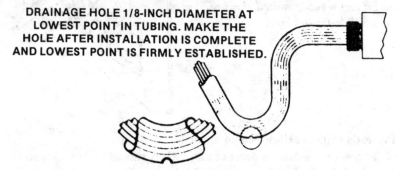

Figure 8-18. A drain hole should be provided at the low point in the protective plastic tubing.

Protection of Wires in Wheel Well Area

Wires located in wheel wells are subject to many additional hazards, such as exposure to fluids, pinching, and severe flexing in service. All wire bundles should be protected by sleeves of flexible tubing securely held at each end, and there should be no relative movement at points where flexible tubing is secured. These wires and the insulating tubing should be inspected carefully at frequent intervals, and wires or tubing should be replaced at the first sign of wear. There should be no strain on attachments when parts are fully extended, but slack should not be excessive.

Routing Precautions

When wiring must be routed parallel to combustible fluid or oxygen lines for short distances, as much fixed separation as possible should be maintained. The wires should be on a level with, or above, the plumbing lines. Clamps should be spaced so that if a wire is broken at a clamp it will not contact the line. Where a 6-in. separation is not possible, both the wire bundle and the plumbing line can be clamped to the same structure to prevent any relative motion. If the separation is less than 2-in. but more than ½-in., a polyethylene sleeve may be used over the wire bundle to give further protection. Also two cable clamps back-to-back, as shown in figure 8-19, can be used to maintain a rigid separation only, and not for support of the bundle. No wire should be routed so that it is located nearer than ½-in. to a plumbing line. Neither should a wire or wire bundle be supported from a plumbing line that carries flammable fluids or oxygen.

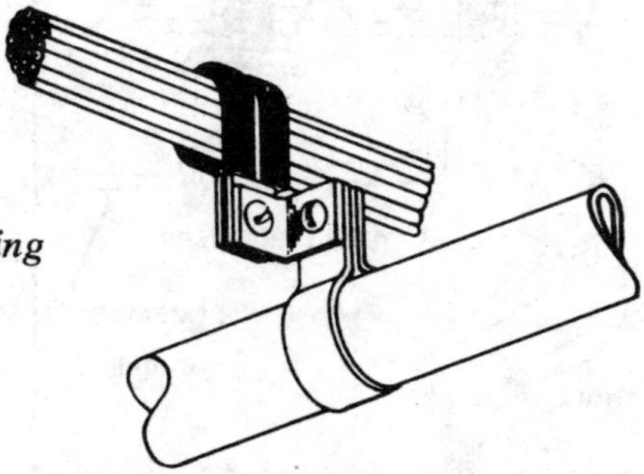

Figure 8-19. Method of separating wires from plumbing lines.

Wiring should be routed to maintain a minimum clearance of at least 3 in. from control cables. If this cannot be accomplished, mechanical guards should be installed to prevent contact between wiring and control cables.

Installation of Cable Clamps

Cable clamps should be installed with regard to the proper angle, as shown in figure 8-20. The mounting screw should be above the wire bundle. It is also desirable that the back of the cable clamp rest against a structural member where practicable.

Figure 8-21 shows some typical mounting hardware used in installing cable clamps.

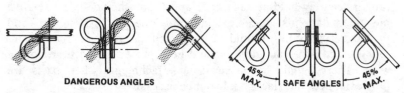

DANGEROUS ANGLES   45% MAX. SAFE ANGLES 45% MAX.

Figure 8-20. Proper and improper angles for installation of cable clamps.

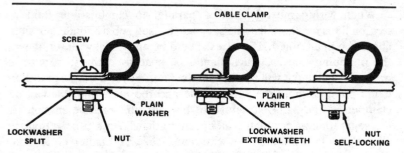

Figure 8-21. Various methods of mounting cable clamps.

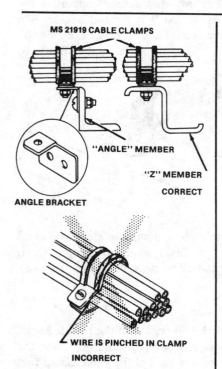

Figure 8-22. Mounting cable clamp to structure.

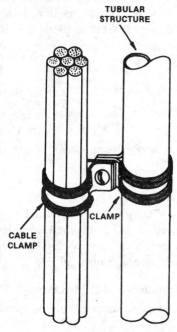

Figure 8-23. Installation of cable clamp to tubular structure.

Care should be taken that wires are not pinched in cable clamps. Where possible, mount the cables directly to structural members, as shown in figure 8-22.

Clamps can be used with rubber cushions to secure wire bundles to tubular structures as shown in figure 8-23. Such clamps must fit tightly, but should not be deformed when locked in place.

LACING AND TYING WIRE BUNDLES

Wire groups and bundles are laced or tied with cord to provide ease of installation, maintenance, and inspection. This section describes and illustrates recommended procedures for lacing and tying wires with knots which will hold tightly under all conditions. For the purposes of this discussion, the following terms are defined:

(1) Tying is the securing together of a group or bundle of wires by individual pieces of cord tied around the group or bundle at regular intervals.

(2) Lacing is the securing together of a group or bundle of wires by a continuous piece of cord forming loops at regular intervals around the group or bundle.

(3) A wire group is two or more wires tied or laced together to give identity to an individual system.

(4) A wire bundle is two or more wires or groups tied or laced together to facilitate maintenance.

The material used for lacing and tying is either cotton or nylon cord. Nylon cord is moisture- and fungus-resistant, but cotton cord must be waxed before using to give it these necessary protective characteristics.

Single-Cord Lacing

Figure 8-24 shows the step in lacing a wire bundle with a single cord. The lacing procedure is started at the thick end of the wire group or bundle with a knot consisting of a clove hitch with an extra loop. The lacing is then continued at regular intervals with half hitches along the wire group or bundle and at each point where a wire or wire group branches off. The half hitches should be spaced so that the bundle is neat and secure. The lacing is ended by tying a knot consisting of a clove hitch with an extra loop. After the knot is tied, the free ends of the lacing cord should be trimmed to approximately ⅜ in.

Double-Cord Lacing

Figure 8-25 illustrates the procedure for double-cord lacing. The lacing is started at the thick end of the wire group or bundle with a bowline-on-a-bight knot (A of figure 8-25). At regular intervals along the wire group or bundle, and at each point where a wire branches off, the lacing is continued using half hitches, with both cords held firmly together. The half hitches should be spaced so that the group or bundle is neat and secure. The lacing is ended with a knot consisting of a half hitch, continuing one of the cords clockwise and the other counterclockwise and then tying the cord ends with a square knot. The free ends of the lacing cord should be trimmed to approximately ⅜ in.

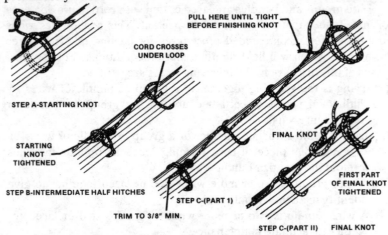

Figure 8-24. Procedure for single-cord lacing of a wire bundle.

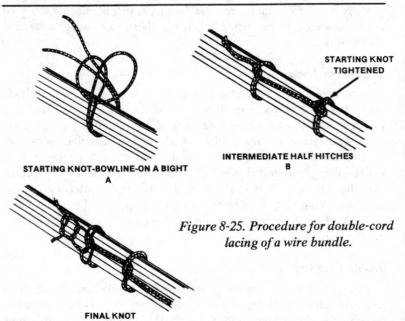

Figure 8-25. Procedure for double-cord lacing of a wire bundle.

Lacing Branch-Offs

Figure 8-26 illustrates a recommended procedure for lacing a wire group that branches off the main wire bundle. The branch-off lacing is started with a knot located on the main bundle just past the branch-off point. Continue the lacing along the branched-off wire group, using regularly spaced half hitches. If a double cord is used, both cords should be held snugly together. The half hitches should be spaced to lace the bundle neatly and securely. The lacing is ended with the regular terminal knot used in single- or double-cord lacing. The free ends of the lacing cord should be neatly trimmed.

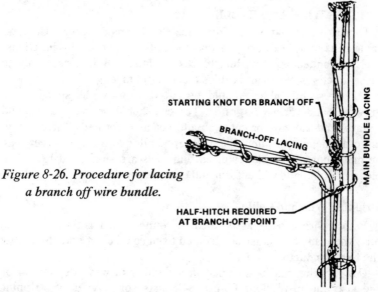

STARTING KNOT FOR BRANCH OFF

BRANCH-OFF LACING

MAIN BUNDLE LACING

HALF-HITCH REQUIRED
AT BRANCH-OFF POINT

*Figure 8-26. Procedure for lacing
a branch off wire bundle.*

Tying

All wire groups or bundles should be tied where supports are more than 12 in. apart. Figure 8-27 illustrates a recommended procedure for tying a wire group or bundle. The tie is started by wrapping the cord around the wire group to tie a clove-hitch knot. Then a square knot with an extra loop is tied, and the free ends of the cord are trimmed.

Temporary ties are sometimes used in making up and installing wire groups and bundles. Colored cord is normally used to make temporary ties, since they are removed when the installation is complete.

Whether laced or tied, bundles should be secured to prevent slipping, but not so tightly that the cord cuts into or deforms the insulation. This applies especially to coaxial cable, which has a soft dielectric insulation between the inner and outer conductor.

The part of a wire group or bundle located inside a conduit is not tied or laced, but wire groups or bundles inside enclosures, such as junction boxes, should be laced only.

Figure 8-27. Details for tying a wire group or bundle.

CUTTING WIRE AND CABLE

To make installation, maintenance, and repair easier, wire and cable runs in aircraft are broken at specified locations by junctions, such as connectors, terminal blocks, or buses. Before assembly to these junctions, wires and cables must be cut to length.

All wires and cables should be cut to the lengths specified on drawings and wiring diagrams. The cut should be made clean and square, and the wire or cable should not be deformed. If necessary, large-diameter wire should be re-shaped after cutting. Good cuts can be made only if the blades of cutting tools are sharp and free from nicks. A dull blade will deform and extrude wire ends.

Stripping Wire and Cable

Before wire can be assembled to connectors, terminals, splices, etc., the insulation must be stripped from connecting ends to expose the bare conductor.

Copper wire can be stripped in a number of ways depending on the size and insulation. Figure 8-28 lists some types of stripping tools recommended for various wire sizes and types of insulation.

Aluminum wire must be stripped very carefully, using extreme care, since individual strands will break very easily after being nicked.

Stripper	Wire Size	Insulations
Hot-blade	#26—#4	All except asbestos
Rotary, electric	#26—#4	All
Bench	#20—#6	All
Hand pliers	#26—#8	All
Knife	#2 —#0000	All

Figure 8-28. Types of wire stripping tools recommended for various sizes of copper wire.

The following general precautions are recommended when stripping any type of wire:

244

(1) When using any type of wire stripper, hold the wire so that it is perpendicular to cutting blades.

(2) Adjust automatic stripping tools carefully; follow the manufacturer's instructions to avoid nicking, cutting, or otherwise damaging strands. This is especially important for aluminum wires and for copper wires smaller than No. 10. Examine stripped wires for damage. Cut off and re-strip (if length is sufficient), or reject and replace any wires having more than the allowable number of nicked or broken strands listed in the manufacturer's instructions.

(3) Make sure insulation is clean-cut with no frayed or ragged edges. Trim if necessary.

(4) Make sure all insulation is removed from stripped area. Some types of wires are supplied with a transparent layer of insulation between the conductor and the primary insulation. If this is present, remove it.

(5) When using hand-plier strippers to remove lengths of insulation longer than ¾ in., it is easier to accomplish in two or more operations.

(6) Re-twist copper strands by hand or with pliers, if necessary, to restore natural lay and tightness of strands.

A pair of hand wire strippers is shown in figure 8-29. This tool is commonly used to strip most types of wire.

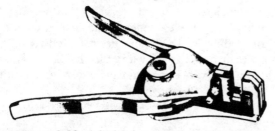

Figure 8-29. A light-duty hand operated wire stripper.

Solderless Terminals and Splices

Splicing of electrical cable should be kept to a minimum and avoided entirely in locations subject to extreme vibrations. Individual wires in a group or bundle can usually be spliced, provided the completed splice is located so that it can be inspected periodically. Splices should be staggered so that the bundle does not become excessively enlarged. Many types of aircraft splice connectors are available for splicing individual wires. Self-insulated splice connectors are usually preferred; however, a noninsulated splice connector can be used if the splice is covered with plastic sleeving secured at both ends. Solder splices may be used, but they are particularly brittle and not recommended.

Electric wires are terminated with solderless terminal lugs to permit easy and efficient connection to and disconnection from terminal blocks, bus bars, or other electrical equipment. Solderless splices join electric wires to form permanent continuous runs. Solderless terminal lugs and splices are made of copper or aluminum and preinsulated or uninsulated, depending on the desired application.

Terminal lugs are generally available in three types for use in different space conditions. These are the flag, straight, and right-angle lugs. Terminal lugs are "crimped" (sometimes called "staked" or "swaged") to the wires by means of hand or power crimping tools.

The following discussion describes recommended methods for terminating copper and aluminum wires using solderless terminal lugs. It also describes the method for splicing copper wires using solderless splices.

Copper Wire Terminals

Copper wires are terminated with solderless, preinsulated straight copper terminal lugs. The insulation is part of the terminal lug and extends beyond its barrel so that it will cover a portion of the wire insulation, making the use of an insulation sleeve unnecessary (figure 8-30).

In addition, preinsulated terminal lugs contain an insulation grip (a metal reinforcing sleeve) beneath the insulation for extra gripping strength on the wire insulation. Preinsulated terminals accommodate more than one size of wire; the insulation is usually color-coded to identify the wire sizes that can be terminated with each of the terminal lug sizes.

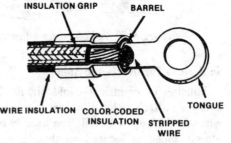

Figure 8-30. A preinsulated terminal lug.

INSULATION GRIP   BARREL

WIRE INSULATION   COLOR-CODED INSULATION   STRIPPED WIRE   TONGUE

Crimping Tools

Hand, portable power, and stationary power tools are available for crimping terminal lugs. These tools crimp the barrel of the terminal lug to the conductor and simultaneously crimp the insulation grip to the wire insulation.

Hand crimping tools all have a self-locking ratchet that prevents opening the tool until the crimp is complete. Some hand crimping tools are equipped with a nest of various size inserts to fit different size terminal lugs. Others are used on one terminal lug size only. All types of hand crimping tools are checked by gages for proper adjustment of crimping jaws. Figure 8-31 shows a terminal lug inserted into a hand tool.

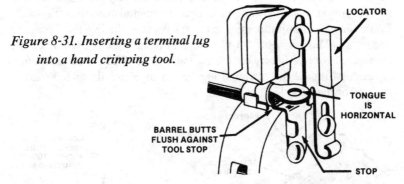

Figure 8-31. Inserting a terminal lug into a hand crimping tool.

Some types of uninsulated terminal lugs are insulated after assembly to a wire by means of pieces of transparent flexible tubing called "sleeves." The sleeve provides electrical and mechanical protection at the connection. When the size of the sleeving used is such that it will fit tightly over the terminal lug, the sleeving need not be tied; otherwise, it should be tied with lacing cord as illustrated in figure 8-32.

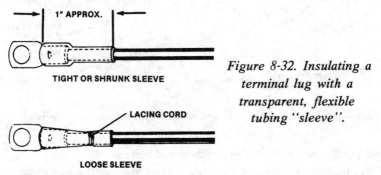

Figure 8-32. Insulating a terminal lug with a transparent, flexible tubing "sleeve".

Aluminum Wire Terminals

The use of aluminum wire in aircraft systems is increasing because of its weight advantage over copper. However, bending aluminum will cause "work hardening" of the metal, making it brittle. This results in failure or breakage of strands much sooner than in a similar case with copper wire. Aluminum also forms a high-resistant oxide film immediately upon exposure to air. To compensate for these disadvantages, it is important to use the most reliable installation procedures.

Only aluminum terminal lugs are used to terminate aluminum wires. They are generally available in three types: (1) Straight, (2) right-angle, and (3) flag. All aluminum terminals incorporate an inspection hole (figure 8-33) which permits checking the depth of wire insertion. The barrel of aluminum terminal lugs is filled with a petrolatum-zinc dust compound. This compound removes the oxide film from the aluminum by a grinding process during the crimping operation. The compound will also minimize later oxidation of the completed connection by excluding moisture and air. The compound is retained inside the terminal lug barrel by a plastic or foil seal at the end of the barrel.

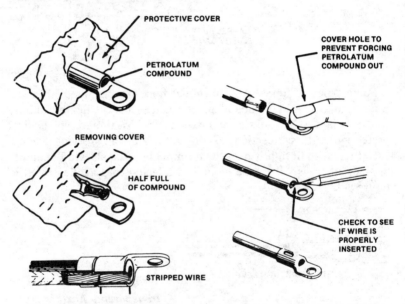

Figure 8-33. Inserting aluminum wire into aluminum terminal lugs.

Splicing Copper Wires Using Preinsulated Splices

Preinsuluated permanent copper splices join small wires of sizes 22 through 10. Each splice size can be used for more than one wire size. Splices are usually color-coded in the same manner as pre-insulated small copper terminal lugs. Some splices are insulated with white plastic. Splices are also used to reduce wire sizes (figure 8-34).

Crimping tools are used to accomplish this type of splice. The crimping procedures are the same as those used for terminal lugs, except that the crimping operation must be done twice, once for each end of the splice.

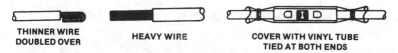

THINNER WIRE
DOUBLED OVER

HEAVY WIRE

COVER WITH VINYL TUBE
TIED AT BOTH ENDS

Figure 8-34. Method of reducing wire size with a permanent splice.

EMERGENCY SPLICING REPAIRS

Broken wires can be repaired by means of crimped splices, by using terminal lugs from which the tongue has been cut off, or by soldering together and potting broken strands. These repairs are applicable to copper wire. Damaged aluminum wire must not be temporarily spliced. These repairs are for temporary emergency use only and should be replaced as soon as possible with permanent repairs. Since some manufacturers prohibit splicing, the applicable manufacturer's instructions should always be consulted.

Splicing with Solder and Potting Compound

When neither a permanent splice nor a terminal lug is available, a broken wire can be repaired as follows (figure 8-35):

(1) Install a piece of plastic sleeving about 3 in. long, and of the proper diameter to fit loosely over the insulation, on one piece of the broken wire.
(2) Strip approximately 1½ in. from each broken end of the wire.
(3) Lay the stripped ends side by side and twist one wire around the other with approximately four turns.
(4) Twist the free end of the second wire around the first wire with approximately four turns. Solder wire turns together, using 60/40 tin-lead resin-core solder.
(5) When solder is cool, draw the sleeve over the soldered wires and tie at one end. If potting compound is available, fill the sleeve with potting material and tie securely.
(6) Allow the potting compound to set without touching for 4 hrs. Full cure and electrical characteristics are achieved in 24 hrs.

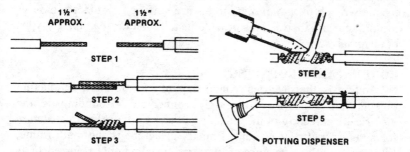

Figure 8-35. Procedure for repairing a broken wire by soldering and potting.

CONNECTING TERMINAL LUGS TO TERMINAL BLOCKS

Terminal lugs should be installed on terminal blocks so that they are locked against movement in the direction of loosening (figure 8-36).

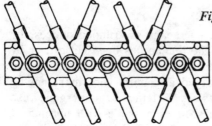

Figure 8-36. Connecting terminals to a terminal block.

Terminal blocks are normally supplied with studs secured in place by a plain washer, an external tooth lockwasher, and a nut. In connecting terminals, a recommended practice is to place copper terminal lugs directly on top of the nut, followed with a plain washer and elastic stop nut, or with a plain washer, split steel lockwasher, and plain nut.

Aluminum terminal lugs should be placed over a plated brass plain washer, followed with another plated brass plain washer, split steel lockwasher, and plain nut or elastic stop nut. The plated brass washer should have a diameter equal to the tongue width of the aluminum terminal lug. Consult the manufacturer's instructions for recommended dimensions of these plated brass washers. Do not place any washer in the current path between two aluminum terminal lugs or between two copper terminal lugs. Also, do not place a lockwasher directly against the tongue or pad of the aluminum terminal.

To join a copper terminal lug to an aluminum terminal lug, place a plated brass plain washer over the nut which holds the stud in place; follow with the aluminum terminal lug, a plated brass plain washer, the copper terminal lug, plain washer, split steel lockwasher, and plain nut or self-locking, all-metal nut. As a general rule use a torque wrench to tighten nuts to ensure sufficient contact pressure. Manufacturer's instructions provide installation torques for all types of terminals.

BONDING AND GROUNDING

Bonding is the electrical connecting of two or more conducting objects not otherwise adequately connected. Grounding is the electrical connecting of a conducting object to the primary structure for a return path for current. Primary structure is the main frame, fuselage, or wing structure of the aircraft, commonly referred to as ground. Bonding and grounding connections are made in aircraft electrical systems to:

(1) Protect aircraft and personnel against hazards from lightning discharge.

(2) Provide current return paths.

(3) Prevent development of radio-frequency potentials.

(4) Protect personnel from shock hazards.

(5) Provide stability of radio transmission and reception.

(6) Prevent accumulation of static charge.

General Bonding and Grounding Procedures

The following general procedures and precautions are recommended when making bonding or grounding connections:

(1) Bond or ground parts to the primary aircraft structure where practicable.

(2) Make bonding or grounding connections so that no part of the aircraft structure is weakened.

(3) Bond parts individually if possible.

(4) Install bonding or grounding connections against smooth, clean surfaces.

(5) Install bonding or grounding connections so that vibration, expansion or contraction, or relative movement in normal service will not break or loosen the connection.

(6) Install bonding and grounding connections in protected areas whenever possible.

Bonding jumpers should be kept as short as practicable. The jumper should not interfere with the operation of movable aircraft elements, such as surface controls; normal movement of these elements should not result in damage to the bonding jumper.

Electrolytic action can rapidly corrode a bonding connection if suitable precautions are not observed. Aluminum alloy jumpers are recommended for most cases; however, copper jumpers can be used to bond together parts made of stainless steel, cadimum-plated steel, copper, brass, or bronze. Where contact between dissimilar metals cannot be avoided, the choice of jumper and hardware should be such that corrosion is minimized, and the part most likely to corrode will be the jumper or associated hardware. Figure 8-37 illustrates some proper hardware combinations for making bonding connections. At locations where finishes are removed, a protective finish should be applied to the completed connection to prevent corrosion.

The use of solder to attach bonding jumpers should be avoided. Tubular members should be bonded by means of clamps to which the jumper is attached. The proper choice of clamp material minimizes the probability or corrosion. When bonding jumpers carry a substantial amount of ground return current, the current rating of the jumper should be adequate, and it should be determined that a

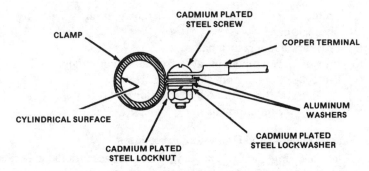

A. COPPER JUMPER CONNECTION TO TUBULAR STRUCTURE.

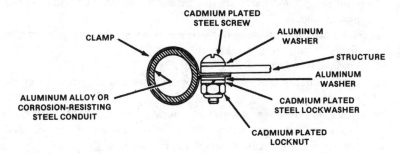

B. BONDING CONDUIT TO STRUCTURE.

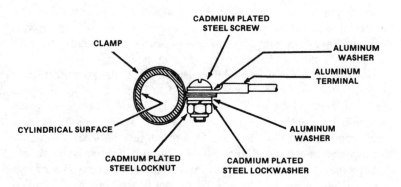

C. ALUMINUM JUMPER CONNECTION TO TUBULAR STRUCTURE.

Figure 8-37. Various hardware combinations for use in making bonding connections.

negligible voltage drop is produced.

Bonding and grounding connections are normally made to flat surfaces by means of through-bolt or screws where there is easy access for installation. Other general types of bolted connections are as follows:

(1) In making a stud connection (figure 8-38), a bolt or screw is

locked securely to the structure, thus becoming a stud. Grounding or bonding jumpers can be removed or added to the shank of the stud without removing the stud from the structure.

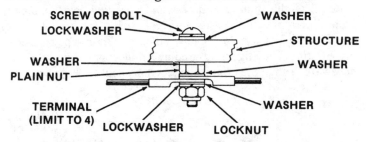

Figure 8-38. Stud bonding or grounding to a flat surface.

(2) Nut plates are used where access to the nut for repairs is difficult. Nut plates are riveted or welded to a clean area of the structure (figure 8-39).

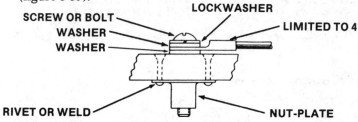

Figure 8-39. Nut plate bonding or grounding to a flat surface.

Bonding and grounding connections are also made to a tab riveted to a structure. In such cases it is important to clean the bonding or grounding surface and make the connection as through the connection were being made to the structure. If it is necessary to remove the tab for any reason, the rivets should be replaced with rivets one size larger, and the mating surfaces of the structure and the tab should be clean and free of anodic film.

Bonding or grounding connections can be made to aluminum alloy, magnesium, or corrosion-resistant steel tubular structure as shown in figure 8-40, which shows the arrangement of hardware for bonding with an aluminum jumper. Because of the ease with which aluminum is deformed, it is necessary to distribute the screw and nut pressure by means of plain washers.

Hardware used to make bonding or grounding connections should be selected on the basis of mechanical strength, current to be carried, and ease of installation. If connection is made by aluminum or copper jumpers to the structure of a dissimilar material, a washer of suitable material should be installed between the dissimilar metals so that any corrosion will occur on the washer, which is expendable.

Hardware material and finish should be selected on the basis of the material of the structure to which attachment is made and on the material of the jumper and terminal specified for the bonding or grounding connection. Either a screw or bolt of the proper size for the specified jumper terminal should be used. When repairing or replacing existing bonding or grounding connections, the same type of hardware used in the original connection should always be used.

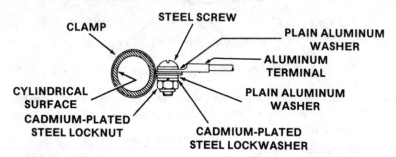

Figure 8-40. Bonding or grounding connections to a cylindrical surface.

Testing Grounds and Bonds

The resistance of all bond and ground connections should be tested after connections are made before re-finishing. The resistance of each connection should normally not exceed 0.003 ohm. Resistance measurements need to be of limited nature only for verification of the existence of a bond, but should not be considered as the sole proof of satisfactory bonding. The length of jumpers, methods, and materials used, and the possibility of loosening the connections in service should also be considered.

CONNECTORS

Connectors (plugs and receptacles) facilitate maintenance when frequent disconnection is required. Since the cable is soldered to the connector inserts, the joints should be individually installed and the cable bundle firmly supported to avoid damage by vibration. Connectors have been particularly vulnerable to corrosion in the past, due to condensation within the shell. Special connectors with waterproof features have been developed which may replace non-waterproof plugs in areas where moisture causes a problem. A connector of the same basic type and design should be used when replacing a connector. Connectors susceptible to corrosion difficulties may be treated with a chemcially inert waterproof jelly. When replacing connector assemblies, the socket-type insert should be used on the half which is "live" or "hot" after the connector is disconnected, to prevent unintentional grounding.

Types of Connectors

Connectors are identified by AN numbers and are divided into classes with the manufacturer's variations in each class. The manufacturer's variations are differences in appearance and in the method of meeting a specification. Some commonly used connectors are shown in figure 8-41. There are five basic classes of AN connectors used in most aircraft. Each class of connector has slightly different construction characteristics. Classes A, B, C, and D are made of aluminum, and class K is made of steel.

AN3100
WALL RECEPTACLE

AN3101
CABLE RECEPTACLE

AN3102
BOX RECEPTACLE

AN3107
MCK DISCONNECT
PLUG

AN3106
STRAIGHT PLUG

AN3106
STRAIGHT PLUG

AN3108
ANGLE PLUG

AN3106
ANGLE PLUG

Figure 8-41. A few typical AN connectors.

Class A—Solid, one-piece back shell, general-purpose connector.
Class B—Connector back shell separates into two parts lengthwise. Used primarily where it is important that the soldered connectors be

readily accessible. The back shell is held together by a threaded ring or by screws.

Class C—A pressurized connector with inserts that are not removable. Similar to a class A connector in appearance, but the inside sealing arrangement is sometimes different. It is used on walls of bulkheads of pressurized equipment.

Class D—Moisture- and vibration-resistant connector which has a sealing grommet in the back shell. Wires are threaded through tight-fitting holes in the grommet, thus sealing against moisture.

Class K—A fireproof connector used in areas where it is vital that the electric current is not interrupted, even though the connector may be exposed to continuous open flame. Wires are crimped to the pin or socket contacts and the shells are made of steel. This class of connector is normally longer than other classes of connectors.

Connector Identification

Code letters and numbers are marked on the coupling ring or shell to identify a connector. This code (figure 8-42) provides all the information necessary to obtain the correct replacement for a defective or damaged part.

Many special-purpose connectors have been designed for use in aircraft applications. These include subminiature and rectangular shell connectors, and connectors with short body shells or split-shell construction.

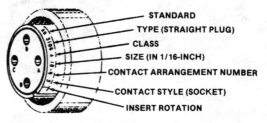

Figure 8-42. Standard procedure for AN connector marking.

STANDARD
TYPE (STRAIGHT PLUG)
CLASS
SIZE (IN 1/16-INCH)
CONTACT ARRANGEMENT NUMBER
CONTACT STYLE (SOCKET)
INSERT ROTATION

Installation of Connectors

The following procedures outline one recommended method of assembling connectors to receptacles.

(1) Locate the proper position of the plug in relation to the receptacle by aligning the key of one part with the groove or keyway of the other part.

(2) Start the plug into the receptacle with a light forward pressure and engage the threads of the coupling ring and receptacle.

(3) Alternately push in the plug and tighten the coupling ring until the plug is completely seated.

(4) Use connector pliers to tighten coupling rings one sixteenth to one eighth turn beyond fingertight if space around the connector

is too small to obtain a good finger grip.

(5) Never use force to mate connectors to receptacles. Do not hammer a plug into its receptacle; and never use a torque wrench or pliers to lock coupling rings.

A connector is generally disassembled from a receptacle in the following manner:

(1) Use connector pliers to loosen coupling rings which are too tight to be loosened by hand.

(2) Alternately pull on the plug body and unscrew the coupling ring until the connector is separated.

(3) Protect disconnected plugs and receptacles with caps or plastic bags to keep debris from entering and causing faults.

(4) Do not use excessive force, and do not pull on attached wires.

CONDUIT

Conduit is used in aircraft installations for the mechanical protection of wires and cables. It is available in metallic and nonmetallic materials in both rigid and flexible form.

When selecting conduit size for a specific cable bundle application, it is common practice to allow for ease in maintenance and possible future circuit expansion by specifying the conduit inner diameter about 25% larger than the maximum diameter of the conductor bundle. The nominal diameter of a rigid metallic conduit is the outside diameter. Therefore, to obtain the inside diameter, subtract twice the tube wall thickness.

From the abrasion standpoint, the conductor is vulnerable at the conduit ends. Suitable fittings are affixed to the conduit ends in such a manner that a smooth surface comes in contact with the conductor within the conduit. When fittings are not used, the conduit end should be flared to prevent wire insulation damage. The conduit is supported by clamps along the conduit run.

Many of the common conduit installation problems can be avoided by proper attention to the following details:

(1) Do not locate conduit where it can be used as a handhold or footstep.

(2) Provide drain holes at the lowest point in a conduit run. Drilling burrs should be carefully removed from the drain holes.

(3) Support the conduit to prevent chafing against the structure and to avoid stressing its end fittings.

Damaged conduit sections should be repaired to prevent damage to the wires or wire bundle. The minimum acceptable tube bend radii for rigid conduit as prescribed by the manufacturer's instructions should be followed carefully. Kinked or wrinkled bends in a rigid conduit are normally not acceptable.

Flexible aluminum conduit is widely available in two types: (1) Bare flexible and (2) rubber-covered conduit. Flexible brass conduit is normally used instead of flexible aluminum conduit, where necessary to minimize radio interference. Flexible conduit may be used where it is impractical to use rigid conduit, such as areas that have motion between conduit ends or where complex bends are necessary. Transparent adhesive tape is recommended when cutting flexible tubing with a hacksaw to minimize fraying of the braid.

ELECTRICAL EQUIPMENT INSTALLATION

This section provides general procedures and safety precautions for installation of commonly used aircraft electrical equipment and components. Electrical load limits, acceptable means of controlling or monitoring electrical loads, and circuit protection devices are subjects with which mechanics must be familiar to properly install and maintain aircraft electrical systems.

Electrical Load Limits

When installing additional electrical equipment that consumes electrical power in an aircraft, the total electrical load must be safely controlled or managed within the rated limits of the affected components of the aircraft's power-supply system.

Before any aircraft electrical load is increased, the associated wires, cables, and circuit protection devices (fuses or circuit breakers) should be checked to determine that the new electrical load (previous maximum load plus added load) does not exceed the rated limits of the existing wires, cables, or protection devices.

The generator or alternator output ratings prescribed by the manufacturer should be compared with the electrical loads which can be imposed on the affected generator or alternator by installed equipment. When the comparison shows that the probable total connected electrical load can exceed the output load limits of the generator(s) or alternator(s), the load should be reduced so that an overload cannot occur. When a storage battery is part of the electrical power system, ensure, that the battery is continuously charged in flight, except when short, intermittent loads are connected such as a radio transmitter, a landing-gear motor, or other similar devices which may place short-time demand loads on the battery.

Controlling or Monitoring the Electrical Load

Placards are recommended to inform crewmembers of an aircraft about the combination of electrical loads that can safely be connected to the power source.

In installations where the ammeter is in the battery lead, and the regulator system limits the maximum current that the generator or alternator can deliver, a voltmeter can be installed on the system bus. As long as the ammeter does not read "discharge" (except for short, intermittent loads such as operating the gear and flaps) and the voltmeter remains at "system voltage," the generator or alternator will not be overloaded.

In installations where the ammeter is in the generator or alternator lead, and the regulator system does not limit the maximum current that the generator or alternator can deliver, the ammeter can be redlined at 100% of the generator or alternator rating. If the ammeter reading is never allowed to exceed the red line, except for short, inermittent loads, the generator or alternator will not be overloaded.

Where the use of placards or monitoring devices is not practicable or desired, and where assurances is needed that the battery in a typical small aircraft generator/battery power source will be charged in flight, the total continuous connected electrical load may be held to approximately 80% of the total rated generator output capacity. (When more than one generator is used in parallel, the total rated output is the combined output of the installed generators.)

When two or more generators are operated in parallel and the total connected system load can exceed the rated output of one generator, means must be provided for quickly coping with the sudden overloads which can be caused by generator or engine failure. A quick load reduction system, or a specified procedure whereby the total load can be reduced to a quantity which is within the rated capacity of the remaining operable generator(s), can be employed.

Electrical loads should be connected to inverters, alternators, or similar aircraft electrical power sources in such a manner that the rated limits of the power source are not exceeded, unless some type of effective monitoring means is provided to keep the load within prescribed limits.

Circuit Protection Devices

Conductors should be protected with circuit breakers or fuses located as close as possible to the electrical power source bus. Normally, the manufacturer of the electrical equipment specifies the fuse or circuit breaker to be used when installing equipment.

The circuit breaker or fuse should open the circuit before the conductor emits smoke. To accomplish this, the time current characteristic of the protection device must fall below that of the associated conductor. Circuit protector characteristics should be matched to obtain the maximum utilization of the connected equipment.

Figure 8-43 shows an example of the chart used in selecting the circuit breaker and fuse protection for copper conductors. This

Wire AN gage copper	Circuit breaker amperage	Fuse amp.
22	5	5
20	7.5	5
18	10	10
16	15	10
14	20	15
12	30	20
10	40	30
8	50	50
6	80	70
4	100	70
2	125	100
1		150
0		150

Figure 8-43. Typical wire and circuit protector chart.

limited chart is applicable to a specific set of ambient temperatures and wire bundle sizes, and is presented as a typical example only. It is important to consult such guides before selecting a conductor for a specific purpose. For example, a wire run individually in the open air may be protected by the circuit breaker of the next higher rating to that shown on the chart.

All re-settable circuit breakers should open the circuit in which they are installed regardless of the position of the operating control when an overload or circuit fault exists. Such circuit breakers are referred to as "trip-free." Automatic re-set circuit breakers automatically re-set themselves. They should not be used as circuit protection devices in aircraft.

Switches

A specifically designed switch should be used in all circuits where a switch malfunction would be hazardous. Such switches are of rugged construction and have sufficient contact capacity to break, make, and carry continuously the connected load current. Snap-action design is generally preferred to obtain rapid opening and closing of contacts regardless of the speed of the operating toggle or plunger, thereby minimizing contact arcing.

The nominal current rating of the conventional aircraft switch is usually stamped on the switch housing. This rating represents the continuous current rating with the contacts closed. Switches should be derated from their nominal current rating for the following types of circuits:

(1) High rush-in circuits—Circuits containing incandescent lamps can draw an initial current which is 15 times greater than the continuous current. Contact burning or welding may occur when the switch is closed.

(2) Inductive circuits—Magnetic energy stored in solenoid coils or relays is released and appears as an arc when the control switch is opened.

(3) Motors—Direct-current motors will draw several times their rated current during starting, and magnetic energy stored in their armature and field coils is released when the control switch is opened.

The chart in figure 8-44 is typical of those available for selecting the proper nominal switch rating when the continuous load current is known. This selection is essentially a derating to obtain reasonable switch efficiency and service life.

Hazardous errors in switch operation can be avoided by logical and consistent installation. Two-position "on-off" switches should be mounted so that the "on" position is reached by an upward or forward movement of the toggle. When the switch controls movable aircraft elements, such as landing gear or flaps, the toggle should move in the same direction as the desired motion. Inadvertent operation of a switch can be prevented by mounting a suitable guard over the switch.

Nominal system voltage	Type of load	Derating factor
24 v. d.c.	Lamp	8
24 v. d.c.	Inductive (Relay-Solenoid)	4
24 v. d.c.	Resistive (Heater)	2
24 v. d.c.	Motor	3
12 v. d.c.	Lamp	5
12 v. d.c.	Inductive (Relay-Solenoid)	2
12 v. d.c.	Resistive (Heater)	1
12 v. d.c.	Motor	2

Figure 8-44. Switch derating factors.

Relays

Relays are used as switching devices where a weight reduction can be achieved or electrical controls can be simplified. A relay is an electrically operated switch and is therefore subject to dropout under low system voltage conditions. The foregoing discussion of switch ratings is generally applicable to relay contact ratings.

MAINTENANCE AND INSPECTION OF WIRING SYSTEMS

Inspection of an aircraft's wiring systems normally includes checking the condition and security of all visible wiring, connections, terminals, fuses, and switches. A continuity light or meter can be used in making these checks, since the cause of many troubles can often be located by systematically testing each circuit for continuity.

Circuit testing, commonly known as troubleshooting is a means of systematically locating faults in an electrical system. These faults are usually of three kinds:

(1) Open circuits in which leads or wires are broken.
(2) Shorted circuits in which grounded leads cause current to be returned by shortcuts to the source of power.
(3) Low power in circuits causing lights to burn dimly and relays to chatter. Electrical troubles may develop in the unit or wiring.

The equipment generally used in testing circuits in an aircraft consists of a voltmeter, test light, continuity meter, and ohmmeter.

Although any standard d.c. voltmeter with flexible leads and test prods is satisfactory for testing circuits, portable voltmeters especially designed for test purposes are usually used.

The test lamp consists of a low wattage aircraft light. Two leads are used with this light.

Continuity testers vary somewhat. One type consists of a small lamp connected in series with two small batteries (flashlight batteries are very suitable) and two leads. (See A of figure 8-45.) Another type of continuity tester contains two batteries connected in series with a d.c. voltmeter and two test leads. A completed circuit will be registered by the voltmeter.

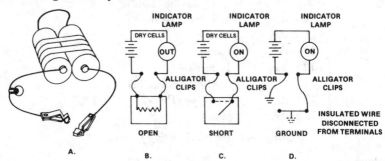

Figure 8-45. Continuity testing of a circuit with a simple continuity tester.

Whenever generator or battery voltage is available, the voltmeter and the test light can be used in circuit testing, since these sources of power will activate the test light and the voltmeter.

If no electrical power is available (the circuit is dead), then the continuity tester is used. The self-contained batteries of the continuity tester force current through the circuit, causing the continuity meter to indicate when the circuit being tested is completed. When using the continuity meter, the circuit being tested should always be isolated from all other circuits by removing the fuse, by opening the switch, or by disconnecting the wires.

Figure 8-45 illustrates techniques which may be used in checking circuits. The continuity tester contains a light to serve as an indicator. When the test leads are touched together, a complete circuit is established and the indicator light illuminates. When the leads are brought into contact with a resistor or other circuit element, as shown in B of figure 8-45, and the light does not illuminate, then the circuit being tested is open.

For the open test to be conclusive, be sure the resistance of the unit tested is low enough to permit the lamp to light. In a test in which the resistance is too high, usually more than 10 ohms, connect a voltmeter in the circuit in place of the lamp. If the voltmeter pointer fails to deflect, an open circuit is indicated.

The test for shorts (C of figure 8-45) shows the continuity tester connected across the terminals of a switch in the "open" position. If the tester lamp lights, there is a short circuit in the switch.

To determine whether a length of wire is grounded at some point between its terminals, disconnect the wire at each end and hook one test clip to the wire at one end and ground the other test clip (D of figure 8-45). If the wire is grounded, the lamp will light. To locate the ground, check back at intervals toward the other end. The lighting of the lamp will indicate the section of the wire that is grounded.

The ohmmeter, although primarily designed to measure resistance, is useful for checking continuity. With an ohmmeter, the resistance of a circuit can be determined directly by scale. Since an open circuit has infinite resistance, a zero reading on the ohmmeter indicates circuit continuity.

As illustrated in figure 8-46, the ohmmeter uses a battery as the source of voltage. There are fixed resistors, which are of such value that when the test prods are shorted together, the meter will read full scale. The variable resistor, in parallel with the meter, and the fixed resistors compensate for changes in voltage of the battery. The variable resistor provides for zero adjustment on the meter control panel.

On the meter there may be several scales, which are made possible by various values of resistance and battery voltage. The desired scale is selected by a selector switch on the face of the ohmmeter. Each scale reads low resistances at the upper end. Greater resistance in a circuit is indicated by less deflection of the indicator on the scale.

When using an ohmmeter to check continuity, connect the leads across the circuit. A zero ohm reading indicates circuit continuity. For checking resistance, a scale should be chosen which will contain the resistance of the element being measured. In general, a scale should be selected on which the reading will fall in the upper half of the scale. Short the leads together and set the meter to read zero

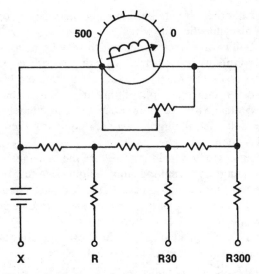

Figure 8-46. Typical ohmmeter internal circuity.

ohm by the zero adjustment. If a change in scales is made anytime, remember to re-adjust the meter to zero ohm.

When making circuit tests with the ohmmeter, never attempt to check continuity or measure the resistance in a circuit while it is connected to a source of voltage. Disconnect one end of an element when checking resistance, so that the ohmmeter will not read the resistance of parallel paths.

The following summary of continuity testing of circuits is recommended, using either an ohmmeter or any other type of continuity tester.

(1) Check the fuse or circuit breaker. Be sure it is the correct one for the circuit being tested.

(2) Check the electrical unit.

(3) If fuse or circuit breaker and electrical unit are in good condition, check at the most accessible point for an open or short in the circuit.

(4) Never guess. Always locate the trouble in the positive lead of a circuit, the operating unit, or the negative lead before removing any equipment or wires.

Chapter 9

Aircraft Painting and Finishing

TOPCOAT SYSTEMS

OLDER AIRCRAFT FINISHING SYSTEMS

Most older aircraft are usually finished with a nitrocellulose lacquer or a conventional enamel; however, many new manufacture aircraft are still finished with a conventional enamel.

Lacquer is a fast drying finish which cures by the evaporation of its solvents. An enamel however, cures by the chemical combining of some of its solvents by oxidation, catalytic action or heat. These older enamels were essentially standard paint pigments suspended in an oil type varnish.

Nitrocellulose Lacquer

Nitrocellulose lacquers are available in both glossy and flat finishes. They are also available in either clear or pigmented form. These materials can be applied over either old type zinc chromate or the newer modified zinc chromate primer. The lacquer finish is applied in two coats; a mist coat first, with a full, wet cross coat applied within 20 to 30 min. afterward. The lacquer finishes should be thinned as necessary, using cellulose nitrate dope and lacquer thinner. Lacquer should never be applied over paint, enamel, or varnish because it tends to remove such material.

Enamel

Enamels are special types of varnish having either an oil base or nitrocellulose base as the solvent. Enamel finishes are generally glossy, although flat enamel finishes are available. Enameled surfaces are hard, resist scratching and the action of oils or water, and certain grades resist high temperatures. Enamel can be applied by spraying or brushing and is suitable for either interior or exterior application.

MODERN AIRCRAFT FINISHING SYSTEMS

High volume production combined with requirements for durable

and attractive finishes for modern high speed aircraft, have resulted in the development of two widely used finishing systems based on:
- Acrylic lacquers
- Polyurethane Enamels

Acryclic Nitrocellulose Lacquer

This is the most common topcoat in use today, available either in flat or glossy finish. Both types of material are required in refinishing conventional aircraft. Anti-glare areas generally require the use of flat finishes. The remaining surfaces usually are finished with glossy materials to reduce heat absorption. The base materials should be thinned as necessary for spray application with acrylic nitrocellulose thinner.

Acrylic lacquer can be applied over wash primer, generally used for new production; or over any of the epoxy primers. It should not be applied over zinc chromate as the solvents in the acrylic may lift the zinc chromate.

Polyurethane Finishes

Another type of paint becoming increasingly common is a Military Specification epoxy finish or proprietary epoxy primer and topcoats. These finishes ordinarily consist of a conventional wash primer coat and two coats of epoxy material.

The high gloss inherent with this system is primarily due to the slow flowing resins used. The thinners flash off quickly but the resins continue to flow for three to five days. It is this long flow-out time and the even cure throughout the film that gives the pigment and the film time to form a truly flat surface, one that reflects light and has the glossy "wet" look which makes them so popular.

Polyurethane finish is used on agricultural aircraft and seaplanes because of its abrasion resistance and resistance to chemical attack. Hydraulic fluid, which quite actively attacks and softens other finishes, has only minimal effect on polyurethanes. Even acetone will not dull the finish. Paint strippers must be held to the surface for a good while to give the active ingredients time to break through the film and attack the primer.

The epoxy material presently in use is a two-package system that consists of a resin and a converter which must be mixed in definite proportions just before application. Since the proportions will vary between colors used and also with sources of procurement, it is important that instructions on the specific container be observed carefully. The converter should always be added to the resin, **never resin to the converter.** Also, do not mix materials from two different manufacturers. The mixture should be allowed to stand at least 15 minutes before initial use. During use of this mixture an 8-hour pot life should be observed.

Polyurethane enamels are manufactured under various proprietory names such as:

- "Ranthane," manufactured by Randolf Products Company.
- "Alumigrip," manufactured by U.S. Paint Lacquer and Chemical Company.
- "Imron," manufactured by E.I. Du Pont de Nemours & Company.
- Skymaster" polyurethane coatings by Sterling Lacquer Manufacturing Company.

FINISHING PROCEDURES
(Replacement of Existing Finish)

PAINT REMOVAL

One of the most important jobs is the stripping of old paint finishes preparatory to applying a new surface cover coat. An original finish may have to be removed in any of the following cases:

- If a panel or other area on the aircraft has badly deteriorated paint surfaces.
- If repair materials are not compatible with the existing finish, thereby precluding touchup repair.
- If corrosion is evident or suspected under an apparently good paint coating.

The area to be stripped must be cleaned of grease, oil, dirt, or preservatives to assure maximum efficiency of the stripping compound. The selection of the type of cleaning materials to be used will depend on the nature of the matter to be removed. Dry-cleaning solvent or naptha may be used for removing oil, grease, and soft preservative compounds. For heavy duty removal of thick or dried preservatives, other compounds of the solvent-emulsion type are available.

In general, paint stripping materials are toxic and must be used with care. The use of a general-purpose, water-rinsable stripper is recommended for most field applications. Wherever practicable, paint removal from any large area should be done out of doors and preferably in shaded areas. If indoor removal is necessary, adequate ventilation must be assured. Synthetic rubber surfaces, including aircraft tires, fabric, and acrylics, must be thoroughly protected against possible contact with paint remover. Care must be taken when using paint remover around gas- or water-tight seam sealants, since this material will soften and destroy the integrity of the sealants.

Mask any opening that would permit stripper to get into aircraft interiors or critical cavities. Paint stripper is toxic and contains ingredients harmful to both skin and eyes. Rubber gloves, aprons of acid repellent material, and goggle type eyeglasses should be worn if any extensive paint removal is to be done. A general stripping procedure is discussed in the following paragraphs.

No prepared paint remover should be used on aircraft fabric or be allowed to come in contact with any fiberglass reinforced parts such as radomes, radio antenna, or any component such as fiberglass reinforced wheel pants or wing tips. The active agents will attack and soften the binder in these parts.

CAUTION: Any time you use a paint stripper, always wear protective goggles and rubber gloves. If any stripper is splashed on your skin, wash it off immediately with water; and if any comes in contact with your eyes, flood them repeatedly with water and CALL A PHYSICIAN.

Brush the entire area to be stripped with a cover of stripper to a depth of 1/32 in. to 1/16 in. Any paint brush makes a satisfactory applicator, except that the bristles will be loosened by the effect of paint remover on the binder. The brush should not be used for other purposes after being exposed to paint remover.

After applying the stripping compound, it may be covered with an inexpensive polyethane drop cloth. Covering prevents rapid evaporation of the solvents and facilitates penetration of the paint film.

Allow the stripper to remain on the surface for a sufficient length of time to wrinkle and lift the paint. This may vary from 10 min. to several hours, depending on the temperature, humidity, and the condition of the paint coat being removed. Scrub the paint-remover-wet surface with a bristle brush saturated with paint remover to further loosen any finish that may still be adhering to the metal.

Re-apply the stripper as necessary in areas that remain tight or where the material has dried, and repeat the above process. Non-metallic scrapers may be used to assist in removing persistent paint finishes.

Remove the loosened paint and residual stripper by washing and scrubbing the surface with water. If water spray is available, use a low-to-medium pressure stream of water directly on the scrubbing broom. If steam cleaning equipment is available and the area is sufficiently large, this equipment, together with a solution of steam cleaning compound, may be used for cleaning. On small areas, any method may be used that will assure complete rinsing of the cleaned area.

After washing and scrubbing with water and/or steam, the entire surface should be scrubbed with a solvent such as methyl-ethyl-ketone (MEK) or acetone. The use of xylol, toluol or lacquer thinner is not recommended.

SURFACE PREPARATION (Conversion Coating)

After the aircraft surfaces have been thoroughly cleaned and/or stripped, the bare aluminum skin should be treated with a conversion coating in order to:

- Microscopically roughen the surface so that the subsequent primer coats will adhere.
- Provide maximum protection against corrosion.

Three types of conversion materials are in general use:

(1) Phosphoric acid etch.
(2) Chromic acid conversion coating per MIL-C-5541.
(3) Alodizing (Alodine solution treatment).

Phosphoric Acid Etch Application

The etching material should be applied with a rag, wiping a 4 × 8 foot section at a time. The etching material should be removed by a water rinse paying particular attention to seams, fasteners and riveted areas. In no instance should etching material remain on the skin for over 5 minutes. The skin should be wiped dry, as any remaining phosphate residue on the skin will cause "crawling" of a polyurethane system and can be the seeds for future corrosion.

After the skin is dry, it should be wiped with MEK. It is now ready for application of a primer.

Chromic Acid Conversion Coating

Apply the chromic acid solution to the cleaned surface with an acid-resistant brush. Keep the surface wet with the solution for 2 to 5 minutes. Rinse the treated area with water. Allow the area to dry, or force-dry with filtered clean air. Pay particular attention to seams and rivet areas. The skin is now ready for application of a primer.

Alodizing

Alodizing is a simple chemical treatment for all aluminum alloys to increase their corrosion resistance and to improve their paint-bonding qualities.

The process consists of precleaning with an acidic or alkaline metal cleaner that is applied by either dipping or spraying. The parts are then rinsed with fresh water under pressure for 10 or 15 seconds. After thorough rinsing, alodine is applied by dipping, spraying or brushing. A thin, hard coating results which ranges in color from light, bluish-green with a slight iridescence on copper-free alloys to an olive green on copper-bearing alloys. The alodine is first rinsed with clear, cold or warm water for a period of 15 to 30 seconds. An additional 10 to 15 second rinse is then given in a Deoxylyte bath. This bath is to counteract alkaline material and to make the alodyzed aluminum surface slightly acid in drying.

APPLICATION OF PRIMER

After the skin has been pre-treated as described immediately above, a primer is applied to provide a bond between the metal and the topcoats.

The three types of primers in general use are:

(1) Wash Primer
(2) Zinc Chromate Primer
(3) Epoxy Primer

Standard Wash Primer

Acrylic lacquer, conventional enamel, and polyurethane enamel include a standard wash primer undercoat. Wash primer can be applied directly to properly cleaned bare aluminum skin without the conversion coating described previously. However, when wash primer is applied over a conversion coating, the organic film of the wash primer combines with the inorganic film of the conversion coating to provide greater adhesion between the topcoats and the skin. Better surface protection also results.

Wash primer is a two-part material consisting of resin and alcoholic phosphoric acid, which is added just prior to application. The two components should be mixed very slowly and carefully and allowed to stand at least 30 min. before use. The primer should be used within a total time of 4 hrs. Any necessary thinning is done with a 25/75 to 50/50 mixture of butyl alcohol and ethyl alcohol, respectively. The percentage of butyl alcohol used will be determined by the evaporation rate. The percentage of butyl alcohol should be kept to the minimum possible under local temperature and humidity conditions. It is particularly important that the ratio of acid to resin in the wash primer be maintained. Any decrease in acid will result in poor coat formation. An excess of acid will cause serious brittleness.

Zinc Chromate Primer

Zinc chromate primer is applied to metallic surfaces, before the application of conventional enamel or lacquer, as a corrosion-resistant covering and as a base for protective topcoats. Older type zinc chromate primer is distinguishable by its bright yellow color compared to the green cast of the modified primers currently used. The old type primer will adhere well to bare metal, however, improved adhesion is obtained by first providing an Alodine conversion coating to the cleaned bare metal. It is still specified as an acceptable coating for internal surfaces, and it forms a part of the old type nitrocellulose system finishes. It can be applied by brush or spray and should be thinned for spraying as necessary with toluene. When this material is to be applied by brush, it should be thinned to brushing consistency with xylene to give better wet-edge retention.

It dries adequately for overcoating within an hour. Zinc chromate primer is satisfactory for use under oilbase enamels or nitrocellulose lacquers.

Epoxy Primer

Epoxy primer is an optional primer for use between a standard wash primer and the new polyurethane finishes. A finishing system using epoxy primers is normally used for float planes, agricultural airplanes or other applications requiring maximum corrosion protection. Epoxy primers are used on aluminum, steel or fiberglass surfaces.

Epoxy primers are not normally used on production aircraft since a waiting period of from 5 to 12 hours is necessary before applying the topcoats of acrylic lacquer or enamel. However, polyurethane enamels can be applied after a wait of only one hour. The polyurethane enamel softens the epoxy surface slightly, thus forming a chemical bond with the primer.

FINISHING PROCEDURES
(Touchup of Existing Finish)
PAINT TOUCHUP

A good intact paint finish is one of the most effective barriers available for placement between metal surfaces and corrosive media. Touching up the existing paint finish and keeping it in good condition will eliminate most general corrosion problems.

When touching up paint, confine paint coverage to the smallest area possible. Acrylic primer or lacquer may be used, but adhesion is usually poor. Epoxy coatings, as well as the older type of zinc chromate primer, may be used for touchup on bare metal.

When a paint surface has deteriorated badly, it is best to strip and repaint the entire panel rather than attempt to touchup the area. Touchup materials should be the same as the original finish. Surfaces to be painted should be thoroughly cleaned and free from grease, oil, or moisture. Where conditions are not suitable for painting, preservatives may be used as temporary coatings until good painting conditions are restored. Paint finishes should not be too thick since thickness promotes cracking in service.

Much of the effectiveness of a paint finish and its adherence depends on the careful preparation of the surface prior to touchup and repair. It is imperative that surfaces be clean and that all soils, lubricants, or preservatives be removed.

Cleaning procedures for paint touchup are much the same as the procedures for cleaning before inspection. Many types of cleaning compounds are available.

IDENTIFICATION OF PAINT FINISHES

Existing finishes on current aircraft may be any one of several types, combinations of two or more types, or combinations of general finishes with special proprietary coatings. The maintenance manuals for some modern aircraft provide detailed information on the finishing systems applied at the factory.

Any of the finishes may be present at any given time, and repairs may have been made using materials from several different types. Some detailed information for the identification of each finish is necessary to assure adequate repair procedures. A simple test is valuable in confirming the nature of the coatings present. The following tests will aid in paint finish identification.

Apply a coating of engine oil (Military Specification MIL-L-7808, or equal) to a small area of the surface to be checked. Old nitrocellulose finishes will soften within a period of a few minutes. Acrylic and epoxy finishes will show no effects. Another worthwhile test is to rub the finish with some thinner used to reduce the material for spraying. If it softens the finish, the material is a nitrocellulose lacquer. If not, it is probably an enamel.

If not identified, next wipe down a small area of the surface in question with a rag wet with MEK (methyl ethyl ketone). MEK will pick up the pigment from an acrylic finish, but will have no effect on an epoxy coating. Wipe the surface; do not rub. Heavy rubbing will pick up even epoxy pigment from coatings that are not thoroughly cured. Do not use MEK on nitrocellulose finishes.

REPLACEMENT OF NITROCELLULOSE LACQUER EXISTING FINISH

When an existing nitrocellulose finish is extensively deteriorated, the entire aircraft may have to be stripped of paint and a complete new paint finish applied. When such damage is confined to one or more panels, the stripping and application of the new finish may be limited to such areas by masking to the nearest seam line.

The complete nitrocellulose lacquer finish is begun with the application of standard wash primer undercoat. The wash primer should be applied in a thin coat, with the texture of the metal still visible through the coating. If absorption of water results and the coat shows evidence of blushing, successive coatings will not adhere. The area should be resprayed with butyl alcohol to re-deposit the wash primer. If blushing is still evident, it should be stripped and re-sprayed. After 20 min. drying time, adherence of the film should be checked with a thumbnail test. A moderate thumbnail scratch should not remove the prime coat.

The wash primer must be applied over a precleaned surface that has been wiped with a volatile solvent such as MEK, naphtha, or paint and lacquer thinners just before paint application. Evaporation of the solvent should be complete before the prime coat is added. Better results will be obtained if the solvent wipe-down is followed by a detergent wash.

Lacquer primer is a modified alkyd-type zinc chromate developed for its adherence to the wash primer. Lacquer primer does not adhere well to bare metal, but works effectively as a sandwich between the wash coat primer and the nitrocellulose topcoating, and can be thinned as necessary for spray application with cellulose nitrate thinner. In areas where the relative humidity is high, it may be more desirable to use acrylic nitrocellulose thinner. For best results, lacquer primer should be topcoated within 30 to 45 min. after its application.

The old type primer will adhere well to bare metal and is still specifed as an acceptable coating for internal surfaces as well as a part of the nitrocellulose finishes. Apply by brush or spray; thin for spraying with toluene. When this material is to be applied by brush, thin to brushing consistency with xylene to give better wet-edge retention. Overcoating may be applied within an hour.

Nitrocellulose lacquers are availabe in both glossy and nonspecular finishes. The lacquer finish is applied in two coats: a mist coat first, with a full wet crosscoat applied within 20 to 30 min. The lacquer should be thinned as necessary, using cellulose nitrate dope and lacquer thinner.

Cellulose nitrate dope and lacquer thinner (Federal Specification TT-T-266) is both explosive and toxic, as well as damaging to most paint finishes. Dope and lacquer thinner may be used for hand removal of lacquer or primer overspray, is an approved thinner for nitrocellulose lacquers, and is a mixture of ketones, alcohols, and hydrocarbons.

If the old finish is not to be completely stripped, the existing surface must be prepared to receive the new cover coat after cleaning. If good adhesion is to be obtained, all loose paint should be brushed off, giving particular attention to overpaint usually found in wheel wells and wing butt areas. Curled or flaky edges must be removed and feathered to provide about ½ in. of overlap. A fine abrasive approved for aircraft use should be used and extreme care taken to ensure that existing surface treatments are not damaged.

After sanding, sanded areas and bare metal should be wiped with either mineral spirits, alcohol, aliphatic naphtha, or dry-cleaning solvent. Following complete evaporation of these solvents, a detergent wash using a nonionic detergent/isoproply alcohol mixture should be applied just prior to painting. This will improve paint adhesion.

REPLACEMENT OF EXISTING ACRYLIC NITROCELLULOSE LACQUER FINISH

This finish includes a wash primer coat, modified zinc chromate primer coat, and an acrylic nitrocellulose lacquer topcoat. This finish may be applied only in the sequence specified in the manufacturer's instructions and will not adhere to either the old nitrocellulose coatings or the new epoxy finishes. Even when finishes are applied over old acrylic coatings during touchup, a softening of the old film with a compatible thinner is required.

When a finish is being rebuilt from bare metal, the steps through the application of the modified primer are the same as for nitrocellulose finishes, except that old type zinc chromate primer may not be used. As with the nitrocellulose finish, the acrylic nitrocellulose topcoat should be applied within 30 to 45 min. The finish coatings are usually applied in two coats over the modified primer: the first a mist coat, and the second a wet, full-hiding crosscoat, with 20 to 30 min. drying time allowed between the two coatings. Once the paint finish has set, paint stripper is necessary for its removal.

Acrylic nitrocellulose lacquer thinner is used in thinning acrylic nitrocellulose lacquers to spray consistency.

When rebuilding acrylic finishes, use two separate thinners: (1) Cellulose nitrate dope and lacquer thinner to thin the modified primer, and (2) acrylic nitrocellulose lacquer thinner to reduce the topcoat material. Make sure that the thinner materials are used properly and that the two are not mixed.

Touchup of Acrylic Nitrocellulose Finishes

After removal of damaged paint, the first step before application of touchup acrylic nitrocellulose lacquer is preparing the old coat to receive the new. Acrylic nitrocellulose lacquer thinner may be effectively used to wipe small areas prior to painting. This will soften the edges of the base paint film around damaged areas, which in turn will assure improved adhesion of the touchup coating. However, the thinner contains toulene and ketones and should never be used indiscriminately for cleaning painted surfaces.

When softening old, good-condition acrylic nitrocellulose finishes with thinner, care should be taken to avoid penetration and separation of the old primer coats. The new acrylic lacquer coat should be applied directly over the softened surface without the use of primers between the old and new coats.

REPLACEMENT OF EXISTING ENAMEL FINISHES

- Mask windows with a double thickness of paper. Cover all openings where paint might enter aircraft.
- Clean airplane surface to be painted with solvent (lacquer thinner

or methyl ethyl keotone) to remove shop primer, exposed sealer, silicon deposits, and other contaminants which could adversely affect the paint finish.

- Wipe the cleaned surface with a tacky rag to remove dust. Do not touch the surface to be painted with your hands or contact the surface with your clothing.
- Apply one light wet coat of pretreatment wash primer. Mix the wash primer to the manufacturer's directions. Keep air pressure at a minimum during application of the primer to prevent over-spray. **Temperature and humidity will affect drying time of the wash primer. It should dry at least 15 minutes before the zinc chromate primer is applied.**
- After a sufficient drying time has elasped for the wash primer, tacky the surface and apply a wet coat of zinc chromate primer. The zinc chromate is thinned one part primer to two parts toluol. Mix only enough primer for use within an 8 hour period. Primer mixed longer than 8 hours must be discarded.
- With a fine grit sandpaper (400 to 600), very lightly sand the zinc chromate primer surface and remove the sanding dust with a tacky rag.
- The exterior surfaces are now ready for the color coat. Cross-coat the color application until complete coverage is obtained.

Touch-up of Enamel Finishes
- Mask around the skin containing the damaged area.
- Remove any loose edges of paint by using a high tack adhesive tape around the edge of the damaged area.
- Using a coarse sandpaper, fair the edge of the damaged area with the metal.
- When the edge of the paint begins to "feather" into a smooth joint, use a fine grade of sandpaper to eliminate the sand scratches left by the coarse paper so that the finish will be perfectly smooth. Take care to avoid removing any more metal than is absolutely necessary.
- Wash the sanded area with a solvent, such as naphtha. Change the wash cloths used for this purpose frequently so that all the sanding dust will be picked up.
- After the area to be touched up has been cleaned with solvent until all trace of discoloration is gone, apply a coat of pretreatment primer to the damaged area.
- Spray two or three coats of zinc chromate primer, for a heavier than normal build-up.
- After the primer has dried, sand the area being repaired with a medium fine sandpaper. Sand the edge of the repair area until the indention where the metal and the old paint meet is gone. If it is

necessary, apply additional primer until the junction of the paint and metal is no longer visible.
- Spray on two thin topcoats of finish paint.

REPLACEMENT OF EXISTING EPOXY PAINT FINISH

Beside forming a tougher film than enamel or lacquer, epoxy has a very lustrous finish. However, the painted surface oxidizes a little faster than enamel or lacquer, and must be polished more frequently to retain the sheen. Oxidation is accelerated by exposure to the sun, hence, in hot weather oxidation will occur faster than in cold weather. A good coat of wax will protect the aircraft surface from the sun's rays and keep the surface from oxiding as fast. Any good automotive polish or wax can be used.

At temperatures below 70 degrees F, the paint cure time required for any of the paints used in this procedure will extend beyond the time normally required. Under no circumstances should the paint be applied at temperatures below 60 degrees F, since the paint will not cure.

The skin may be finished with pretreatment (wash) primer, epoxy primer, and a topcoat of epoxy enamel. The following procedures include cleaning, paint stripping, prepaint preparation, priming, epoxy painting, and an alternate method for small repairs that does not involve paint stripping. Careful observance of these procedures should result in a smooth, high lustre finish with firm adhesion for maximum life.

Paint Stripping and Cleaning

Epoxy paints and primer are difficult to strip because of their resistance to chemicals and solvents, therefore, a paint stripper made specifically for epoxy paints should be used.

If an epoxy stripper is not available, use a good enamel stripper. Removing the finish with such a substitute will require several applications and working the stripper with a stiff brush or wooden scraper.
- Mask around the edge of the skin containing the damaged area. Use a double thickness of heavy paper to prevent accidental splashes of paint stripper from penetrating the masking.
- Apply epoxy stripper as indicated by the manufacturer's directions. Try to stay approximately ⅛ inch away from the masking tape. This will necessitate a little more clean up upon finishing. but will prevent any damage to the finish on the next skin. The stripper will not attack aluminum during the stripping process and can be neutralized by rinsing the affected area with water.

CAUTION

Epoxy stripper usually contains acids that will irritate or burn the skin. Wear rubber gloves and eye protection when using the stripper.
- Rinse the area with water and dry.
- Wash the stripped area carefully with a solvent such as acetone, methyl ethyl ketone, or lacquer thinner. This will prevent tiny particles of loose paint from adhering to the stripped area.
- Using a nylon scratch pad dipped in clean water, clean the surface with a cleanser such as Bon Ami, Ajax, Comet Cleanser, etc. A good scouring will leave the surface completely clean.
- Rinse thoroughly with clean water and dry the affected area carefully. If the stripped area includes several joints or skin laps, let the aircraft sit until all moisture has dried. This may be accelerated by blowing the skin laps with compressed air. Wet masking should be replaced.

Pretreatment (Wash) Primer

An acid etching primer that conforms to specification MIL-C-8514 should be applied to improve adhesion of the finishing coats.
- Mix the primer in accordance with the manufacturers instructions.
- Apply a thin wet coat of primer. It should dry for at least an hour, but not over 6 hours before applying epoxy primer.

Epoxy Primer

- Mix epoxy primer in accordance with the manufacturers instructions. For the best results these directions must be followed carefully, since some manufacturers require that the primers be allowed to set for ½ hour after the catalyst and base have been mixed while others allow immediate use after mixing.
- Apply a thin coat of epoxy primer with a spray gun using 35 to 40 psi of air pressure. A dappled appearance indicates that the coat is too thin.
- If the initial coat is allowed to cure for more than 24 hours before topcoating, sand the primer slightly to roughen the surface to assure adhesion. Wipe off the surface with a cloth dampened with a solvent (such as lacquer thinner), then apply the topcoat.

Applying Epoxy Topcoat

- Mix the paint and catalyst as directed by the manufacturer.
- Apply the topcoat with a spray gun at 35 to 45 psi of air pressure. Two coats are normally required to fully conceal the primer and build up the topcoat film to a thickness necessary for adequate service life and beauty. The epoxy finish will normally cure to

approximately 85% of its full hardness in 24 hours at temperatures of 80 degrees F or higher.

Epoxy Touch-up Paint Repair

- Mask around the skin containing the damaged area.
- Remove any loose edges of paint by using a high tack adhesive tape around the edge of the damaged area.
- Using a coarse sandpaper, fair the edge of the damaged area with the metal.
- When the edge of the paint begins to fair into a smooth joint, use a fine grade of sandpaper to eliminate the sand scratches left by the coarse paper so that the finish will be perfectly smooth. Take care to avoid removing any more metal than is absolutely necessary.
- Wash the sanded area with a solvent, such as lacquer thinner or methyl ethyl ketone. Change the wash cloths used for this purpose frequently so that all of the sanding dust will be picked up.
- After the area to be touched up has been cleaned with solvent until all trace of discoloration is gone, apply a thin coat of pretreatment primer to the damaged area.

Note

If a metal conversion coating such as iridite or alodine is used, the wash primer coating can be dispensed with. If the metal has not been treated with a metal conversion coating but no wash primer is available, carefully clean the surface to be touched up and apply epoxy primer to the bare metal. This will produce a satisfactory undercoat for the repair area.

- Spray two or three coats of epoxy for a heavier than normal buildup of primer.
- After the epoxy primer has cured for 24 hours, sand the area being repaired with a medium fine sandpaper. Sand the edge of the repair area until the indentation where the metal and the old paint meet is gone. If necessary, apply additional epoxy primer until the conjunction of old paint with metal is no longer visible.
- Spray on two topcoats.

REPLACEMENT OF EXISTING POLYURETHANE (URETHANE) FINISHES

The surfaces may be finished with pretreatment (wash) primer, urethane primer, and a topcoat of urethane enamel. The following procedures include cleaning, paint stripping, prepaint preparation, priming, applying a urethane topcoat, and an alternate method for small repairs not requiring paint stripping. Careful observance of these procedures should result in a smooth, hard, glossy finish with firm adhesion for maximum life.

Paint Stripping and Cleaning Urethane Paint

Because of their resistance to chemicals and solvents, urethane paints and primers require a special paint stripper. If a urethane stripper is not available, a good enamel stripper may be used. Removing the finish with such a substitute will require several applications while working the stripper in with a stiff brush or wooden scraper.

- Mask around the edge of the skin or skins containing the damaged area. Use a double thickness of heavy paper to prevent accidental splashes of paint stripper from penetrating the masking.
- Apply urethane stripper as indicated by the manufacturer's directions. Try to stay approximately ⅛ inch away from the masking tape. This will necessitate a little more cleanup upon finishing, but will prevent damage to the finish on the next skin. The strippers will not attack aluminum during the stripping process and can be neutralized afterwards by rinsing the affected area with water.

Urethane strippers usually contain acids that irritate or burn the skin. Wear rubber gloves and eye protection when using the stripper.

- Rinse the area with water and dry.
- Wash the stripped area carefully with a solvent such as acetone, methyl ethyl ketone, or lacquer thinner. This will prevent tiny particles of loose paint from adhering to the stripped area.
- Using a nylon scratch pad dipped in clean water, clean the surface with a cleanser such as Bon Ami, Ajax, Comet Cleanser, etc. A good scouring will leave the surface completely clean.
- Thoroughly rinse with clean water and carefully dry the affected area. If the stripped area includes several joints of skin laps, let the aircraft sit until all moisture has dried. This may be accelerated by blowing the skin laps and seams with compressed air. Wet masking should be replaced.

Pretreatment (Wash) Primer for Urethane Paint

An acid etching primer that conforms to Specification MIL-C-8514 should be applied to improve adhesion of the finishing coats.

- Mix the primer in accordance with the manufacturers instructions.
- Apply a thin wet coat of primer. It should be permitted to dry for at least one hour, but not over six hours, before the next coat of urethane primer is applied.

Urethane Primer

- Mix the urethane catalyst and base in accordance with the manufacturers instructions when preparing the primer.

For the best results these directions must be followed carefully, for some manufacturers require that the primer be allowed to set for ½ hour after the catalyst and base have been mixed while others recommend immediate use after mixing.

- Apply a coat of urethane primer with a spray gun using 35 to 40 psi of air pressure. A dappled appearance only indicates that the coat is thin.
- If the initial coat is allowed to cure for more than 24 hours before the topcoat is applied, sand the primer slightly to roughen the surface and assure adhesion. Wipe off the surface with a cloth dampened with a solvent (such as lacquer thinner), then apply the topcoat.

Applying Optional Urethane Topcoats

- Mix the paint and catalyst as directed by the manufacturer.
- Apply the topcoat with a spray gun at 35 to 45 psi of air pressure. Two coats are required to fully conceal the primer and build up the topcoat film necessary for adequate service life and beauty. The urethane finish will normally cure to approximately 85% of its full hardness in 24 hours at temperatures of 80 degrees F or higher.

Urethane Touch-Up Repair

- Mask around the skin containing the damage area.
- Remove all loose edges of paint by using a high tack adhesive tape around the edge of the damaged area.
- Using a coarse sandpaper, fair the edge of the damaged area with the metal.
- When the edge of the paint begins to fair into a smooth joint, use a fine grade of sandpaper to eliminate the scratches left by the coarse paper. Take care to avoid removing any more metal than is absolutely necessary.
- Wash the sanded area with a solvent, such as lacquer thinner or methyl ethyl ketone. Change the wash cloths used for this purpose often so that all the sanding dirt will be picked up.
- After the area to be touched up has been cleaned with solvent until all traces of discoloration are gone, apply a thin coat of pretreatment primer to the damaged area.

If a metal conversion coating such as iridite or alodine is used, the wash primer coating can be dispensed with. If the metal has not been treated with a metal conversion coating but no wash primer is available, carefully clean the surface to be touched up and apply urethane primer to the bare metal. This should produce a satisfactory undercoat for the repair area.

- After the urethane primer has cured for 24 hours, sand the area under repair with medium fine sandpaper. Sand the edge of the repair area until the indentation where the metal and old paint meet is gone. If necessary, apply additional urethane primer until the juncture of old paint with metal is no longer visible.

Note

The time normally required for urethane paint to cure must be extended at temperatures below 70 degrees F. The paint will not cure at temperatures below 60 degrees F.

PAINT SYSTEM COMPATIBILITY

The use of several different types of paint, coupled with several proprietary coatings, makes repair of damaged and deteriorated areas particularly difficult, since paint finishes are not necessarily compatible with each other. The following general rules for constituent compatibility are included for information and are not necessarily listed in the order of importance:

- Old type zinc chromate primer may be used directly for touchup of bare metal surfaces and for use on interior finishes. It may be overcoated with wash primers if it is in good condition. Acrylic lacquer finishes will not adhere to this material.
- Modified zinc chromate primer will not adhere satisfactorily to bare metal. It must never be used over a dried film of acrylic nitrocellulose lacquer.
- Nitrocellulose coatings will adhere to acrylic finishes, but the reverse is not true. Acrylic nitrocellulose lacquers may not be used over old nitrocellulose finishes.
- Acrylic nitrocellulose lacquers will adhere poorly to both nitrocellulose and epoxy finishes and to bare metal generally. For best results the lacquers must be applied over fresh, successive coatings of wash primer and modified zinc chromate. They will also adhere to freshly applied epoxy coatings (dried less than 6 hrs.).
- Epoxy topcoats will adhere to all the paint systems that are in good condition and may be used for general touchup, including touchup of defects in baked enamel coatings.
- Old wash primer coats may be overcoated directly with epoxy finishes. A new second coat of wash primer must be applied if an acrylic finish is to be applied.
- Old acrylic finishes may be refinished with new acrylic if the old coating is thoroughly softened using acrylic nitrocellulose thinner before paint touchup.
- Damage to epoxy finishes can best be repaired by using more epoxy, since neither of the lacquer finishes will stick to the epoxy surface. In some instances, air-drying enamels may be used for

touchup of epoxy coatings if edges of damaged areas are first roughened with abrasive paper.

METHODS OF APPLYING FINISHES

There are several methods of applying aircraft finishes. Among the most common are dipping, brushing, and spraying. Spraying however, is the most practical method for use by the field mechanic.

Spray Painting

All spray systems have several basic similarities. There must be an adequate source of compressed air, a reservoir or feed tank to hold a supply of the finishing material, and a device for controlling the combination of air and finishing material ejected in an atomized cloud or spray against the surface to be coated.

There are two main types of spray equipment. A spray gun with integral paint container as shown in figure 9-1 is satisfactory when painting small areas. When large areas are painted, pressure-feed equipment is usually preferred, since a large supply of finishing material can be provided under constant pressure to a pressure-feed type of spray gun.

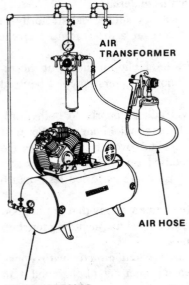

AIR TRANSFORMER

AIR HOSE

AIR COMPRESSOR

Figure 9-1.

A typical suction type spray gun, water extractor, regulator, hose and air compressor.

The air-pressure supply must be entirely free from water or oil to obtain good spray painting. Oil and water traps as well as suitable filters must be incorporated in the air pressure supply line. These filters and traps must be serviced on a regular basis.

The spray gun can be adjusted to give a circular or fan type of spray pattern. Figure 9-2 shows the spray pattern at various dial settings. When covering large surfaces, set the gun just below maximum width of the fan spray. The circular spray is suitable for "spotting-in" small areas.

The gun should be held 6 to 10 in. away from the surface and the contour of the work carefully followed. It is important that the gun be kept at right angles to the surface. Each stroke of the spray gun should be straight and the trigger released just before completing the stroke. The speed of movement should be regulated to deposit an even, wet, but not too heavy, coat.

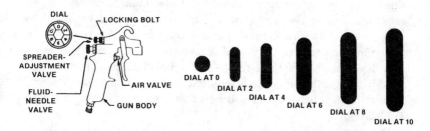

Figure 9-2. Spray patterns at various dial settings.

Each stroke of the gun should be overlapped to keep a wet film, thus absorbing the dry edges of the previous stroke.

The spray should be applied as an even, wet coat that will flow out smoothly and be free from "spray dust." Inadequate coverage results from spraying too lightly and "runs" and "sags" from spraying too heavily.

To aid in obtaining good results, make sure the air pressure to the spray gun is between 40 and 80 p.s.i., depending on the material being used. With air pressures below 40 p.s.i. spraying is slow and tedious. Also, with viscous materials, full atomization is not obtained. Above 80 p.s.i. "dust" and blowback become troublesome.

When using pressure-feed equipment, adjust the air pressure in the container according to the viscosity of the paint and the length of the fluid hose used. The pressure must be such that the material reaches the spray gun head in a gentle and continuous flow. Generally, a pressure between 5 and 15 p.s.i. should be used. Higher pressures lead to runs and sags caused by the delivery of too much paint.

PREPARATION OF PAINT

Before paint is used, it must be stirred thoroughly so that any pigment which may have settled to the bottom of the container is brought into suspension and distributed evenly throughout the paint.

If a film, called "skinning," has formed over the paint, the skin must be completely removed before stirring. A mechanical agitator or tumbler may be used. However, as tumbling does not always remove pigment caked at the bottom of the container, a test with a stirrer should be made to ensure that the pigment is completely held in suspension. For hand stirring, a flat-bladed, nonferrous stirrer should be used.

The degree of thinning depends on the type of spray equipment, air pressure, atmospheric conditions and the type of paint being used. No hard and fast rule for thinning ratios can be applied. Because of the importance of accurate thinning, some manufacturers recommend the use of viscosity control. This is usually accomplished by using a viscosity (flow) cup. When the right proportion of thinner is mixed into the material, a cupful of material will flow out completely in a designated number of seconds. The finishing manufacturer can specify the number of seconds required for a given material. Material thinned using this method will be of the correct viscosity for best application.

In many cases manufacturers recommend that all materials should be strained before use. A 60- to 90-mesh strainer is suitable for this purpose. Strainers are available in metal gauze, paper, or nylon mesh.

COMMON PAINT TROUBLES

Poor Adhesion

Paint properly applied to correctly pretreated surfaces should adhere satisfactorily, and when it is thoroughly dry, it should not be possible to remove it easily, even by firm scratching with the fingernail. poor adhesion may result from one of the following:

(1) Inadequate cleaning and pretreatment.
(2) Inadequate stirring of paint or primer.
(3) Coating at incorrect time intervals.
(4) Application under adverse conditions.
(5) Bad application.

Spray Dust

Spray dust is caused by the atomized particles becoming dry before reaching the surface being painted and thus failing to flow into a continuous film. The usual causes are incorrect air pressure or the distance the gun is held from the work.

Sags and Runs

Sags and runs result from too much paint being applied causing the film of wet paint to move by gravity and presenting a sagging appearance. Incorrect viscosity, air pressure, and gun handling are frequent causes. However, inadequate surface preparation may also be repsonsible.

Spray Mottle

Sometimes known as "orange peel" or "pebble," spray mottle is usually caused by incorrect paint viscosity, air pressure, spray gun setting, or the distance the gun is held from the work.

Blushing

Blushing is one of the most common troubles experienced and appears as a "clouding" or "blooming" of the paint film. It is more common with the cellulose than synthetic materials. It may be caused by moisture in the air supply line, adverse humidity, drafts, or sudden changes in temperature.

PAINTING TRIM AND IDENTIFICATION NUMBERS

When an aircraft is being painted, the predominate color usually is applied first over the entire surface. The trim colors are applied over the base color after it dries. When the top of the fuselage is to be painted white with a dark color adjoining it, the light color is applied and feathered into the area to be painted with the dark color. When the light color has dried, masking tape and paper are placed along the line of separation and the dark color is then sprayed on.

Allow the paint to dry for several hours before removing the masking tape. Remove the tape by pulling slowly parallel to the surface. This will reduce the possibility of peeling off the finish with the tape.

All aircraft are required to display nationality and registration marks. These marks may be painted on or affixed using self-adhering plastic figures. The marks must be formed of solid lines using a color that contrasts with the background. No ornamentation may be used with the markings, and they must be affixed with a material or paint that produces a degree of permanence. Aircraft scheduled for immediate delivery to a foreign purchaser may display marks that can be easily removed. Aircraft manufactured in the United States for delivery outside the U.S. may display identification marks required by the State of registry of the aircraft. The aircraft may be operated only for test and demonstration flights for a limited period of time or for delivery to the purchaser.

Aircraft registered in the United States must display the Roman capital letter "N" followed by the registration number of the aircraft. The location and size of the identification marks vary according to the type of aircraft. The location and size are prescribed in the Federal Aviation Regulations.

CLEANING AND WAXING THE AIRCRAFT FINISH

Because the wax seals the paint from the outside air, a new paint job **should not be waxed for a period of 90 days** to allow the paint to cure. For uncured painted surfaces, wash only with cold or lukewarm (never hot) water and a mild nondetergent soap. Any rubbing of the painted surface should be done gently and held to a minimum to avoid cracking the paint film.

After the paint cures a thorough waxing will protect painted and unpainted metal surfaces from a variety of highly corrosive elements. Flush loose dirt away first with clear water, then wash the airplane with a mild soap and water. Harsh, abrasive or alkaline soaps or detergents should never be used. Use soft cloths or chamois to prevent scratches when cleaning and polishing. Any good trade automobile wax may be used to preserve painted surfaces. To remove stubborn oil and grease, use a soft cloth dampened with naphtha. After cleaning with naphtha, the surface should be rewaxed and polished.

Piper Seminole

Chapter 10
Assembly and Rigging

This chapter includes both assembly and rigging since the subjects are directly related. Assembly involves putting together the component sections of the aircraft, such as wing sections, empennage units, nacelles, and landing gear. Rigging is the final adjustment and alignment of the various component sections to provide the proper aerodynamic reaction.

Two important considerations in all assembly and rigging operations are: (1) Proper operation of the component in regard to its aerodynamic and mechanical function, and (2) maintaining the aircraft's structural integrity by the correct use of materials, hardware, and safetying devices. Improper assembly and rigging may result in certain members being subjected to loads greater than those for which they were designed.

Assembly and rigging must be done in accordance with the requirements prescribed by the aircraft manufacturer. These procedures are usually detailed in the applicable maintenance or service manuals. The Aircraft Specification or Type Certificate Data Sheets also provide valuable information regarding control surface travel.

The rigging of control systems varies with each type of aircraft, therefore, it would be impracticable to define a precise procedure. However, certain principles apply in all situations and these will be discussed in this chapter. **It is essential that the aircraft manufacturer's instructions be followed when rigging an aircraft.**

CONTROL SYSTEMS

Three types of control systems commonly used are: (1) The cable, (2) push-pull, and (3) the torque tube system. The cable system is the most widely used because deflections of the structure to which it is attached do not affect its operation. Many aircraft incorporate control systems that are combinations of all three types.

Flight Control System Hardware, Mechanical Linkage, and Mechanisms

The systems which operate the control surfaces, tabs, and flaps include flight control system hardware, linkage, and mechanisms. These items connect the control surfaces to the cockpit controls. Included in these systems are cable assemblies, cable guides, linkage, adjustable stops, control surface snubber or locking devices, surface control booster units, actuators operated by electric motors, and actuators operated by hydraulic motors.

Cables are the most widely used linkage in primary flight control systems. Cable-type linkage is also used in engine controls, emergency extension systems for the landing gear, and various other systems throughout the aircraft.

CABLE ASSEMBLY

The conventional cable assembly consists of flexible cable, terminals (end fittings) for attaching to other units, and turnbuckles.

Cable-type linkage has several advantages over the other types. It is strong and light in weight, and its flexibility makes it easy to route through the aircraft. An aircraft cable has a high mechanical efficiency and can be set up without backlash, which is very important for precise control.

Cable linkage also has some disadvantages. Tension must be adjusted frequently due to stretching and temperature changes.

Aircraft control cables are fabricated from carbon steel or stainless steel.

Cable Construction

The basic component of a cable is a wire. The diameter of the wire determines the total diameter of the cable. A number of wires are preformed into a helical or spiral shape and then formed into a strand. These preformed strands are laid around a straight center strand to form a cable.

Cable designations are based on the number of strands and the number of wires in each strand. The most common aircraft cables are the 7 X 7 and 7 X 19.

The 7 X 7 cable consists of seven strands of seven wires each. Six of these strands are laid around the center strand (see figure 10-1). This is a cable of medium flexibility and is used for trim tab controls, engine controls, and indicator controls.

The 7 x 19 cable is made up of seven strands of 19 wires each. Six of these strands are laid around the center strand (see figure 10-1). This cable is extra flexible and is used in primary control systems and in other places where operation over pulleys is frequent.

Aircraft control cables vary in diameter, ranging from 1/16 to ⅜ inch. The diameter is measured as shown in figure 10-1.

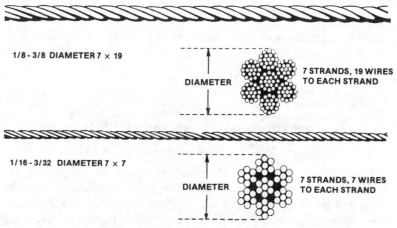

1/8 - 3/8 DIAMETER 7 × 19

DIAMETER

7 STRANDS, 19 WIRES TO EACH STRAND

1/16 - 3/32 DIAMETER 7 × 7

DIAMETER

7 STRANDS, 7 WIRES TO EACH STRAND

Figure 10-1. The most common aircraft cables are 7x7 of medium flexibility and 7x19, extra flexible.

Cable Fittings

Cables may be equipped with several different types of fittings such as terminals, thimbles, bushings, and shackles.

Terminal fittings are generally of the swaged type. They are available in the threaded end, fork end, eye end, single-shank ball end, and double-shank ball end. The threaded end, fork end, and eye end terminals are used to connect the cable to a turnbuckle, bellcrank, or other linkage in the system. The ball-end terminals are used for attaching cables to quadrants and special connections where space is limited. Figure 10-2 illustrates the various types of terminal fittings.

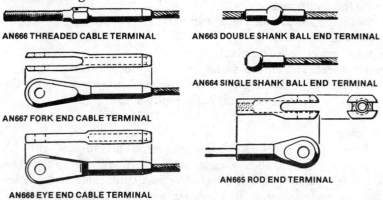

AN666 THREADED CABLE TERMINAL

AN663 DOUBLE SHANK BALL END TERMINAL

AN664 SINGLE SHANK BALL END TERMINAL

AN667 FORK END CABLE TERMINAL

AN665 ROD END TERMINAL

AN668 EYE END CABLE TERMINAL

Figure 10-2. Various types of terminal fittings.

The thimble, bushing, and shackle fittings may be used in place of some types of terminal fittings when facilities and supplies are limited and immediate replacement of the cable is necessary.

Turnbuckles

A turnbuckle assembly is a mechanical screw device consisting of two threaded terminals and a threaded barrel. Figure 10-3 illustrates a typical turnbuckle assembly.

Figure 10-3. A typical turnbuckle assembly.

Turnbuckles are fitted in the cable assembly for the purpose of making minor adjustments in cable length and for adjusting cable tension. One of the terminals has right-hand threads and the other has left-hand threads. The barrel has matching right- and left-hand internal threads. The end of the barrel with the left-hand threads can usually be identified by a groove or knurl around that end of the barrel.

When installing a turnbuckle in a control system, it is necessary to screw both of the terminals an equal number of turns into the barrel. It is also essential that all turnbuckle terminals be screwed into the barrel until not more than three threads are exposed on either side of the turnbuckle barrel.

After a turnbuckle is properly adjusted, it must be safetied. The methods of safetying turnbuckles are discussed later in this chapter.

FABRICATING A CABLE ASSEMBLY

Terminals for aircraft control cables are normally fabricated using three different processes:
- Swaging as used in all modern aircraft
- Nicopress process
- Hand woven splice terminal.

Hand woven splices are found on many older aircraft; however, this is a time consuming process considered unnecessary with the availability of mechanically fabricated splices.

Swaging

Swage type terminals, manufactured in accordance with Air Force-Navy Aeronautical Standard Specifications, are suitable for use in civil aircraft up to and including maximum cable loads. When swaging tools are used, it is important that all the manufacturers' instructions, including "go and no-go" dimensions, be followed in detail to avoid defective and inferior swaging. Observance of all instructions should result in a terminal developing the full rated strength of the cable. Critical dimensions, both before and after swaging, are shown in figure 10-4.

Cable size (inches)	Wire strands	Before swaging				After swaging	
		Outside diameter	Bore diameter	Bore length	Swaging length	Minimum breaking strength (pounds)	Shank diameter*
1/16	7×7	0. 160	0. 078	1. 042	0. 969	480	0. 138
3/32	7×7	. 218	. 109	1. 261	1. 188	920	. 190
1/8	7×19	. 250	. 141	1. 511	1. 438	2, 000	. 219
5/32	7×19	. 297	. 172	1. 761	1. 688	2, 800	. 250
3/16	7×19	. 359	. 203	2. 011	1. 938	4, 200	. 313
7/32	7×19	. 427	. 234	2. 261	2. 188	5, 600	. 375
1/4	7×19	. 494	. 265	2. 511	2. 438	7, 000	. 438
9/32	7×19	. 563	. 297	2. 761	2. 688	8, 000	. 500
5/16	7×19	. 635	. 328	3. 011	2. 938	9, 800	. 563
3/8	7×19	. 703	. 390	3. 510	3. 438	14, 400	. 625

*Use gages in kit for checking diameters.

Figure 10-4. Straight-shank terminal dimensions for AN-666, 667, 668 and 669 terminal fittings.

When swaging terminals onto cable ends, observe the following procedure:

• Cut the cable to the proper length, allowing for growth during swaging. Apply a preservative compound to the cable ends before insertion into the terminal barrel. Never solder cable ends to prevent fraying since the presence of the solder will greatly increase the tendency of the cable to pull out of the terminal.

• Insert the cable into the terminal approximately one inch, and bend toward the terminal; straighten the cable back to normal position and then push the cable end entirely into the terminal barrel. See figure 10-5. The bending action puts a kink or bend in the cable end and provides enough friction to hold the terminal in place until the swaging operation can be performed. Bending also tends to separate the strands inside the barrel, thereby reducing the strain on them. If the terminal is drilled completely through, push the cable into the terminal until it reaches the approximate position shown in figure 10-5. If the hole is not drilled through, insert the cable until the end rests against the bottom of the hole.

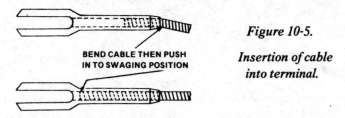

BEND CABLE THEN PUSH
IN TO SWAGING POSITION

Figure 10-5.

Insertion of cable into terminal.

• Accomplish the swaging operation in accordance with the instrutions furnished by the manufacturer of the swaging equipment.
• Inspect the terminal after swaging to determine that it is free from die marks and splits, and is not out-of-round. Check for cable slippage in the terminal and for cut or broken wire strands.
• Using a "go no-go" gauge or a micrometer, check the terminal barrel diameter as shown in figure 10-6.

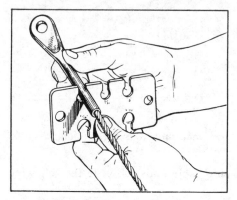

Figure 10-6.

Using a "go, no-go" gauge for checking the terminal shank after swaging.

• Test the cable by proof-loading it to 60 percent of its rated breaking strength.

Completely severed cables, or those badly damaged in a localized area, may be repaired by the use of an eye terminal bolted to a clevis terminal. (See figure 10-7a.) However, this type of splice can only be used in free lengths of cable which do not pass over pulleys or through fair-leads.

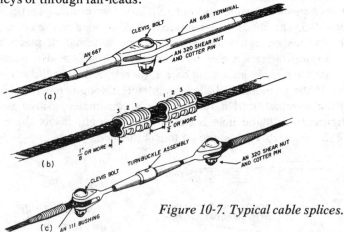

Figure 10-7. Typical cable splices.

On some aircraft cables, swaged ball terminals are used for attaching cables to quadrants and special connections where space is limited. Single shank terminals are generally used at the cable ends, and double shank fittings may be used at either the end or in the center of the cable. Dies are supplied with the swaging machines for attaching these terminals to cables in the following manner:

• The steel balls and shanks have a hole through the center, and are slipped over the cable and positioned in the desired location.

• Perform the swaging operation in accordance with the instructions furnished by the manufacturer of the swaging equipment.

• Check the swaged fitting with a "go no-go" gauge to see that the fitting is properly compressed. (See figure 10-8.) Also inspect the physical condition of the finished terminal.

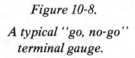

Figure 10-8.

A typical "go, no-go" terminal gauge.

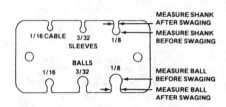

Ensure that the cable is properly inserted in the terminal after the swaging operation is completed. Instances have been noted wherein only ¼ inch of the cable was swaged in the terminal. Observance of the following precautions should minimize this possibility:

(a) Measure the length of the terminal end of the fitting to determine the proper length of cable to be inserted into the barrel of the fitting.

(b) Lay off this length at the end of the cable and mark with masking tape. Since the tape will not slip, it will provide a positive marking during the swaging process.

(c) After swaging, check the tape marker to make certain that the cable did not slip during the swaging operation.

(d) Remove the tape and, using red paint, paint the junction of the swaged fitting and cable.

(e) At all subsequent service inspections of the swaged fittings, check for a gap in the painted section to see if cable slippage has occurred.

Nicopress Process

A patented process using copper sleeves may be used up to the full rated strength of the cable when the cable is looped around a thimble. This process may also be used in place of the five-tuck splice on cables up to and including ⅜-inch diameter. The use of sleeves that are fabricated of materials other than copper will require engineering approval of the specific application by a representative of the Federal Aviation Administration.

Before undertaking a nicopress splice, determine the proper

tool and sleeve for the cable to be used. Refer to figures 10-9 and 10-11 for details on sleeves, tools, and the number of presses required for the various sizes of aircraft cable. The tool must be in good working condition and properly adjusted to assure a satisfactory splice.

Cable size	Copper oval sleeve stock No.		Manual tool No.	Sleeve length before compression (approx.) (inches)	Sleeve length after compression (approx.) (inches)	Number of presses	Tested strength (pounds)
	Plain	Plated*					
3/64	18-11-B4	28-11-B4	51-B4-887	3/8	3/16	1	340
1/16	18-1-C	28-1-C	51-C-887	3/8	3/16	1	550
3/32	18-2-G	28-2-G	51-G-887	7/16	1/2	1	1,180
1/8	18-3-M	28-3-M	51-M-850	9/16	3/4	3	2,300
5/32	18-4-P	28-4-P	51-P-850	3/4	7/8	3	3,050
3/16	18-6-X	28-6-X	51-X-850	1	1 1/4	4	4,350
7/32	18-8-F2	28-8-F2	51-F2-850	7/8	1 1/16	4	5,790
1/4	18-10-F6	28-10-F6	3-F6-950	1 1/4	1 1/2	3	7,180
5/16	18-13-G9	28-13-G9	3-G9-950	1 1/4	1 5/8	3	11,130
			No. 635 Hydraulic tool dies				
3/8	18-23-H5	28-23-H5	Oval H5	1 1/2	1 7/8	1	16,800
7/16	18-24-J8	28-24-J8	Oval J8	1 3/4	2 3/8	2	19,700
1/2	18-25-K8	28-25-K8	Oval K8	1 3/4	2 1/2	2	25,200
9/16	18-27-M1	28-27-M1	Oval M1	2	2 5/8	3	31,025
5/8	18-28-N5	28-28-N5	Oval N5	2 3/8	3 1/4	3	39,200

*Required on stainless cable.

Figure 10-9. Copper oval sleeve data.

Figure 10-10. A typical nicopress thimble-eye splice. The sleeve should be compressed in the 1-2-3 sequence shown.

Figure 10-11.

Copper stop sleeve data.

Cable size (inch)	Sleeve No.	Tool No.	Sleeve length (inch)	Sleeve O.D. (inch)	Tested strength (pounds)
3/64	871-12-B4	51-B4-887	7/32	11/64	280
1/16	871-1-C	51-C-887	7/32	13/64	525
3/32	871-17-J (Yellow)	51-MJ	5/16	21/64	600
1/8	871-18-J (Red)	51-MJ	5/16	21/64	800
5/32	871-19-M	51-MJ	5/16	27/64	1,200
3/16	871-20-M (Black)	51-MJ	5/16	27/64	1,600
7/32	871-22-M	51-MJ	5/8	7/16	2,300
1/4	871-23-F6	3-F6-950	11/16	21/32	3,500
5/16	871-26-F6	3-F6-950	11/16	21/32	3,800

NOTE: All stop sleeves are plain copper—certain sizes are colored for identification.

To compress a sleeve, have it well centered in the tool groove with the major axis of the sleeve at right angles to the tool. If the sleeve appears to be out of line after the press is started, open the tool, re-center the sleeve, and complete the press.

Initially position the cable so that the end will extend slightly beyond the sleeve, as the sleeve will elongate somewhat when it is compressed. If the cable end is inside the sleeve, the splice may not hold the full strength of the cable. It is desirable that the oval sleeve be placed in close proximity to the thimble points, so that when compressed the sleeve will contact the thimble as shown in figure 10-10. The sharp ends of the thimble may be cut off before being used; however, make certain the thimble is firmly secured in the cable loop after the splice has been completed. When using a sleeve requiring three compressions, make the center compression first, the compression next to the thimble second, and the one farthest from the thimble last as shown in figure 10-10.

Lap or running splices may also be made with copper oval sleeves. When making such splices, it is usually necessary to use two sleeves to develop the full strength of the cable. The sleeves should be positioned as shown in figure 10-7b, and the compressions made in the order shown. As in the case of eye splices, it is desirable to have the cable ends extend beyond the sleeves sufficiently to allow for the increased length of the compressed sleeves.

Stop sleeves may be used for special cable end and intermediate fittings and they are installed in the same manner as Nicopress oval sleeves. All stop sleeves are plain copper—certain sizes are colored for identification.

To make a satisfactory copper sleeve installation, it is important that the amount of sleeve pressure be kept uniform. The completed sleeves should be checked periodically with the proper gauge. Hold the gauge so that it contacts the major axis of the sleeve. The compressed portion at the center of the sleeve should enter the gauge opening with very little clearance, as shown in figure 10-12. If it does not, the tool must be adjusted accordingly.

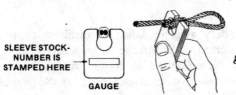

SLEEVE STOCK-
NUMBER IS
STAMPED HERE

GAUGE

Figure 10-12.

Typical "go, no-go" gauge for nicopress terminals.

Hand Fabricated Cable Assemblies

Figure 10-13 shows the general procedure for hand fabricating a cable splice. Due to its limited use in the light of mechanical fabrication, detail discussion of hand fabrication of a cable splice will not be presented.

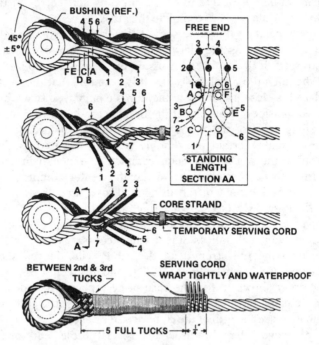

Figure 10-13. Preparation of a woven cable splice.

SAFETY METHODS FOR TURNBUCKLES

After a turnbuckle has been properly adjusted, it must be safetied. There are several methods of safetying turnbuckles; however, only two methods will be discussed in this section. These methods are illustrated in figure 10-14 (A) and 10-14 (B). The clip-locking method is used only on the most modern aircraft. The older type aircraft still use the type turnbuckles that require the wire-wrapping method.

Double-Wrap Method

Of the methods using safety wire for safetying turnbuckles, the double-wrap method is preferred, although the single-wrap methods described are satisfactory. The method of double-wrap safetying is shown in figure 10-14 (B). Use two separate lengths of the proper wire as shown in figure 10-15. Run one end of the wire through the hole in the barrel of the turnbuckle and bend the ends of the wire towards opposite ends of the turnbuckle. Then pass the second length of the wire into the hole in the barrel and bend the ends along the barrel on the side opposite the first. Then pass the wires at

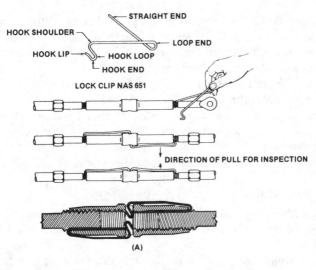

LOCK CLIP NAS 651

DIRECTION OF PULL FOR INSPECTION

(A)

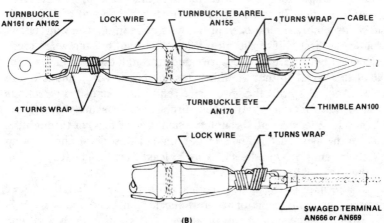

(B)

Figure 10-14. Methods of safetying turnbuckles.

Cable size (in.)	Type of wrap	Diameter of safety wire (in.)	Material (annealed condition)
1/16	Single	.020	Stainless steel
3/32	Single	.040	Copper, brass[1]
1/8	Single	.040	Stainless steel
1/8	Double	.040	Copper, brass[1]
1/8	Single	.057 min	Copper, brass[1]
5/32 and greater	Single	.057	Stainless steel

1. GALVANIZED OR TINNED STEEL, OR SOFT IRON WIRES ARE ALSO ACCEPTABLE.

Figure 10-15. Guide for selecting turnbuckle safety wire.

the end of the turnbuckle in opposite directions through the holes in
the turnbuckle eyes or between the jaws of the turnbuckle fork, as

297

applicable. Bend the laid wires in place before cutting off the wrapped wire. Wrap the remaining length of safety wire at least four turns around the shank and cut it off. Repeat the procedure at the opposite end of the turnbuckle.

When a swaged terminal is being safetied, pass the ends of both wires, if possible, through the hole provided in the terminal for this purpose and wrap both ends around the shank as described above.

If the hole is not large enough to allow passage of both wires, pass the wire through the hole and loop it over the free end of the other wire, and then wrap both ends around the shank as described.

Single-wrap Method

The single-wrap safetying methods described in the following paragraphs are acceptable but are not the equal of the double-wrap methods.

Pass a single length of wire through the cable eye or fork, or through the hole in the swaged terminal at either end of the turnbuckle assembly. Spiral each of the wire ends in opposite directions around the first half of the turnbuckle barrel so that the wires cross each other twice. Thread both wire ends through the hole in the middle of the barrel so that the third crossing of the wire ends is in the hole. Again, spiral the two wire ends in opposite directions around the remaining half of the turnbuckle, crossing them twice. Then, pass one wire end through the cable eye or fork, or through the hole in the swaged terminal. In the manner described above, wrap both wire ends around the shank for at least four turns each, cutting off the excess wire.

An alternate to the above method is to pass one length of wire through the center hole of the turnbuckle and bend the wire ends toward opposite ends of the turnbuckle. Then pass each wire end through the cable eye or fork, or through the hole in the swaged terminal and wrap each wire end around the shank for at least four turns, cutting off the excess wire. After safetying, no more than three threads of the turnbuckle threaded terminal should be exposed.

Cable Connectors

In addition to turnbuckles, cable connectors are used in some systems. These connectors enable a cable length to be quickly connected or disconnected from a system. Figure 10-16 illustrates one type of cable connector in use. This type is connected or disconnected by compressing the spring.

CABLE GUIDES

Cable guides (figure 10-17) consist primarily of fairleads, pressure seals, and pulleys.

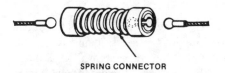

SPRING CONNECTOR

Figure 10-16.

Spring type of cable connector.

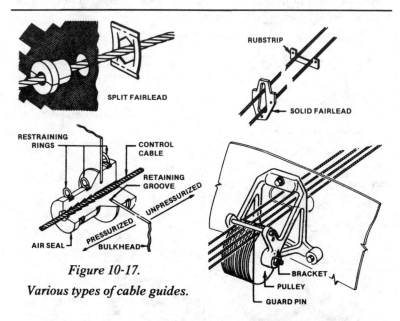

RUBSTRIP

SPLIT FAIRLEAD

SOLID FAIRLEAD

RESTRAINING RINGS

CONTROL CABLE

RETAINING GROOVE

UNPRESSURIZED

PRESSURIZED

AIR SEAL

BULKHEAD

Figure 10-17.

Various types of cable guides.

BRACKET

PULLEY

GUARD PIN

A fairlead may be made from a nonmetallic material, such as phenolic or a metallic material such as soft aluminum. The fairlead completely encircles the cable where it passes through holes in bulkheads or other metal parts. Fairleads are used to guide cables in a straight line through or between structural members of the aircraft. Fairleads should never deflect the alignment of a cable more than 3 degrees from a straight line.

Pressure seals are installed where cables (or rods) move through pressure bulkheads. The seal grips tightly enough to prevent excess air pressure loss but not enough to hinder movement of the cable. Pressure seals should be inspected at regular intervals to determine that the retaining rings are in place. If a retaining ring comes off, it may slide along the cable and cause jamming of a pulley.

Pulleys are used to guide cables and also to change the direction of cable movement. Pulley bearings are sealed, and need no lubrication other than the lubrication done at the factory. Brackets fastened to the structure of the aircraft support the pulleys. Cables passing over pulleys are kept in place by guards. The guards are close-fitting to prevent jamming or to prevent the cables from slipping off when they slacken due to temperature variations.

MECHANICAL LINKAGE

Various mechanical linkages connect the cockpit controls to control cables and surface controls. These devices either transmit motion or change the direction of motion of the control system. The linkage consists primarily of control (push-pull) rods, torque tubes, quadrants, sectors, bellcranks, and cable drums.

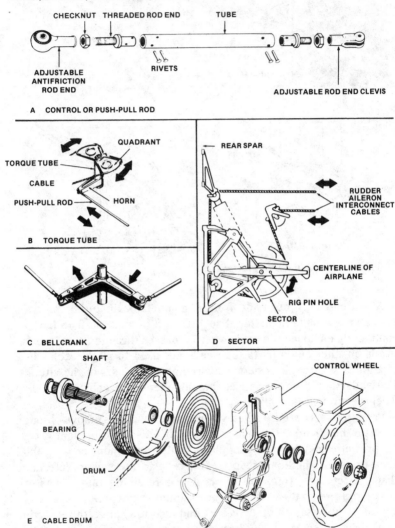

Figure 10-18. Flight control system mechanical linkages.

Control rods are used as links in flight control systems to give a push-pull motion. They may be adjusted at one or both ends. View A of figure 10-18 shows the parts of a control rod. Notice that it consists of a tube having threaded rod ends. An adjustable antifriction rod end, or rod end clevis, attaches at each end of the tube. The rod end, or clevis, permits attachment of the tube to flight control system parts. The checknut, when tightened, prevents the rod end or clevis from loosening.

Control rods should be perfectly straight, unless designed to be otherwise, when they are installed. The bellcrank to which they are attached should be checked for freedom of movement before and after attaching the control rods. The assembly as a whole should be checked for correct alignment. When the rod is fitted with self-aligning bearings, free rotational movement of the rods must be obtained in all positions.

TORQUE TUBES

Where an angular or twisting motion is needed in a control system, a torque tube is installed. View B of figure 10-18 shows how a torque tube is used to transmit motion in opposite directions.

Quadrants, bellcranks, sectors, and drums change direction of motion and transmit motion to parts such as control rods, cables, and torque tubes. The quadrant shown in figure 10-18B is typical of flight control system linkages used by various manufacturers. Figure 10-18C and D illustrate a bellcrank and a sector. View E illustrates a cable drum. Cable drums are used primarily in trim tab systems. As the trim tab control wheel is moved clockwise or counterclockwise, the cable drum winds or unwinds to actuate the trim tab cables.

STOPS

Adjustable and nonadjustable stops (whichever the case requires) are used to limit the throw-range or travel movement of the ailerons, elevator, and rudder. Usually there are two sets of stops for each of the three main control surfaces, one set being located at the control surface, either in the snubber cylinders or as structural stops (figure 10-19), and the other at the cockpit control. Either of these may serve as the actual limit stop. However, those situated at the control surface usually perform this function. In other words, the control surface should always contact its stops before the control column contacts its stops. The other stops do not normally contact each other, but are adjusted to a definite clearance when the control surface is at the full extent of its travel. These work as over-ride stops to prevent stretching of cables and damage to the control system during violent maneuvers. **When rigging control systems, refer to the applicable maintenance manual for the sequence of steps for adjusting these stops to limit the control surface travel.**

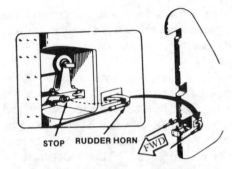

Figure 10-19.
Adjustable rudder stops.

STOP   RUDDER HORN   FWD

CONTROL SURFACE SNUBBERS AND LOCKING DEVICES

Various types of devices are in use to lock the control surfaces when the aircraft is parked or moored. Locking devices prevent damage to the control surfaces and their linkages from gusts and high-velocity winds. Common devices that are in use are the internal locking brake (sector brake) spring-loaded plunger, and external control surface locks.

Tension Regulators

Cable tension regulators are used in some flight control systems because there is considerable difference in temperature expansion of the aluminum aircraft structure and the steel control cables. Some large aircraft incorporate tension regulators in the control cable systems to automatically maintain a given cable tension. The unit consists of a compression spring and a locking mechanism which allows the spring to make correction in the system only when the cable system is in neutral.

AIRCRAFT RIGGING

Control surfaces should move a certain distance in either direction from the neutral position. These movements must be synchronized with the movement of the cockpit controls. The flight control system must be adjusted (rigged) to obtain these requirements.

Generally speaking, the rigging consists of the following: (1) Positioning the flight control system in neutral and temporarily locking it there with rig pins or blocks, and (2) adjusting surface travel, system cable tension, linkages, and adjustable stops to the aircraft manufacturer's specifications.

When rigging flight control systems, certain items of rigging equipment are needed. Primarily, this equipment consists of tensiometers, cable rigging tension charts, protractors, rigging fixtures, contour templates, and rulers.

Measuring Cable Tension

To determine the amount of tension on a cable, a tensiometer (figure 10-20) is used. When properly maintained, a tensiometer is 98% accurate. Cable tension is determined by measuring the amount of force needed to make an offset in the cable between two hardened steel blocks, called anvils. A riser or plunger is pressed against the cable to form the offset. Several manufacturers make a variety of tensiometers, each type designed for different kinds of cable, cable sizes, and cable tensions.

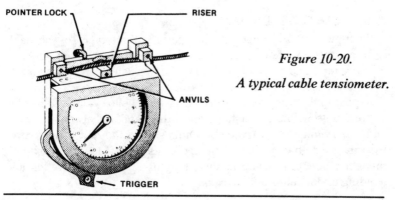

Figure 10-20.

A typical cable tensiometer.

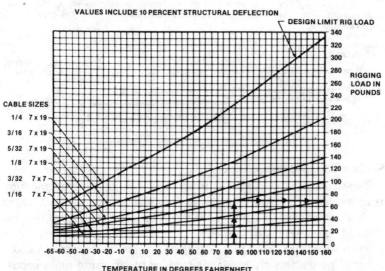

Figure 10-21. Typical cable rigging chart.

Cable rigging tension charts (figure 10-21) are graphic tools used to compensate for temperature variations. They are used when establishing cable tensions in flight control systems, landing gear systems, or any other cable-operated systems.

To use the chart, determine the size of the cable that is to be adjusted and the ambient air temperature. For example, assume that the cable size is ⅛-in. in diameter, that it is a 7 x 19 cable, and the ambient air temperature is 85 degrees F. Follow the 85 degrees F. line upward to where it intersects the curve for ⅛-in. cable. Extend a horizontal line from the point of intersection to the right edge of the chart. The value at this point indicates the tension (rigging load in pounds) to establish on the cable. The tension for this example is 70 lbs.

PUSH-PULL TUBE LINKAGE

Push-pull tubes are used as linkage in various types of mechanically operated systems. This type linkage eliminates the problem of varying tension and permits the transfer of either compression or tension stress through a single tube.

A push-pull tube assembly consists of a hollow aluminum alloy or steel tube with an adjustable end fitting and a checknut at either end. (See figure 10-22.) The checknuts secure the end fittings after the tube assembly has been adjusted to its correct length. Push-pull tubes are generally made in short lengths to prevent vibration and bending under compression loads.

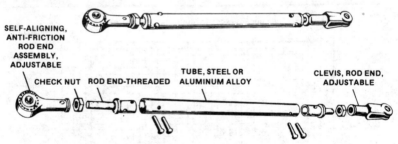

Figure 10-22. Push-pull tube assembly.

Surface Travel Measurement

The tools for measuring surface travel primarily include protractors, rigging fixtures, contour templates, and rulers. These tools are used when rigging flight control systems to assure that the desired travel has been obtained.

Protractors are tools for measuring angles in degrees. Various types of protractors are used to determine the travel of flight control surfaces. One protractor that can be used to measure aileron, elevator, or wing flap travel is the universal propeller protractor as shown in figure 10-23.

Rigging fixtures and templates are special tools (gages) designed by the manufacturer to measure control surface travel. Markings on the fixture or template indicate desired control surface travel.

These are described in detail in the aircraft maintenance manual.

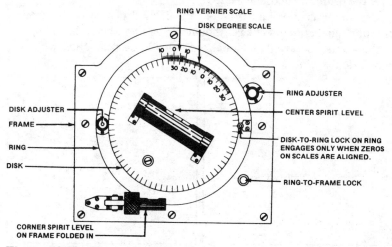

Figure 10-23. The universal propeller protractor can be used to measure control surface travel.

RIGGING CHECKS

The purpose of this section is to explain the methods of checking the relative alignment and adjustment of an aircraft's main structural components. It is not intended to imply that the procedures are exactly as they may be in a particular aircraft. **When rigging an aircraft, always follow the procedures and methods specified by the aircraft manufacturer in the service manual.**

Structural Alignment

The position or angle of the main structural components is related to a longitudinal datum line parallel to the aircraft center line and a lateral datum line parallel to a line joining the wing tips. Before checking the position or angle of the main components, the aircraft should be leveled.

Small aircraft usually have fixed pegs or blocks attached to the fuselage parallel to or coincident with the datum lines. A spirit level and a straight edge are rested across the pegs or blocks to check the level of the aircraft. See figure 10-24. This method of checking aircraft level also applies to many of the larger types of aircraft. However, the grid method is sometimes used on large aircraft. The grid plate (figure 10-25) is a permanent fixture installed on the aircraft floor or supporting structure. When the aircraft is to be leveled, a plumb bob is suspended from a predetermined position in the ceiling of the aircraft over the grid plate. The adjustments to the jacks necessary to level the aircraft are indicated on the grid scale. The aircraft is level when the plumb bob is suspended over the center point of the grid.

Certain precautions must be observed in all instances. Normally, rigging and alignment checks should not be undertaken in the open. If this cannot be avoided, the aircraft should be positioned with the nose into the wind.

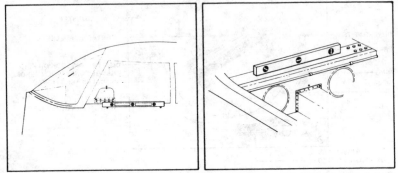

Figure 10-24. A typical longitudinal and lateral leveling provision. (From Piper Cherokee Service Manual.)

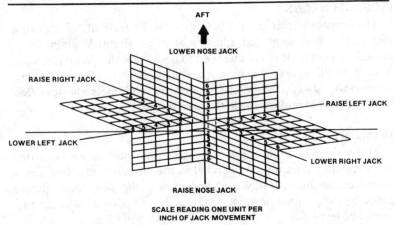

Figure 10-25. Typical leveling grid plate used on large aircraft.

The weight and loading of the aircraft should be exactly as described in the manufacturer's manual. In all cases, the air-craft should not be jacked until it is ensured that the maximum jacking weight (if any) specified by the manufacturer is not exceeded.

With a few exceptions, **the dihedral and incidence angles of conventional modern aircraft cannot be adjusted.** Some manu-facturers permit adjusting the wing angle of incidence to correct for a wing-heavy condition. The dihedral and incidence angles should be checked after hard landings or after experiencing abnormal flight loads to ensure that the components are not distorted and that the angles are within the specified limits.

There are several methods for checking structural alignment and rigging angles. Special rigging boards which incorporate, or on which can be placed, a special instrument (spirit level or clinometer) for determining the angle are used on some aircraft. On a number of aircraft the alignment is checked using a transit and plumb bobs or a theodolite and sighting rods. The particular equipment to use is usually specified in the manufacturer's manuals.

When checking alignment, a suitable sequence should be developed and followed to be certain that the checks are made at all the positions specified. The alignment checks specified usually include:

(1) Wing dihedral angle.
(2) Wing incidence angle.
(3) Engine alignment.
(4) Horizontal stabilizer incidence.
(5) Horizontal stabilizer dihedral.
(6) Verticality of the fin.
(7) A symmetry check.

ADJUSTMENT OF CONTROL SURFACES

In order for a control system to function properly, it must be correctly adjusted. Correctly rigged control surfaces will move through a prescribed arc (surface-throw) and be synchronized with the movement of the cockpit controls.

Rigging any system requires that the step-by-step procedures be followed as outlined in the aircraft maintenance manual. Although the complete rigging procedure for most aircraft is of a detailed nature that requires several adjustments, the basic method follows three steps:

(1) Lock the cockpit control, bellcranks, and the control surfaces in the neutral position.
(2) Adjust the cable tension, maintaining the rudder, elevators, or ailerons in the neutral position.
(3) Adjust the control stops to limit the control surface travel to the dimensions given for the aircraft being rigged.

The range of movement of the controls and control surfaces should be checked in both directions from neutral.

The rigging of the trim tab systems is performed in a similar manner. The trim tab control is set to the neutral (no trim) position, and the surface tab is usually adjusted to streamline with the control surface. However, on some aircraft the trim tabs may be offset a degree or two from streamline when in the "neutral" position. After the tab and tab control are in the neutral position, adjust the control cable tension.

Pins, usually called rig pins, are sometimes used to simplify the setting of pulleys, levers, bellcranks, etc., in their neutral positions. A rig pin is a small metallic pin or clip. When rig pins are not provided, the neutral positions can be established by means of alignment marks, by special templates, or by taking linear measurements.

If the final alignment and adjustment of a system are correct, it should be possible to withdraw the rigging pins easily. Any undue tightness of the pins in the rigging holes indicates incorrect tensioning or misalignment of the system.

After a system has been adjusted, the full and synchronized movement of the controls should be checked. When checking the range of movement of the control surface, the controls must be operated from the cockpit and not by moving the control surfaces. During the checking of control surface travel, ensure that chains, cables, etc., have not reached the limit of their travel when the controls are against their respective stops. Where dual controls are installed, they must be synchronized and function satisfactorily when operated from both positions.

Trim tabs and other tabs should be checked in a manner similar to the main control surfaces. The tab position indicator must be checked to see that they are not extended beyond the specified limits when the tab is in its extreme positions.

After determining that the control system functions properly and is correctly rigged, it should be thoroughly inspected to determine that the system is correctly assembled, and will operate freely over the specified range of movement. Make certain that all turnbuckles rod ends, and attaching nuts and bolts are correctly safetied.

WARNING

Be sure all control surfaces move in correct direction when operated by cockpit controls.

BALANCING OR RE-BALANCING CONTROL SURFACES

The ailerons, elevators and rudders of medium to high speed airplanes must be balanced about their hinge lines to prevent flutter or buffeting of the aircraft. This is normally accomplished by the addition of weights forward of the hinge line. Re-balancing is normally only required when a repair results in added material, usually located aft of this hinge line. **It is emphasized that balancing or re-balancing of control surfaces be accomplished in accordance with instructions in the applicable service or maintenance manual.**

Some aircraft specifications may require an underbalance condition where the control surface is trailing edge heavy. This condition is not as prevelant as the overbalanced condition where the control surface is leading edge heavy. **It is emphasized that paint can affect the balanced condition of a control surface.** The maintenance manual usually provides painted and unpainted balance limits.

RE-BALANCING OF MOVABLE SURFACES

The material in this section is presented for familiarization purposes only, and should not be used when re-balancing a control surface. Explicit instructions for the balancing of control surfaces are given in the service and overhaul manuals for the specific aircraft and must be followed closely.

Any time repairs on a control surface add weight fore or aft of the hinge center line, the control surface must be re-balanced. Any control surface that is out of balance will be unstable and will not remain in a streamlined position during normal flight. For example, an aileron that is trailing-edge heavy will move down when the wing deflects upward, and up when the wing deflects downward. Such a condition can cause unexpected and violent maneuvers of the aircraft. In extreme cases, fluttering and buffeting may develop to a degree that could cause the complete loss of the aircraft.

Re-balancing a control surface concerns both static and dynamic balance. A control surface that is statically balanced will also be dynamically balanced.

Static Balance

Static balance is the tendency of an object to remain stationary when supported from its own center of gravity. There are two ways in which a control surface may be out of static balance. They are called underbalance and overbalance.

When a control surface is mounted on a balance stand, a downward travel of the trailing edge below the horizontal position indicates underbalance. Some manufacturers indicate this condition with a plus (+) sign. Figure 10-26A illustrates the underbalance condition of a control surface.

An upward movement of the trailing edge, above the horizontal position (figure 10-26B), indicates overblance. This is designated by a minus(−) sign. These signs show the need for more or less weight in the correct area to achieve a balanced control surface as shown in figure 10-26C.

A tail-heavy condition (static underbalance) causes undesirable flight performance and is not usually allowed. Better flight operations are gained by nose heaviness static overbalance. Most manufacturers advocate the existence of nose-heavy control surfaces.

Dynamic Balance

Dynamic balance is that condition in a rotating body wherein all rotating forces are balanced within themselves so that no vibration is produced while the body is in motion. Dynamic balance as related to control surfaces is an effort to maintain balance when the control surface is submitted to movement on the aircraft in flight. It involves the placing of weights in the correct location along the span of the surfaces. The location of the weights will, in most cases, be forward of the hinge center line.

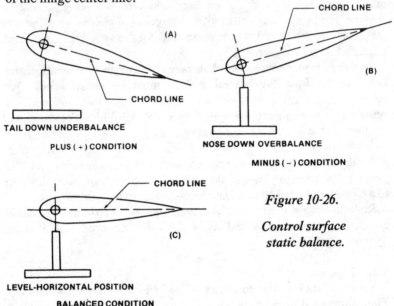

Figure 10-26.

Control surface static balance.

Requirements

Repairs to a control surface or its tabs generally increase the weight aft of the hinge center line, requiring static re-balancing of the control surface system as well as the tabs. Control surfaces to be rebalanced should be removed from the aircraft and supported, from their own points, on a suitable stand, jig, or fixture (figure 10-27).

Trim tabs on the surface should be secured in the neutral position when the control surface is mounted on the stand. The stand must be level and be located in the area free of air currents. The control surface must be permitted to rotate freely about the hinge points without binding. Balance condition is determined by the behavior of the trailing edge when the surface is suspended from its hinge points. Any excessive friction would result in a false reaction as to the overbalance or underbalance of the surface.

When installing the control surface in the stand or jig, a neutral position should be established with the chord line of the surface in a horizontal position (figure 10-28). Use a bubble protractor to determine the neutral position before continuing balancing procedures. Sometimes a visual check is all that is needed to determine whether the surface is balanced or unbalanced.

Any trim tabs or other assemblies that are to remain on the surface during balancing procedures should be in place. If any assemblies or parts must be removed before balancing, they should be removed.

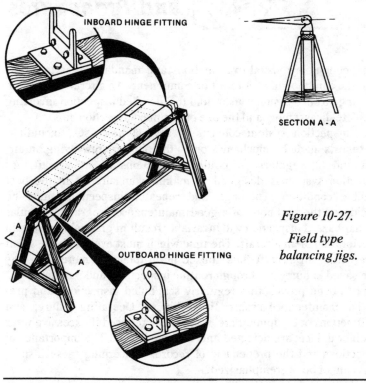

INBOARD HINGE FITTING

SECTION A - A

OUTBOARD HINGE FITTING

Figure 10-27.

Field type balancing jigs.

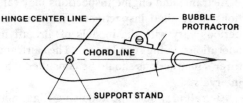

Figure 10-28.

Establishing a neutral position.

HINGE CENTER LINE

BUBBLE PROTRACTOR

CHORD LINE

SUPPORT STAND

Chapter 11

Inspection Techniques and Procedures

Inspections are visual examinations and manual checks to determine the condition of an aircraft or component. An aircraft inspection can range from a casual walkaround to a detailed inspection involving complete disassembly and the use of complex inspection aids.

An inspection system consists of several processes, including: (1) Reports made by mechanics or by the pilot or crew flying an aircraft and (2) regularly scheduled inspections of an aircraft. An inspection system is designed to maintain an aircraft in the best possible condition. Thorough and repeated inspections must be considered the backbone of a good maintenance program. Irregular and haphazard inspection will invariably result in gradual and certain deterioration of an aircraft. The time which must eventually be spent in repairing an aircraft thus abused often totals far more than any time saved in hurrying through routine inspections and maintenance.

It has been proven that regularly scheduled inspections and preventive maintenance assure airworthiness. Operating failures and malfunctions of equipment are appreciably reduced if excessive wear or minor defects are detected and corrected early. The importance of inspections and the proper use of records concerning these inspections cannot be overemphasized.

Airframe and engine inspections may range from preflight inspections to detailed inspections. The time intervals for the inspection periods vary with the models of aircraft involved and the types of operations being conducted. The airframe and engine manufacturer's instructions should be consulted when establishing inspection intervals.

Aircraft may be inspected using flight hours as a basis for scheduling, or on a calendar inspection system. Under the calender inspection system, the appropriate inspection is performed on the expiration of a specified number of calendar weeks. The calendar inspection system is an efficient system from a maintenance management standpoint. Scheduled replacement of components with stated hourly operating limitations is normally accomplished during the calendar inspection falling nearest the hourly limitation.

In some instances, a flight-hour limitation is established to limit the number of hours that may be flown during the calendar interval.

Aircraft operating under the flight-hour system are inspected when a specified number of flight hours are accumulated. Components with stated hourly operating limitations are normally replaced during the inspection that falls nearest the hourly limitation.

REQUIRED INSPECTIONS

Federal Aviation Regulations (FAR) provide for the inspection of all civil aircraft at specific intervals, depending generally upon the type of operations in which they are engaged, for the purpose of determining their overall condition. Some aircraft must be inspected at last once each 12 calendar months, while inspection is required for others after each 100 hours of flight. In other instances, an aircraft may be inspected in accordance with an inspection system set up to provide for total inspection of the aircraft over a calendar or flight-time period.

In order to determine the specific inspection requirements and rules for the preformance of inspections, reference should be made to the Federal Aviation Regulations which prescribe the requirements for the inspection and maintenance of aircraft in various types of operations.

INSPECTION PROCEDURES

Before starting an inspection, be certain all plates, access doors, fairings, and cowling have been opened or removed and the structure cleaned. When opening inspection plates and cowling, and before cleaning the area take note of any oil or other evidence of fluid leakage.

Always use a checklist when performing the inspection. The check-list may be of your own design, one provided by the manufacturer of the equipment being inspected, or one obtained from some other source. The checklist should include the following:

1. Fuselage and hull group.
   - Fabric and skin—for deterioration, distortion, other evidence of failure, and defective or insecure attachment of fittings.
   - Systems and components—for proper installation, apparent defects, and satisfactory operation.
2. Cabin and cockpit group.
   - Generally—for cleaness and loose equipment that should be secured.
   - Seats and safety belts—for condition and security.
   - Windows and windshields—for deterioration and breakage.
   - Instrument—for condition, mounting, marking, and (where practical) for proper operation.

- Flight and engine controls—for proper installation and operation.
- Batteries—for proper installation and charge.
- All systems—for proper installation, general condition, apparent defects, and security of attachment.

3. Engine and nacelle group.
   - Engine section—for visual evidence of excessive oil, fuel, or hydraulic leaks, and sources of such leaks.
   - Studs and nuts—for proper torquing and obvious defects.
   - Internal engine—for cylinder compression and for metal particles of foreign matter on screens and sump drain plugs. If cylinder compression is weak, check for improper internal condition and improper internal tolerances.
   - Engine mount—for cracks, looseness of mounting, and looseness of engine to mount.
   - Flexible vibration dampeners—for condition and deterioration.
   - Engine controls—for defects proper travel, and proper safetying.
   - Lines, hoses, and clamps—for leaks, condition, and looseness.
   - Exhaust stacks—for cracks, defects, and proper attachment.
   - Accessories—for apparent defects in security of mounting.
   - All systems—for proper installation, general condition defects, and secure attachment.
   - Cowling—for cracks and defects.
   - Ground runup and functional check—check all powerplant controls and systems for correct response, all instruments for proper operation and indication.

4. Landing gear group.
   - All units—for condition and security of attachment.
   - Shock absorbing devices—for proper oleo fluid level.
   - Linkage, trusses, and members—for undue or excessive wear, fatigue, and distortion.
   - Retracting and locking mechanism—for proper operation.
   - Hydraulic lines—for leakage.
   - Electrical system—for chafing and proper operation of switches.
   - Wheels—for cracks defects, and condition of bearings.
   - Tires—for wear and cuts.
   - Brakes—for proper adjustment.
   - Floats and skis—for security of attachment and obvious defects.

5. Wing and center section.
   - All components—for condition and security.
   - Fabric and skin—for deterioration, distortion, other evidence of failure, and security of attachment.
   - Internal structure (spars, ribs compression members)—for cracks, bends, and security.

- Movable surfaces—for damage or obvious defects, unsatisfactory fabric or skin attachment and proper travel.
- Control mechanism—for freedom of movement, alignment, and security.
- Control cables—for proper tension, fraying, wear and proper routing through fairleads and pulleys.

6. Empénnage group.
- Fixed surfaces—for damage or obvious defects, loose fasteners, and security of attachment.
- Movable control surfaces—for damage or obvious defects, loose fasteners, loose fabric, or skin distortion.
- Fabric or skin—for abrasion, tears, cuts or defects, distortion, and deterioration.

7. Propeller group.
- Propeller assembly—for cracks, nicks, bends, and oil leakage.
- Bolts—for proper torquing, and safetying.
- Anti-icing devices—for proper operations and obvious defects.
- Control mechanisms—for proper operation, secure mounting, and travel.

8. Communication and navigation group.
- Radio and electronic equipment—for proper installation and secure mounting.
- Wiring and conduits—for proper routing, secure mountings, and obvious defects.
- Bonding and shielding—for proper installation and condition.
- Antennas—for condition, secure mounting and proper operation.

9. Miscellaneous.
- Emergency and first-aid equipment—for general condition and proper stowage.
- Parachutes, life rafts, flares, etc.—inspect in accordance with the manufacturer's recommendations.
- Autopilot system—for general condition, security of attachment, and proper operation.

AIRCRAFT LOGS

"Aircraft logs" as used in this handbook is an inclusive term which applies to the aircraft logbook and all supplemental records concerned with the aircraft. The logs and records provide a history of maintenance and operation, control of maintenance schedules, and data for time replacements of components or accessories.

The aircraft logbook is the record in which all data concerning the aircraft is recorded. Information gathered in this log is used to determine the aircraft condition, date of inspections, time on airframe and engines. It reflects a history of all significant events occuring to the airframe, its components, and accessories, and provides a place for indicating compliance with FAA Airworthiness Directives or manufacturers' service bulletins.

SPECIAL INSPECTIONS

During the service life of an aircraft, occasions may arise when landings are made in an overweight condition or part of a flight must be made through severe turbulence. Rough landings are also experienced for a number of reasons.

When these situations are encountered, special inspection procedures should be followed to determine if any damage to the aircraft structure has occurred. The procedures outlined on the following pages are general in nature and are intended to acquaint the aviation mechanic with the areas which should be inspected. As such, they are not all inclusive. When performing any one of these special inspections, always follow the detailed procedures in the aircraft maintenance manual.

Hard or Overweight Landing Inspection

The structural stress induced by a landing depends not only upon the gross weight at the time but also upon the severity of impact. However, because of the difficulty in estimating vertical velocity at the time of contact, it is hard to judge whether or not a landing has been sufficiently severe to cause structural damage. For this reason, a special inspection should be performed after a landing is made at a weight known to exceed the design landing weight or after a rough landing, even though the latter may have occurred when the aircraft did not exceed the design landing weight.

Wrinkled wing skin is the most easily detected sign of an excessive load having been imposed during a landing. Another indication which can be detected easily is fuel leaks along riveted seams. Other possible locations of damage are spar webs, bulkheads, nacelle skin and attachments, firewall skin, and wing and fuselage stringers.

If none of these areas show adverse effects, it is reasonable to assume that no serious damage has occurred. If damage is detected, a more extensive inspection and alignment check may be necessary.

Severe Turbulence Inspection

When an aircraft encounters a gust condition, the airload on the wings exceeds the normal wingload supporting the aircraft weight. The gust tends to accelerate the aircraft while its inertia acts to resist this change. If the combination of gust velocity and airspeed is too severe, the induced stress can cause structural damage.

A special inspection should be performed after a flight through severe turbulence. Emphasis should be placed upon inspecting the upper and lower wing surfaces for excessive buckles or wrinkles with permanent set. Where wrinkles have occurred, remove a few rivets and examine the rivet shanks to determine if the rivets have sheared or were highly loaded in shear.

Inspect all spar webs from the fuselage to the tip, through the inspection doors and other accessible openings. Check for buckling, wrinkles, and sheared attachments. Inspect for buckling in the area around the nacelles and in the nacelle skin, particularly at the wing leading edge.

Check for fuel leaks. Any sizeable fuel leak is an indication that an area may have received overloads which have broken the sealant and opened the seams.

If the landing gear was lowered during a period of severe turbulence, inspect the surrounding surfaces carefully for loose rivets, cracks, or buckling. The interior of the wheel well may give further indications of excessive gust conditions.

Inspect the top and bottom fuselage skin. An excessive bending moment may have left wrinkles of a diagonal nature in these areas.

Inspect the surface of the empennage for wrinkles, buckling, or sheared attachments. Also, inspect the area of attachment of the empennage to the fuselage.

The above inspections cover the critical areas. If excessive damage is noted in any of the areas mentioned, the inspection should be continued until all damage is detected.

PUBLICATIONS

Aeronautical publications are the sources of information for guiding aviation mechanics in the operation and maintenance of aircraft and related equipment. The proper use of these publications will greatly aid in the efficient operation and maintenance of all aircraft. These include manufacturers' service bulletins, manuals, and catalogs, as well as FAA regulations, airworthiness directives, advisory circulars, and aircraft, engine and propeller specifications. See Appendix II.

Service Bulletins

Service bulletins are one of several types of publications issued by airframe, engine, and component manufacturers.

The bulletins may include: (1) The purpose for issuing the publication; (2) the name of the applicable airframe, engine, or component; (3) detailed instructions for service, adjustment, modification or inspection, and source of parts, if required; and (4) the estimated number of manhours required to accomplish the job.

Maintenance Manual

The aircraft maintenance manual provided by the manufacturer contains complete instructions for maintenance of all systems and components installed in the aircraft. See figure 11-1. It contains information for the mechanic who normally works on units, assemblies, and systems, while they are installed in the aircraft, and not for the overhaul mechanic. A typical aircraft maintenance manual contains: (1) A description of the systems such as electrical, hydraulic, fuel, control, etc.; (2) lubrication instructions setting forth the frequency and the lubricants and fluids which are to be used in the various systems; (3) pressures and electrical loads applicable to the various systems; (4) tolerances and adjustments necessary to proper functioning of the airplane; (5) methods of leveling, raising, and towing; (6) methods of balancing control surfaces; (7) identification of primary and secondary structures; (8) frequency and extent of inspections necessary to the proper operation of the airplane; (9) special repair methods applicable to the airplane; (10) special inspection techniques requiring X-ray, ultrasonic, or magnetic particle inspection; and (11) a list of special tools.

Figure 11-1.

Aircraft manufacturers provide complete instructions for maintenance of all systems and components. (Courtesy Cessna Aircraft Company.)

Overhaul Manual

The manufacturer's overhaul manual contains brief descriptive information and detailed step-by-step instructions covering work normally performed on a unit away from the aircraft. Simple, inexpensive items, such as switches and relays, on which overhaul is uneconomical, are not covered in the overhaul manual.

Structural Repair Manual

This manual contains information and specific instructions from the manufacturer for repairing primary and secondary structure. Typical skin, frame, rib, and stringer repairs are covered in this manual. Also included are material and fastener substitutions and special repair techniques.

Illustrated Parts Catalog

This catalog presents component breakdowns of structure and equipment in disassembly sequence. Also included are exploded views or cutaway illustrations for all parts and equipment manufactured by the aircraft manufacturer. See figure 11-2.

Figure 11-2.

An illustrated Parts Catalog. (Courtesy Cessna Aircraft Company.)

Federal Aviation Regulations (FAR)

Federal Aviation Regulations were established by law to provide for the safe and orderly conduct of flight operations and to prescribe airmen privileges and limitations. A knowledge of the FARs is necessary during the performance of maintenance, since all work done on aircraft must comply with FAR provisions.

Airworthiness Directives

A primary safety function of the Federal Aviation Administration is to require correction of unsafe conditions found in an aircraft, aircraft engine, propeller, or appliance when such conditions exists and are likely to exist or develop in other products of the same design. The unsafe condition may exist because of a design defect, maintenance, or other causes. FAR Part 39, Airworthiness Directives, defines the authority and responsibility of the administrator for requiring the necessary corrective action. The Airworthiness Directives (AD) are the media used to notify aircraft owners and other interested persons of unsafe conditions and to prescribe the conditions under which the product may continue to be operated.

Airworthiness Directives are Federal Aviation Regulations and must be complied with, unless specific exemption is granted.

Airworthiness Directives may be divided into two categories: (1) Those of an emergency nature requiring immediate compliance upon receipt and (2) those of a less urgent nature requiring compliance within a relatively longer period of time.

The contents of ADs include the aircraft, engine, propeller, or appliance model and serial numbers affected. Also included are the compliance time or period, a description of the difficulty experienced, and the necessary corrective action.

Type Certificate Data Sheets

The type certificate data sheet describes the type design and sets forth the limitations prescribed by the applicable Federal Aviation Regulations. It also includes any other limitations and information found necessary for type certification of a particular model aircraft.

Type certificate data sheets are numbered in the upper right-hand corner of each page. This number is the same as the type certificate number. The name of the type certificate holder, together with all of the approved models, appears immediately below the type certificate number. The issue date completes this group, which is enclosed in a box to set it off.

The data sheet is separated into one or more sections. Each section is identified by a Roman numeral followed by the model designation of the aircraft to which the section pertains. The category or categories in which the aircraft can be certificated are shown in parentheses following the model number. Also included is the approval date shown on the type certificate.

The data sheet contains information regarding:

1. Model designation for all engines for which the aircraft manufacturer obtained approval for use with this model aircraft.
2. Minimum fuel grade to be used.
3. Maximum continuous and takeoff ratings of the approved engines, including manifold pressure (when used), r.p.m., and horsepower (hp.).
4. Name of the manufacturer and model designation for each propeller for which the aircraft manufacturer obtained approval will be shown together with the propeller limits and any operating restrictions peculiar to the propeller or propeller-engine combination.
5. Airspeed limits in both m.p.h. and knots.
6. Center of gravity range for the extreme loading conditions of the aircraft is given in inches from the datum. The range may also be stated in percent of MAC (Mean Aerodynamic Chord) for transport category aircraft.
7. Empty weight c.g. range (when established) will be given as fore and aft limits in inches from the datum. If no range exists, the word "none" will be shown following the heading on the data sheet.
8. Location of the datum.
9. Means provided for leveling the aircraft.
10. All pertinent maximum weights.

11. Number of seats and their moment arms.
12. Oil and fuel capacity.
13. Control surface movements.
14. Required equipment.
15. Additional or special equipment found necessary for certification.
16. Information concerning required placards.

It is not within the scope of this handbook to list all the items that can be shown on the type certificate data sheets. Those items listed above are merely to acquaint aviation mechanics with the type of information generally included on the data sheets.

CONTROL CABLE SYSTEM INSPECTION

CABLES

At each regular inspection period, cables should be inspected for broken wires by passing a cloth along their length and observing points where the cloth snags. The absence of snags however, is not positive evidence that broken wires do not exist. Figure 11-3 shows a cable with broken wires that were not detected by wiping, but were found during a visual inspection. The damage became readily apparent when the cable was removed and bent using the technique depicted in figure 11-3.

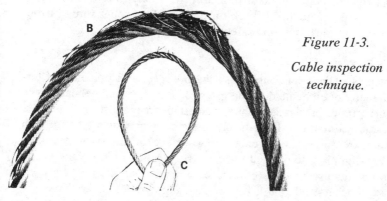

Figure 11-3.

Cable inspection technique.

To thoroughly inspect the cable, move the surface control to its extreme travel limits. This will reveal the cable in pulley, fairlead, and drum areas. If the surface of the cable is corroded, relieve cable tension. Then carefully force the cable open by reverse twisting, and visually inspect the interior for corrosion. Corrosion on the interior strands of the cable indicates failure of the cable and requires re-placement of the cable. If there is no internal corrosion, remove external corrosion with a coarseweave rag or fiber brush. Never use metallic wools or solvents to clean flexible cable. Metallic wools imbed dissimilar metal particles, which cause further corrosion.

Solvents remove the internal cable lubricant, which also results in further corrosion. After thoroughly cleaning the flexible cable, apply corrosion-preventive compound. This compound preserves and lubricates the cable.

Breakage of wires occurs most frequently where cables pass over pulleys and through fairleads. Typical breakage points are shown in figure 11-4. Control cables and wires should be replaced if worn, distorted, corroded, or otherwise damaged.

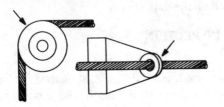

Figure 11-4.

Typical cable breakage points.

CABLE FITTINGS

Check swaged treminal reference marks for an indication of cable slippage within the fitting. Inspect the fitting assembly for distortion and/or broken strands at the terminal. Assure that all bearings and swivel fittings (bolted or pinned) pivot freely to prevent binding and subsequent failure. Check turnbuckles for proper thread exposure and broken or missing safety wires/clips.

PULLEYS

Inspect pulleys for roughness, sharp edges, and presence of foreign material embedded in the grooves. Examine pulley bearings to assure proper lubrication, smooth rotation, freedom from flat spots, dirt, and paint spray. Periodically rotate pulleys, which turn through a small arc, to provide a new bearing surface for the cable. Maintain pulley alignment to prevent the cable from riding on the flanges and chafing against guards, covers, or adjacent structure. Check all pulley brackets and guards for damage, alignment, and security.

Various cable system malfunctions may be detected by analyzing pulley conditions. These include such discrepancies as too much tension, misalignment, pulley bearing problems, and size mismatches between cables and pulleys. Examples of these conditions are shown in figure 11-5.

FAIRLEADS

Inspect fairleads for wear, breakage, alignment, cleanness, and security. Examine cable routing at fairleads to assure that deflection angles are no greater than 3 degrees maximum. Determine that all guides and anti-abrasion strips are secure and in good condition.

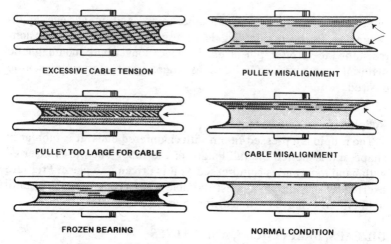

Figure 11-5. Typical pulley wear patterns.

Labels in figure: EXCESSIVE CABLE TENSION, PULLEY MISALIGNMENT, PULLEY TOO LARGE FOR CABLE, CABLE MISALIGNMENT, FROZEN BEARING, NORMAL CONDITION

GENERAL SAFETY WIRING RULES AND PROCEDURES

Safety methods for bolts and nuts, are presented in Chapter 4, Fastening Devices and Processes. Turnbuckle safetying is discussed in Chapter 7, Assembly and Rigging. Additional types of safetying are presented in the following paragraphs.

PINS

The three main types of pins used in aircraft structures are the taper pin, flathead pin, and cotter pin. Pins are used in shear applications and for safetying. Roll pins are finding increasing uses in aircraft construction.

Taper Pins

Plain and threaded taper pins (AN385 and AN386) are used in joints which carry shear loads and where absence of play is essential. The plain taper pin is drilled and usually safetied with wire. The threaded taper pin is used with a taper-pin washer (AN975) and shear nut (safetied with cotter pin) or self-locking nut.

Flathead Pin

Commonly called a clevis pin, the flathead pin (MS20392) is used with tie-rod terminals and in secondary controls which are not subject to continuous operation. The pin is customarily installed with the head up so that if the cotter pin fails or works out, the pin will remain in place.

Cotter Pins

The AN380 cadmium-plated, low-carbon steel cotter pin is used for safetying bolts, screws, nuts, other pins, and in various applications where such safetying is necessary. The AN381 corrosion-resistant steel cotter pin is used in locations where nonmagnetic material is required, or in locations where resistance to corrosion is desired.

Rollpins

The rollpin is a pressed-fit pin with chamfered ends. It is tubular in shape and is slotted the full length of the tube. The pin is inserted with hand tools and is compressed as it is driven into place. Pressure exerted by the roll pin against the hole walls keeps it in place, until deliberately removed with a drift punch or pin punch.

OIL CAPS, DRAIN COCKS, AND VALVES

These units are safety wired as shown in figure 11-6. In the case of the oil cap, the wire is anchored to an adjacent fillister head screw.

This system applies to any other unit which must be safety wired individually. Ordinarily, anchorage lips are conveniently located near these individual parts. When such provision is not made, the safety wire is fastened to some adjacent part of the assembly.

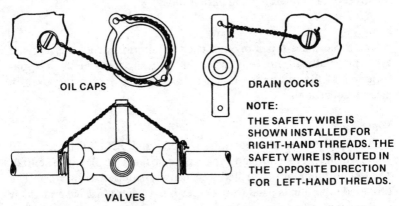

OIL CAPS

DRAIN COCKS

NOTE:
THE SAFETY WIRE IS SHOWN INSTALLED FOR RIGHT-HAND THREADS. THE SAFETY WIRE IS ROUTED IN THE OPPOSITE DIRECTION FOR LEFT-HAND THREADS.

VALVES

Figure 11-6. Safety wiring oil caps, drain cocks and valves.

Electrical Connectors

Under conditions of severe vibration, the coupling nut of a connector may vibrate loose, and with sufficient vibration the connector may come apart. When this occurs, the circuit carried by the cable opens. The proper protective measure to prevent this occurrence is by safety wiring as shown in figure 11-7. The safety wire should be as short as practicable and must be installed in such a manner that the pull on the wire is in the direction which tightens the nut on the plug.

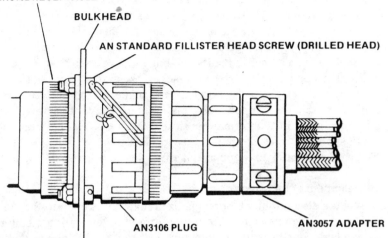

Figure 11-7. Safety wiring attachment for electrical plug connectors.

DETAIL INSPECTION PROCEDURES

These procedures are generally applicable to highly stressed components disassembled from the aircraft such as an engine crankshaft, or forged landing gear strut. Their main purpose is to detect internal and surface cracks which cannot be detected by a normal visual inspection. Inasmuch as these procedures generally require special equipment and a skilled operator, a brief discussion only, will be presented in this manual. The inspection equipment's operations manual should be consulted for detailed inspection procedures.

MAGNETIC PARTICLE INSPECTION

Magnetic particle inspection is a method of detecting invisible cracks and other defects in ferromagnetic materials, such as iron and steel. This method of inspection is a nondestructive test, which means it is performed on the actual part without damage to the part. It is not applicable to nonmagnetic materials.

In rapidly rotating, reciprocating, vibrating, and other highly stressed aircraft parts, small defects often develop to the point that they cause complete failure of the part. Magnetic particle inspection has proved extremely reliable for the rapid detection of such defects located on or near the surface. In using this method of inspection, the approximate size and shape are outlined.

The inspection process consists of magnetizing the part and then applying ferromagnetic particles to the surface area to be inspected. The ferromagnetic particles (indicating medium) may be held in suspension in a liquid that is flushed over the part; the part may be immersed in the suspension liquid; or the particles, in dry powder form, may be dusted over the surface of the part. The wet process is more commonly used in the inspection of aircraft parts.

If a discontinuity is present, the magnetic lines of force will be disturbed and opposite poles will exist on either side of the discontinuity. The magnetized particles thus form a pattern in the magnetic field between the opposite poles. This pattern known as an "indication," assumes the approximate shape of the surface projection of the discontinuity. A discontinuity may be defined as an interruption in the normal physical structure or configuration of a part such as a crack, forging lap, seam, inclusion, porosity, and the like. A discontinuity may or may not affect the usefulness of a part.

Development of Indications

When a discontinuity in a magnetized material is open to the surface and a magnetic substance in the form of an indicating medium is available on the surface, the flux leakage at the discontinuity tends to form the indicating medium into a path of higher permeability. (Permeability is a term used to refer to the ease with which a magnetic flux can be established in a given magnetic circuit.) Because of the magnetism in the part and the adherence of the magnetic particles to each other, the indication remains on the surface of the part in the form of an approximate outline of the discontinuity that is immediately below it.

The same action takes place when the discontinuity is not open to the surface, but since the amount of flux leakage is less, fewer particles are held in place and a fainter and less sharply defined indication is obtained.

If the discontinuity is very far below the surface, there may be no flux leakage and, therefore, no indication on the surface. The flux leakage at a transverse discontinuity is shown in figure 11-8. The flux leakage at a longitudinal discontinuity is shown in figure 11-9.

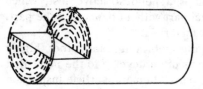

Figure 11-8.

Flux leakage at transverse discontinuity.

Figure 11-9.

Flux leakage at longitudinal discontinuity.

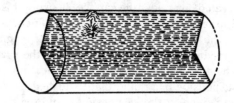

326

Types of Discontinuities Disclosed

The following types of discontinuities are normally detected by the magnetic particle test: cracks, laps, seams, cold shuts, inclusions, splits, tears, pipes, and voids. All these may affect the reliability of parts in service.

Cracks, splits, bursts, tears, seams, voids, and pipes are formed by an actual parting or rupture of the solid metal. Cold shuts and laps are folds that have been formed in the metal, interrupting its continuity.

Inclusions are foreign material formed by impurities in the metal during the metal processing stages. They may consist, for example, of bits of furnace lining picked up during the melting of the basic metal or of other foreign constituents. Inclusions interrupt the continuity of the metal because they prevent the joining or welding of adjacent faces of the metal.

Figure 11-10 shows a general-purpose magnetizing unit, while figures 11-11, 11-12 and 11-13 show various engine components installed in the magnetizing unit.

An operator inspecting parts using the magnetic particle inspection procedure, should be skilled and experienced in judging which defects are cause for rejection.

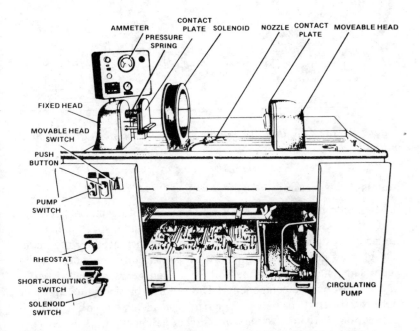

Figure 11-10. General-purpose magnetizing unit.

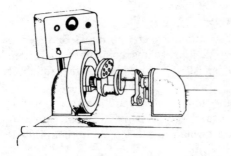

Figure 11-11.

Circular magnetization of crankshaft.

Figure 11-12.

Circular magnetization of piston pin with conductor bar.

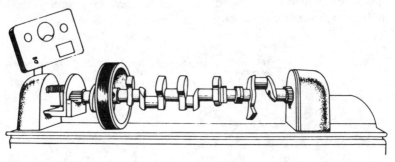

Figure 11-13. Longitudinal magnetization of crankshaft (solenoid method).

Magnaglo Inspection

Magnaglo inspection is similar to the preceding method, except that a fluorescent particle solution is used and the inspection is made under black light. Efficiency of inspection is increased by the neon-like glow of defects, and smaller flaw indications are more readily seen. This is an excellent method for use on gears, threaded parts, and aircraft engine components. The reddish brown liquid spray or bath that is used consists of Magnaglo paste mixed with a light oil at the ratio of .10 to .25 ounce of paste per gallon of oil.

After inspection, the part must be demagnetized and rinsed with a cleaning solvent.

DYE-PENETRANT INSPECTION

Penetrant inspection is a nondestructive test for defects open to the surface in parts made of any nonporous material. It is used with equal success on such metals as aluminum, magnesium, brass, copper, cast iron, stainless steel, and titanium. It may also be used on ceramics, plastics, molded rubber, and glass.

Penetrant inspection will detect such defects as surface cracks or porosity. These defects may be caused by fatigue cracks, shrinkage cracks, shrinkage porosity, cold shuts, grinding and heat-treat cracks seams, forging laps, and bursts. Penetrant inspection will also indicate a lack of bond between joined metals.

The main disadvantage of penetrant inspection is that the defect must be open to the surface in order to let the penetrant get into the defect. For this reason, if the part in question is made of material which is magnetic, the use of magnetic particle inspection is generally recommended.

Penetrant inspection depends for its success upon a penetrating liquid entering the surface opening and remaining in that opening, making it clearly visible to the operator. It calls for visual examination of the part after it has been processed, but the visibility of the defect is increased so that it can be detected. Visibility of the penetrating material is increased by the addition of dye which may be either one or two types—visible or fluorescent.

The visible penetrant kit consists of dye penetrant, dye remover-emulsifier and developer. The fluorescent penetrant inspection kit contains a black light assembly as well as spray cans of penetrant, cleaner, and developer. The light assembly consists of a power transformer, a flexible power cable, and a hand-held lamp. Due to its size, the lamp may be used in almost any position or location.

Briefly, the steps to be taken when performing a penetrant inspection are:

1. Thorough cleaning of the metal surface.
2. Applying penetrant.
3. Removing penetrant with remover-emulsifier or cleaner.
4. Drying the part.
5. Applying the developer.
6. Inspecting and interpreting results.

RADIOGRAPHY

X- and gamma radiations, because of their unique ability to penetrate material and disclose discontinuities, have been applied to the radiographic (X-ray) inspection of metal fabrications and nonmetallic products.

The penetrating radiation is projected through the part to be inspected and produces an invisible or latent image in the film. When processed, the film becomes a radiograph or shadow picture of the object. This inspection medium, in a portable unit, provides a fast and reliable means for checking the integrity of airframe structures and engines.

Radiographic inspection techniques are used to locate defects or flaws in airframe structures or engines with little or no disassembly. This is in marked contrast to other types of nondestructive testing, which usually require removal, disassembly, and stripping of paint from the suspected part before it can be inspected. Due to the nature of X-ray, extensive training is required to become a qualified radiographer, and only qualified radiographers are allowed to operate the X-ray units.

Three major steps in the X-ray process are: (1) Exposure to radiation, including preparation, (2) processing of film, and (3) interpretation of the radiograph.

ULTRASONIC TESTING

Ultrasonic detection equipment has made it possible to locate defects in all types of materials without damaging the material being inspected. Minute cracks, checks, and voids, too small to be seen by X-ray, are located by ultrasonic inspection. An ultrasonic test instrument requires access to only one surface of the material to be inspected and can be used with either straight line or angle beam testing techniques.

Two basic methods are used for ultrasonic inspection. The first of these methods is immersion testing. In this method of inspection, the part under examination and the search unit are totally immersed in a liquid couplant, which may be water or any other suitable fluid.

The second method is called contact testing, which is readily adapted to field use. In this method the part under examination and the search unit are coupled with a viscous material, liquid or a paste, which wets both the face of the search unit and the material under examination.

There are two basic ultrasonic systems: (1) pulsed and (2) resonance. The pulsed system may be either echo or through-transmission; the echo is the most versatile of the two pulse systems.

VISUAL INSPECTION

Nondestructive testing by visual means is the oldest method of inspection. Defects which would escape the naked eye can be magnified so they will be visible. Telescopes, borescopes, and magnifying glasses aid in performing visual inspection.

Appendix I
Standard Parts

Since the manufacture of aircraft requires a large number of miscellaneous small fasteners and other items usually called "hardware", some degree of standardization is required. These standards have been derived by the various military organizations and described in detail in a set of specifications with applicable identification codes. These military standards have been universally adopted by the civil aircraft industry.

The derivation of a uniform "standard" is of necessity an evolutionary process. Originally, each of the military services derived their own standards. The old Army Air Corps set up AC (Air Corps) standards whereas the Navy used NAF (Naval Aircraft Factory) standards. In time, these were consolidated into AN (Air Force-Navy) standards and NAS (National Aerospace Standards). Still later these were consolidated into MS (Military Standard) designations.

At present, the three most common standards are:
- AN, Army-Navy
- MS, Military Standard
- NAS (National Aerospace Standards)

The aircraft mechanic however, will also occasionally be confronted with the following standard parts on older aircraft:
- AC (Air Corps)
- NAF (Naval Aircraft Factory)

Each of these standard parts is identified by its specification number and various dash numbers and letters to fully describe its name, size and material.

Additional information on AN, MS, NAS as well as AMS and AND specifications and schedule of prices for specification sheets can be obtained from: National Standards Association, 1321 Fourteenth St. N.W., Washington, D.C. 20005.

Also, a relatively complete summary of standard parts can be found in: Aircraft Hardware Standards Manual & Engineering Reference by Stanley J. Dzik. Published by: Aviation Publications, P.O. Box 357, Appleton, Wisconsin 54911.

The most commonly used bolts, nuts, washers and rivets are illustrated and described in Chapter 4.

The following pages describe and illustrate some of the more commonly used standard parts. However, all the variations in dash numbers for size and letter designations for material, are not presented.

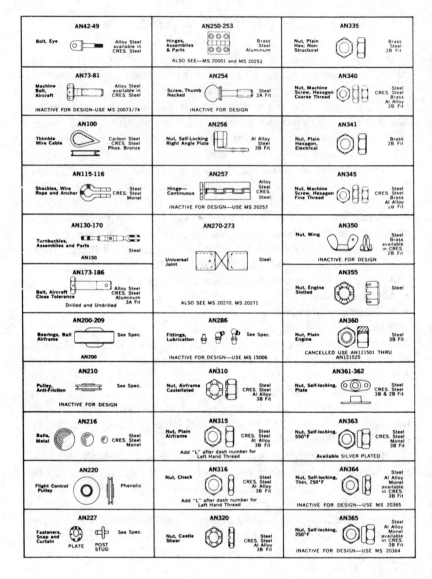

AN42-49		AN250-253		AN335	
Bolt, Eye	Alloy Steel available in CRES. Steel	Hinges, Assemblies & Parts	Brass Steel Aluminum	Nut, Plain Hex; Non-Structural	Brass Steel 2B Fit
		ALSO SEE—MS 20001 and MS 20253			
AN73-81		**AN254**		**AN340**	
Machine Bolt, Aircraft	Alloy Steel available in CRES. Steel	Screw, Thumb Necked	Steel 2A Fit	Nut, Machine Screw, Hexagon Coarse Thread	Steel CRES. Steel Brass Al Alloy 2B Fit
INACTIVE FOR DESIGN-USE MS 20073/74		INACTIVE FOR DESIGN			
AN100		**AN256**		**AN341**	
Thimble Wire Cable	Carbon Steel CRES. Steel Phos. Bronze	Nut, Self-Locking Right Angle Plate	Al Alloy Steel 3B Fit	Nut, Plain Hexagon, Electrical	Brass 2B Fit
AN115-116		**AN257**		**AN345**	
Shackles, Wire Rope and Anchor	Steel CRES. Steel Monel	Hinge— Continuous	Alloy Steel CRES. Steel	Nut, Machine Screw, Hexagon Fine Thread	Steel CRES. Steel Brass Al Alloy 2B Fit
		INACTIVE FOR DESIGN—USE MS 20257			
AN130-170		**AN270-273**		**AN350**	
Turnbuckles, Assemblies and Parts	Steel	Universal Joint	Steel	Nut, Wing	Steel Brass available in CRES. 2B Fit
AN150				INACTIVE FOR DESIGN	
AN173-186				**AN355**	
Bolt, Aircraft Close Tolerance	Alloy Steel CRES. Steel Aluminum 3A Fit			Nut, Engine Slotted	Steel
Drilled and Undrilled		ALSO SEE MS 20270, MS 20271			
AN200-209		**AN286**		**AN360**	
Bearings, Ball Airframe	See Spec.	Fittings, Lubrication	See Spec.	Nut, Plain Engine	Steel 3B Fit
AN200		INACTIVE FOR DESIGN—USE MS 15006		CANCELLED USE AN121501 THRU AN121525	
AN210		**AN310**		**AN361-362**	
Pulley, Anti-Friction	See Spec.	Nut, Airframe Castellated	Steel CRES. Steel Al Alloy 3B Fit	Nut, Self-locking, Plate	Steel CRES. Steel 3B & 2B Fit
INACTIVE FOR DESIGN					
AN216		**AN315**		**AN363**	
Balls, Metal	Steel CRES. Steel Monel	Nut, Plain Airframe	Steel CRES. Steel Al Alloy 3B Fit	Nut, Self-locking, 550°F	Steel CRES. Steel 3B Fit
		Add "L" after dash number for Left Hand Thread		Available SILVER PLATED	
AN220		**AN316**		**AN364**	
Flight Control Pulley	Phenolic	Nut, Check	Steel CRES. Steel Al Alloy 3B Fit	Nut, Self-locking, Thin, 250°F	Steel Al Alloy Monel available in CRES. 3B Fit
		Add "L" after dash number for Left Hand Thread		INACTIVE FOR DESIGN—USE MS 20365	
AN227		**AN320**		**AN365**	
Fasteners, Snap and Curtain	See Spec.	Nut, Castle Shear	Steel CRES. Steel Al Alloy 3B Fit	Nut, Self-locking, 250°F	Steel Al Alloy Monel available in CRES. 3B Fit
PLATE POST STUD				INACTIVE FOR DESIGN—USE MS 20364	

(Illustrations from AIMSCO catalog)

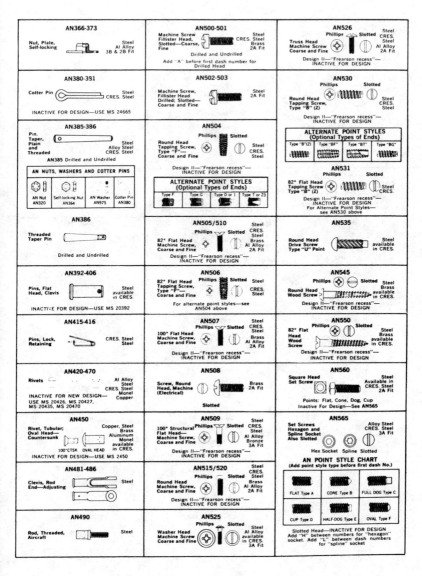

AN366-373	AN500-501	AN526
Nut, Plate, Self-locking — Steel, Al Alloy, 3B & 2B Fit	Machine Screw Fillister Head, Slotted—Coarse and Fine — Steel, CRES. Steel, Brass, 2A Fit. Drilled and Undrilled. Add "A" before first dash number for Drilled Head	Truss Head Machine Screw Coarse and Fine — Phillips, Slotted — Steel, CRES. Steel, Al Alloy, 2A Fit. Design II—"Frearson recess"—INACTIVE FOR DESIGN

AN366-373 — Nut, Plate, Self-locking — Steel, Al Alloy, 3B & 2B Fit

AN380-391 — Cotter Pin — Steel, CRES. Steel — INACTIVE FOR DESIGN—USE MS 24665

AN385-386 — Pin, Taper, Plain and Threaded — Steel, Alloy Steel, CRES. Steel — AN385 Drilled and Undrilled

AN NUTS, WASHERS AND COTTER PINS

AN Nut AN320	Self-locking Nut AN364	AN Washer AN975	Cotter Pin AN380

AN386 — Threaded Taper Pin — Steel, Alloy Steel, CRES. Steel — Drilled and Undrilled

AN392-406 — Pins, Flat Head, Clevis — Steel available in CRES. — INACTIVE FOR DESIGN—USE MS 20392

AN415-416 — Pins, Lock, Retaining — CRES. Steel, Steel

AN420-470 — Rivets — Al Alloy, Steel, CRES. Steel, Monel, Copper — INACTIVE FOR NEW DESIGN USE MS 20426, MS 20427, MS 20435, MS 20470

AN450 — Rivet, Tubular; Oval Head—Countersunk — Copper, Steel, Brass, Aluminum, Monel available in CRES. 100°CTSK. OVAL HEAD — INACTIVE FOR DESIGN—USE MS 2450

AN481-486 — Clevis, Rod End—Adjusting — Steel

AN490 — Rod, Threaded, Aircraft — Steel

AN500-501 — Machine Screw Fillister Head, Slotted—Coarse Fine — Steel, CRES. Steel, Brass, 2A Fit. Drilled and Undrilled. Add "A" before first dash number for Drilled Head

AN502-503 — Machine Screw, Fillister Head Drilled; Slotted—Coarse and Fine — Steel, 2A Fit

AN504 — Round Head Tapping Screw, Type "F"—Coarse and Fine — Phillips, Slotted — Steel, CRES. Steel — Design II—"Frearson recess"—INACTIVE FOR DESIGN

ALTERNATE POINT STYLES (Optional Types of Ends)

Type F	Type G	Type D or 1	Type T or 23

AN505/510 — 82° Flat Head Machine Screw, Coarse and Fine — Phillips, Slotted — Steel, CRES. Steel, Brass, Al Alloy, 2A Fit — Design II—"Frearson recess"—INACTIVE FOR DESIGN

AN506 — 82° Flat Head Tapping Screw, Type "F"—Coarse and Fine — Phillips, Slotted — Steel, CRES. Steel — For alternate point styles—see AN504 above

AN507 — 100° Flat Head Machine Screw, Coarse and Fine — Phillips, Slotted — Steel, CRES. Steel, Brass, Al Alloy, 2A Fit — Design II—"Frearson recess"—INACTIVE FOR DESIGN

AN508 — Screw, Round Head, Machine (Electrical) — Brass, 2A Fit — Slotted

AN509 — 100° Structural Flat Head Machine Screw, Coarse and Fine — Phillips, Slotted — Steel, CRES. Steel, Al Alloy, Bronze, 3A Fit — Design II—"Frearson recess"—INACTIVE FOR DESIGN

AN515/520 — Round Head Machine Screw, Coarse and Fine — Phillips, Slotted — Steel, CRES. Steel, Brass, Al Alloy, 2A Fit — Design II—"Frearson recess"—INACTIVE FOR DESIGN

AN525 — Washer Head Machine Screw, Coarse and Fine — Phillips, Slotted — Steel, Al Alloy available in CRES. 3A Fit

AN526 — Truss Head Machine Screw Coarse and Fine — Phillips, Slotted — Steel, CRES. Steel, Al Alloy, 2A Fit — Design II—"Frearson recess"—INACTIVE FOR DESIGN

AN530 — Round Head Tapping Screw, Type "B" (Z) — Phillips, Slotted — Steel, CRES. Steel — Design II—"Frearson recess"—INACTIVE FOR DESIGN

ALTERNATE POINT STYLES (Optional Types of Ends)

Type "B"(Z)	Type "BF"	Type "BT"	Type "BG"

AN531 — 82° Flat Head Tapping Screw, Type "B" (Z) — Phillips, Slotted — Steel, CRES. — Design II—"Frearson recess"—INACTIVE FOR DESIGN. For Alternate Point Styles—see AN530 above

AN535 — Round Head Drive Screw, Type "U" Point — Steel available in CRES.

AN545 — Round Head Wood Screw — Phillips, Slotted — Steel, Brass available in CRES. — Design II—"Frearson recess"—INACTIVE FOR DESIGN

AN550 — 82° Flat Head Wood Screw — Phillips, Slotted — Steel, Brass available in CRES. — Design II—"Frearson recess"—INACTIVE FOR DESIGN

AN560 — Square Head Set Screw — Steel Available in CRES. Steel, 2A Fit — Points: Flat, Cone, Dog, Cup — Inactive For Design—See AN565

AN565 — Set Screws Hexagon and Spline Socket Also Slotted — Alloy Steel, CRES. Steel, 3A Fit — Hex Socket, Spline, Slotted

AN POINT STYLE CHART (Add point style type before first dash No.)

FLAT Type A	CONE Type B	FULL DOG Type C
CUP Type D	HALF-DOG Type E	OVAL Type F

Slotted Head—INACTIVE FOR DESIGN. Add "H" between numbers for "hexagon" socket. Add "L" between dash numbers for "spline" socket

(Illustrations from AIMSCO catalog)

333

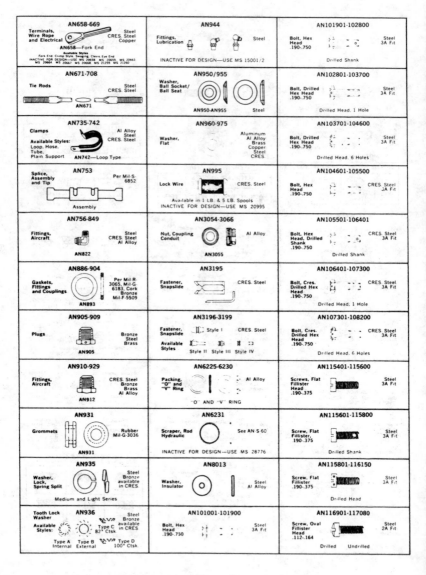

AN658-669 Terminals, Wire Rope and Electrical — Steel, CRES. Steel, Copper AN658—Fork End <small>Available Styles</small> <small>Fork End. Crimp Style. Swaging. Clevis Eye End</small> <small>INACTIVE FOR DESIGN—USE MS 20658 MS 20659 MS 20663</small> <small>MS 20664 MS 20667 MS 20668 MS 21259 MS 21260</small>	**AN944** Fittings, Lubrication — Steel INACTIVE FOR DESIGN—USE MS 15001/2	**AN101901-102800** Bolt, Hex Head — Steel 3A Fit .190-.750 Drilled Shank
AN671-708 Tie Rods — Steel, CRES. Steel AN671	**AN950-955** Washer, Ball Socket/ Ball Seat — Steel AN950-AN955	**AN102801-103700** Bolt, Drilled Hex Head — Steel 3A Fit .190-.750 Drilled Head. 1 Hole
AN735-742 Clamps — Al Alloy, Steel, CRES. Steel Available Styles: Loop. Hose. Tube. Plain Support AN742—Loop Type	**AN960-975** Washer, Flat — Aluminum, Al Alloy, Brass, Copper, Steel, CRES.	**AN103701-104600** Bolt, Drilled Hex Head — Steel 3A Fit .190-.750 Drilled Head. 6 Holes
AN753 Splice, Assembly and Tip — Per Mil-S-6852 Assembly	**AN995** Lock Wire — CRES. Steel Available in 1 LB. & 5 LB. Spools INACTIVE FOR DESIGN—USE MS 20995	**AN104601-105500** Bolt, Hex Head — CRES. Steel JA Fit .190-.750
AN756-849 Fittings, Aircraft — Steel, CRES. Steel, Al Alloy AN822	**AN3054-3066** Nut, Coupling Conduit — Al Alloy AN3055	**AN105501-106401** Bolt, Hex Head, Drilled Shank — CRES. Steel 3A Fit .190-.750 Drilled Shank
AN886-904 Gaskets, Fittings and Couplings — Per Mil-R-3065, Mil-G-6183, Cork, Bronze, Mil-F-5509 AN893	**AN3195** Fastener, Snapslide — CRES. Steel	**AN106401-107300** Bolt, Cres. Drilled Hex Head — CRES. Steel 3A Fit .190-.750 Drilled Head. 1 Hole
AN905-909 Plugs — Bronze, Steel, Brass AN905	**AN3196-3199** Fastener, Snapslide — Style I — CRES. Steel Available Styles Style II Style III Style IV	**AN107301-108200** Bolt, Cres. Drilled Hex Head — CRES. Steel 3A Fit .190-.750 Drilled Head. 6 Holes
AN910-929 Fittings, Aircraft — CRES. Steel, Bronze, Brass, Al Alloy AN912	**AN6225-6230** Packing, "O" and "V" Ring — Al Alloy "O" AND "V" RING	**AN115401-115600** Screws, Flat Fillister Head — Steel 3A Fit .190-.375
AN931 Grommets — Rubber, Mil-G-3036 AN931	**AN6231** Scraper, Rod Hydraulic — See AN S-60 INACTIVE FOR DESIGN—USE MS 28776	**AN115601-115800** Screw, Flat Fillister, Head — Steel 3A Fit .190-.375 Drilled Shank
AN935 Washer, Lock, Spring Split — Steel, Bronze, available in CRES Medium and Light Series	**AN8013** Washer, Insulator — Steel, Al Alloy	**AN115801-116150** Screw, Flat Fillister Head — Steel 3A Fit .190-.375 Drilled Head
AN936 Tooth Lock Washer — Steel, Bronze available in CRES Available Styles: Type A Internal Type B External Type C 82° Ctsk Type D 100° Ctsk	**AN101001-101900** Bolt, Hex Head — Steel 3A Fit .190-.750	**AN116901-117080** Screw, Oval Fillister Head — Steel 2A Fit .112-.164 Drilled Undrilled

(Illustrations from AIMSCO catalog)

AN121501-121550	AN150201-150400	MS 9060-9066
Nut, Plain — Steel CRES. Steel 3B Fit	Pin, Lock — Steel Brass / E1 Marking	Bolt, Machine 12 Point Ext. Washer Head High Temp. — AMS 5735 (A-286) / EH19 Head Marking
AN121551-121600	**AN150401-150450**	**MS 9068**
Nut, Castle — Steel CRES. Steel 3B Fit	Nut-Hex, Check and Shear Slotted — Steel 3B Fit	Packing "O" Ring — Silicone Rubber AMS 3304
AN121601-121925	**AN150501-170900**	**MS 9081**
Pin, Flat Head Clevis .125-.500 — Steel / Drilled Shank	Stud-Stepped — Steel 3A Fit	Washer, Key-Double — Steel
AN122576-122600	**MS 9012-9014**	**MS 9088-9094**
Washer, Plain — Steel	Retaining Rings — Beryllium Copper Steel / Superceded by MS 16624/5 / External Internal	Bolt, Machine 12 Point Head Drilled — Steel / E 11 Head Marking
AN122676-122775	**MS 9016-MS 9017**	**MS 9099-9100**
Pin, Dowel — Steel	Bushing Screw, Slotted — Steel	Nut, Hex Connection — Aluminum CRES. Steel / E 12 Marking Aluminum E 10 Marking CRES.
AN123020-123119	**MS 9018**	**MS 9101-9104**
Gasket — Aluminum-Asbestos Annular	Insert, 18-1.5MM Aviation Spark Plug, Helical Coil — CRES. Steel / SEE DESIGN STANDARD MS 9071	Bracket, 90° Angle .190-.375 Bolt — AMS 5510
AN123151-123750	**MS 9020-9021**	**MS 9105**
Rivet, Solid Universal Head and 100° CTSK Head — CRES. Steel Inconel	Packing "O" Ring — Rubber	Pin, Lock — CRES. Steel
AN123851-124050	**MS 9024-9025**	**MS 9122-9123**
Seal, Packing "O" Ring — Rubber	Clamp, Loop Types — AMS 6350 AMS 5510	Slotted Hex Head Machine Screw — Steel / E 11 Head Marking
AN124951-125550	**MS 9033-9039**	**MS 9146-9163**
Rivet, Solid Universal Head and 100° CTSK Head — CRES. Steel	Bolt, 12 Point High Temp. — AMS 5735 (A-286) / EH19 Head Marking	Bolt, Machine 12 Point Head — Steel / E 11 Head Marking
AN125551-125700	**MS 9047-9048**	**MS 9164**
Rivet, Solid Universal Head — Steel	Pin, Spring — Steel	Pin, Dowel Oversize — Steel
AN125951-130774	**MS 9058**	**MS 9165-9168**
Studs-Straight .250-.625 — Steel 3A Fit / Drilled and Undrilled	Ring, Back-Up — AMS 3651	Bolt, Brackets — Steel / ALSO SEE MS 9101-04/MS 9228-31

(Illustrations from AIMSCO catalog)

335

MS 9169-9175	MS 9318/9	MS 9391-9395
Bolt, Machine 12 Point Head Drilled — Steel E 11 Head Marking	Rivets 100° Flush Head and Universal Head — Monel	Clamp, Loop; Cushion; Strap Back Plate — CRES. Steel AMS 3303 MS 9391
MS 9177/8-9183-9192	**MS 9320-9321**	**MS 9403**
Bolt, Machine Drilled and Undrilled — AMS 5735 (A-286) Steel EH 19 A-286 Head Marking E 11 Steel Head Marking	Washer, Flat — Steel CRES. Steel	Rivet, Universal Head — AMS 5737 (A-286)
MS 9200-9201	**MS 9352-MS 9353/4**	**MS 9440-9459**
Nut, Plain Hex, Connection — Aluminum CRES. Steel E 12 Aluminum EH 5 CRES.	Clamp, Loop — Aluminum	Bolt, Machine Hexagon Head Drilled and Undrilled — Steel
MS 9224	**MS 9355**	**MS 9460**
Bolt, Machine 12 Point Head — AMS 5735 (A-286) EH 19 A-286 Head Marking	Packing "O" Ring — Rubber AMS 7272	Rivet, Solid 100° Flush Head — AMS 7235
MS 9228-9231	**MS 9356/7**	**MS 15000-15006**
Bracket, 90° Angle .190-.375 Bolt — AMS 5504	Nut, Plain Hexagon — CRES. Steel A-286	Fittings, Lubrication — Steel Monel
MS 9241	**MS 9358/9**	**MS 15795**
Packing "O" Ring — Rubber AMS 7272	Nut, Castellated Hexagon — CRES. Steel A-286	Washer, Flat — CRES. Steel Monel Copper Brass Al Alloy
MS 9245	**MS 9360**	**MS 15820**
Cotter Pin — CRES. Steel Optional Ends	Nut, Plain Hex, Drilled Silver Plated — AMS 5735 (A-286)	Washers, Lock (Special Design) — per Spec.
MS 9274	**MS 9361/2**	**MS 15986-15988**
Washer, Key- Double — CRES. Steel	Nut, Plain Hexagon, Check (also Silver Plated) — CRES. Steel A-286	Stud, Plain Full Body — Steel Brass Monel
MS 9303-9312	**MS 9363/4**	**MS 16036**
Stud, Shouldered Hex, Wrenching Drilled and Undrilled — Steel E 11 Marking	Nut, Slotted Hexagon, Shear (also Silver Plated) — CRES. Steel A-286	Bolt, Aircraft Safety — See Mil-B-18461 (Wep) Complete Assembly and Individual Parts
	MS 9365-9367	**MS 16107**
	Bracket, Bolt, Flat — CRES. Steel	Jacks, Tip, High Voltage — See Spec. (Ships) Color Coded
MS 9316/7	**MS 9389/90**	**MS 16108**
Screw, Machine Hexagon Head Slotted — Steel 2A Fit E 37 Head Marking	Dowel Pin — AMS 5735 (A-286)	Jacks, Tip, Low Voltage — Bronze Copper

(Illustrations from AIMSCO catalog)

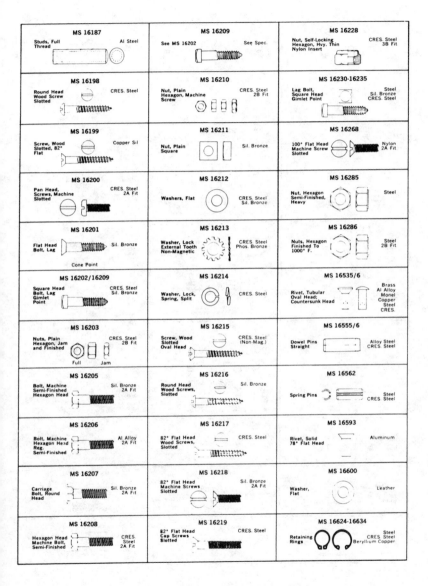

MS 16187	MS 16209	MS 16228
Studs, Full Thread — Al Steel	See MS 16202 — See Spec.	Nut, Self-Locking Hexagon, Hvy. Thin Nylon Insert — CRES. Steel 3B Fit
MS 16198 Round Head Wood Screw Slotted — CRES. Steel	**MS 16210** Nut, Plain Hexagon, Machine Screw — CRES. Steel 2B Fit	**MS 16230-16235** Lag Bolt, Square Head Gimlet Point — Steel Sil. Bronze CRES. Steel
MS 16199 Screw, Wood Slotted, 82° Flat — Copper Sil	**MS 16211** Nut, Plain Square — Sil. Bronze	**MS 16268** 100° Flat Head Machine Screw Slotted — Nylon 2A Fit
MS 16200 Pan Head, Screws, Machine Slotted — CRES. Steel 2A Fit	**MS 16212** Washers, Flat — CRES. Steel Sil. Bronze	**MS 16285** Nut, Hexagon Semi-Finished, Heavy — Steel
MS 16201 Flat Head Bolt, Lag — Sil. Bronze Cone Point	**MS 16213** Washer, Lock External Tooth Non-Magnetic — CRES. Steel Phos. Bronze	**MS 16286** Nuts, Hexagon Finished To 1000° F. — Steel 2B Fit
MS 16202/16209 Square Head Bolt, Lag Gimlet Point — CRES. Steel Sil. Bronze	**MS 16214** Washer, Lock, Spring, Split — CRES. Steel	**MS 16535/6** Rivet, Tubular Oval Head; Countersunk Head — Brass Al Alloy Monel Copper Steel CRES.
MS 16203 Nuts, Plain Hexagon, Jam and Finished — CRES. Steel 2B Fit Full Jam	**MS 16215** Screw, Wood Slotted Oval Head — CRES. Steel (Non-Mag.)	**MS 16555/6** Dowel Pins Straight — Alloy Steel CRES. Steel
MS 16205 Bolt, Machine Semi-Finished Hexagon Head — Sil. Bronze 2A Fit	**MS 16216** Round Head Wood Screws, Slotted — Sil. Bronze	**MS 16562** Spring Pins — Steel CRES. Steel
MS 16206 Bolt, Machine Hexagon Head Reg. Semi-Finished — Al Alloy 2A Fit	**MS 16217** 82° Flat Head Wood Screws, Slotted — CRES. Steel	**MS 16593** Rivet, Solid 78° Flat Head — Aluminum
MS 16207 Carriage Bolt, Round Head — Sil. Bronze 2A Fit	**MS 16218** 82° Flat Head Machine Screws Slotted — Sil. Bronze 2A Fit	**MS 16600** Washer, Flat — Leather
MS 16208 Hexagon Head Machine Bolt, Semi-Finished — CRES. Steel 2A Fit	**MS 16219** 82° Flat Head Cap Screws Slotted — CRES. Steel	**MS 16624-16634** Retaining Rings — Steel CRES. Steel Beryllium Copper

(Illustrations from AIMSCO catalog)

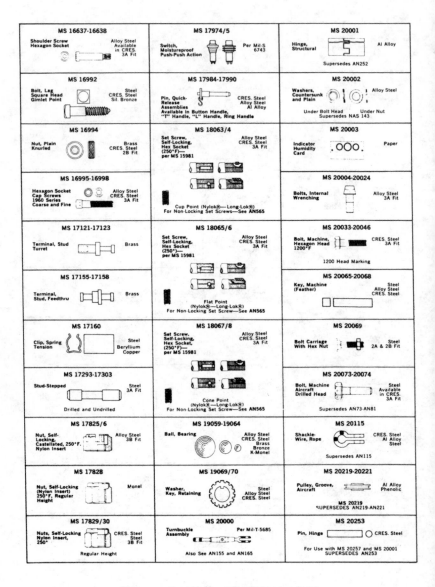

MS 16637-16638	MS 17974/5	MS 20001
Shoulder Screw Hexagon Socket — Alloy Steel, Available in CRES. 3A Fit	Switch, Moistureproof Push-Push Action — Per Mil-S 6743	Hinge, Structural — Al Alloy. Supersedes AN252
MS 16992 — Bolt, Lag Square Head Gimlet Point — Steel, CRES. Steel, Sil. Bronze	**MS 17984-17990** — Pin, Quick-Release Assemblies Available in Button Handle, "T" Handle, "L" Handle, Ring Handle — CRES. Steel, Alloy Steel, Al Alloy	**MS 20002** — Washers, Countersunk and Plain — Alloy Steel. Under Bolt Head. Under Nut. Supersedes NAS 143
MS 16994 — Nut, Plain Knurled — Brass, CRES. Steel 2B Fit	**MS 18063/4** — Set Screw, Self-Locking, Hex Socket (250°F)— per MS 15981 — Alloy Steel, CRES. Steel 3A Fit. Cup Point (Nylok®—Long-Lok®) For Non-Locking Set Screws—See AN565	**MS 20003** — Indicator Humidity Card — Paper
MS 16995-16998 — Hexagon Socket Cap Screws 1960 Series Coarse and Fine — Alloy Steel, CRES. Steel 3A Fit		**MS 20004-20024** — Bolts, Internal Wrenching — Alloy Steel 3A Fit
MS 17121-17123 — Terminal, Stud Turret — Brass	**MS 18065/6** — Set Screw, Self-Locking, Hex Socket (250°F)— per MS 15981 — Alloy Steel, CRES. Steel 3A Fit. Flat Point (Nylok®—Long-Lok®) For Non-Locking Set Screw—See AN565	**MS 20033-20046** — Bolt, Machine, Hexagon Head 1200°F — CRES. Steel 3A Fit. 1200 Head Marking
MS 17155-17158 — Terminal, Stud, Feedthru — Brass		**MS 20065-20068** — Key, Machine (Feather) — Steel, Alloy Steel, CRES. Steel
MS 17160 — Clip, Spring Tension — Steel, Beryllium Copper	**MS 18067/8** — Set Screw, Self-Locking, Hex Socket, (250°F)— per MS 15981 — Alloy Steel, CRES. Steel 3A Fit. Cone Point (Nylok®—Long-Lok®) For Non-Locking Set Screw—See AN565	**MS 20069** — Bolt Carriage With Hex Nut — Steel 2A & 2B Fit
MS 17293-17303 — Stud-Stepped — Steel 3A Fit. Drilled and Undrilled		**MS 20073-20074** — Bolt, Machine Aircraft Drilled Head — Steel, Available in CRES. 3A Fit. Supersedes AN73-AN81
MS 17825/6 — Nut, Self-Locking, Castellated, 250°F. Nylon Insert — Alloy Steel 3B Fit	**MS 19059-19064** — Ball, Bearing — Alloy Steel, CRES. Steel, Brass, Bronze, K-Monel	**MS 20115** — Shackle-Wire, Rope — CRES. Steel, Al Alloy, Steel. Supersedes AN115
MS 17828 — Nut, Self-Locking (Nylon Insert) 250°F, Regular Height — Monel	**MS 19069/70** — Washer, Key, Retaining — Steel, Alloy Steel, CRES. Steel	**MS 20219-20221** — Pulley, Groove, Aircraft — Al Alloy, Phenolic. MS 20219 SUPERSEDES AN219-AN221
MS 17829/30 — Nuts, Self-Locking Nylon Insert, 250° — CRES. Steel, Steel 3B Fit. Regular Height	**MS 20000** — Turnbuckle Assembly — Per Mil-T-5685. Also See AN155 and AN165	**MS 20253** — Pin, Hinge — CRES. Steel. For Use with MS 20257 and MS 20001 SUPERSEDES AN253

(Illustrations from AIMSCO catalog)

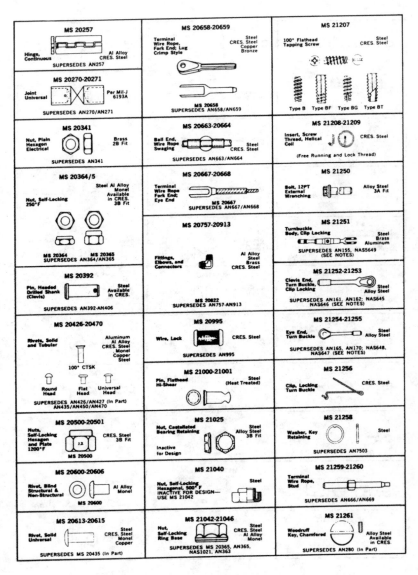

MS 20257
Hinge, Continuous — Al Alloy, CRES. Steel
SUPERSEDES AN257

MS 20270-20271
Joint Universal — Per Mil-J 6193A
SUPERSEDES AN270/AN271

MS 20341
Nut, Plain Hexagon Electrical — Brass 2B Fit
SUPERSEDES AN341

MS 20364/5
Nut, Self-Locking 250°F — Steel Al Alloy Monel Available in CRES. 3B Fit
MS 20364   MS 20365
SUPERSEDES AN364/AN365

MS 20392
Pin, Headed Drilled Shank (Clevis) — Steel Available in CRES.
SUPERSEDES AN392-AN406

MS 20426-20470
Rivets, Solid and Tubular — Aluminum Al Alloy CRES. Steel Monel Copper Steel
100° CTSK
Round Head   Flat Head   Universal Head
SUPERSEDES AN426/AN427 (In Part) AN435/AN450/AN470

MS 20500-20501
Nuts, Self-Locking Hexagon and Plate 1200°F — CRES. Steel 3B Fit
MS 20500

MS 20600-20606
Rivet, Blind Structural & Non-Structural — Al Alloy Monel
MS 20600

MS 20613-20615
Rivet, Solid Universal — Steel CRES. Steel Monel Copper
SUPERSEDES MS 20435 (In Part)

MS 20658-20659
Terminal Wire Rope, Fork End; Lug Crimp Style — Steel CRES. Steel Copper Bronze
MS 20658
SUPERSEDES AN658/AN659

MS 20663-20664
Ball End, Wire Rope Swaging — Steel CRES. Steel
SUPERSEDES AN663/AN664

MS 20667-20668
Terminal Wire Rope Fork End; Eye End —
MS 20667
SUPERSEDES AN667/AN668

MS 20757-20913
Fittings, Elbows, and Connecters — Al Alloy Steel Brass CRES. Steel
MS 20822
SUPERSEDES AN757-AN913

MS 20995
Wire, Lock — CRES. Steel
SUPERSEDES AN995

MS 21000-21001
Pin, Flathead Hi-Shear — Steel (Heat Treated)

MS 21025
Nut, Castellated Bearing Retaining — Steel Alloy Steel 3B Fit
Inactive for Design

MS 21040
Nut, Self-Locking Hexagonal, 500°F INACTIVE FOR DESIGN— USE MS 21042 — Steel

MS 21042-21046
Nut, Self-Locking Ring Base — Steel CRES. Steel Al Alloy Monel
SUPERSEDES MS 20365, AN365, NAS1021, AN363

MS 21207
100° Flathead Tapping Screw — Steel CRES. Steel
Type B   Type BF   Type BG   Type BT

MS 21208-21209
Insert, Screw Thread, Helical Coil — CRES. Steel
(Free Running and Lock Thread)

MS 21250
Bolt, 12PT External Wrenching — Alloy Steel 3A Fit

MS 21251
Turnbuckle Body, Clip Locking — Steel Brass Aluminum
SUPERSEDES AN155, NAS5649 (SEE NOTES)

MS 21252-21253
Clevis End, Turn Buckle, Clip Locking — Steel Alloy Steel
SUPERSEDES AN161, AN162; NAS645 NAS646 (SEE NOTES)

MS 21254-21255
Eye End, Turn Buckle — Steel Alloy Steel
SUPERSEDES AN165, AN170; NAS648, NAS647 (SEE NOTES)

MS 21256
Clip, Locking Turn Buckle — CRES. Steel

MS 21258
Washer, Key Retaining — Steel
SUPERSEDES AN7503

MS 21259-21260
Terminal Wire Rope, Stud —
SUPERSEDES AN666/AN669

MS 21261
Woodruff Key, Chamfered — Alloy Steel Available in CRES.
SUPERSEDES AN280 (In Part)

(Illustrations from AIMSCO catalog)

339

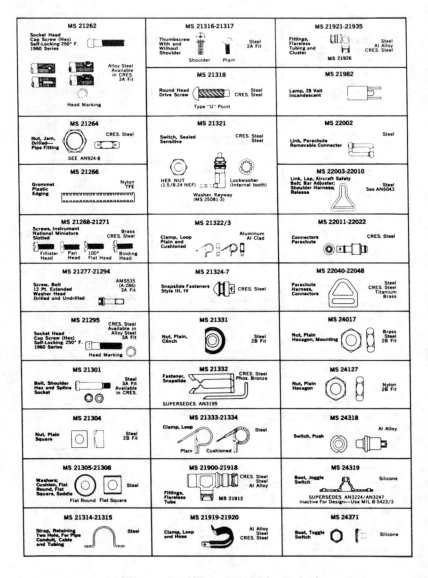

MS 21262	MS 21316-21317	MS 21921-21935
Socket Head Cap Screw (Hex) Self-Locking 250° F. 1960 Series — Alloy Steel Available in CRES. 3A Fit — Head Marking	Thumbscrew With and Without Shoulder — Steel 2A Fit — Shoulder Plain	Fittings, Flareless Tubing and Cluster — Steel Al Alloy CRES. Steel — MS 21926

MS 21318	MS 21982
Round Head Drive Screw — Steel CRES. Steel — Type "U" Point	Lamp, 28 Volt Incandescent

MS 21264	MS 21321	MS 22002
Nut, Jam, Drilled— Pipe Fitting — CRES. Steel — SEE AN924-8	Switch, Sealed Sensitive — CRES. Steel Steel — HEX NUT (1-5/8-24 NEF) / Lockwasher (Internal tooth) — Washer, Keyway (MS 25081-3)	Link, Parachute Removable Connector — Steel

MS 21266	MS 22003-22010
Grommet Plastic Edging — Nylon TFE	Link, Lap, Aircraft Safety Belt; Bar Adjuster; Shoulder Harness; Release — Steel See AN6043

MS 21268-21271	MS 21322/3	MS 22011-22022
Screws, Instrument National Miniature Slotted — Brass CRES. Steel — Fillister Head, Pan Head, 100° Flat Head, Binding Head	Clamp, Loop Plain and Cushioned — Aluminum Al Clad	Connectors Parachute — CRES. Steel

MS 21277-21294	MS 21324-7	MS 22040-22048
Screw, Bolt 12 Pt. Extended Washer Head Drilled and Undrilled — AMS535 (A-286) 3A Fit	Snapslide Fasteners Style III, IV — CRES. Steel	Parachute Harness, Connectors — Steel CRES. Steel Titanium Brass

MS 21295	MS 21331	MS 24017
Socket Head Cap Screw (Hex) Self-Locking 250° F. 1960 Series — CRES. Steel Available in Alloy Steel 3A Fit — Head Marking	Nut, Plain Clinch — Steel 2B Fit	Nut, Plain Hexagon, Mounting — Brass Steel 2B Fit

MS 21301	MS 21332	MS 24127
Bolt, Shoulder Hex and Spline Socket — Steel 3A Fit Available in CRES.	Fastener, Snapslide — CRES. Steel Phos. Bronze — SUPERSEDES AN3195	Nut, Plain Hexagon — Nylon 2B Fit

MS 21304	MS 21333-21334	MS 24318
Nut, Plain Square — Steel 2B Fit	Clamp, Loop — Steel — Plain Cushioned	Switch, Push — Al Alloy

MS 21305-21308	MS 21900-21918	MS 24319
Washers: Cushion, Flat Round, Flat Square, Saddle — Steel — Flat Round Flat Square	Fittings, Flareless Tube — CRES. Steel Steel Al Alloy — MS 21912	Boot, Joggle Switch — Silicone — SUPERSEDES AN3224/AN3247 Inactive For Design—Use MIL-B-5423/3

MS 21314-21315	MS 21919-21920	MS 24371
Strap, Retaining Two Hole, For Pipe Conduit, Cable and Tubing — Steel	Clamp, Loop and Hose — Al Alloy Steel CRES. Steel	Boot, Toggle Switch — Silicone

(Illustrations from AIMSCO catalog)

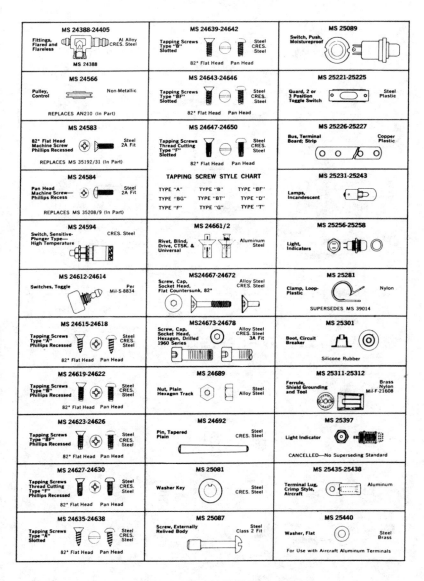

MS 24388-24405 Fittings, Flared and Flareless — Al Alloy, CRES. Steel MS 24388	**MS 24639-24642** Tapping Screws Type "B" Slotted — Steel, CRES. Steel 82° Flat Head Pan Head	**MS 25089** Switch, Push, Moistureproof
MS 24566 Pulley, Control — Non-Metallic REPLACES AN210 (In Part)	**MS 24643-24646** Tapping Screws Type "BF" Slotted — Steel, CRES. Steel 82° Flat Head Pan Head	**MS 25221-25225** Guard, 2 or 3 Position Toggle Switch — Steel, Plastic
MS 24583 82° Flat Head Machine Screw Phillips Recessed — Steel, 2A Fit REPLACES MS 35192/31 (In Part)	**MS 24647-24650** Tapping Screws Thread Cutting Type "F" Slotted — Steel, CRES. Steel 82° Flat Head Pan Head	**MS 25226-25227** Bus, Terminal Board; Strip — Copper, Plastic
MS 24584 Pan Head Machine Screw— Phillips Recess — Steel, 2A Fit REPLACES MS 35208/9 (In Part)	**TAPPING SCREW STYLE CHART** TYPE "A" TYPE "B" TYPE "BF" TYPE "BG" TYPE "BT" TYPE "D" TYPE "F" TYPE "G" TYPE "T"	**MS 25231-25243** Lamps, Incandescent
MS 24594 Switch, Sensitive-Plunger Type— High Temperature — CRES. Steel	**MS 24661/2** Rivet, Blind, Drive, CTSK. & Universal — Aluminum, Steel	**MS 25256-25258** Light, Indicators
MS 24612-24614 Switches, Toggle — Per Mil-S-8834	**MS24667-24672** Screw, Cap, Socket Head, Flat Countersunk, 82° — Alloy Steel, CRES. Steel	**MS 25281** Clamp, Loop-Plastic — Nylon SUPERSEDES MS 39014
MS 24615-24618 Tapping Screws Type "A" Phillips Recessed — Steel, CRES. Steel 82° Flat Head Pan Head	**MS24673-24678** Screw, Cap, Socket Head, Hexagon, Drilled 1960 Series — Alloy Steel, CRES. Steel, 3A Fit	**MS 25301** Boot, Circuit Breaker Silicone Rubber
MS 24619-24622 Tapping Screws Type "B" Phillips Recessed — Steel, CRES. Steel 82° Flat Head Pan Head	**MS 24689** Nut, Plain Hexagon Track — Steel, Alloy Steel	**MS 25311-25312** Ferrule, Shield Grounding and Tool — Brass, Nylon Mil-F-21608
MS 24623-24626 Tapping Screws Type "BF" Phillips Recessed — Steel, CRES. Steel 82° Flat Head Pan Head	**MS 24692** Pin, Tapered Plain — Steel, CRES. Steel	**MS 25397** Light Indicator CANCELLED—No Superseding Standard
MS 24627-24630 Tapping Screws Thread Cutting Type "F" Phillips Recessed — Steel, CRES. Steel 82° Flat Head Pan Head	**MS 25081** Washer Key — Steel, CRES. Steel	**MS 25435-25438** Terminal Lug, Crimp Style, Aircraft — Aluminum
MS 24635-24638 Tapping Screws Type "A" Slotted — Steel, CRES. Steel 82° Flat Head Pan Head	**MS 25087** Screw, Externally Relived Body — Steel, Class 2 Fit	**MS 25440** Washer, Flat — Steel, Brass For Use with Aircraft Aluminum Terminals

(Illustrations from AIMSCO catalog)

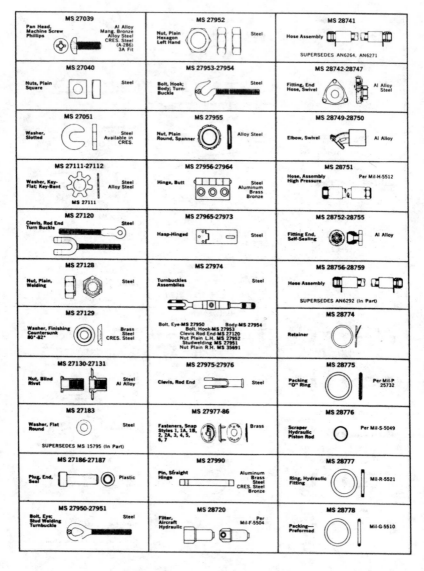

MS 27039	MS 27952	MS 28741
Pan Head, Machine Screw Phillips — Al Alloy, Mang. Bronze, Alloy Steel, CRES. Steel (A-286), 3A Fit	Nut, Plain Hexagon Left Hand — Steel	Hose Assembly — SUPERSEDES AN6264, AN6271
MS 27040 — Nuts, Plain Square — Steel	MS 27953-27954 — Bolt, Hook; Body; Turn-Buckle — Steel	MS 28742-28747 — Fitting, End Hose, Swivel — Al Alloy, Steel
MS 27051 — Washer, Slotted — Steel Available in CRES.	MS 27955 — Nut, Plain Round, Spanner — Alloy Steel	MS 28749-28750 — Elbow, Swivel — Al Alloy
MS 27111-27112 — Washer, Key-Flat; Key-Bent — Steel, Alloy Steel — MS 27111	MS 27956-27964 — Hinge, Butt — Steel, Aluminum, Brass, Bronze	MS 28751 — Hose, Assembly High Pressure — Per Mil-H-5512
MS 27120 — Clevis, Rod End Turn Buckle — Steel	MS 27965-27973 — Hasp-Hinged — Steel	MS 28752-28755 — Fitting End, Self-Sealing — Al Alloy
MS 27128 — Nut, Plain, Welding — Steel	MS 27974 — Turnbuckles Assemblies — Steel	MS 28756-28759 — Hose Assembly — SUPERSEDES AN6292 (In Part)
MS 27129 — Washer, Finishing Countersunk 80°-82° — Brass, Steel, CRES. Steel	Bolt, Eye-MS 27950, Body-MS 27954, Bolt, Hook-MS 27953, Clevis Rod End-MS 27120, Nut Plain L.H. MS 27952, Studwelding MS 27951, Nut Plain R.H. MS 35691	MS 28774 — Retainer
MS 27130-27131 — Nut, Blind Rivet — Steel, Al Alloy	MS 27975-27976 — Clevis, Rod End — Steel	MS 28775 — Packing "O" Ring — Per Mil-P 25732
MS 27183 — Washer, Flat Round — Steel — SUPERSEDES MS 15795 (In Part)	MS 27977-86 — Fasteners, Snap Styles 1, 1A, 1B, 2, 2A, 3, 4, 5, 6, 7 — Brass	MS 28776 — Scraper Hydraulic Piston Rod — Per Mil-S-5049
MS 27186-27187 — Plug, End, Seal — Plastic	MS 27990 — Pin, Straight Hinge — Aluminum, Brass, Steel, CRES. Steel, Bronze	MS 28777 — Ring, Hydraulic Fitting — Mil-R-5521
MS 27950-27951 — Bolt, Eye; Stud Welding Turnbuckle — Steel	MS 28720 — Filter, Aircraft Hydraulic — Per Mil-F-5504	MS 28778 — Packing—Preformed — Mil-G-5510

(Illustrations from AIMSCO catalog)

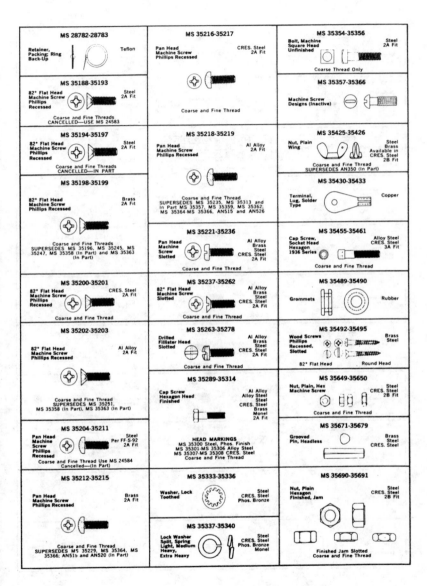

MS 28782-28783	MS 35216-35217	MS 35354-35356
Retainer, Packing; Ring Back-Up — Teflon	Pan Head Machine Screw Phillips Recessed — CRES. Steel 2A Fit Coarse and Fine Thread	Bolt, Machine Square Head Unfinished — Steel 2A Fit Coarse Thread Only
MS 35188-35193 82° Flat Head Machine Screw Phillips Recessed — Steel 2A Fit Coarse and Fine Threads CANCELLED—USE MS 24583		**MS 35357-35366** Machine Screw Designs (Inactive)
MS 35194-35197 82° Flat Head Machine Screw Phillips Recessed — Steel 2A Fit Coarse and Fine Threads CANCELLED—IN PART	**MS 35218-35219** Pan Head Machine Screw Phillips Recessed — Al Alloy 2A Fit Coarse and Fine Thread SUPERSEDES MS 35235, MS 35313 and In Part MS 35357, MS 35359, MS 35362; MS 35364-MS 35366, AN515 and AN526	**MS 35425-35426** Nut, Plain Wing — Steel Brass Available in CRES. Steel 2B Fit Coarse and Fine Thread SUPERSEDES AN350 (In Part)
MS 35198-35199 82° Flat Head Machine Screw Phillips Recessed — Brass 2A Fit Coarse and Fine Threads SUPERSEDES MS 35196, MS 35245, MS 35247, MS 35358 (In Part) and MS 35363 (In Part)		**MS 35430-35433** Terminal, Lug, Solder Type — Copper
	MS 35221-35236 Pan Head Machine Screw Slotted — Al Alloy Brass Steel CRES. Steel 2A Fit Coarse and Fine Thread	**MS 35455-35461** Cap Screw, Socket Head Hexagon 1936 Series — Alloy Steel CRES. Steel 3A Fit Coarse and Fine Thread
MS 35200-35201 82° Flat Head Machine Screw Phillips Recessed — CRES. Steel 2A Fit Coarse and Fine Thread	**MS 35237-35262** 82° Flat Head Machine Screw Slotted — Al Alloy Brass Steel CRES. Steel 2A Fit Coarse and Fine Thread	**MS 35489-35490** Grommets — Rubber
MS 35202-35203 82° Flat Head Machine Screw Phillips Recessed — Al Alloy 2A Fit Coarse and Fine Thread SUPERSEDES MS 35251, MS 35358 (In Part), MS 35363 (In Part)	**MS 35263-35278** Drilled Fillister Head Slotted — Al Alloy Brass Steel CRES. Steel 2A Fit Coarse and Fine Thread	**MS 35492-35495** Wood Screws Phillips Recessed, Slotted — Brass Steel 82° Flat Head — Round Head
	MS 35289-35314 Cap Screw Hexagon Head Finished — Al Alloy Alloy Steel Steel CRES. Steel Brass Monel 2A Fit	**MS 35649-35650** Nut, Plain, Hex Machine Screw — Steel CRES. Steel 2B Fit Coarse and Fine Thread
MS 35204-35211 Pan Head Machine Screw Phillips Recessed — Steel Per FF-S-92 2A Fit Coarse and Fine Thread Use MS 24584 Cancelled—(In Part)	**HEAD MARKINGS** MS 35300 Steel, Phos. Finish MS 35301-MS 35306 Alloy Steel MS 35307-MS 35308 CRES. Steel Coarse and Fine Thread	**MS 35671-35679** Grooved Pin, Headless — Brass Steel CRES. Steel
MS 35212-35215 Pan Head Machine Screw Phillips Recessed — Brass 2A Fit Coarse and Fine Thread SUPERSEDES MS 35229, MS 35364, MS 35366; AN515 and AN520 (In Part)	**MS 35333-35336** Washer, Lock Toothed — Steel CRES. Steel Phos. Bronze	**MS 35690-35691** Nut, Plain Hexagon Finished, Jam — Steel CRES. Steel 2B Fit Finished Jam Slotted Coarse and Fine Thread
	MS 35337-35340 Lock Washer Split, Spring Light, Medium Heavy, Extra Heavy — Steel CRES. Steel Phos. Bronze Monel	

(Illustrations from AIMSCO catalog)

343

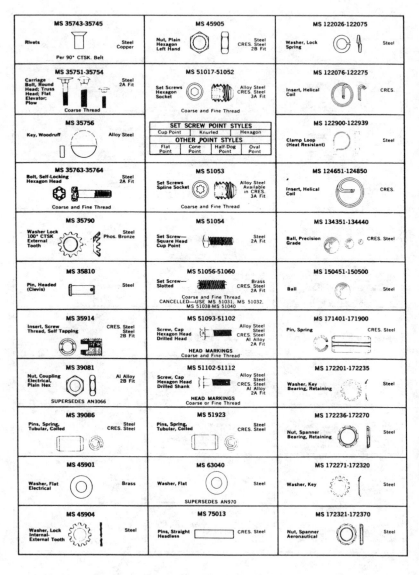

MS 35743-35745	MS 45905	MS 122026-122075
Rivets — Steel Copper — Per 90° CTSK. Belt	Nut, Plain Hexagon Left Hand — Steel CRES. Steel 2B Fit	Washer, Lock Spring — Steel
MS 35751-35754 — Carriage Bolt; Round Head; Truss Head; Flat Elevator; Plow — Steel 2A Fit — Coarse Thread	**MS 51017-51052** — Set Screws Hexagon Socket — Alloy Steel CRES. Steel 3A Fit — Coarse and Fine Thread	**MS 122076-122275** — Insert, Helical Coil — CRES.
MS 35756 — Key, Woodruff — Alloy Steel	**SET SCREW POINT STYLES** — Cup Point / Knurled / Hexagon — **OTHER POINT STYLES** — Flat Point / Cone Point / Half-Dog Point / Oval Point	**MS 122900-122939** — Clamp Loop (Heat Resistant) — Steel
MS 35763-35764 — Bolt, Self-Locking Hexagon Head — Steel 2A Fit — Coarse and Fine Thread	**MS 51053** — Set Screws Spline Socket — Alloy Steel Available in CRES. 3A Fit — Coarse and Fine Thread	**MS 124651-124850** — Insert, Helical Coil — CRES.
MS 35790 — Washer Lock 100° CTSK External Tooth — Steel Phos. Bronze	**MS 51054** — Set Screw— Square Head Cup Point — Steel 2A Fit	**MS 134351-134440** — Ball, Precision Grade — CRES. Steel
MS 35810 — Pin, Headed (Clevis) — Steel	**MS 51056-51060** — Set Screw— Slotted — Brass CRES. Steel 2A Fit — Coarse and Fine Thread CANCELLED—USE MS 51031, MS 51032, MS 51038-MS 51040	**MS 150451-150500** — Ball — Steel
MS 35914 — Insert, Screw Thread, Self Tapping — CRES. Steel Steel 2B Fit	**MS 51093-51102** — Screw, Cap Hexagon Head Drilled Head — Alloy Steel Steel CRES. Steel Al Alloy 2A Fit — **HEAD MARKINGS** Coarse and Fine Thread	**MS 171401-171900** — Pin, Spring — CRES. Steel
MS 39081 — Nut, Coupling Electrical, Plain Hex — Al Alloy 2B Fit — SUPERSEDES AN3066	**MS 51102-51112** — Screw, Cap Hexagon Head Drilled Shank — Alloy Steel Steel CRES. Steel Al Alloy 2A Fit — **HEAD MARKINGS** Coarse or Fine Thread	**MS 172201-172235** — Washer, Key Bearing, Retaining — Steel
MS 39086 — Pins, Spring, Tubular, Coiled — Steel CRES. Steel	**MS 51923** — Pins, Spring, Tubular, Coiled — Steel CRES. Steel	**MS 172236-172270** — Nut, Spanner Bearing, Retaining — Steel
MS 45901 — Washer, Flat Electrical — Brass	**MS 63040** — Washer, Flat — Steel — SUPERSEDES AN970	**MS 172271-172320** — Washer, Key — Steel
MS 45904 — Washer, Lock Internal- External Tooth — Steel	**MS 75013** — Pins, Straight Headless — CRES. Steel	**MS 172321-172370** — Nut, Spanner Aeronautical — Steel

(Illustrations from AIMSCO catalog)

344

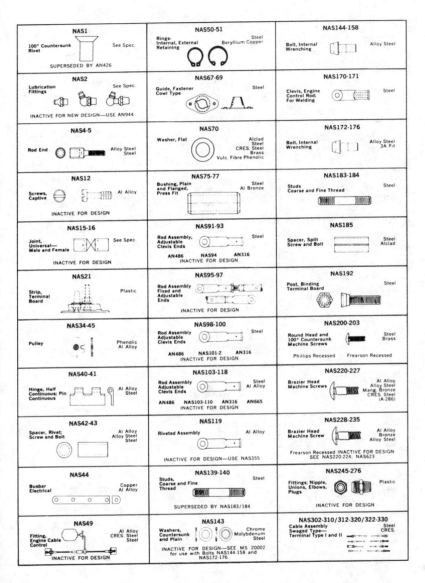

NAS1	NAS50-51	NAS144-158
100° Countersunk Rivet — See Spec. SUPERSEDED BY AN426	Rings- Internal, External Retaining — Steel, Beryllium Copper	Bolt, Internal Wrenching — Alloy Steel
NAS2 Lubrication Fittings — See Spec. INACTIVE FOR NEW DESIGN—USE AN944	**NAS67-69** Guide, Fastener Cowl Type — Steel	**NAS170-171** Clevis, Engine Control Rod; For Welding — Steel
NAS4-5 Rod End — Alloy Steel, Steel	**NAS70** Washer, Flat — Alclad, Steel, CRES. Steel, Brass, Vulc. Fibre Phenolic	**NAS172-176** Bolt, Internal Wrenching — Alloy Steel 3A Fit
NAS12 Screws, Captive — Al Alloy INACTIVE FOR DESIGN	**NAS75-77** Bushing, Plain and Flanged, Press Fit — Steel, Al Bronze	**NAS183-184** Studs Coarse and Fine Thread — Steel
NAS15-16 Joint, Universal—Male and Female — See Spec. INACTIVE FOR DESIGN	**NAS91-93** Rod Assembly, Adjustable Clevis Ends — Steel AN486 NAS94 AN316 INACTIVE FOR DESIGN	**NAS185** Spacer, Split Screw and Bolt — Steel, Alclad
NAS21 Strip, Terminal Board — Plastic	**NAS95-97** Rod Assembly Fixed and Adjustable Ends INACTIVE FOR DESIGN	**NAS192** Post, Binding Terminal Board — Steel
NAS34-45 Pulley — Phenolic, Al Alloy	**NAS98-100** Rod Assembly Adjustable Clevis Ends — Steel AN486 NAS101-2 AN316 INACTIVE FOR DESIGN	**NAS200-203** Round Head and 100° Countersunk Machine Screws — Steel, Brass Phillips Recessed Frearson Recessed
NAS40-41 Hinge, Half Continuous; Pin Continuous — Al Alloy, Steel	**NAS103-118** Rod Assembly Adjustable Clevis Ends — Steel, Al Alloy AN486 NAS103-110 AN316 AN665 INACTIVE FOR DESIGN	**NAS220-227** Brazier Head Machine Screws — Al Alloy, Alloy Steel, Mang. Bronze, CRES. Steel (A-286)
NAS42-43 Spacer, Rivet; Screw and Bolt — Al Alloy, Alloy Steel, Steel	**NAS119** Riveted Assembly — Al Alloy INACTIVE FOR DESIGN—USE NAS355	**NAS228-235** Brazier Head Machine Screw — Al Alloy, Bronze, Alloy Steel Frearson Recessed INACTIVE FOR DESIGN SEE NAS220-224; NAS623
NAS44 Busbar Electrical — Copper, Al Alloy	**NAS139-140** Studs, Coarse and Fine Thread — Steel SUPERSEDED BY NAS183/184	**NAS245-276** Fittings; Nipple, Unions, Elbows, Plugs — Plastic INACTIVE FOR DESIGN
NAS49 Fitting, Engine Cable Control — Al Alloy, CRES. Steel, Steel INACTIVE FOR DESIGN	**NAS143** Washers, Countersunk and Plain — Chrome, Molybdenum, Steel INACTIVE FOR DESIGN—SEE MS 20002 for use with Bolts NAS144-158 and NAS172-176	**NAS302-310/312-320/322-330** Cable Assembly Swaged Type—Terminal Type I and II — Steel, CRES.

(Illustrations from AIMSCO catalog)

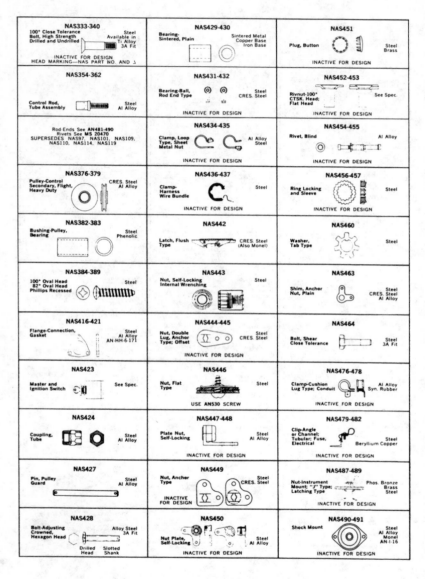

NAS333-340	NAS429-430	NAS451
100° Close Tolerance Bolt, High Strength Drilled and Undrilled — Steel, Available in Ti. Alloy, 3A Fit. INACTIVE FOR DESIGN. HEAD MARKING—NAS PART NO. AND ⅃	Bearing-Sintered, Plain — Sintered Metal Copper Base, Iron Base	Plug, Button — Steel, Brass. INACTIVE FOR DESIGN
NAS354-362	NAS431-432	NAS452-453
Control Rod, Tube Assembly — Steel, Al Alloy	Bearing-Ball, Rod End Type — Steel, CRES. Steel. INACTIVE FOR DESIGN	Rivnut-100° CTSK. Head; Flat Head — See Spec. INACTIVE FOR DESIGN
Rod-Ends See AN481-490. Rivets See MS 20470. SUPERSEDES NAS97, NAS101, NAS109, NAS110, NAS114, NAS119	NAS434-435	NAS454-455
	Clamp, Loop Type, Sheet Metal Nut — Al Alloy, Steel. INACTIVE FOR DESIGN	Rivet, Blind — Al Alloy. INACTIVE FOR DESIGN
NAS376-379	NAS436-437	NAS456-457
Pulley-Control Secondary, Flight, Heavy Duty — CRES. Steel, Al Alloy	Clamp-Harness Wire Bundle — Steel. INACTIVE FOR DESIGN	Ring Locking and Sleeve — Steel. INACTIVE FOR DESIGN
NAS382-383	NAS442	NAS460
Bushing-Pulley, Bearing — Steel, Phenolic	Latch, Flush Type — CRES. Steel (Also Monel)	Washer, Tab Type — Steel
NAS384-389	NAS443	NAS463
100° Oval Head 82° Oval Head Phillips Recessed — Steel	Nut, Self-Locking Internal Wrenching — Steel	Shim, Anchor Nut, Plain — Steel, CRES. Steel, Al Alloy
NAS416-421	NAS444-445	NAS464
Flange-Connection, Gasket — Steel, Al Alloy, AN-HH-6-171	Nut, Double Lug, Anchor Type; Offset — Steel, CRES. Steel. INACTIVE FOR DESIGN	Bolt, Shear Close Tolerance — Steel, 3A Fit
NAS423	NAS446	NAS476-478
Master and Ignition Switch — See Spec.	Nut, Flat Type — Steel. USE AN530 SCREW	Clamp-Cushion Lug Type; Conduit — Al Alloy, Syn. Rubber. INACTIVE FOR DESIGN
NAS424	NAS447-448	NAS479-482
Coupling, Tube — Steel, Al Alloy	Plate Nut, Self-Locking — Steel, Al Alloy. INACTIVE FOR DESIGN	Clip-Angle or Channel; Tubular; Fuse, Electrical — Steel, Beryllium Copper. INACTIVE FOR DESIGN
NAS427	NAS449	NAS487-489
Pin, Pulley Guard — Steel, Al Alloy	Nut, Anchor Type — Steel, CRES. Steel. INACTIVE FOR DESIGN	Nut-Instrument Mount; "J" Type; Latching Type — Phos. Bronze, Brass, Steel. INACTIVE FOR DESIGN
NAS428	NAS450	NAS490-491
Bolt-Adjusting Crowned, Hexagon Head — Alloy Steel, 3A Fit. Drilled Head, Slotted Shank	Nut Plate, Self-Locking — Steel, Al Alloy. INACTIVE FOR DESIGN	Shock Mount — Steel, Al Alloy, Monel, AN-I-16. INACTIVE FOR DESIGN

(Illustrations from AIMSCO catalog)

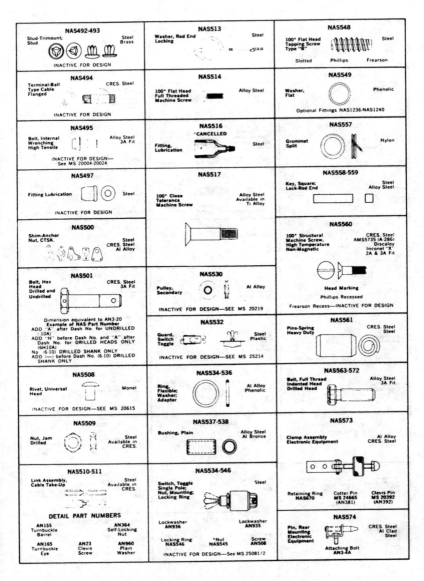

NAS492-493	NAS513	NAS548
Stud-Trimount; Stud — Steel, Brass	Washer, Rod End Locking — Steel	100° Flat Head Tapping Screw Type "B" — Steel
INACTIVE FOR DESIGN		Slotted Phillips Frearson
NAS494	**NAS514**	**NAS549**
Terminal-Ball Type Cable Flanged — CRES. Steel	100° Flat Head Full Threaded Machine Screw — Alloy Steel	Washer, Flat — Phenolic
INACTIVE FOR DESIGN		Optional Fittings NAS1236-NAS1240
NAS495	**NAS516** "CANCELLED"	**NAS557**
Bolt, Internal Wrenching High Tensile — Alloy Steel 3A Fit	Fitting, Lubrication — Steel	Grommet Split — Nylon
INACTIVE FOR DESIGN— See MS 20004-20024		
NAS497	**NAS517**	**NAS558-559**
Fitting Lubrication — Steel	100° Close Tolerance Machine Screw — Alloy Steel Available in Ti Alloy	Key, Square; Lock-Rod End — Steel, Alloy Steel
INACTIVE FOR DESIGN		
NAS500	**NAS517**	**NAS560**
Shim-Anchor Nut, CTSK. — Steel, CRES. Steel, Al Alloy		100° Structural Machine Screw, High Temperature Non-Magnetic — CRES. Steel AMS5735 (A 286) Discaloy Inconel "X" 2A & 3A Fit
NAS501	**NAS530**	
Bolt, Hex Head Drilled and Undrilled — CRES. Steel 3A Fit	Pulley, Secondary — Al Alloy	Head Marking
	INACTIVE FOR DESIGN—SEE MS 20219	Phillips Recessed
Dimension equivalent to AN3-20 Example of NAS Part Number ADD "A" after after No. for UNDRILLED (-10A) ADD "H" before Dash No. and "A" after Dash No. for DRILLED HEADS ONLY (6H10A) No. (6-10) DRILLED SHANK ONLY ADD (—) before Dash No. (6-10) DRILLED SHANK ONLY	**NAS532**	Frearson Recess—INACTIVE FOR DESIGN
	Guard, Switch Toggle — Steel, Plastic	**NAS561**
		Pins-Spring Heavy Duty — CRES. Steel, Steel
	INACTIVE FOR DESIGN—SEE MS 25214	
NAS508	**NAS534-536**	**NAS563-572**
Rivet, Universal Head — Monel	Ring, Flexible; Washer; Adapter — Al Alloy Phenolic	Bolt, Full Thread Indented Head Drilled Head — Alloy Steel 3A Fit
INACTIVE FOR DESIGN—SEE MS 20615		
NAS509	**NAS537-538**	**NAS573**
Nut, Jam Drilled — Steel Available in CRES.	Bushing, Plain — Alloy Steel Al Bronze	Clamp Assembly Electronic Equipment — Al Alloy CRES. Steel
NAS510-511	**NAS534-546**	
Link Assembly, Cable Take-Up — Steel Available in CRES.	Switch, Toggle Single Pole; Nut, Mounting; Locking Ring — Steel	
		Retaining Ring NAS670 Cotter Pin MS 24665 (AN381) Clevis Pin MS 20392 (AN392)
DETAIL PART NUMBERS	Lockwasher AN936 Lockwasher AN935	**NAS574**
AN155 Turnbuckle Barrel AN364 Self-Locking Nut	Locking Ring NAS546 *Nut NAS545 Screw AN508	Pin, Rear Mounting Electronic Equipment — CRES. Steel Al Clad Steel
AN165 Turnbuckle Eye AN23 Clevis Screw AN960 Plain Washer	INACTIVE FOR DESIGN—See MS 25081/2	Attaching Bolt AN3-4A

(Illustrations from AIMSCO catalog)

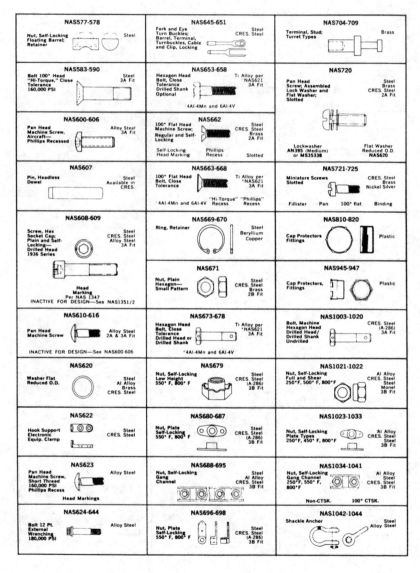

NAS577-578	NAS645-651	NAS704-709
Nut, Self-Locking Floating Barrel; Retainer — Steel	Fork and Eye Turn Buckles; Barrel, Terminal, Turnbuckles, Cable and Clip, Locking — Steel, CRES. Steel	Terminal, Stud; Turret Types — Brass
NAS583-590 Bolt 100° Head "Hi-Torque," Close Tolerance 160,000 PSI — Steel 3A Fit	**NAS653-658** Hexagon Head Bolt, Close Tolerance Drilled Shank Optional — Ti Alloy per *NAS621 3A Fit 4Al-4Mn and 6Al-4V	**NAS720** Pan Head Screw; Assembled Lock Washer and Flat Washer; Slotted — Steel, Brass, CRES. Steel 2A Fit
NAS600-606 Pan Head Machine Screw, Aircraft- Phillips Recessed — Alloy Steel 3A Fit	**NAS662** 100° Flat Head Machine Screw; Regular and Self-Locking — Steel, CRES. Steel, Brass 2A Fit Self-Locking Head Marking — Phillips Recess — Slotted	Lockwasher AN395 (Medium) or MS35338 — Flat Washer Reduced O.D. NAS620
NAS607 Pin, Headless Dowel — Steel Available in CRES.	**NAS663-668** 100° Flat Head Bolt, Close Tolerance — Ti Alloy per *NAS621 3A Fit *4Al-4Mn and 6Al-4V — "Hi-Torque" Recess — "Phillips" Recess	**NAS721-725** Miniature Screws Slotted — CRES. Steel, Brass, Nickel Silver Fillister — Pan — 100° flat — Binding
NAS608-609 Screw, Hex Socket Cap; Plain and Self-Locking— Drilled Head 1936 Series — Steel, CRES. Steel, Alloy Steel 3A Fit Head Marking Per NAS 1347 INACTIVE FOR DESIGN—See NAS1351/2	**NAS669-670** Ring, Retainer — Steel, Beryllium Copper	**NAS810-820** Cap Protectors Fittings — Plastic
	NAS671 Nut, Plain Hexagon— Small Pattern — Steel, CRES. Steel, Brass 2B Fit	**NAS945-947** Cap Protectors, Fittings — Plastic
NAS610-616 Pan Head Machine Screw — Alloy Steel 2A & 3A Fit INACTIVE FOR DESIGN—See NAS600-606	**NAS673-678** Hexagon Head Bolt, Close Tolerance Drilled Head or Drilled Shank — Ti Alloy per *NAS621 3A Fit *4Al-4Mn and 6Al-4V	**NAS1003-1020** Bolt, Machine Hexagon Head Drilled Head / Drilled Shank Undrilled — CRES. Steel (A-286) 3A Fit
NAS620 Washer Flat Reduced O.D. — Steel, Al Alloy, Brass, CRES. Steel	**NAS679** Nut, Self-Locking Low Height 550° F, 800° F — Steel (A-286) 3B Fit	**NAS1021-1022** Nut, Self-Locking Full and Shear 250°F, 500° F, 800°F — Al Alloy, CRES. Steel, Monel 3B Fit
NAS622 Hook Support Electronic Equip. Clamp — Steel, CRES. Steel	**NAS680-687** Nut, Plate Self-Locking 550° F, 800° F — Steel, CRES. Steel (A-286) 3B Fit	**NAS1023-1033** Nut, Self-Locking Plate Types 250°F, 450° F, 800°F — Al Alloy, CRES. Steel, Steel 3B Fit
NAS623 Pan Head Machine Screw, Short Thread 160,000 PSI Phillips Recess — Alloy Steel Head Markings	**NAS688-695** Nut, Self-Locking Gang Channel — Steel, Al Alloy, CRES. Steel 3B Fit	**NAS1034-1041** Nut, Self-Locking Gang Channel 250°F, 550° F, 800° F — Al Alloy, Steel, CRES. Steel 3B Fit Non-CTSK. — 100° CTSK.
NAS624-644 Bolt 12 Pt. External Wrenching 180,000 PSI — Alloy Steel	**NAS696-698** Nut, Plate Self-Locking 550° F, 800° F — Steel, CRES. Steel (A-286) 3B Fit	**NAS1042-1044** Shackle Anchor — Steel, Alloy Steel

(Illustrations from AIMSCO catalog)

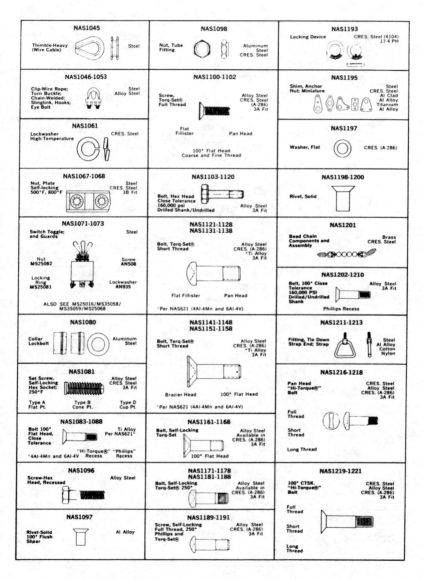

NAS1045			NAS1098			NAS1193	
Thimble-Heavy (Wire Cable)		Steel	Nut, Tube Fitting		Aluminum Steel CRES. Steel	Locking Device	CRES. Steel (4104) 17 4 PH

NAS1046-1053

Clip-Wire Rope; Turn Buckle; Chain-Welded; Slinglink, Hooks; Eye Bolt — Steel / Alloy Steel

NAS1100-1102

Screw, Torq-Set® Full Thread — Alloy Steel / CRES. Steel / (A-286) / 3A Fit

Flat Fillister — Pan Head

100° Flat Head
Coarse and Fine Thread

NAS1195

Shim, Anchor / Nut; Miniature — Steel / CRES. Steel / Al Clad / Al Alloy / Titanium / Al Alloy

NAS1061

Lockwasher High-Temperature — CRES. Steel

NAS1197

Washer, Flat — CRES. (A-286)

NAS1067-1068

Nut, Plate Self-locking 500°F, 800°F — Steel / CRES. Steel / 3B Fit

NAS1103-1120

Bolt, Hex Head Close Tolerance 160,000 psi Drilled Shank/Undrilled — Alloy Steel / 3A Fit

NAS1198-1200

Rivet, Solid

NAS1071-1073

Switch Toggle; and Guards — Steel

Nut MS25082

Locking Ring MS25081

Screw AN508

Lockwasher AN935

ALSO SEE MS25016/MS35058/ MS35059/MS25068

NAS1121-1128
NAS1131-1138

Bolt, Torq-Set® Short Thread — Alloy Steel / CRES. (A-286) / *Ti Alloy / 3A Fit

Flat Fillister — Pan Head

*Per NAS621 (4Al-4Mn and 6Al-4V)

NAS1201

Bead Chain Components and Assembly — Brass / CRES. Steel

NAS1202-1210

Bolt, 100° Close Tolerance 160,000 PSI Drilled/Undrilled Shank — Alloy Steel / 3A Fit

Phillips Recess

NAS1080

Collar Lockbolt — Aluminum / Steel

NAS1141-1148
NAS1151-1158

Bolt, Torq-Set® Short Thread — Alloy Steel / CRES. (A-286) / *Ti Alloy / 3A Fit

Brazier Head — 100° Flat Head

*Per NAS621 (4Al-4Mn and 6Al-4V)

NAS1211-1213

Fitting, Tie Down Strap End; Strap — Steel / Al Alloy / Cotton / Nylon

NAS1081

Set Screw, Self-Locking Hex Socket; 250°F — Alloy Steel / CRES. Steel / 3A Fit

Type A — Flat Pt. / Type B — Cone Pt. / Type D — Cup Pt.

NAS1216-1218

Pan Head "Hi-Torque®" Bolt — CRES. Steel / Alloy Steel / CRES. (A-286) / 3A Fit

Full Thread

Short Thread

Long Thread

NAS1083-1088

Bolt 100° Flat Head, Close Tolerance — Ti Alloy / Per NAS621*

"Hi-Torque®" Recess — "Phillips" Recess

*4Al-4Mn and 6Al-4V

NAS1161-1168

Bolt, Self-Locking Torq-Set — Alloy Steel / Available in / CRES. (A-286) / 3A Fit

100° Flat Head

NAS1219-1221

100° CTSK. "Hi-Torque®" Bolt — CRES. Steel / Alloy Steel / CRES. (A-286) / 3A Fit

Full Thread

Short Thread

Long Thread

NAS1096

Screw-Hex Head, Recessed — Alloy Steel

NAS1171-1178
NAS1181-1188

Bolt, Self-Locking Torq-Set® 250° — Alloy Steel / Available in / CRES. (A-286) / 3A Fit

NAS1097

Rivet-Solid 100° Flush Shear — Al Alloy

NAS1189-1191

Screw, Self-Locking Full Thread, 250° Phillips and Torq-Set® — Alloy Steel / CRES. (A-286) / 3A Fit

(Illustrations from AIMSCO catalog)

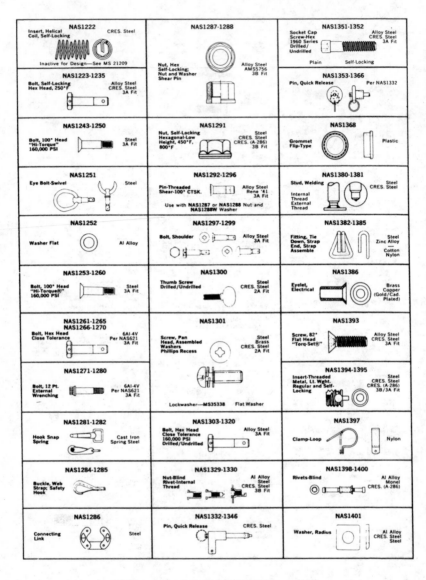

NAS1222 Insert, Helical Coil, Self-Locking — CRES. Steel — Inactive for Design—See MS 21209	**NAS1287-1288** Nut, Hex Self-Locking; Nut and Washer Shear Pin — Alloy Steel AMS5756 3B Fit	**NAS1351-1352** Socket Cap Screw-Hex 1960 Series Drilled/ Undrilled — Alloy Steel CRES. Steel 3A Fit — Plain Self-Locking
NAS1223-1235 Bolt, Self-Locking Hex Head, 250°F — Alloy Steel CRES. Steel 3A Fit		**NAS1353-1366** Pin, Quick Release — Per NAS1332
NAS1243-1250 Bolt, 100° Head "Hi-Torque" 160,000 PSI — Steel 3A Fit	**NAS1291** Nut, Self-Locking Hexagonal-Low Height, 450°F, 800°F — Steel CRES. Steel CRES. (A-286) 3B Fit	**NAS1368** Grommet Flip-Type — Plastic
NAS1251 Eye Bolt-Swivel — Steel	**NAS1292-1296** Pin-Threaded Shear-100° CTSK. — Alloy Steel Rene '41 3A Fit — Use with NAS1287 or NAS1288 Nut and NAS1288W Washer	**NAS1380-1381** Stud, Welding — Steel CRES. Steel — Internal Thread External Thread
NAS1252 Washer Flat — Al Alloy	**NAS1297-1299** Bolt, Shoulder — Alloy Steel 3A Fit	**NAS1382-1385** Fitting, Tie Down, Strap End, Strap Assemble — Steel Zinc Alloy Cotton Nylon
NAS1253-1260 Bolt, 100° Head "Hi-Torque®" 160,000 PSI — Steel 3A Fit	**NAS1300** Thumb Screw Drilled/Undrilled — Steel CRES. Steel 2A Fit	**NAS1386** Eyelet, Electrical — Brass Copper (Gold/Cad. Plated)
NAS1261-1265 NAS1266-1270 Bolt, Hex Head Close Tolerance — 6Al-4V Per NAS621 3A Fit	**NAS1301** Screw, Pan Head, Assembled Washers Phillips Recess — Steel Brass CRES. Steel 2A Fit	**NAS1393** Screw, 82° Flat Head "Torq-Set®" — Alloy Steel CRES. Steel 3A Fit
NAS1271-1280 Bolt, 12 Pt. External Wrenching — 6Al-4V Per NAS621 3A Fit		**NAS1394-1395** Insert-Threaded Metal, Lt. Wght. Regular and Self-Locking — Steel CRES. Steel CRES. (A-286) 3B/3A Fit
NAS1281-1282 Hook Snap Spring — Cast Iron Spring Steel	Lockwasher—MS35338 Flat Washer	**NAS1397** Clamp-Loop — Nylon
NAS1284-1285 Buckle, Web Strap; Safety Hook	**NAS1303-1320** Bolt, Hex Head Close Tolerance 160,000 PSI Drilled/Undrilled — Alloy Steel 3A Fit	**NAS1398-1400** Rivets-Blind — Al Alloy Monel CRES. (A-286)
	NAS1329-1330 Nut-Blind Rivet-Internal Thread — Al Alloy Steel CRES. Steel 3B Fit	
NAS1286 Connecting Link — Steel	**NAS1332-1346** Pin, Quick Release — CRES. Steel	**NAS1401** Washer, Radius — Al Alloy CRES. Steel Steel

(Illustrations from AIMSCO catalog)

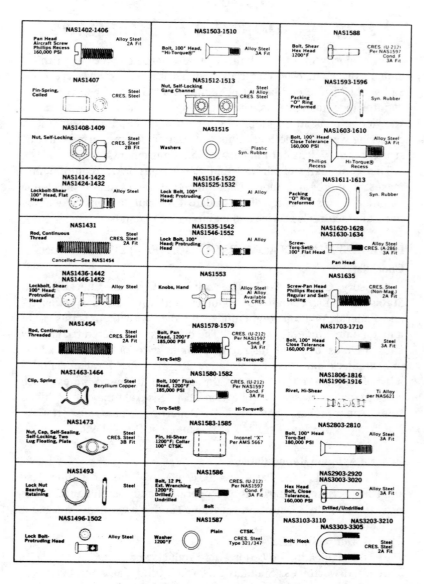

NAS1402-1406	NAS1503-1510	NAS1588
Pan Head Aircraft Screw Phillips Recess 160,000 PSI — Alloy Steel 2A Fit	Bolt, 100° Head, "Hi-Torque®" — Alloy Steel 3A Fit	Bolt, Shear Hex Head 1200°F — CRES. (U 212) Per NAS1597 Cond. F 3A Fit
NAS1407 Pin-Spring, Coiled — Steel CRES. Steel	**NAS1512-1513** Nut, Self-Locking Gang Channel — Steel Al Alloy CRES. Steel	**NAS1593-1596** Packing "O" Ring Preformed — Syn. Rubber
NAS1408-1409 Nut, Self-Locking — Steel CRES. Steel 2B Fit	**NAS1515** Washers — Plastic Syn. Rubber	**NAS1603-1610** Bolt, 100° Head Close Tolerance 160,000 PSI — Alloy Steel 3A Fit Phillips Recess — Hi-Torque® Recess
NAS1414-1422 NAS1424-1432 Lockbolt-Shear 100° Head, Flat Head — Alloy Steel	**NAS1516-1522 NAS1525-1532** Lock Bolt, 100° Head; Protruding Head — Al Alloy	**NAS1611-1613** Packing "O" Ring Preformed — Syn. Rubber
NAS1431 Rod, Continuous Thread — Steel CRES. Steel 2A Fit Cancelled—See NAS1454	**NAS1535-1542 NAS1546-1552** Lock Bolt, 100° Head; Protruding Head — Al Alloy	**NAS1620-1628 NAS1630-1634** Screw-Torq-Set® 100° Flat Head — Alloy Steel CRES. (A-286) 3A Fit Pan Head
NAS1436-1442 NAS1446-1452 Lockbolt, Shear 100° Head; Protruding Head — Alloy Steel	**NAS1553** Knobs, Hand — Alloy Steel Al Alloy Available in CRES.	**NAS1635** Screw-Pan Head Phillips Recess Regular and Self-Locking — CRES. Steel (Non-Mag.) 2A Fit
NAS1454 Rod, Continuous Threaded — Steel CRES. Steel 2A Fit	**NAS1578-1579** Bolt, Pan Head, 1200°F 185,000 PSI — CRES. (U-212) Per NAS1597 Cond. F 3A Fit Torq-Set® — Hi-Torque®	**NAS1703-1710** Bolt, 100° Head Close Tolerance 160,000 PSI — Steel 3A Fit
NAS1463-1464 Clip, Spring — Steel Beryllium Copper	**NAS1580-1582** Bolt, 100° Flush Head, 1200°F 185,000 PSI — CRES. (U-212) Per NAS1597 Cond. F 3A Fit Torq-Set® — Hi-Torque®	**NAS1806-1816 NAS1906-1916** Rivet, Hi-Shear — Ti. Alloy per NAS621
NAS1473 Nut, Cap, Self-Sealing, Self-Locking, Two Lug Floating, Plate — Steel CRES. Steel 3B Fit	**NAS1583-1585** Pin, Hi-Shear 1200°F; Collar 100° CTSK. — Inconel "X" Per AMS 5667	**NAS2803-2810** Bolt, 100° Head Torq-Set 180,000 PSI — Alloy Steel 3A Fit
NAS1493 Lock Nut Bearing, Retaining — Steel	**NAS1586** Bolt, 12 Pt. Ext. Wrenching 1200°F; Drilled/Undrilled — CRES. (U-212) Per NAS1597 Cond. F 3A Fit Bolt	**NAS2903-2920 NAS3003-3020** Hex Head Bolt, Close Tolerance, 160,000 PSI — Alloy Steel 3A Fit Drilled/Undrilled
NAS1496-1502 Lock Bolt-Protruding Head — Alloy Steel	**NAS1587** Washer 1200°F — Plain CTSK. CRES. Steel Type 321/347	**NAS3103-3110 NAS3203-3210 NAS3303-3305** Bolt; Hook — Steel CRES. Steel 2A Fit

(Illustrations from AIMSCO catalog)

Appendix II
Regulations and Publications

The majority of aircraft built today are more complex than those built in the past. New materials and fabrication methods are used and sophisticated equipment is being installed, all of which require maintenance instructions and techniques which are not common knowledge or used on older aircraft. In addition, FAA regulations prescribe specific methods and procedures for repairing aircraft structures as well as defining inspection requirements.

This complexity of aircraft and the various FAA requirements, makes it more and more important that the aviation mechanic maintain a small library of up-to-date FAA publications as well as the manufacturer's service and maintenance manuals.

FEDERAL AVIATION ADMINISTRATION (FAA) PUBLICATIONS
Checklist

Advisory Circular 00-2, **The Advisory Circular Checklist and Status of FARs,** contains a list of current FAA advisory circulars and Federal Aviation Regulations, together with their status as of a given date, contents, and cost. The checklist is updated triannually and provides detailed instructions on how to obtain both advisory circulars and Federal Aviation Regulations. It also contains a list of GPO bookstores located throughout the United States which stock many government publications. The checklist may be obtained **free** upon request from the U.S. Department of Transportation, Publications Section, TAD 443.1, Washington, D.C. 20590.

Federal Aviation Regulations.

The following FAR Parts are those you may be most interested in. They pertain primarily to the operation and maintenance of the aircraft and to obtain an airframe and powerplant mechanic certificate.

Part 1   Definitions and Abbreviations
Part 21   Certification Procedures for Products and Parts
Part 23   Airworthiness Standards: Normal, Utility, and Acrobatic
          Category Aircraft
Part 33   Airworthiness Standards: Aircraft Engines
Part 35   Airworthiness Standards: Propellers
Part 39   Airworthiness Directives
Part 43   Maintenance, Preventive Maintenance, Rebuilding, and
          Alteration

Part 45 Identification and Registration Marking
Part 47 Aircraft Registration
Part 65 Certification: Airmen Other Than Flight Crewmembers
Part 91 General Operating and Flight Rules

The Advisory Circulars

Advisory circulars are issued by the FAA to inform the aviation public, in a systematic way of nonregulatory material of interest. The contents of advisory circulars are not binding on the public unless incorporated into a regulation by reference.

The following Advisory Circulars in particular should be available to the aviation mechanic:

Acceptable Methods. Techniques, and Practices. These advisory circulars replace the policy material formerly contained in CAM 18.

(1) AC 43.13-1A Acceptable Methods. Techniques, and Practices— Aircraft Inspection and Repair.

(2) AC 43.13-2 Acceptable Methods, Techniques, and Practices— Aircraft Alterations.

Inspection Aids

An FAA publication, The General Aviation Inspection Aids, AC 20-7, provides the aviation community with a means for interchanging service difficulty information. The Aids are prepared for pilots, mechanics, operators of repair agencies, and others participating in inspection and maintenance of general aviation aircraft. The information is brief and advisory. Compliance is not mandatory. It is, however, intended to alert you to service experience and, when pertinent, direct your attention to the manufacturer's recommended corrective measures.

The articles contained in the Aids are derived from the Service Difficulty or Malfunction and Defect Reports submitted by aircraft owners, pilots, mechanics, repair stations, and air taxi operators. The FAA reviews the reports and selects pertinent items for publication in the Aids.

Airworthiness Directives

A primary safety function of the Federal Aviation Administration is to require correction of unsafe conditions found in an aircraft, aircraft engine, propeller, or appliance when such conditions exist and are likely to exist or develop in other products of the same design. The unsafe conditions may exist because of a design defect, maintenance, or other causes. FAR Part 39, Airworthiness Directives, defines the authority and responsibility of the Administrator for requiring the necessary corrective action. The Airworthiness

Directives (ADs) are the media used to notify aircraft owners and other interested persons of unsafe conditions and to prescribe the conditions under which the product may continue to be operated.

Airworthiness Directives may be divided into two categories: (1) those of an emergency nature requiring immediate compliance upon receipt, and (2) those of a less urgent nature requiring compliance within a relatively longer period of time.

Airworthiness Directives are Federal Aviation Regulations and must be complied with, unless specific exemption is granted. It is the aircraft owner's or operator's responsibility to assure compliance with all pertinent ADs. This includes those ADs that may require a repetitive inspection each 50 hours of operation, meaning the particular inspection shall be accomplished and recorded **every** 50 hours of time in service.

Federal Aviation Regulations require a record to be maintained that shows the current status of applicable airworthiness directives, including the method of compliance, and the signature and certificate number of the repair station or mechanic who performed the work. For ready reference, many aircraft owners have a chronological listing of the pertinent ADs in the back of their aircraft and engine records.

The Airworthiness Directives Summary contains all the valid ADs previously published and biweekly supplements. The Summary is divided into two volumes. Volume I includes directives applicable to small aircraft (12,500 pounds or less maximum certificated takeoff weight). Volume II includes directives applicable to large aircraft (over 12,500 pounds).

Other Technical Data

Aircraft Type Certificate Data Sheets and Specifications. Basic subscription consists of specifications and type certification data sheets in all weight groups.

Aircraft Engine and Propeller Type Certificate Data Sheets and Specifications. Basic subscription consists of engine and propeller specifications.

MANUFACTURER'S MANUALS

All aircraft manufacturer's publish service and maintenance manuals and parts catalogs for all their aircraft. These manuals are described in Chapter 1, Introduction of this handbook.